PARKIN◆KING

ECONOMICS

STUDY GUIDE

SECOND EDITION

PARKIN ◆ KING
ECONOMICS

STUDY GUIDE

SECOND EDITION

Brian Atkinson *University of Central Lancashire*

and

Avi J. Cohen *York University*

Harvey B. King *University of Regina*

with contributions by

David E. Spencer *Brigham Young University*

 ADDISON-WESLEY PUBLISHERS LIMITED

WOKINGHAM, ENGLAND ◆ READING, MASSACHUSETTS ◆ MENLO PARK, CALIFORNIA ◆ NEW YORK
DON MILLS, ONTARIO ◆ AMSTERDAM ◆ BONN ◆ SYDNEY ◆ SINGAPORE ◆ TOKYO
MADRID ◆ SAN JUAN ◆ MILAN ◆ PARIS ◆ MEXICO CITY ◆ SEOUL ◆ TAIPEI

Cover designed by Anthony Leung and Designers & Partners
Typeset by Meridian Phototypesetting Limited, Pangbourne
Artwork by Margaret Macknelly Design, Tadley
Printed and bound in Great Britain by William Clowes Ltd, Beccles, Suffolk

First printed in 1995

British Library Cataloguing in Publication Data
A catalogue record for this book is available from
the British Library

ISBN: 0-201-42785-0

Acknowledgements
The publishers wish to thank the following for permission to reproduce material: The Guardian; Commission of
the European Union; Datastream International; Economics Association; Associated Examining Board; Philip Allan
Publishers Ltd; Times Newspapers Ltd; University of London Examinations and Assessment Council; Addison-
Wesley Publishing Company, Inc, Reading, MA; Central Statistical Office; Organization for Economic Co-operation
and Development (Paris); The Controller of Her Majesty's Stationery Office; Macmillan Ltd; George Weidenfield &
Nicholson Ltd; Cambridge University Press.

CONTENTS

INTRODUCTION

Before You Begin . . .

Our experience has taught us that what first-year economics students want most from a study guide is help in mastering course material in order to do well in examinations. We have developed this *Study Guide* to respond specifically to that demand. Using this *Study Guide* alone, however, is not enough to guarantee that you will do well in your course. In order to help you overcome the problems and difficulties that most first-year students encounter, we have some general advice on how to study, as well as some specific advice on how best to use this *Study Guide*.

Some Friendly Advice

The study of economics requires a different style of thinking from what you may encounter in other courses. Economists make extensive use of assumptions to break down complex problems into simple, analytically manageable, parts. This analytical style, while not ultimately more demanding than the styles of thinking in other disciplines, feels unfamiliar to most students and requires practice. In order to do well we suggest:

Don't rely solely on your previous knowledge of economics. If you have taken economics before you will have seen the material on supply and demand on which your tutor will lecture in the first few weeks. Don't be lulled into feeling that the course will be easy. Your previous knowledge of economic concepts will be very useful, but it will not be enough to guarantee high marks in exams. Your tutors will demand much more detailed knowledge of concepts and ask you to apply them in new circumstances.

Keep up with the course material on a weekly basis. Read the appropriate chapter in the textbook *before*

your tutor lectures on it. In this initial reading, don't worry about details or arguments you can't quite follow – just try and get a general understanding of the basic concepts and issues. You may be amazed at how your tutor's ability to teach improves when you come to class prepared. As soon as your tutor has finished covering a chapter, complete the corresponding *Study Guide* chapter. Avoid cramming the day before or even just the week before an exam. Because economics requires practice, cramming is an almost certain recipe for failure.

Keep a good set of lecture notes. Good lecture notes are vital for focusing your studying. Your tutor will only lecture on a subset of topics from the textbook. The topics your tutor covers in a lecture should usually be given priority when studying. You should also give priority to studying the figures and graphs covered in lectures.

Use your tutor for help. When you have questions or problems with course material, ask for help. Remember, tutors are there to help you learn. We are often amazed at how few students come to see us to ask for help. Don't be shy. The personal contact that comes from one-to-one tutoring is professionally gratifying for us as well as (hopefully) beneficial for you.

Form a study group. A very useful way to motivate your studying and to learn economics is to discuss the course material and problems with other students. Explaining the answer to a question *out loud* is a very effective way of discovering how well you understand the question. When you answer a question in your head only, you often skip steps in the chain of reasoning without realizing it. When you are forced to explain your reasoning aloud, gaps and mistakes quickly appear, and you (and your fellow group members) can quickly correct your reasoning. The Short Answer questions in the *Study Guide* and the Review questions at the end of each textbook chapter are good study group material. You also might get together *after* having worked the problems in the *Study Guide* chapter, but *before* looking at the answers, and help each other solve unsolved problems.

Work old exams. One of the most effective ways of studying is to work through exams your tutor has given in previous years. Old exams give you a feel for the style of question your instructor may ask, and give you the opportunity to get used to time pressure if you force yourself to do the exam in the allotted time. Some institutions keep old exams in the library, others in the department. Students who have previously taken the course are usually a good source as well. Remember, though, that old exams are a useful study aid only if you use them to *understand* the reasoning behind each question. If you simply memorize answers in the hopes that your instructor will repeat the identical question, you are likely to fail. From year to year, examiners routinely change the questions or change the numerical values for similar questions.

Use the other study aids. In addition to the *Study Guide* you will benefit from using *Economics in Action* software. This is truly interactive tutorial software available for IBM-compatible computers, adapted for this text by Robin Bade. The software includes modules on core concepts such as graphing, production possibilities and opportunity cost, demand and supply, elasticity, utility and demand, product curves and cost curves, perfect competition, monopoly, macroeconomic performance, aggregate demand and aggregate supply, expenditure multipliers, money and banking and international trade.

Four interactive modes take full advantage of the computer's capacity to facilitate critical thinking skills. First, a tutorial mode walks students through the central concepts. Second, a quiz mode enables guided self-testing. Third, a free mode enables students and professors to interact with economic models by changing parameters and observing the effects on the graph. Fourth, an evaluation mode allows students to construct and complete a multiple-choice test and keep a (read-only) record of their score.

In addition to its emphasis on interaction, the software is also closely integrated with the text. The art style is the same, the terminology is consistent, and supporting material in the text is cross-referenced in the software. The software has a user's manual and has been tested and reviewed for accuracy.

Using the Study Guide

You should only attempt to complete a chapter in the *Study Guide* after you have read the corresponding textbook chapter once and listened to your instructor lecture on the material. Each *Study Guide* chapter contains the following sections.

Chapter in Perspective. The purpose of this first section is to briefly situate the material of a particular textbook chapter in the context of what has come before and what will follow. Since you will see so much detailed information throughout the course, we try to paint the bigger picture for you in broad strokes so that you don't feel lost. This is the 'look at the forest instead of the trees' section.

Helpful Hints. Where you encounter difficulty in mastering concepts or techniques, you will not be alone. Many students find certain concepts difficult and often make the same kinds of mistakes. We have seen these common mistakes often enough to have learned how to help students avoid them. These hints point out these mistakes and offer tips for avoiding them. The hints focus on the most important concepts, equations and techniques for problem solving.

Key Figures and Tables. In the textbook, key figures and tables are identified with the textbook icon. Here, we group together summaries of the key figures and tables to help you focus your study on the most important diagrams. The summaries in this section are similar to those in the textbook captions, but use slightly different language. If you are having trouble understanding particular figures, these additional summaries should prove helpful. If you have understood the figure or table in the textbook, you may skip or skim the summary here.

Self-Test. Besides the Helpful Hints, this will be the most useful section of the *Study Guide*. The questions are designed to give you practice and to test the skills and techniques you must master to do well in exams. There are plenty of the types of questions you are most likely to encounter in your course exams – True/False and Multiple-Choice questions.

There are other types of questions, described below, each with a specific pedagogical purpose. Before we describe the six parts of the Self-Test section, here are some general tips that apply to all of the parts.

Use a pencil to write your answers in the *Study Guide*. This will allow you to erase your mistakes and have neat, completed pages from which to study.

Draw graphs wherever they are applicable. Some questions will ask explicitly for graphs; many others will not but require a chain of reasoning that involves shifts of curves on a graph. *Always draw the graph*. Don't try and work through the reasoning in your head – you are much more likely to make mistakes that way. Whenever you draw a graph, even in the margins of the *Study Guide*, label the axes. You may think that you can keep the labels in your head, but you will be confronting many different graphs with many different variables on the axes. Avoid confusion and label. As an added incentive, remember that on exams where graphs are required, examiners will deduct marks for unlabelled axes.

Do the Self-Test questions as if they were real exam questions, which means do them *without looking at the answers*. This is the single most important tip we can give you about effectively using the *Study Guide* to improve your exam performance. Struggling for the answers to questions that you find difficult is one of the most effective ways to learn. The athletic adage – no pain, no gain – applies equally well to studying. You will learn the most from right answers you had to struggle for and from your wrong answers and mistakes. Only after you have attempted all of the questions should you look at the answers. When you finally do check the answers, be sure to understand where you went wrong and why the right answer is correct.

If you want to impose time pressure on yourself to simulate the conditions of a real exam, allow two minutes for each Multiple-Choice question and one minute for each True/False question. The other types of question vary considerably in their time requirements, so it is difficult to give generally applicable time estimates for them. However, we believe that such time pressure is probably not a good idea for *Study Guide* questions. A state of mind of relaxed concentration is best for work in the *Study Guide*. Use old exams if you want practice with time pressure.

The six parts of the Self-Test section are:

Concept Review.
This part contains simple 'recall' questions, designed to check your memory of basic terms and concepts. These questions should build your confidence. If you have understood the terms and concepts in the chapter, you should get very few of these questions wrong. This part is not a test of deep understanding or of mastery of analytical skills.

True or False.
These questions test your basic knowledge of chapter concepts as well as your ability to apply the concepts. These are the first questions to challenge your understanding to see if you can identify mistakes in statements using basic concepts.

Multiple-Choice.
These more difficult questions test your analytical abilities by asking you to apply concepts to new situations, to manipulate information and to solve numerical and graphical problems.

Read each question and all five choices carefully before you answer. Many of the choices will be plausible and will differ only slightly. You must choose the one *best* answer. A useful strategy in working these questions is first to eliminate any obviously wrong choices and then to focus on the remaining alternatives. Be aware that sometimes the correct answer will be 'none of the above choices is correct'. Don't get frustrated or think that you are dim if you can't immediately see the correct answer. These questions are designed to make you work to find the correct choice.

Short Answer.
Each chapter contains several Short Answer questions. These are straightforward, confidence-building questions about basic concepts. They can generally be answered in a few sentences or, at most, in one paragraph. These questions are useful to answer out loud in a study group.

Problems.
The best way to learn to do economics is to do problems. Each Self-Test includes numerical or graphical problems. In many chapters, this will be the most challenging part of the Self-Test. It is also likely to be particularly helpful for deepening your understanding of the chapter material. We have, however, designed the questions to teach as much as to test. We have purposefully arranged the parts of each question to lead you through the problem-solving analysis in a gradual and sequential fashion, from easier to more difficult parts.

Data Questions.
Each chapter includes a data question. These have been chosen to test your ability to apply economic concepts to 'real life situations'. Since real life does not come in well-defined chapters, the questions often require you to use ideas from earlier chapters. For reasons of space, the answers are not always set out in full but instead refer you to parts of the main text.

Answers. The Self-Test is followed by answers to all of the questions. Be sure not to look at the answers until you have attempted to answer all of the questions. When you do finally look at the answers, use them to understand where you went wrong and why the right answer is correct. The detailed answers to the Problems should be especially useful in clarifying and illustrating typical chains of reasoning involved in economics analysis. If the answers alone do not clear up your confusion, go back to the appropriate sections of the textbook. If that still does not suffice, ask your tutor for help or go to your study group members, and get help and clarification.

If you effectively combine the use of the textbook and the *Study Guide*, you will be well prepared for exams. Equally importantly, you will also have developed analytical skills and powers of reasoning that will benefit you throughout your life and in whatever career you choose.

Do You Have Any Friendly Advice For Us?

We have attempted to make this *Study Guide* as clear as possible, and to avoid errors. No doubt, we have not succeeded entirely, and you are the only judges who count in evaluating our attempt. If you discover errors, or if you have other suggestions for improving the *Study Guide*, please write to us. In future editions, we will try and acknowledge the names of all students whose suggestions help us improve the *Study Guide*. Send your correspondence to:

Brian Atkinson
Department of International Business
University of Central Lancashire
Preston PR1 2TQ

Acknowledgements

This *Study Guide* has benefited from help and advice from many sources. In particular it has drawn on the American and Canadian Study Guides, and I would like to thank all those who helped in preparing these editions.

Brian Atkinson
March 1995

Chapter 1   What is Economics?

Chapter In Perspective, Text Pages 4–27

The fundamental economic problem is scarcity. Because wants exceed the resources available to satisfy them, we cannot have everything we want and must make choices. This problem leads to economizing behaviour – choosing the best or optimal use of the resources available. Economics, as a subject, is the study of how we use limited resources to try to satisfy unlimited wants.

    This chapter also introduces the *method* of economics: how economists use economic theory and models to answer economic questions and to analyse and understand how people and economic systems cope with the fundamental problem of scarcity.

Helpful Hints

1 The definition of economics (the study of how people use limited resources to try to satisfy unlimited wants) leads us directly to three important economic concepts – choice, opportunity cost and competition. If wants exceed resources, we cannot have everything we want and therefore must make *choices* among alternatives. In making a choice, we forgo other alternatives, and the *opportunity cost* of any choice is the value of the best forgone alternative. Also, if wants exceed resources, then wants and individuals must *compete* against each other for the scarce resources.

2 Scientists use theory to abstract from the complex descriptive facts of the real world and focus only on those elements essential for understanding. Those essential elements are fashioned into models – highly simplified representations of the real world.

Economic models attempt to focus on the essential forces (competition, self-interest) operating in the economy while abstracting from less important forces (whims, advertising, altruism). Unlike physicists, economists cannot perform controlled experiments to test their models. As a result, it is difficult conclusively to prove or disprove a theory and its models.

3 Remember that economic models are not claims that the real world is as simple as the model. Models claim to capture the simplified effect of some real force operating in the economy. Before drawing conclusions about the real economy from a model, we must be careful to consider whether, when we reinsert all the real-world complexities we have omitted from the model, the conclusions will be the same as in the model.

4 The most important purpose of studying economics is not to learn lots of economic facts, but rather *how* to think about economics. The value of an economics education is the ability to think critically about economic problems and *to understand how* an economy works. This understanding of the essential forces governing how an economy works comes through the mastery of economic theory and model-building.

Key Figure

Figure 1.2   A Picture of an Economy with Households, Firms and Governments, text page 14

This illustrates the flow of goods and services as well as flows of money in the economy. There are three groups of decision makers (households, firms and governments) and two groups of markets (goods markets and factor markets). Households supply factors of production to firms through factor markets for which they receive payment of wages, interest, rent and profits. Firms supply goods and services to households through goods markets for which they receive money payments. Governments collect taxes (money flows) from both households and firms and supply goods and services to both in addition to other benefits (transfer payments) to households and subsidies to firms.

Figure 1.2 is important because it highlights the *interdependence* between households, firms and governments. What any one group can do depends on what the other groups do. This interdependence is coordinated through competition and the market mechanism.

SELF-TEST

CONCEPT REVIEW

1 The fundamental and pervasive fact that gives rise to economic problems is _____ . This simply means that human wants _____ the resources available to satisfy them. The inescapable consequence is that people must make _____ .

2 When we choose an action, the value of the best forgone alternative is the _____ cost of that action.

3 The process of evaluating the costs and benefits of our choices in order to do the best we can with limited resources is called _____ or _____ .

4 An economy is a mechanism that determines _____ is produced, _____ it is produced and _____ it is produced.

5 The three groups of decision makers in the economy are _____ , _____ and _____ .

6 Factors of production are classified under three general headings. The physical and mental resources of human beings are called _____ . Natural resources are called _____ . Manufactured goods used in production (for example, machines and factories) are called _____ .

7 While all economies must have some way of coordinating choices, there are two fundamental mechanisms. The _____ mechanism relies on the authority of some kind of central planning, while the _____ mechanism relies on the adjustment of _____ in economic markets. A _____ economy has elements of both of these fundamental mechanisms.

8 An economy that is economically linked with other economies in the world is called _____ .

9 Statements about what *is* are called _____ statements, while those about what *ought* to be are called _____ statements.

10 The branch of economics that studies the choices of individual households and firms is called _____ , while the branch that studies behaviour of the economy as a whole is called _____ .

TRUE OR FALSE

1 Scarcity is a problem only for capitalist (market) economies.

2 Economics is the study of how to use unlimited resources to satisfy limited wants.

3 The notion of opportunity cost is illustrated by the fact that because Fred studied for his economics examination last night he was unable to see a movie with his friends.

4 Competition is a contest for command over scarce resources.

5 The opportunity cost of any action is the cost of all forgone alternatives.

6 The pair of scissors a barber uses to cut hair is an example of capital as a factor of production.

7 A mixed economy is one in which there is both internal and international trade.

8 The United Kingdom is a pure market economy.

9 Careful and systematic observation and measurement are basic components of any science.

10 Economics is not a science since it deals with the study of wilful human beings and not inanimate objects in nature.

11 An increase in the income tax rate will cause total tax revenue to fall. This is an example of a positive statement.

12 A positive statement is about what *is*, while a normative statement is about what *will* be.

13 Economic models are of very limited value in helping us understand the real world because they abstract from the complexity of the real world.

14 Microeconomics is concerned with the economy as a whole.

15 Macroeconomics includes the study of the causes of inflation.

16 Testing an economic model requires comparing its predictions against real-world events.

17 When the predictions of a model conflict with the relevant facts, a theory must be discarded or modified.

MULTIPLE-CHOICE

1 The fact that human wants cannot be fully satisfied with available resources is called the problem of
a opportunity cost.
b scarcity.
c normative economics.
d what to produce.
e for whom to produce.

2 The problem of scarcity exists
a only in economies which rely on the market mechanism.
b only in economies which rely on the command mechanism.
c in all economies.
d only when people have not optimized.
e now but will be eliminated with economic growth.

3 When the government chooses to use resources to build a dam, those resources are no longer available to build a road. This illustrates the concept of
a a market mechanism.
b macroeconomics.
c opportunity cost.
d a closed economy.
e cooperation.

4 Renata has the chance either to attend an economics lecture or to play tennis. If she chooses to attend the lecture, the value of playing tennis is
a greater than the value of the lecture.
b not comparable to the value of the lecture.
c equal to the value of the lecture.
d the opportunity cost of attending the lecture.
e zero.

5 Which of the following is an example of capital as a factor of production?
a money held by Shell
b a Shell bond
c a building owned by Shell
d all of the above
e none of the above

6 All of the following are factors of production except
a natural resources.
b tools.
c labour.
d government.
e land.

7 A closed economy is one that has
   a more exports than imports.
   b more imports than exports.
   c strict government control of production.
   d no economic links between households and government.
   e no economic links with other economies.

8 A normative statement is a statement regarding
   a what is usually the case.
   b the assumptions of an economic model.
   c what ought to be.
   d the predictions of an economic model.
   e what is.

9 'The rich face higher income tax rates than the pool' is an example of
   a a normative statement.
   b a positive statement.
   c a descriptive statement.
   d a theoretical statement.
   e **b** and **c**.

10 An economic model is tested by
   a examining the realism of its assumptions.
   b comparing its predictions with the facts.
   c comparing its descriptions with the facts.
   d the Royal Economic Society.
   e all of the above.

11 When economists say that people are rational, it means they
   a do not make errors of judgement.
   b make the best decision from their perspective.
   c act on complete information.
   d will not later regret any decision made now.
   e do not let emotion influence decisions.

12 The branch of economics that studies the decisions of individual households and firms is called
   a macroeconomics.
   b microeconomics.
   c positive economics.
   d normative economics.
   e home economics.

13 All of the following are microeconomic questions *except*
   a technological change.
   b wages and earnings.
   c distribution of wealth.
   d production.
   e consumption.

14 Equilibrium is
   a a balance of opposing forces.
   b a situation in which everyone has economized.
   c a situation where all choices are mutually compatible.
   d the solution of an economic model.
   e all of the above.

SHORT ANSWER

1 What is meant by scarcity and why does the existence of scarcity mean that we must make choices?

2 If all people would only economize, that would solve the problem of scarcity. Agree or disagree and explain why.

3 Explain the interdependence that exists between households and firms in textbook Figure 1.1 on page 12.

4 Why are European economies considered to be mixed?

PROBLEMS

1 Assume that it takes one hour to travel from London to Glasgow by aeroplane and five hours by train. Further, suppose that the air fare is £100 and the train fare is £60. Which mode of transport has the lower opportunity cost for the following people?
   a a person who can earn £5 an hour
   b a person who can earn £10 an hour
   c a person who can earn £12 an hour

2 Suppose the government builds and staffs a hospital in order to provide 'free' medical care.
   a What is the opportunity cost of the free medical care?
   b Is it free from the perspective of society as a whole?

3 Indicate whether each of the following statements is positive or normative. If it is normative (positive), rewrite it so that it becomes positive (normative).
   a The government ought to reduce the size of the deficit in order to lower interest rates.
   b Government imposition of a tax on tobacco products will reduce their consumption.

4 Suppose we examine a model of plant growth which predicts that, given the amount of water and sunlight, the application of fertilizer stimulates plant growth.
a How might you test the model?
b How is the test different from what an economist could do to test an economic model?

DATA QUESTIONS

1 Two-thirds of the Netherlands lies below sea level. In 1953 a huge storm flooded large parts of the country, killing more than 2,000 people. This caused the Dutch to devote huge resources to the 'Delta Project' – a massive sea barrage which prevents the sea encroaching on to the land.

But the problem remains. If global warming becomes a reality, then the sea levels will rise and the Netherlands will again become vulnerable to storms. Hence it is not surprising that the Dutch are world leaders in the search for sources of energy that do not pollute the atmosphere and for measures to reduce the effects of pollution. Thus the Dutch propose to plant large numbers of trees across the world to absorb carbon dioxide.

a What is meant by 'opportunity cost'? How can this concept be related to the above passage?
b Distinguish between command and market economies. Which decision making mechanism do you think was used by the Dutch in making the decisions outlined above? Why did they choose this mechanism?

2 Saving lives costs money. More important, it needs resources. There are lots of examples of this. Every year children are killed when they run on to the road. It would be quite possible to reduce this number by improving road safety education and by building safety barriers along the road side. This is often done outside schools, but it could be done on a much wider scale. Similarly 'sleeping policemen' would reduce the speed of cars on housing estates.

Another example of how more resources could save lives is in medicine. If everyone had regular medical check-ups then diseases would be caught early and treatment would be more successful.

a Why don't governments take such measures and so save lives?
b How do you think market mechanisms would approach the problem of allocating resources to medicine?

ANSWERS

CONCEPT REVIEW

1 scarcity; exceed; choices

2 opportunity

3 optimizing; economizing

4 what; how; for whom

5 households; firms; government

6 labour; land; capital

7 command; market; prices; mixed

8 open

9 positive; normative

10 microeconomics; macroeconomics

TRUE OR FALSE

1 **F** Scarcity is a universal fact.

2 **F** It is the study of limited resources and unlimited wants.

3 **T** The opportunity cost is the alternative forgone.

4 **T** True by definition.

5 **F** It is the best alternative forgone.

6 **T** All tools are capital.

7 **F** A mixed economy uses markets and command mechanisms.

8 **F** It is a mixed economy.

9 **T** All sciences have these characteristics.

10 F Science is not defined by subject but by method.

11 T Positive because it can be tested.

12 F Normative statements are about what *ought* to be.

13 F The abstraction is what makes them useful.

14 F 'Micro' means small.

15 T Inflation affects the whole society.

16 T Test predictions, not assumptions.

17 T A model's predictions must be consistent with the facts to become part of accepted theory.

MULTIPLE-CHOICE

1 b Definition.

2 c With infinite wants and limited resources, scarcity will never be eliminated.

3 c The road is a forgone alternative.

4 d Choosing the lecture means its value is greater than tennis. Tennis is the best alternative forgone.

5 c Capital defined as manufactured goods used in production.

6 d Government is a decision maker, not a factor.

7 e Definition.

8 c Key word for normative statements is *ought*.

9 e Positive statements describe facts about what is.

10 b If its predictions do not match the facts, it is discarded.

11 b Rational choice is an individual's best choice based on available information.

12 b Definition.

13 c c is a macroeconomic topic.

14 e Definition.

SHORT ANSWER

1 Scarcity is the universal condition that human wants always exceed the resources available to satisfy them. The fact that goods and services are scarce means that individuals cannot have all of everything they want. It is therefore necessary to choose among alternatives.

2 Disagree. If everyone economized, then we would be making the best possible use of our resources and would be achieving the greatest benefits or satisfaction

possible, given the limited quantity of resources. But this does not mean that we would be satisfying all of our limitless needs. The problem of scarcity can never be 'solved' as long as people have infinite needs and finite resources for satisfying those needs.

3 Firms depend on households for the supply of factors of production. In exchange, households depend on firms for income. Households use that income to buy goods and services from firms, while firms depend on the money they get from household purchases to be able to purchase more factors of production in the next period and start the circular flow all over again.

4 European economies are mixed because they rely on both market and command mechanisms. Most coordination is carried out through the market mechanism, but there are many economic decisions which are either made or regulated by governments or by the European Union.

PROBLEMS

1 The point here is to recognize that the opportunity cost of travel includes the best alternative value of travel time as well as the train or air fare.

  a Thus, if the opportunity cost of the time spent travelling is the £5 an hour that could have been earned (but wasn't), the opportunity cost of train travel (in pounds) is the £60 train fare plus the £25 (£5 an hour × 5 hours) in forgone income for a total of £85.

  b In this case, the opportunity cost of air travel is the £100 air fare plus £5 in forgone income, for a total of £105. Therefore, for a person whose best alternative use of time is to earn £5 an hour, the opportunity cost of travelling by train is less than the opportunity cost of travelling by air.

  c For a person who could have earned £12 an hour the opportunity cost of train travel (£120) exceeds the opportunity cost of air travel (£112).

2 a Even though medical care may be offered without charge ('free'), there are still opportunity costs. The opportunity cost of providing such health care is the best alternative use of the resources used in the construction of the hospital and the best alternative use of the resources (including human resources) used in the operation of the hospital.

  b These resources are no longer available for other activities and therefore represent a cost to society.

3 a The given statement is normative. The following is positive: if the government reduces the size of the deficit, interest rates will fall.

b The given statement is positive. The following is normative: the government ought to impose a tax on tobacco products.

4 a The prediction of the model can be tested by conducting the following controlled experiment and carefully observing the outcome. Select a number of similar plots of ground which will be subject to the same amount of water and sunlight. Plant equal quantities of seeds in all the plots. In some of the plots apply no fertilizer and in some of the plots apply (perhaps varying amounts of) fertilizer. When the plants have grown, measure their size and compare growth in the fertilized plots and the unfertilized plots. If plant growth is greater in fertilized plots, we provisionally accept the model and the theory on which it is based. If plant growth is *not* greater in fertilized plots, we discard the theory (model), or modify its assumptions. Perhaps the effective use of fertilizer requires more water. Then construct a new model which predicts that given more water (and the same amount of sunlight), fertilized plants will grow larger than equivalently watered unfertilized plants. Test that model and continue modifying assumptions until predictions are consistent with the facts.

b Economists cannot perform such controlled experiments and must instead change one assumption at a time in alternative models and compare the resulting outcomes. Such differences in outcomes can then be tested only against variations in data that occur naturally in the economy. This is a more difficult and less precise model-building and testing procedure than exists for the controlled fertilizer experiment.

DATA QUESTIONS

1 a The opportunity cost of any action is the best alternative forgone. In this case the resources used to build the Delta Project and to plant trees could have been used for other purposes.

b When command mechanisms are used, decisions are made by the government while market mechanisms allocate resources through markets. In this example it was the Dutch government which made the decisions. Hence it is an example of the command mechanism. They did this because they decided that the market mechanism would not work in this case.

2 a Governments don't take such measures because resources are scarce. The land, labour and capital used to implement life-saving measures would have to be paid for by giving up something else.

b Markets would allocate resources to medicine just as they would to any other good or service – if people wanted some medical service, it would be provided if they could pay. Command economies would involve the government deciding which services should be provided, perhaps as a result of political pressure. Neither system would be able to provide all the medical services which everyone would like because the opportunity cost would be too high.

Chapter 2

Making and Using Graphs

Chapter In Perspective, Text Pages 28–49

As a science, economics is characterized by systematic observation and measurement as well as by the development of economic theory. In both of these components of economic science, the use of graphs plays an important role.

Economic theory describes relationships among economic variables, and graphs offer a very convenient way to represent such relationships. Moreover, representing data graphically can be extremely useful for quickly conveying information about general characteristics of economic behaviour. As we will see in the next few chapters, graphical analysis of economic relationships is especially helpful when we are interested in discovering the theoretical consequences of a change in economic circumstances.

This chapter reviews all the concepts and techniques you will need to construct and use graphs in this course.

Helpful Hints

1 The chapters of the text discuss numerous relationships among economic variables. Many of these relationships will be represented and analysed graphically. Thus an understanding of graphs will greatly facilitate mastery of the economic analysis of later chapters.

2 If your experience with graphical analysis is limited, this chapter is crucial to your ability to understand readily later economic analysis. If you are experienced in the construction and use of graphs this chapter may be 'old hat'. Even in this case, the chapter should be skimmed and the Self-Test in this *Study Guide* completed. The main point is that you should be thoroughly familiar with the basic concepts and techniques of this chapter.

3 Slope is a *linear* concept since it is a property of a straight line. For this reason, the slope is constant along a straight line but is different at different points on a curved (non-linear) line. When we are interested in the slope of a curved line, we actually calculate the slope of a straight line. The text presents two ways of choosing such a straight line and thus two ways of calculating the slope of a curved line: **(1)** slope across an arc, and **(2)** slope at a point. The first of these calculates the slope of the *straight line* formed by the arc between two points on the curved line. The second calculates the slope of the *straight line* that just touches (is tangent to) the curve at a point.

4 A straight line on a graph can also be described by a simple equation. The general form for the equation of a straight line is:

$$y = a + bx$$

If you are given such an equation, you can graph the line by finding the y-intercept (where the line intersects the vertical y-axis), finding the x-intercept (where the line intersects the horizontal x-axis), and then connecting those two points with a straight line.

To find the y-intercept, set $x = 0$.

$$y = a + b(0)$$
$$y = a$$

To find the x-intercept, set $y = 0$.

$$0 = a + bx$$
$$x = -a/b$$

Connecting these two points $((x = 0, y = a)$ and $(x = -a/b, y = 0))$ or $((0, a)$ and $(-a/b, 0))$ yields the line in Fig. 2.1.

Figure 2.1

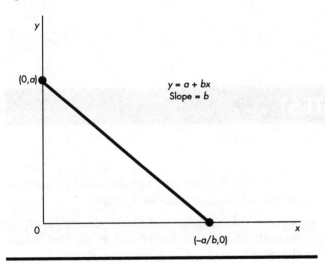

For any straight line with the equation of the form $y = a + bx$, the slope of the line is b.

To see how to apply this general equation, consider this example:

$$y = 4 - 2x$$

To find the y-intercept, set $x = 0$.

$$y = 4 - 2(0)$$
$$y = 4$$

To find the x-intercept, set $y = 0$.

$$0 = 4 - 2x$$
$$x = 2$$

Connecting these two points, (0,4) and (2,0), yields the line in Fig. 2.2.

Figure 2.2

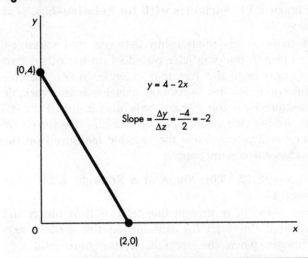

The slope of this line is –2. Since the slope is negative, there is a negative relationship between the variables x and y.

Key Figures

Figure 2.8 Positive Relationships, text page 36
Variables that move up and down together are positively related. Three different positive relationships are illustrated in Fig. 2.8. In each case, as the variable measured on the horizontal axis increases, the variable measured on the vertical axis also increases. Part (a) illustrates a positive linear relationship while parts (b) and (c) illustrate positive relationships that are not linear.

Figure 2.9 Negative Relationships, text page 37
This is a companion to Fig. 2.8 and illustrates negative relationships. Variables that move in opposite directions are negatively related. Three different negative relationships are illustrated in this figure. In each case, as the variable measured on the horizontal axis increases, the variable measured on the vertical axis decreases.

Figure 2.10 Maximum and Minimum Points, text page 38
The relationship in part (a) reaches a maximum. As the variable measured on the horizontal axis increases, the

value of the variable measured on the vertical axis increases, reaches a maximum at point *a* and then decreases. Similarly, the relationship in part (b) reaches a minimum at point *b*.

Figure 2.11 Variables with No Relationship, text page 39

If there is no relationship between two variables, changes in one will have no effect on the other. Part (a) illustrates the fact that changes in the variable measured on the horizontal axis leave the variable measured on the vertical axis unchanged. Part (b) illustrates that changes in the variable measured on the vertical axis leave the variable measured on the horizontal axis unchanged.

Figure 2.12 The Slope of a Straight Line, text page 42

The slope of a straight line tells us how much and in what direction the variable on the vertical axis changes when the variable on the horizontal axis changes. The slope is computed by dividing the change in y (the 'rise') by the change in x (the 'run').

Figure 2.13 The Slope of a Curve, text page 43

Slope is a linear concept, so even when we measure the slope of a curve, we do so by calculating the slope of a straight line. This figure illustrates the two ways of choosing a straight line to do this. Part (a) calculates the slope of the straight line that just touches (is tangent to) the curve at a point. Part (b) calculates the slope of the straight line formed by the arc between two points on the curved line.

Figure 2.14 Graphing a Relationship Between Three Variables, text page 45

When graphing a relationship between three variables, we can reduce the problem to graphing the relationship between two variables by holding one of the variables constant and graphing the relationship between the other two. This is illustrated in Fig. 2.14 using as an example the relationship between ice cream consumption, the price of a scoop of ice cream and air temperature.

SELF-TEST

CONCEPT REVIEW

1 A graph that measures an economic variable on the vertical axis and time on the horizontal axis is called a(n) _____ - _____ graph.

2 The tendency for a variable to rise or fall over time is called the _____ of the variable.

3 Suppose the value of one economic variable is measured on the *x*-axis and the value of a second is measured on the *y*-axis. A diagram that plots the value of one variable corresponding to the value of the other is called a(n) _____ diagram.

4 If two variables tend to move up or down together they exhibit a(n) _____ relationship. Such a relationship is represented graphically by a line that slopes _____ (to the right).

5 Two variables that move in opposite directions exhibit a(n) _____ relationship. Such a relationship is represented graphically by a line that slopes _____ (to the right).

6 Suppose variables *A* and *B* are unrelated. If we measure *A* on the *y*-axis and *B* on the *x*-axis, the graph of *A* as we increase *B* will be a(n) _____ line.

7 The slope of a line is calculated as the change in the value of the variable measured on the _____ axis divided by the change in the value of the variable measured on the _____ axis.

8 A straight line exhibits _____ slope at all points.

9 To graph a relationship among more than two variables, we simply graph the relationship between _____ variables, holding all other variables constant.

TRUE OR FALSE

___ **1** A time-series graph measures time on the horizontal axis.

___ **2** A time-series graph gives information about the level of the relevant economic variable, as well as information about changes and the speed of those changes.

___ **3** A two-variable time-series graph can help us see if the two variables tend to move together over time.

___ **4** A one-dimensional graph that represents measured rainfall along a horizontal line is an example of a scatter diagram.

___ **5** If the graph of the relationship between two variables slopes upward (to the right), the variables move up and down together.

___ **6** If variable a rises when variable b falls and falls when b rises, then the relationship between a and b is negative.

___ **7** The graph of the 'relationship' between two variables that are in fact unrelated will be either horizontal or vertical.

___ **8** The slope of a straight line is calculated by dividing the change in the value of the variable measured on the horizontal axis by the change in the value of the variable measured on the vertical axis.

___ **9** The slope of a curved line is not constant.

___ **10** If we want to graph the relationship among three variables, we must hold two of them constant as we represent the third.

___ **11** In Fig. 2.3, the relationship between y and x is first negative, reaches a minimum, and then becomes positive as x increases.

___ **12** In Fig. 2.3, the slope of the curve is increasing as we move from point b to point c.

___ **13** In Fig. 2.3, the slope of the curve is approaching zero as we move from point a to point b.

___ **14** In Fig. 2.3, the value of x is a minimum at point b.

Figure 2.3

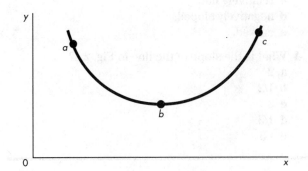

MULTIPLE-CHOICE

Table 2.1

Year	x	y
1990	6.2	143
1991	5.7	156
1992	5.3	162

1 From the information in Table 2.1, it appears that
a x and y tend to exhibit a negative relationship.
b x and y tend to exhibit a positive relationship.
c there is no relationship between x and y.
d there is first a negative and then a positive relationship between x and y.
e there is first a positive and then a negative relationship between x and y.

2 If variables x and y move up and down together, they are said to be
a positively related.
b negatively related.
c conversely related.
d unrelated.
e trendy.

3 The relationship between two variables that move in opposite directions is shown graphically by a line that is
a positively sloped.
b relatively steep.
c relatively flat.
d negatively sloped.
e curved.

4 What is the slope of the line in Fig. 2.4?
a 2
b 1/2
c 3
d 1/3
e −3

Figure 2.4

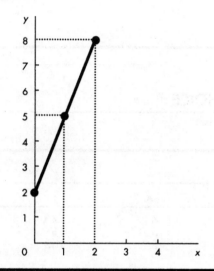

---

5 If the line in Fig. 2.4 were to continue down to the x-axis, what would the value of x be when y is zero?
a 0
b 2
c 2/3
d −2/3
e −3/2

6 If the price of an umbrella is low and the number of rainy days per month is large, more umbrellas will be sold each month. On the other hand, if the price of an umbrella is high and there are few rainy days per month, fewer umbrellas will be sold each month. On the basis of this information, which of the following statements is true?

a The number of umbrellas sold and the price of an umbrella are positively related, holding the number of rainy days constant.
b The number of umbrellas sold and the price of an umbrella are negatively related, holding the number of rainy days constant.
c The number of rainy days and the number of umbrellas sold are negatively related, holding the price of an umbrella constant.
d The number of rainy days and the price of an umbrella are negatively related, holding the number of umbrellas sold constant.
e None of the above statements is true.

7 Given the data in Table 2.2, holding income constant, the graph relating the price of strawberries (vertical axis) to the purchases of strawberries (horizontal axis)
a is a vertical line.
b is a horizontal line.
c is a positively-sloped line.
d is a negatively-sloped line.
e reaches a minimum.

Table 2.2

Weekly family income (pounds)	Price per box of strawberries (pounds)	Number of boxes purchased per week
300	1.00	5
300	1.25	3
300	1.50	2
400	1.00	7
400	1.25	5
400	1.50	4

8 Consider the data in Table 2.2. Suppose family income decreases from £400 to £300 per week. Then the graph relating the price of strawberries (vertical axis) to the purchases of strawberries (horizontal axis) will
a become negatively sloped.
b become positively sloped.
c shift to the right.
c shift to the left.
e no longer exist.

9 Given the data in Table 2.2, holding price constant, the graph relating family income (vertical axis) to the purchases of strawberries (horizontal axis) is

a a vertical line.
b a horizontal line.
c a positively-sloped line.
d a negatively-sloped line.
e a positively- or negatively-sloped line, depending on the price that is held constant.

10 If the equation of a straight line is $y = 6 + 3x$, then the slope is
a −3 and the y-intercept is 6.
b −3 and the y-intercept is −2.
c 3 and the y-intercept is 6.
d 3 and the y-intercept is −2.
e 3 and the y-intercept is −6.

SHORT ANSWER

1 Draw a two-variable time-series graph that illustrates two variables that have a tendency to move up and down together. What would the scatter diagram for these two variables look like?

2 Draw a graph of variables x and y that illustrates each of the following relationships:
a x and y move up and down together.
b x and y move in opposite directions.
c as x increases y reaches a maximum.
d as x increases y reaches a minimum.
e x and y move in opposite directions, but as x increases y decreases by larger and larger increments for each unit increase in x.
f y is independent of the value of x.
g x is independent of the value of y.

3 What does it mean to say that the slope of a line is −2/3?

4 Explain how we measure the slope of a curved line
a at a point.
b across an arc.

5 How do we graph a relationship among more than two variables using a two-dimensional graph?

PROBLEMS

1 Consider the data in Table 2.3.
a Draw a time-series graph for the interest rate.

b Draw a two-variable time-series graph for both the inflation rate and the interest rate.
c Draw a scatter diagram for the inflation rate (horizontal axis) and the interest rate (vertical axis).
d Would you describe the general relationship between the inflation rate and the interest rate as positive, negative or unrelated?

Table 2.3

Year	Inflation rate (per cent)	Interest rate (per cent)
1985	5.4	6.4
1986	3.2	4.3
1987	3.4	4.1
1988	8.3	7.0
1989	11.8	7.9
1990	6.7	5.8
1991	4.9	5.0
1992	6.5	5.3
1993	8.6	7.2
1994	12.3	10.0

2 Compute the slope of the lines in Fig. 2.5 (a) and (b).

Figure 2.5

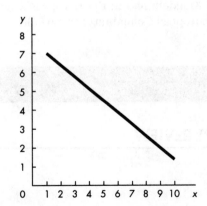

(a)

(b)

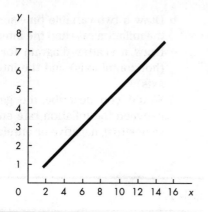

3 Draw each of the following:
a a straight line with slope −10 and passing through the point (2,80).
b a straight line with slope 2 and passing through the point (6,10).

4 The equation for a straight line is $y = 6 - 2x$.
a Calculate:
  i the y-intercept
  ii the x-intercept
  iii the slope
b Draw the graph of the line.

5 Use the graph in Fig. 2.6 to compute the slope
a across the arc between points a and b.
b at point b.
c at point c, and explain your answer.

DATA QUESTIONS

Table 2.4 shows the percentage unemployment rate in the United Kingdom and in the European Union (formerly the European Community) as a whole.

Table 2.4

	1984	1985	1986	1987	1988	1989	1990	1991	1992	1993
UK	11.7	11.2	11.2	10.2	8.5	7.1	6.9	8.7	9.9	10.3
EU	10.9	11.1	10.8	10.5	9.9	9.0	8.4	8.6	9.5	10.7

Source: *Economic Survey of Europe*, UN.

Graph this data and answer the following questions:

1 In what year was unemployment lowest in the United Kingdom? In the European Union as a whole?

2 In what year was unemployment highest in the United Kingdom? In the European Union?

3 Would this data support the hypothesis that unemployment was caused by international factors or by influences in one country?

4 Was the unemployment record better in the United Kingdom or in the European Union as a whole?

Figure 2.6

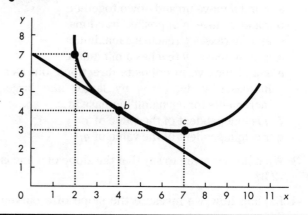

ANSWERS

CONCEPT REVIEW

1 time-series

2 trend

3 scatter

4 positive; upward

5 negative; downward

6 horizontal

7 vertical (y); horizontal (x)

8 constant

9 two

TRUE OR FALSE

1 T Other variables are plotted on the vertical axis.

2 T The graph enables us to see the changes.

3 T A visual representation allows comparison.

4 F A scatter diagram shows the relationship between variables.

5 T This illustrates a positive relationship.

6 T A rise in one variable and a fall in another represents a negative relationship.

7 T Such a relationship can take any pattern.

8 F Slope is the change in the variable on the vertical axis divided by the change in the variable on the horizontal axis.

9 T Slope of a straight line is constant.

10 F Changes in more than one variable can be shown.

11 T Arc ab would have a negative slope, arc bc a positive slope.

12 T The curve becomes steeper showing the change in y increases faster than the change in x, so the slope is increasing.

13 T At point b the curve is horizontal.

14 F The value of y is at a minimum.

MULTIPLE CHOICE

1 a Higher values of x are associated with lower values of y.

2 a Definition.

3 d Graph may be steep, flat or curved, but must have a negative slope.

4 c Change in vertical axis is 3 for each change in horizontal.

5 d Minus, because it is to the left of the y-axis.

6 b **c** would be true if we change 'negatively' to 'positively'. Can't judge **d** without additional information.

7 d Higher price is associated with lower purchases.

8 d At each price fewer boxes will be purchased.

9 c Sales increase as income increases.

10 c Use formula $y = a + bx$. Slope = b, y intercept = a.

SHORT ANSWER

1 Figure 2.7(a) illustrates a two-variable time-series graph of two variables with a tendency to move up and down together. Figure 2.7(b) illustrates a scatter diagram for such variables.

Figure 2.7

(a)

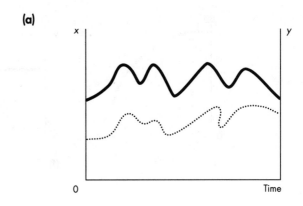

(b)

2 Figures 2.8(a) to (g) illustrate the desired graphs.

Figure 2.8

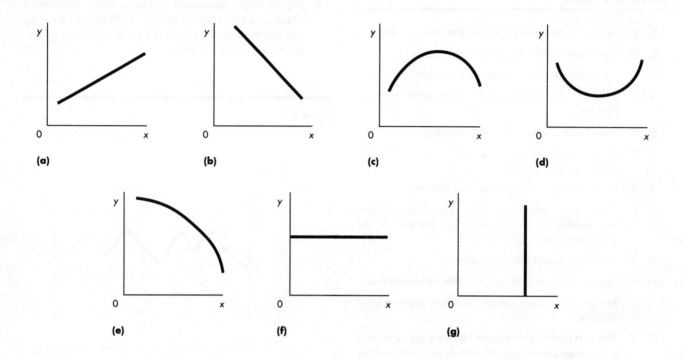

---

3 The negative sign in the slope of –2/3 means that there is a negative relationship between the two variables. The value of 2/3 means that when the variable measured on the vertical axis decreases by 2 units (the 'rise' or 'delta' y), the variable measured on the horizontal axis increases by 3 units (the 'run' or 'delta' x).

4 In both cases we actually measure the slope of a straight line.
  a The slope at a point is measured by calculating the slope of the straight line that is tangent to (just touches) the curved line at the point.
  b The slope across an arc is measured by calculating the slope of the straight line that forms the arc.

5 To graph a relationship among more than two variables, we hold all of the variables but two constant, and graph the relationship between the remaining two. Thus, we can graph the relationship between any pair of variables, given the constant values of the other variables.

PROBLEMS

1 **a** A time-series graph for the interest rate is given in Fig. 2.9(a).
  b Figure 2.9(b) is a two-variable time-series graph for both the inflation rate and the interest rate.
  c The scatter diagram for the inflation rate and the interest rate is given in Fig. 2.9(c).
  d From the graphs in parts (b) and (c), we see that the relationship between the inflation rate and the interest rate is generally positive.

Figure 2.9

(a)

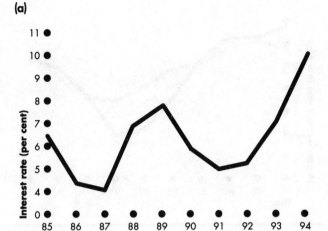

(b)

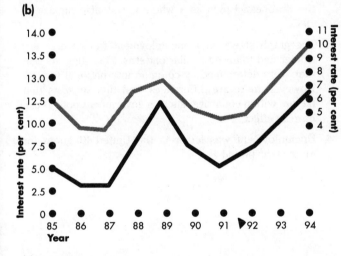

(c)

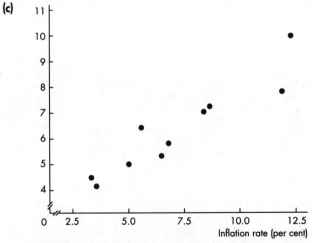

2 The slope of the line in Fig. 2.5(a) is –2/3 and the slope of the line in Fig. 2.5(b) is 2.

3 a The requested straight line is graphed in Fig. 2.10(a).
 b The requested straight line is graphed in Fig. 2.10(b).

Figure 2.10

(a)

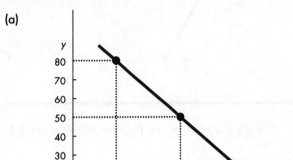

(b)

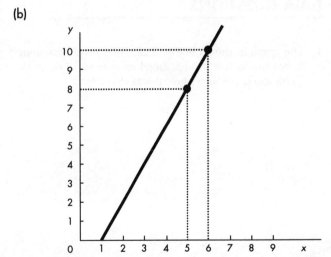

4 a i To find the y-intercept, set $x = 0$.
$$y = 6 - 2(0)$$
$$y = 6$$

ii To find the x-intercept, set $y = 0$.
$$0 = 6 - 2x$$
$$x = 3$$

iii The slope of the line is –2, the value of the b coefficient on x.

b The graph of the line is shown in Fig. 2.11.

Figure 2.11

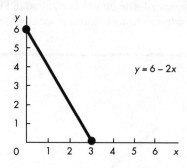

$y = 6 - 2x$

5 a The slope across the arc between points *a* and *b* is −3/2.

b The slope at point *b* is −3/4.

c The slope at point *c* is zero because it is a minimum point. Near a minimum point the slope changes from negative to positive and must pass through zero, or no slope, to do so.

DATA QUESTIONS

1 The graph is shown in Fig. 2.12. The lowest unemployment rate in the United Kingdom was in 1990; in the European Union as a whole it was also 1990.

Figure 2.12

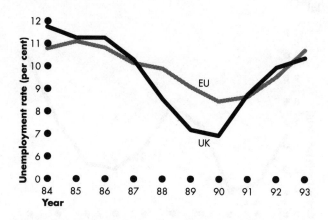

2 The rate was highest in the United Kingdom in 1984; in the European Union as a whole it was also highest in 1985.

3 The graph shows that unemployment rates were very similar and followed similar patterns. This suggests that they were determined by common international factors. However, there are differences, and this suggests that factors within countries (such as government policy) can have an effect.

4 Unemployment was lower in the United Kingdom for most of the period.

Chapter 3 **Production, Specialization and Exchange**

Chapter in Perspective, Text Pages 50–71

In Chapter 1 we learned that the existence of scarcity is the fundamental and pervasive social problem giving rise to economic activity. Because all individuals and all economies are faced with scarce resources choices must be made, each of which has an opportunity cost. Specialization in production is the key to obtaining maximum output from scarce resources, and leads to lowest opportunity costs. Since workers specialize as producers but consume a variety of goods and services, exchange is a necessary complement to specialization.

This chapter explains why specialization and exchange are the natural consequences of attempts to get the most from scarce resources (that is, to optimize). It also discusses the critical role of opportunity cost in explaining both why individuals and countries specialize in the production of goods and services and why tremendous gains occur from specialization and exchange.

Helpful Hints

1 This chapter reviews the absolutely critical concept of *opportunity cost* – the best alternative forgone – which was introduced in Chapter 1. A formula for opportunity cost, which works well in solving problems that involve moving up or down a production possibility frontier is:

$$\text{Opportunity cost} = \frac{\text{Give up}}{\text{Get}}$$

Opportunity cost equals the quantity of goods you must give up divided by the quantity of goods you will get.

Opportunity cost can also be related to the slope of the production possibility frontier (PPF). As we move down between any two points on the PPF, the opportunity cost of an additional unit of the good on the *horizontal* axis is:

$$\mid \text{slope of PPF} \mid$$

The slope of the PPF is negative, but economists like to describe opportunity cost in terms of a positive quantity of forgone goods. Therefore, we must use the *absolute value* of the slope to calculate the desired positive number.

As we move up between any two points on the PPF, the opportunity cost of an additional unit of the good on the *vertical* axis is:

$$\left| \frac{1}{\text{slope of PPF}} \right|$$

2 A production possibility frontier represents the boundary between attainable and unattainable levels of production for a fixed quantity of resources and a given state of technology. It indicates the best that can be done with existing resources and technology. Thus, the production possibility frontier will shift out if the quantity of resources increases (for example, an increase in the stock of capital goods) or if there is an increase in the ability to produce (that is, a technological improvement).

3 The text defines absolute advantage as a situation where one person has greater productivity than another in the production of all goods. We can also define *absolute advantage in the production of one good*. In comparing the productivity of two persons, this narrower concept of absolute advantage can be defined in terms of either greater output of the good per unit of inputs, or fewer inputs per unit of output. The text shows that the gains from trade depend on differing comparative advantages. People have a comparative advantage in producing a good if they can produce it at lower opportunity cost than others.

4 This chapter gives us our first chance to develop and use an economic model. The model developed in the chapter is a representation of the production possibilities in the two-person and two-good world of Jane and Joe. The model abstracts greatly from the complexity of the real world in which there are billions of people and numerous different kinds of goods and services. The model allows us to explain a number of phenomena that we observe in the world such as specialization and exchange. The model also has some implications or predictions. For example, countries that devote a larger proportion of their resources to capital accumulation will have more rapidly expanding production possibilities. The model can be subjected to 'test' by comparing these predictions with the facts we observe in the real world.

Key Figures

Figure 3.1 Jane's Production Possibility Frontier, text page 54

A production possibility frontier is the boundary between attainable and unattainable levels of production for a fixed quantity of resources and a given state of technology. Figure 3.1 illustrates the production possibility frontier for Jane, who produces corn and cloth. Each point on the frontier shows the *maximum* combinations of corn and cloth she can produce with her resources and technology. Points beyond the frontier are unattainable. Points inside the production possibility frontier are attainable but inferior.

Figure 3.2 Jane's Opportunity Cost of Cloth, text page 56

The opportunity cost of a good is not constant. In Fig. 3.2 it varies with the quantity produced – the opportunity cost of cloth changes as Jane produces more or less cloth. The first metre of cloth she gives up costs her 2 kilograms of corn, the last costs her 6 kilograms.

Figure 3.3 Economic Growth on Jane's Island, text page 59

If resources are used to produce capital goods (for example, tools), productive capacity will increase. This is represented by an outward shift of the production possibility frontier. The greater the proportion of resources used to produce capital goods, the faster the production possibility frontier will shift out. Figure 3.3 illustrates this concept using the example of Jane's production of corn and cloth. Jane can choose to use all resources to produce corn and cloth (point *e*). In this case, her production possibility frontier remains in its initial position, since Jane's ability to produce will not change. If, however, Jane decides to reduce her current production of corn and cloth in order to produce tools, her future productive ability will increase, and so her production possibility frontier will shift out. Figure 3.3 clearly illustrates that the opportunity cost of increasing future production possibilities by producing tools is forgone current production (consumption) of corn and cloth.

SELF-TEST

CONCEPT REVIEW

1 The process of converting resources into goods and services is called _____ .

2 Resources such as iron ore and running rivers are examples of _____ resources, the skill of a computer programmer and the physical strength of a bricklayer are examples of _____ resources, and a shoe factory and an olive-pitting machine are examples of _____ resources.

3 The graphical representation of the boundary between attainable and unattainable production levels is called the _____ _____ _____ .

4 The _____ _____ of a choice is the value of the best forgone alternative choice.

5 Two key activities that can shift the production possibility frontier out are _____ progress and _____ accumulation.

6 The opportunity cost of producing capital goods now in order to expand future production is forgone current _____ goods.

7 If Marta can produce salad forks at a lower opportunity cost than Jill, we say that Marta has a(n) _____ advantage in the production of salad forks.

8 The economic system that permits private individuals to own the capital resources used in production is called _____ .

9 A system in which goods are traded directly for goods is known as _____ .

10 In order for exchange to take place in such a system there must be a double _____ of wants.

11 _____ is defined as a medium of exchange.

TRUE OR FALSE

___ 1 Increasing opportunity cost results from the equal usefulness of scarce resources in all activities.

Refer to the production possibility frontier in Fig. 3.1 for Questions 2 to 7.

Figure 3.1

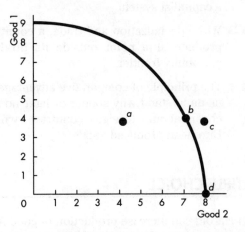

___ 2 At point d, 9 units of good 1 and 8 units of good 2 are produced.

___ 3 Point a is not attainable.

___ 4 The opportunity cost of increasing the production of good 2 from 7 to 8 units is 4 units of good 1.

___ 5 Point c is not attainable.

___ 6 In moving from point b to point d, the opportunity cost of increasing the production of good 2 equals the absolute value of the slope of the production possibility frontier between b and d.

___ 7 The bowed out (concave) shape of a PPF reflects decreasing opportunity cost as we increase production of either good.

___ 8 Reducing the current production of consumption goods in order to produce more capital goods will shift the production possibility frontier inward in the future.

___ 9 Consider an economy with two goods, X and Y, and two producers, Bill and Joe. If Bill has a comparative advantage in the production of X then Joe must have a comparative advantage in the production of Y.

___ **10** Any time two individuals have different opportunity costs they can both gain from specialization and trade.

___ **11** The incentives for specialization and exchange do not depend on property rights but only on differing opportunity costs.

___ **12** Any system that uses capital in production is a capitalist system.

___ **13** With specialization and trade, a country can produce at a point outside its production possibility frontier.

___ **14** The principle of comparative advantage helps us understand why sooner or later no one in cheap-labour foreign countries will buy European-produced goods.

MULTIPLE CHOICE

1 If Harold can increase production of good X without decreasing the production of any other good, then Harold
  a is producing on his production possibility frontier.
  b is producing outside his production possibility frontier.
  c is producing inside his production possibility frontier.
  d must have a linear production possibility frontier.
  e must prefer good X to any other good.

2 The bowed out (concave) shape of a production possibility frontier
  a is due to the equal usefulness of resources in all activities.
  b is due to capital accumulation.
  c is due to technological improvement.
  d reflects the existence of increasing opportunity cost.
  e reflects the existence of decreasing opportunity cost.

3 The economy is at point b on the production possibility frontier in Fig. 3.2. The opportunity cost of producing one more unit of X is
  a 1 unit of Y.
  b 20 units of Y.
  c 1 unit of X.

  d 8 units of X.
  e 20 units of X.

4 The economy is at point b on the production possibility frontier in Fig. 3.2. The opportunity cost of increasing the production of Y to 50 units is
  a 2 units of X.
  b 6 units of X.
  c 8 units of X.
  d 20 units of Y.
  e 30 units of Y.

Figure 3.2

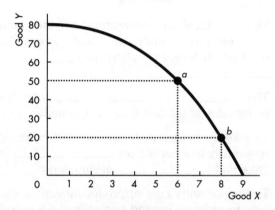

5 Because productive resources are scarce, we must give up some of one good in order to acquire more of another. This is the essence of the concept of
  a specialization.
  b monetary exchange.
  c comparative advantage.
  d absolute advantage.
  e opportunity cost.

6 In general, the higher the proportion of resources devoted to technological research in an economy the
  a greater will be current consumption.
  b faster the production possibility frontier will shift outward.
  c faster the production possibility frontier will shift inward.
  d closer it will come to having a comparative advantage in the production of all goods.
  e more bowed out will be the shape of the frontier.

In an eight-hour day, Andy can produce either 24 loaves of bread or 8 pounds of butter. In an eight-hour day, Rolfe can produce either 8 loaves of bread or 8 pounds of butter. Use this information to answer Questions 7 and 8.

7 Which of the following statements is true?
  a Andy has an absolute advantage in butter production.
  b Rolfe has an absolute advantage in butter production.
  c Andy has an absolute advantage in bread production.
  d Andy has a comparative advantage in butter production.
  e Rolfe has a comparative advantage in bread production.

8 Andy and Rolfe
  a can gain from exchange if Andy specializes in butter production and Rolfe specializes in bread production.
  b can gain from exchange if Andy specializes in bread production and Rolfe specializes in butter production.
  c cannot gain from exchange.
  d can exchange, but only Rolfe will be able to gain.
  e can exchange, but only Andy will be able to gain.

9 Anything that is generally acceptable in exchange for goods and services is
  a a commodity.
  b a medium of exchange.
  c private property.
  d a barter good.
  e called an exchange resource.

10 Which of the following is an advantage of a monetary exchange system over barter?
  a A monetary exchange system eliminates the basis for comparative advantage.
  b A monetary exchange system does not require a medium of exchange.
  c Only in a monetary exchange system can gains from trade be realized.
  d A monetary system exchange does not require a double coincidence of wants.
  e All of the above are advantages of a monetary exchange system over barter.

11 Norway and the United Kingdom produce both oil and apples using labour only. A barrel of oil can be produced with 4 hours of labour in Norway and 8 hours of labour in the United Kingdom. A bushel of apples can be produced with 8 hours of labour in Norway and 12 hours of labour in the United Kingdom. The United Kingdom has
  a an absolute advantage in oil production.
  b an absolute advantage in apple production.
  c a comparative advantage in oil production.
  d a comparative advantage in apple production.
  e none of the above.

Suppose a society produces only two goods – guns and butter. Three alternative combinations on its production possibility frontier are given in Table 3.1.

Table 3.1 Production Possibilities

Possibility	Units of butter	Units of guns
a	8	0
b	6	1
c	0	3

Use the information in Table 3.1 to answer Questions 12 and 13.

12 In moving from combination b to combination c, the opportunity cost of producing *one* additional unit of guns is
  a 2 units of butter.
  b 1/2 unit of butter.
  c 6 units of butter.
  d 1/6 unit of butter.
  e 3 units of butter.
  f 1/3 unit of butter.

13 According to this production possibility frontier
  a a combination of 6 butter and 1 gun would not employ all resources.
  b a combination of 0 butter and 4 guns is attainable.
  c resources are homogeneous.
  d the opportunity cost of producing guns increases as more guns are produced.
  e the opportunity cost of producing guns decreases as more guns are produced.

14 In Germany, the opportunity cost of 1 bale of wool is 3 bottles of wine. In the United Kingdom, the opportunity cost of 1 bottle of wine is 3 bales of wool. Given this information
  a the United Kingdom has an absolute advantage in wine production.

b the United Kingdom has an absolute advantage in wool production.

c Germany has a comparative advantage in wine production.

d Germany has a comparative advantage in wool production.

e no trade will occur.

SHORT ANSWER

1 a Why is a production possibility frontier negatively sloped?

b Why is it bowed out?

2 a In an economy with no tool-making possibilities (constant capital goods), what is the opportunity cost of moving from a point inside the production possibility frontier to a point on the frontier? Explain.

b In a tool-making economy, what is the opportunity cost of current consumption?

3 Lawyers earn £100 per hour while secretaries earn £4 per hour. Use the concepts of absolute and comparative advantage to explain why a lawyer who is a better typist than her secretary, will still 'specialize' in doing only legal work and will 'trade' with the secretary for typing services.

4 Explain, using a specific example of exchange, why a monetary exchange system is more efficient than barter.

PROBLEMS

1 Suppose that an economy with unchanged capital goods (no tool-making) has the production possibility frontier shown in Table 3.2.

Table 3.2 Production Possibilities

Possibility	Maximum units of butter per week	Maximum units of guns per week
a	200	0
b	180	60
c	160	100
d	100	160
e	40	200
f	0	220

a On graph paper, plot these possibilities, label the points, and draw the production possibility frontier. (Put guns on the *x*-axis.)

b If the economy moves from possibility *c* to possibility *d*, the opportunity cost *per unit of guns* will be how many units of butter?

c If the economy moves from possibility *d* to possibility *e*, the opportunity cost *per unit of guns* will be how many units of butter?

d In general terms, what happens to the opportunity cost of guns as the output of guns increases?

e In general terms, what happens to the opportunity cost of butter as the output of butter increases? What do the results for possibilities *e* and *f* imply about resources?

f If (instead of the possibilities given) the production possibility frontier were a straight line joining points *a* and *f*, what would that imply about opportunity costs and resources?

g Given the original production possibility frontier you have plotted, is a combination of 140 units of butter and 130 units of guns per week attainable? Would you regard this combination as an efficient one? Explain.

h If the following events occurred (each is a separate event, unaccompanied by any other event), what would happen to the production possibility frontier?

i A new, easily exploited, energy source is discovered.

ii A large number of skilled workers immigrate into the country.

iii The output of butter is increased.

iv A new invention increases output per person in the butter industry but not in the guns industry.

v A new law is passed compelling workers, who could previously work as long as they wanted, to retire at age 60.

2 France and Germany produce both wine and beer, using a single homogeneous input – labour. Their production possibilities are:

France has 100 units of labour and can produce a maximum of 200 bottles of wine *or* 400 bottles of beer.

Germany has 50 units of labour and can produce a maximum of 250 bottles of wine *or* 200 bottles of beer.

Table 3.3

	Bottles produced by 1 unit of labour		Opportunity cost of 1 additional bottle	
	Wine	Beer	Wine	Beer
France				
Germany				

a Complete Table 3.3.

Use the information in part **a** to answer the following questions.

b Which country has an absolute advantage in wine production?
c Which country has an absolute advantage in beer production?
d Which country has a comparative advantage in wine production?
e Which country has a comparative advantage in beer production?
f If trade is allowed, describe what specialization, if any, will occur.

DATA QUESTIONS

The tailor and the shoemaker

It is the maxim of every prudent master of a family never to attempt to make at home what it will cost him more to make than to buy. The tailor does not attempt to make his own shoes, but buys them off the shoemaker. The shoemaker does not attempt to make his own clothes, but employs a tailor…. What is prudence in the conduct of a private family can scarce be folly in that of a great kingdom…. If a foreign country can supply us with a commodity cheaper than we ourselves can make it, better buy it off them with some part of the produce of our own industry…

Source: Adam Smith, *The Wealth of Nations.*

1 Explain what is meant by 'absolute advantage' and 'comparative advantage'. Do either of these concepts relate to the passage above? If so how?

2 Draw production possibility curves for the shoemaker and the tailor.

3 How would they each benefit from specialization?

ANSWERS

CONCEPT REVIEW

1 production
2 natural; human; capital
3 production possibility frontier
4 opportunity cost
5 technological; capital
6 consumption
7 comparative
8 capitalism
9 barter
10 coincidence
11 money

TRUE OR FALSE

1 **F** Unequal usefulness.
2 **F** At *d*, 0 units of good 1 and 8 units of good 2 produced.
3 **F** Attainable but not a maximum.
4 **T** Moving from *b* to *d*, production of good 1 falls by 4 units.
5 **T** Outside PPF.
6 **T** See Helpful Hint 1.
7 **F** Reflects the increasing opportunity cost as increased production of either good.
8 **F** It will shift the PPF *out*ward.
9 **T** Because comparative advantage measures *relative* advantages.

10 T Different opportunity cost means different comparative advantage.

11 F Property rights are a prerequisite for specialization and exchange.

12 F Capital is used in all systems.

13 F Can *consume* at points outside the PPF.

14 F They will buy if European goods are relatively cheaper.

MULTIPLE-CHOICE

1 c For zero opportunity cost, there must be unemployed resources.

2 d **a** would be true if *un*equal resources, **b** and **c** shift PPF.

3 b To increase quantity X to 9, must cut quantity Y from 20 to 0.

4 a To move from *b* to *a* quantity X falls from 8 to 6.

5 e Definition.

6 b Technological progress shifts PPF outward at cost of current consumption.

7 c Andy is three times as efficient in producing bread.

8 b Andy is more efficient in producing bread.

9 b Definition.

10 d Double coincidence of wants is a principal limitation of barter.

11 d The United Kingdom uses relatively few hours to produce apples.

12 e Give up 6 butter to get 2 guns: 6/2 = 3 butter per gun.

13 d Opportunity cost of a gun between *a* and *b* = 2 butter. Between *b* and *c* = 3 butter. **a** is on PPF, **b** outside PPF.

14 c Opportunity cost of wine in terms of bales of wool is Germany 1/3, United Kingdom 3. Opportunity cost of wool in terms of wine – Germany 3, United Kingdom 1/3.

SHORT ANSWER

1 a The negative slope of the production possibility frontier reflects opportunity cost: in order to have more of one good, some of the other must be forgone.

  b It is bowed out because the existence of non-homogeneous resources creates increasing opportunity cost as we increase the production of either good.

2 a In an economy with no tool-making possibilities, a point inside the production possibility frontier represents unemployed or underutilized resources. By moving to a point on the frontier, more output can be produced from the same resources, simply by utilizing the resources more efficiently. Since resources do not have to be withdrawn from the production of any other good, the opportunity cost of moving to a point on the frontier is zero. This is the closest we get to a 'free lunch' in the discipline of economics.

  b In a tool-making economy, we can forgo current consumption to produce capital goods which subsequently increase future production and consumption. By consuming all that is currently produced, we forgo tool-making and, ultimately, increase future consumption.

3 The lawyer has an absolute advantage in producing both legal and typing services relative to the secretary. Nevertheless, she has a comparative advantage in legal services, and the secretary has a comparative advantage in typing. To demonstrate these comparative advantages, we can construct a table of opportunity costs.

Table 3.4 Opportunity Cost of 1 Additional Hour (pounds)

	Legal services	Typing
Lawyer	100	100
Secretary	>100	4

Consider first the lawyer's opportunity costs. The lawyer's best forgone alternative to providing 1 hour of legal services is the £100 she could earn by providing another hour of legal services. If she provides 1 hour of typing, she is also forgoing £100 (1 hour) of legal services. What would the secretary have to forgo to provide 1 hour of legal services? She would have to spend several years as a student, forgoing years of income in addition to the tuition she must pay. Her opportunity cost is a very large number, certainly greater than £100. If she provides 1 hour of typing, her best forgone alternative is the £4 she could have earned at another secretarial job. Thus Table 3.4 shows that the lawyer has a lower opportunity cost (comparative advantage) of providing legal services, and the secretary has a lower opportunity cost (comparative advantage) of providing typing services. It is on the basis of comparative advantage (not absolute advantage) that trade will take place from which both parties gain.

4 The principal reason for the efficiency of a monetary exchange system relative to barter is that the monetary system does not require a double coincidence of wants to complete a successful exchange. For example, suppose you specialize in the production of apples but like to eat bananas. In a barter economy, you would probably not be able to complete an exchange with the first person you found who had bananas to trade. It would be necessary for that person also to want to trade the bananas for apples and not for carrots or some other good. In a monetary economy, you would always be able to make a successful exchange with the first person you found with bananas to trade since that person would be willing to accept money in exchange. Similarly, in a money exchange system, you would be able to sell your apples for money to the first person you found who wanted apples (even if that person did not have bananas to sell).

PROBLEMS

1 a The graph of the production possibility frontier is shown in Fig. 3.3.

Figure 3.3

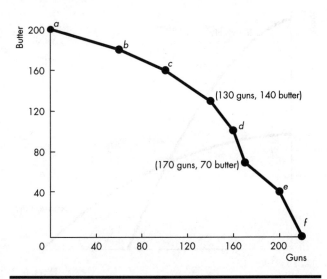

b In moving from c to d, in order to gain 60 units of guns, we must give up $160 - 100 = 60$ units of butter. The opportunity cost per unit of guns is:

$$\frac{60 \text{ units butter}}{60 \text{ units guns}} = 1 \text{ unit butter per } 1 \text{ unit of guns}$$

c In moving from d to e, in order to gain 40 units of guns, we must give up $100 - 40 = 60$ units of butter. The

opportunity cost per unit of guns is:

$$\frac{60 \text{ units butter}}{40 \text{ units guns}} = 1.5 \text{ units butter per } 1 \text{ unit of guns}$$

d The opportunity cost of producing more guns increases as the output of guns increases.

e Likewise, the opportunity cost of producing more butter increases as the output of butter increases.

Increasing opportunity costs imply that resources are non-homogeneous, that is, they are not equally useful in gun and butter production.

f Opportunity costs would always be constant, regardless of the output of guns or butter. The opportunity cost per unit of guns would be:

$$200/220 = 10/11 \text{ units of butter}$$

The opportunity cost per unit of butter would be:

$$220/200 = 1.1 \text{ units of guns}$$

Constant opportunity costs imply that resources are homogeneous, that is, they are equally useful in gun and butter production.

g This combination is outside the frontier and, therefore, is not attainable. Since the economy cannot produce this combination, the question of efficiency is irrelevant.

h **i** Assuming that both goods require energy for their production, the entire frontier shifts out to the north-east (Fig. 3.4).

Figure 3.4

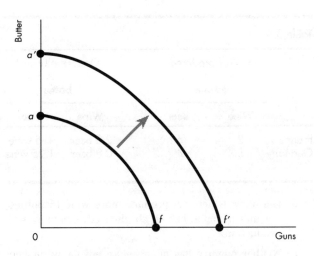

ii Assuming that both goods use skilled labour in their production, the entire frontier shifts out to the north-east.

iii The frontier does not shift. An increase in the output of butter implies a movement *along* the frontier to the left, not a shift of the frontier itself.

iv The new invention implies that for every level of output of guns, the economy can now produce more butter. The frontier swings to the right, but remains anchored at point *f* (Fig. 3.5).

v The entire frontier shifts in towards the origin.

Figure 3.5

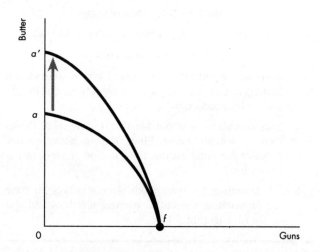

2 a The completed table is shown as Table 3.5:

Table 3.5

	Bottles produced by 1 unit of labour		Opportunity cost of 1 additional bottle	
	Wine	**Beer**	**Wine**	**Beer**
France	2	4	2.0 beer	0.5 wine
Germany	5	4	0.8 beer	1.25 wine

b Germany, which can produce more wine (5 bottles) per unit of input, has an absolute advantage in wine production.

c Neither country has an absolute advantage in beer production, since beer output (4 bottles) per unit of input is the same for both countries.

d Germany, with the lower opportunity cost (0.8 beer), has a comparative advantage in wine production.

e France, with the lower opportunity cost (0.5 wine), has a comparative advantage in beer production.

f The incentive for trade depends only on differences in comparative advantage. Germany will specialize in wine production and France will specialize in beer production.

DATA QUESTIONS

1 Absolute advantage occurs when one person or country has greater productivity than another in the production of all goods. A person has comparative advantage if that person can produce a good at a lower opportunity cost than another person. In the case in question, the shoemaker has a comparative advantage in producing shoes and the tailor in producing clothes.

2 The production possibility curves are shown in Fig. 3.6.

Figure 3.6

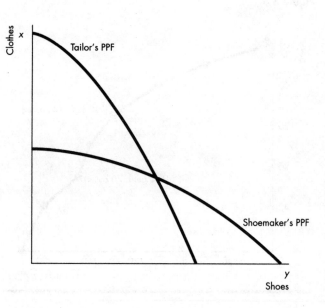

3 Both tailor and shoemaker would benefit if they specialize and exchange their products. In Fig. 3.6, total output would be *x* units of clothes and *y* shoes. This exceeds the output if both tailor and shoemaker produced both clothes and shoes. Self-sufficiency means lower levels of output.

Chapter 4 Demand and Supply

Chapter in Perspective, Text Pages 76–97

Most formal exchange takes place in 'markets' at prices determined by the interaction of buyers (demanders) and sellers (suppliers) in those markets. There are markets for goods (like wheat or textbooks), for services (like haircuts or tattoos), for financial assets (like IBM shares, pounds sterling, or government bonds). Demand and supply are very powerful tools that economists use to explain how much will be traded and at what price. Careful use of these tools will allow us to explain a wide array of economic phenomena and even predict changes in prices and quantities traded.

Helpful Hints

1 Specific examples will help you understand economic ideas. For example, when analysing complementary goods, think about hamburgers and chips; when discussing substitute goods, think about hamburgers and hot dogs. This will help reduce the 'abstractness' of the economic theory.

2 The statement 'price is determined by demand and supply' is a shorthand way of saying that price is determined by all of the factors affecting demand (such as prices of other goods, income, population, preferences) and all of the factors affecting supply (such as prices of other goods, prices of factors of production, technology). The benefit of using demand and supply *curves* is that they allow us systematically to sort out the influences on price of each of these separate factors. Changes in the factors affecting demand shift the demand curve and move us up or down the given supply curve.

Changes in the factors affecting supply shift the supply curve and move us up or down the given demand curve.

Any demand and supply problem requires you to sort out these influences carefully. In so doing, *always draw a graph*, even if it is just a small graph in the margin of a true–false or multiple-choice problem. As you become comfortable with graphs, you will find that they are effective and powerful tools for systematically organizing your thinking.

Note that when you draw a graph, you should be sure to *label* the *axes*. As the course progresses, you will encounter many graphs with different variables on the axes. It is very easy to become confused if you do not develop the habit of labelling the axes.

3 Another very common mistake among students is a failure to *distinguish between a shift in a curve and a movement along a curve* correctly. This distinction applies to both demand and supply curves.

Consider demand curves. The quantity of a good demanded depends on its own price, the prices of related goods, income, population and preferences. The term 'demand' refers to the relationship between the price of a good and the quantity demanded, holding constant all of the other factors on which the quantity demanded depends. This demand relationship is represented graphically by the demand curve. Thus, the effect of a change in price on quantity demanded is already reflected in the slope of the demand curve, that is, the effect of a change in the price of the good itself is given by a movement along the demand curve. This is referred to as a change in quantity demanded.

On the other hand, if one of the other factors affecting the quantity demanded changes, the demand curve itself will shift, that is, the quantity demanded at each price will change. This shift of the demand curve is referred to as a change in demand. The critical thing to remember is that a change in the price of a good will not shift the demand curve, it will only cause a movement along the demand curve. Similarly, it is just as important to distinguish between shifts in the supply curve and movements along the supply curve.

Remember: it is shifts in demand and supply curves that cause the market price to change, not changes in the price that cause demand and supply curves to shift.

4 When analysing the shifts of demand and supply curves in related markets (for example, for substitute goods like beer and wine), it often seems as though the feedback effects from one market to the other can go on endlessly. To avoid confusion, stick to the rule that each curve (demand and supply) for a given market can shift a maximum of *once*.

Key Figures and Tables

Figure 4.1 The Demand Curve, text page 79
A demand schedule is a table that lists the quantities consumers demand at each price, if everything else remains constant. For example, if the price of a tape is £1.60, consumers would be willing to buy 3 million tapes per week, assuming that other things (like income and the price of a Walkman) remain unchanged. The law of demand is illustrated by the fact that as the price of a tape increases, *ceteris*

paribus, the quantity of tapes that consumers would be willing to buy decreases.

A demand curve is the graphical representation of the relationship between the quantity demanded of a good and its price, holding constant all other influences on consumers' planned purchases. Price appears on the vertical axis and quantity demanded on the horizontal axis. The demand curve tells us how many tapes consumers will be willing to buy in a week at each price, other things held constant. The law of demand is reflected in the negative slope of the demand curve.

Figure 4.3 A Change in Demand versus a Change in the Quantity Demanded, text page 82
This distinguishes between a change in demand (represented by a shift in the demand curve) and a change in the quantity demanded (represented by a movement along a given demand curve). Remember that a change in the price of a good or service implies that the quantity demanded changes. Since this is exactly the relationship represented by the demand curve, the change in quantity demanded is represented by a movement along the demand curve. If there is a change in any of the other factors affecting the willingness of consumers to buy at a given price, then we say there is a change in demand which is represented by a shift in the demand curve itself.

Figure 4.4 The Supply Curve, text page 84
A supply schedule is a table that lists the quantities that producers will plan to sell at each price, if everything else remains constant. For example, if the price of a tape is £1.60, producers will plan to sell 5 million tapes per week, assuming that other things (like the technology used to produce tapes) remain unchanged. The law of supply is illustrated by the fact that as the price of a tape increases, *ceteris paribus*, the quantity of tapes that producers plan to supply increases.

A supply curve is the graphical representation of the relationship between the quantity of a good supplied and its price, holding constant all other influences on producers' planned sales. The supply curve tells us how many tapes producers will be willing to sell per week at each price, other things held constant. The law of supply is reflected in the slope of the supply curve.

Figure 4.6 A Change in Supply versus a Change in the Quantity Supplied, text page 86
This distinguishes between a change in supply (represented by a shift in the supply curve) and a change in the quantity supplied (represented by a movement

along a given supply curve). Remember that a change in the price of a good or service implies that the quantity supplied changes. Since this is the relationship represented by the supply curve, the change in quantity supplied is represented by a movement along the supply curve. If there is a change in any of the other factors affecting the willingness of producers to sell at a given price, then we say there is a change in supply which is represented by a shift in the supply curve itself.

Figure 4.7 Equilibrium, text page 90

In this figure, the demand and supply curves are combined in the same graph in order to examine the price and quantity traded that leave both buyers and sellers satisfied. Equilibrium price is defined as that price at which the quantity demanded is equal to the quantity supplied. The equilibrium price (£1.20 in the example) can be identified using either the table or the diagram. The idea of equilibrium as a point of rest is also illustrated. Note that when the price is below the equilibrium price there is a shortage which will cause the price to rise toward equilibrium. When the price is above the equilibrium price, there is a surplus which will cause the price to fall toward equilibrium. Only at the equilibrium price will there be no tendency for the price to change.

Table 4.1 The Demand for Tapes, text page 81

This table specifies the law of demand: the quantity demanded increases as the price of the good or service falls and decreases as the price rises. These changes are represented by movements along the demand curve. The factors that cause changes in demand are also listed. Changes in these factors will cause the demand curve to shift. Note that the table assumes that tapes are a normal good, since a rise in income will cause the demand for tapes to increase. If the good in question is inferior, a rise in income will cause demand to decrease whereas a fall in income will cause demand to increase. As implied by the name, most goods and services are normal.

Table 4.2 The Supply of Tapes, text page 85

In parallel with Table 4.1, this table specifies the law of supply: the quantity supplied increases as the price rises and decreases as the price falls. These changes are represented by movements along the supply curve. The factors that cause changes in supply are also listed. Changes in these factors will cause the supply curve to shift.

SELF-TEST

CONCEPT REVIEW

1 The _____ _____ of a good or service is the amount that consumers are willing and able to purchase at a particular price.

2 The law of demand states that, other things being equal, the higher the _____ of a good, the _____ is the quantity demanded.

3 A demand _____ is a list of the quantities of a good demanded at different _____ .

4 A demand curve illustrates the _____ price that consumers are willing to pay for the last unit of a good purchased.

5 The demand curve for most goods will shift to the right if income _____ , or if the price of

a substitute _____ , or if the price of a complement _____ , or if the size of the population _____ .

6 A good is said to be _____ if the demand for it increases as income increases and _____ if demand decreases as income increases.

7 The amount of a good or service that producers plan to sell at a particular price is called the _____ _____ .

8 The law of supply states that the _____ the price of a good, the _____ the quantity supplied.

9 A supply curve shows the quantity supplied at each given _____ .

10 A decrease in supply is represented by a shift to

the _____ in the supply curve.

11 The supply curve will shift to the right if the price of a complement in production _____ , or if the price of a substitute in production _____ , or if there is a technological _____ , or if the price of a productive resource _____ .

12 An increase in the price of a good will cause an increase in the _____ _____; that is represented by a(n) _____ movement along the supply curve.

13 The price at which the quantity demanded equals the quantity supplied is called the _____ price.

14 If the price is above equilibrium, a(n) _____ will exist, causing the price to _____ .

15 When demand increases, the equilibrium price will _____ and the quantity traded will _____ .

16 When supply increases, the equilibrium price will _____ and the quantity traded will _____ .

17 If demand increases and supply increases, then we know that the quantity traded must _____ ; but equilibrium price may increase, decrease, or remain unchanged.

TRUE OR FALSE

___ **1** The law of demand tells us that as the price of a good rises the quantity demanded decreases.

___ **2** The negative slope of a demand curve is a result of the law of demand.

___ **3** An increase in the price of apples will shift the demand curve for apples to the left.

___ **4** Hamburgers and chips are complements. If Burger Bar reduces the price of chips, the demand for hamburgers will increase.

___ **5** A supply curve shows the maximum price at which the last unit will be supplied.

___ **6** A demand curve is a graphical representation of the relationship between the price of a good and quantity demanded given the level of income, prices of other goods, population and preferences.

___ **7** A cost-reducing technological improvement will shift a supply curve to the right.

___ **8** If we observe a doubling of the price of mozzarella cheese (an ingredient in pizza), we will expect the supply curve for pizzas to shift to the left.

___ **9** When a cow is slaughtered for beef, its hide becomes available to make leather. Thus, beef and leather are substitutes in production.

___ **10** If the price of beef rises, we would expect to see an increase in the supply of leather and in the quantity of beef supplied.

___ **11** If the current price is such that the quantity demanded exceeds the quantity supplied, the price will tend to rise.

___ **12** If demand increases, we would predict an increase in equilibrium price and a decrease in quantity traded.

___ **13** If potatoes are inferior goods, we would expect an increase in income to result in a fall in the price of potatoes.

___ **14** A decrease in the supply of a good will result in a decrease in both the equilibrium price and the quantity traded.

___ **15** Suppose there is a significant decline in the price of iron ore (used in making steel). We would predict that the equilibrium price of steel will fall and the quantity traded will increase.

___ **16** Suppose the demand for personal computers increases while the cost of producing them decreases. With this information, we can definitely predict that the quantity of personal computers traded will increase and the price will fall.

___ **17** When the actual price is above the equilibrium price, a shortage occurs.

MULTIPLE-CHOICE

1 Which of the following could *not* cause an increase in demand for a commodity?
a an increase in income
b a decrease in income
c a decrease in the price of a substitute
d a decrease in the price of a complement
e an increase in preferences for the commodity

2 If Hamburger Helper is an inferior good, then, *ceteris paribus*, a decrease in income will cause
a a leftward shift of the demand curve for Hamburger Helper.
b a rightward shift of the demand curve for Hamburger Helper.
c a movement up along the demand curve for Hamburger Helper.
d a movement down along the demand curve for Hamburger Helper.
e none of the above.

3 Good *A* is a normal good if
a an increase in the price of a complement causes the demand for *A* to decrease.
b an increase in income causes the demand for *A* to increase.
c an increase in the price of a substitute causes the demand for *A* to increase.
d it satisfies the law of demand.
e income and the demand for *A* are negatively correlated.

4 A decrease in quantity demanded is represented by a
a rightward shift of the supply curve.
b rightward shift of the demand curve.
c leftward shift of the demand curve.
d movement upward and to the left along the demand curve.
e movement downward and to the right along the demand curve.

5 The price of a good will tend to fall if
a there is a surplus at the current price.
b the current price is above equilibrium.
c the quantity supplied exceeds the quantity demanded at the current price.
d all of the above are true.
e none of the above is true.

6 The fact that a decline in the price of a good causes producers to reduce the quantity of the good supplied illustrates
a the law of supply.
b the law of demand.
c a change in supply.
d the nature of an inferior good.
e technological improvement.

7 A shift of the supply curve for salami will be caused by
a a change in preferences for salami.
b a change in the price of a related good that is a substitute in consumption for salami.
c a change in income.
d a change in the price of salami.
e none of the above.

8 Which of the following will shift the supply curve for good *X* to the left?
a a decrease in the wages of workers employed to produce *X*
b an increase in the cost of machinery used to produce *X*
c a technological improvement in the production of *X*
d a situation where quantity demanded exceeds quantity supplied
e all of the above

9 If a resource can be used to produce either good *A* or good *B*, then *A* and *B* are
a substitutes in production.
b complements in production.
c substitutes in consumption.
d complements in consumption.
e normal goods.

10 If the market for pencils is in equilibrium, then
a pencils must be a normal good.
b producers would like to sell more at the current price.
c consumers would like to buy more at the current price.
d there will be a surplus.
e quantity traded equals quantity demanded.

11 A shortage is the amount by which quantity
a demanded exceeds quantity supplied.
b traded exceeds quantity supplied.
c traded exceeds quantity demanded.
c demanded exceeds the equilibrium quantity.
e supplied exceeds the equilibrium quantity.

12 A surplus can be eliminated by
   a increasing supply.
   b government raising the price.
   c decreasing the quantity demanded.
   d allowing the price to fall.
   e allowing the quantity traded to fall.

The market for coffee is initially in equilibrium with supply and demand curves of the usual shape. Pepsi is a substitute for coffee; cream is a complement for coffee. Questions 13–15 concern the market for *coffee*.

Assume that all *ceteris paribus* assumptions continue to hold *except* for the event(s) listed. Answer each question without considering the others.

13 Coffee is a normal good. A decrease in income will
   a increase the price of coffee and increase the quantity demanded of coffee.
   b increase the price of coffee and increase the quantity supplied of coffee.
   c decrease the price of coffee and decrease the quantity demanded of coffee.
   d decrease the price of coffee and decrease the quantity supplied of coffee.
   e cause none of the above.

14 An increase in the price of Pepsi will
   a increase the price of coffee and increase the quantity demanded of coffee.
   b increase the price of coffee and increase the quantity supplied of coffee.
   c decrease the price of coffee and decrease the quantity demanded of coffee.
   d decrease the price of coffee and decrease the quantity supplied of coffee.
   e cause none of the above.

15 A technological improvement lowers the cost of producing coffee. At the same time, preferences for coffee decrease. The *quantity traded* of coffee will
   a rise.
   b fall.
   c remain the same.
   d rise or fall depending on whether the price of coffee falls or rises.
   e rise or fall depending on the relative shifts of demand and supply curves.

16 If both demand and supply increase, then
   a price will rise and quantity traded will increase.
   b price will fall and quantity traded will increase.
   c price could either rise or fall and quantity traded will increase.
   d price will rise and quantity traded could either increase or decrease.
   e price will fall and quantity traded could either increase or decrease.

17 Which of the following will definitely cause an increase in the equilibrium price?
   a an increase in both demand and supply
   b a decrease in both demand and supply
   c an increase in demand combined with a decrease in supply
   d a decrease in demand combined with an increase in supply
   e none of the above

SHORT ANSWER

1 Explain the difference between wants and demands.

2 Suppose we observe that the consumption of peanut butter increases at the same time as its price rises. What must have happened in the market for peanut butter? Is the observation consistent with the law of demand?

3 The price of personal computers has continued to fall even in the face of increasing demand. Explain.

4 Brussels sprouts and carrots are substitutes in consumption and, since they can both be grown on the same type of land, substitutes in production too. Suppose there is an increase in the demand for Brussels sprouts. Trace through the effects on price and quantity traded in both the Brussels sprout and carrot markets. (Keep in mind Helpful Hint 4.)

PROBLEMS

1 The information given in Table 4.1 is about the behaviour of buyers and sellers of fish at the market on a particular Saturday.

Table 4.1 Demand and Supply Schedules for Fish

Price per fish (pounds)	Quantity demanded	Quantity supplied
0.75	270	45
1.00	260	135
1.25	245	185
1.50	225	225
1.75	200	250
2.00	170	265
2.25	135	280
2.50	105	290
2.75	80	300
3.00	60	310
3.25	45	315
3.50	35	320

a On graph paper, draw the demand curve and the supply curve. Be sure to label the axes. What is the equilibrium price?

b We will make the usual *ceteris paribus* assumptions about the demand curve so that it does not shift. List four factors that we are assuming do not change.

c We will also hold the supply curve constant by assuming that three factors do not change. List them.

d Explain briefly what would happen if the price were initially set at £2.75.

e Explain briefly what would happen if the price were initially set at £1.

f Explain briefly what would happen if the price were initially set at £1.50.

2 The market for wine in the United Kingdom is initially in equilibrium with supply and demand curves of the usual shape. Beer is a close substitute for wine; cheese and wine are complements. Use demand and supply diagrams to analyse the effect of each of the following (separate) events on the equilibrium price and quantity traded in the UK wine market. Assume that all of the *ceteris paribus* assumptions continue to hold except for the event listed. For both price and quantity traded, you should indicate in each case whether the variable rises, falls, remains the same, or moves ambiguously (may rise or fall).

a The income of consumers falls (wine is a normal good).

b Early frost destroys a large part of the world grape crop.

c A new churning invention reduces the cost of producing cheese.

d A new fermentation technique is invented that reduces the cost of producing wine.

e A government study is published which suggests that wine drinking is linked to higher rates of heart disease.

f Costs of producing both beer and wine increase dramatically.

3 Table 4.2 lists the demand and supply schedules for cases of peanuts.

Table 4.2 Demand and Supply Schedules for Cases of Peanuts per Week

Price per case (pounds)	Quantity demanded (cases)	Quantity supplied (cases)
70	20	140
60	60	120
50	100	100
40	140	80
30	180	60

a Draw the demand and supply curves for peanuts. Be sure to label the axes properly. Label the demand and supply curves D_0 and S_0 respectively.

b What are the equilibrium price and quantity traded in the peanut market? On your diagram, label the equilibrium point a.

c Is there a surplus or shortage at a price of £40? How much?

d Suppose the population grows sufficiently that the demand for peanuts increases by 60 cases per week at every price.

   i Construct a table (price, quantity demanded) of the new demand schedule.

   ii Draw the new demand curve on your original graph and label it D_1.

   iii Label the new equilibrium point b. What are the new equilibrium price and quantity traded?

DATA QUESTIONS

Travel industry seeks safe haven for nervous clients

The travel industry is being restructured because of the war in the Gulf between Iraq and the allies.

The fear that the war may spill over into the neighbouring territories has caused soaring demand for 'safe' holidays in Spain and caused travel operators to scrap package tours to destinations such as Turkey and Cyprus. International airlines similarly face a downturn in transatlantic flights due to American fears of Iraqi terrorism in Europe. The outlook is further confused by the slump in demand for travel caused by the recession.

The Association of British Travel Agents (ABTA) predicts heavy booking for package tours to Majorca and the Costa del Sol. Many resorts could be over booked because Spanish hotel owners have cut the number of beds in an attempt to upgrade the country's tourist image.

Source: Adapted from the *Guardian*, 22 January 1991. Published by permission of The Guardian©.

Draw diagrams to answer the following questions:

1 What was the effect of the war on the price and quantity of holidays in countries near the Gulf such as Turkey?

2 What would be the effect of the war on the price and quantity of holidays in Spain?

3 Earlier, Spanish hoteliers had cut the number of beds. What effect would this have on the price of holidays?

ANSWERS

CONCEPT REVIEW

1 quantity demanded

2 price; lower

3 schedule; prices

4 highest

5 increases; increases; decreases; increases

6 normal; inferior

7 quantity supplied

8 higher; higher

9 price

10 left

11 increases; decreases; improvement; increases

12 quantity supplied; upward

13 equilibrium

14 surplus; fall

15 increase; increase

16 decrease; increase

17 increase

TRUE OR FALSE

1 F As price rises, quantity demanded decreases.

2 T The law of demand states that as price falls, quantity increases.

3 F It will cause a movement *along* the curve.

4 T A meal of hamburger and chips is now cheaper.

5 F Supply curve shows minimum price at which last unit supplied.

6 T The demand curve holds constant all factors except quantity and price.

7 T More will be supplied at each price.

8 T Increase in the price of a factor of production leads to a fall in supply.

9 F Beef and leather are complements in production because they are produced together.

10 T For complements in production, an increase in the price of one good leads to an increase in quantity supplied and an increase in the supply of the other good.

11 T Price rises when demand exceeds supply.

12 F An increase in demand will lead to an increase in quantity.

13 T For inferior goods, an increase in income leads to a fall in demand and a fall in price.

14 F A decrease in supply will lead to a rise in price.

15 T A fall in the price of a factor will shift the supply curve to the right.

16 F Quantity will increase but the effect on price depends on the relative magnitude of shifts in demand and supply.

17 F When actual price is above equilibrium, quantity supplied exceeds quantity demanded.

MULTIPLE-CHOICE

1 c A fall in the price of a substitute causes an increased demand for the substitute and therefore a fall in demand for the other good.

2 b Changes in income shift the demand curve rather than causing moves along it.

3 b Definition.

4 d Decrease in quantity is caused by a change in price and a movement along a curve.

5 d Demand shifts left.

6 a Definition.

7 e **a, b** and **c** affect demand. **d** would cause a move along the supply curve.

8 b A rise in the price of a factor shifts the supply curve left.

9 a As alternatives, they are substitutes.

10 e Definition.

11 a Shortage occurs when demand exceeds supply.

12 d Other answers make surplus larger.

13 d Demand shifts left.

14 b Demand shifts right.

15 e Supply shifts right and demand shifts left.

16 c Both shifts will increase quantity, but have opposite effects on price.

17 c Both shifts will increase price.

SHORT ANSWER

1 Wants reflect our unlimited desires for goods and services without regard to our ability or willingness to make the sacrifices necessary to obtain them. The existence of scarcity means that many of those wants will not be satisfied. On the other hand, demands refer to plans to buy and, therefore, reflect decisions about which wants to satisfy.

2 The observation that the consumption of peanut butter increases at the same time as the price of peanut butter rises is entirely consistent with the law of demand (that is, a negatively-sloped demand curve). It simply reflects the fact that the demand for peanut butter has increased (that is, the demand curve has shifted out to the right).

3 Owing to the tremendous pace of technological advance, not only has the demand for personal computers been increasing, but the supply has been increasing as well. Indeed, supply has been increasing much more rapidly than demand, which has resulted in falling prices. Thus, *much* (but not all) of the increase in sales of personal computers reflects a movement down along a demand curve rather than a shift in demand.

4 The answer to this question requires us to trace through the effects on the two graphs in Fig. 4.1(a) and (b) – one for the Brussels sprout market and one for the carrot market. The sequence of effects occurs in order of the numbers on the graphs.

Figure 4.1

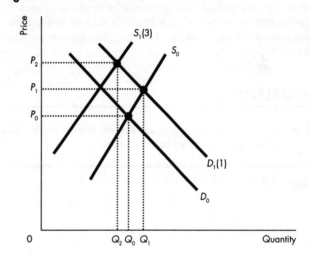

(a) Brussels sprouts

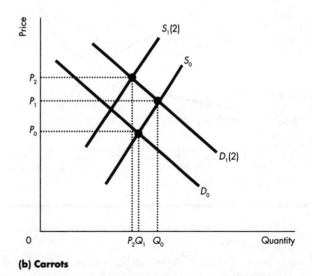

(b) Carrots

Look first at the market for Brussels sprouts. The increase in demand shifts the demand curve to the right from D_0 to D_1 (1), and the price of Brussels sprouts rises. This price rise has two effects (2) on the carrot market. Since Brussels sprouts and carrots ar\e substitutes in consumption, the demand curve for carrots shifts to the right from D_0 to D_1. And, since Brussels sprouts and carrots are substitutes in production, the supply curve of carrots shifts to the left from S_0 to S_1. Both of these shifts in the carrot market raise the price of carrots, causing feedback effects on the Brussels sprout market. But remember the rule (Helpful Hint 4) that each curve (demand and supply) for a given market can shift a maximum of *once*. Since the demand curve for Brussels sprouts has already shifted, we can only shift the supply curve from S_0 to S_1 (3) because of the substitutes in production relationship. Each curve in each market has now shifted once and the analysis must stop. We can predict that the net effects are increases in the equilibrium prices of both Brussels sprouts and carrots, and indeterminate changes in quantities traded in both markets.

PROBLEMS

1 a The demand and supply curves are shown in Fig. 4.2. The equilibrium price is £1.50 per fish.

Figure 4.2

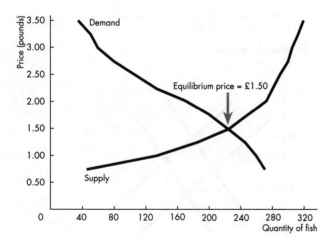

b Prices of other (related) goods; income; population; preferences.

c Prices of other (related) goods; prices of factors of production; technology.

d At a price of £2.75, quantity supplied (300) exceeds quantity demanded (80). Fish sellers find themselves with surplus fish. Rather than be stuck with unsold fish (which yields no revenue), some sellers cut their price in an attempt to increase the quantity of fish demanded. Competition forces other sellers to follow suit, and the price falls until it reaches the equilibrium price of £1.50, while quantity demanded increases until it reaches the equilibrium quantity of 225 units.

e At a price of £1, the quantity demanded (260) exceeds the quantity supplied (135) – there is a shortage. Unrequited fish buyers bid up the price in an attempt to get the 'scarce' fish. As prices continue to be bid up as long as there is excess demand, quantity supplied increases in response to higher prices. Price and quantity supplied both rise until they reach the equilibrium price (£1.50) and quantity (225 units).

f At a price of £1.50, the quantity supplied exactly equals the quantity demanded (225). There is no excess demand (shortage) or excess supply (surplus), and, therefore, no tendency for the price or quantity to change.

2 The demand and supply diagrams for parts (a) to (e) are shown in Fig. 4.3.

Questions like part (f) require the examination of two separate but related markets – the beer and wine markets. Since this kind of question often causes confusion for students, here is a more detailed explanation of the answer.

Look first at the beer market. The increase in the cost of beer production shifts up the supply curve of beer from S_0 to S_1. The resulting rise in the price of beer affects the wine market since beer and wine are substitutes (in consumption).

Turning to the wine market, there are two shifts to examine. The increase in beer prices causes the demand for wine to shift out from D_0 to D_1. The increase in the cost of wine production shifts up the supply curve of wine from S_0 to S_1. This is the end of the analysis, since the question asks only about the wine market. The final result is a rise in the price of wine and an ambiguous change in the quantity traded of wine.

Many students rightfully ask, 'But doesn't the rise in wine prices then shift out the demand curve for beer, causing a rise in beer prices and an additional increase in the demand for wine?' This question, which is correct in principle, is about the dynamics of adjustment, and these graphs are only capable of analysing once-over shifts of demand or supply. We could shift out the demand for beer, but the resulting rise in beer prices would lead us to shift the demand for wine a *second time*. In practice, stick to the rule that each curve (demand and supply) for a given market can shift a maximum of *once*.

3 a The demand and supply curves for peanuts are shown in Fig. 4.4.

b The equilibrium is given at the intersection of the demand and supply curves (labelled point *a*). The equilibrium price is £50 per case and the equilibrium quantity traded is 100 cases per week.

c At a price of £40 there is a shortage of 60 cases per week.

d **i** Table 4.3 also contains the (unchanged) quantity supplied, for reference purposes.
    ii The graph of the new demand curve is shown in Fig. 4.4.
    iii The new equilibrium price is £60 per case and the quantity traded is 120 cases of peanuts per week.

DATA QUESTIONS

1 The war led to a fall in demand for holidays in Turkey. This will shift the demand curve to the left as shown in Fig. 4.5(a). The result is a fall in the price and number of holidays.

2 Figure 4.5(b) shows that the result will be a rise in the demand for holidays in Spain leading to a rise in price and an increase in the number of holidays.

3 The reduction in bed numbers shifts the supply curve to the left as shown in Fig. 4.5(c). The result is a fall in numbers, but a rise in price.

Figure 4.3

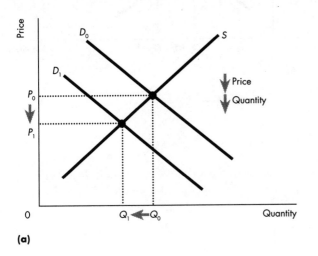

(a)

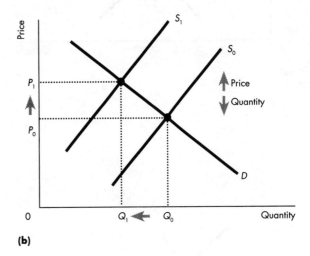

(b)

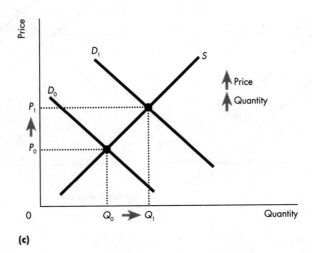

(c)

Figure 4.3

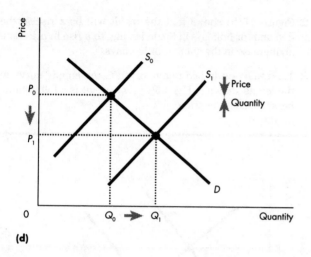

(d)

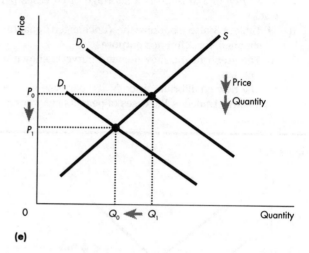

(e)

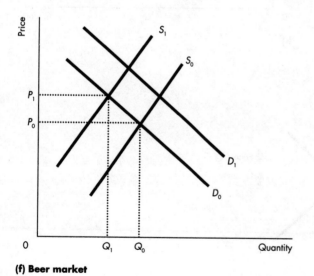

(f) Beer market

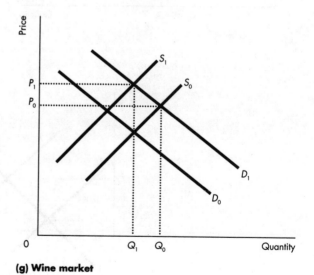

(g) Wine market

Table 4.3 Demand and Supply Schedules for Cases of Peanuts per Week

Price per case (pounds)	Quantity demanded (cases)	Quantity supplied (cases)
70	80	140
60	120	120
50	160	100
40	200	80
30	240	60

Figure 4.4

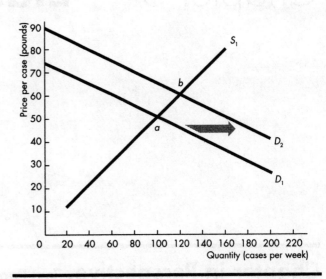

Figure 4.5

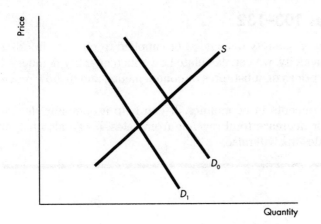

(a)

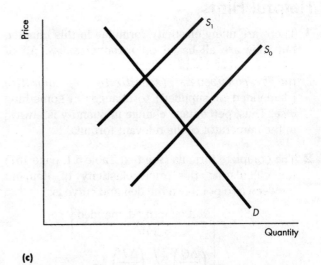

(b)

(c)

Chapter 5 **Elasticity**

Chapter in Perspective, Text Pages 103–132

Elasticity is a measure of the quantitative *responsiveness* of quantity demanded or supplied to changes in other key economic variables. Using different applications of elasticity, we can calculate how much quantity demanded will respond to changes in price, income or changes in the prices of substitutes or complements, and by how much quantity supplied will respond to a change in price.

The elasticity concept is one of the most practical concepts in economics. It can help a company decide whether lowering the price of its product will increase or decrease total revenue from sales. It can also help a government policymaker estimate how much revenue a sales tax will raise.

Helpful Hints

1 There are many elasticity formulae in this chapter, but they are all based on *responsiveness*. All of the demand and supply elasticity formulae measure the *responsiveness (sensitivity) of quantity* (demanded or supplied) to changes in something else. Thus, percentage change in quantity is always in the numerator of the relevant formula.

2 The complete formula (see text Table 5.1, page 107) for calculating the price elasticity of demand between two points on the demand curve is:

$$\eta = \left| \frac{\% \, \Delta \text{ quantity demanded}}{\% \, \Delta \text{ price}} \right|$$

$$= \left| \left(\frac{\Delta Q}{Q_{ave}} \right) \bigg/ \left(\frac{\Delta P}{P_{ave}} \right) \right|$$

The law of demand assures us that price and quantity demanded always move in opposite directions along any demand curve. Thus, without the absolute value sign, the formula for the price elasticity of demand would yield a negative number. Whenever you see the often-used shorthand term, *elasticity of demand*, remember that it means the absolute value of the *price* elasticity of demand.

3 Elasticity is *not* the same as slope (although they are related). Along a straight-line demand curve the slope is constant, but the elasticity varies from infinity to zero as we move down the demand curve.

4 One of the most practical and important uses of the concept of price elasticity of demand is that it allows us to predict the *effect on total revenue* of a change in price. A fall in price will increase total revenue if demand is elastic, leave total revenue unchanged if demand is unit elastic, and decrease total revenue if demand is inelastic. Because price and quantity demanded always move in opposite directions along a demand curve, a fall in price will cause an increase in quantity demanded. Since total revenue equals price × quantity, the fall in price will tend to decrease total revenue, while the increase in quantity demanded will increase total revenue. The net effect depends on which of these individual effects is larger.

The concept of price elasticity of demand conveniently summarizes the net effect. For example, if demand is elastic, the percentage change in quantity demanded is greater than the percentage change in price. Hence, with a fall in price, the quantity effect dominates and total revenue will increase. If, however, demand is inelastic, the percentage change in quantity demanded is less than the percentage change in price. Hence, with a fall in price, the price effect dominates and total revenue will decrease.

5 Two other important elasticity concepts are the income elasticity of demand and the cross elasticity of demand.

Income elasticity of demand:

$$\eta_Y = \left| \frac{\% \, \Delta \text{ quantity demanded}}{\% \, \Delta \text{ income}} \right|$$

$$= \left| \left(\frac{\Delta Q}{Q_{ave}} \right) \Big/ \left(\frac{\Delta Y}{Y_{ave}} \right) \right|$$

Cross elasticity of demand:

$$\eta_X = \left| \frac{\% \, \Delta \text{ quantity demanded of good } A}{\% \, \Delta \text{ price of good } B} \right|$$

$$= \left| \left(\frac{\Delta Q^A}{Q^A_{ave}} \right) \Big/ \left(\frac{\Delta P^B}{P^B_{ave}} \right) \right|$$

Notice that these two elasticity formulae do *not* have absolute value signs and can take on either positive or negative values. In the case of income elasticity of demand, the response of quantity demanded to an increase in income will be positive for a normal good and negative for an inferior good. In the case of cross elasticity of demand, the response of the quantity demanded of good *A* to an increase in the price of good *B* will be positive if the goods are substitutes and negative if the goods are complements.

Key Figures and Tables

Figure 5.3 Elasticity Along a Straight-line Demand Curve, text page 110
While the slope of a straight-line demand curve is constant, the elasticity varies systematically as we move down it. The elasticity decreases as the price of the good falls and the quantity demanded rises. In the price range above the mid-point of a straight-line demand curve, demand is elastic, at the mid-point elasticity is 1 (demand is unit elastic), and in the price range below the mid-point, demand is inelastic.

Figure 5.4 Demand Curves with Constant Elasticity, text page 111
This illustrates three demand curves with constant price elasticity. The first, part (a), is a vertical demand curve which has zero elasticity since any price change will have no effect on quantity demanded. The demand curve in part (b) has constant unitary elasticity. The horizontal demand curve in part (c) is infinitely elastic since a small change in price will have an infinitely large effect on quantity demanded.

Figure 5.5 Income Elasticity of Demand, text page 116
The three graphs in this figure illustrate relationships between income (measured on the horizontal axis) and quantity demanded (measured on the vertical axis). Part (a) shows a relationship in which the quantity demanded increases as income increases, but the quantity demanded increases by a greater percentage than income. Thus the income elasticity is greater than 1. In part (b) quantity demanded and income again increase together but the percentage change in quantity demanded is less than the percentage change in income. The income elasticity is between zero and 1. The first part of the relationship in part (c) is similar to that of part (b). However, as income continues to increase, eventually the quantity demanded reaches a maximum and thereafter decreases. At the point of maximum quantity demand, the income elasticity is zero and it is negative for higher levels of income.

Table 5.1 Calculating the Price Elasticity of Demand, text page 107
The price elasticity of demand is defined as the percentage change in the quantity demanded divided by the percentage change in the price. This table illustrates the procedure for calculating the price elasticity of demand between two points on a demand curve. You must master Table 5.1 to be able to do problems

involving any calculation of elasticity. Although this table presents only the procedure for calculating price elasticity of demand, the procedures for calculating all other elasticity concepts are very similar.

Table 5.6 A Compact Glossary of Elasticities of Demand, text page 119
Three kinds of elasticities of demand are presented in this chapter of the text: price elasticities, income elasticities and cross elasticities of demand. The purpose of this table is to summarize the economic meaning of these measures as they assume values in alternative ranges. Table 5.6 should serve as an excellent study device. You should understand and memorize all of the information contained in the table.

SELF-TEST

CONCEPT REVIEW

1 A units-free measure of the responsiveness of quantity demanded to price changes is given by the _____ _____ of demand.

2 The (price) elasticity of demand is calculated as the percentage change in the _____ _____ divided by the percentage change in the _____ .

3 If the (price) elasticity of demand is between 0 and 1, demand is said to be _____ ; if it is greater than 1, demand is said to be _____ ; if it is equal to 1, demand is said to be _____ _____ .

4 A good that has many good substitutes is likely to have demand that is _____ . If only a small proportion of income is spent on a good, its demand is likely to be _____ .

5 As time passes after a change in the price of a good, demand will tend to become more _____ .

6 If demand is elastic, an increase in the price implies that revenue (expenditures) will _____ .

7 A measure of the responsiveness of the quantity demanded of a good to changes in income is given by the _____ _____ of demand.

8 The income elasticity of demand is calculated as the percentage change in the _____ _____ divided by the percentage change in _____ .

9 The income elasticity is _____ for inferior goods.

10 The responsiveness of the quantity demanded of one good to a change in the price of a complement or substitute is given by the _____ _____ of demand.

11 The cross elasticity of demand with respect to the price of a substitute is _____ . The cross elasticity of demand with respect to the price of a complement is _____ .

12 The elasticity of supply is a measure of the responsiveness of the _____ _____ to changes in _____ .

13 To illustrate the initial change in quantity supplied induced by a sudden change in price we use the _____ supply curve. To illustrate the response of quantity supplied after all technologically possible long-run adjustments in the production process have been made we use the _____ supply curve.

14 The long-run supply curve will generally be more _____ than a short-run supply curve, which will be more _____ than the momentary supply curve.

TRUE OR FALSE

___ 1 The price elasticity of demand measures how responsive prices are to changes in demand.

___ 2 A horizontal demand curve is perfectly inelastic.

___ 3 The demand for petrol is likely to become more inelastic with the passage of time after a price increase.

___ **4** The more readily available are substitutes for a good, the more inelastic will be its demand.

___ **5** If total revenue falls following an increase in price, demand must be inelastic.

___ **6** If your expenditures on toothpaste are a small proportion of your total income, your demand for toothpaste is likely to be inelastic.

___ **7** The more narrowly we define a good, the more elastic is its demand.

___ **8** Long-run demand is more inelastic than short-run demand because there is more opportunity for substitution.

___ **9** If the income elasticity of the demand for turnips is positive, then turnips are an inferior good.

___ **10** The effect of the change in the price of one good on the quantity demanded of another good is measured by the cross elasticity of demand.

___ **11** We would expect the cross elasticity of demand between hamburgers and hot dogs to be negative.

___ **12** If goods *A* and *B* are substitutes, then a decrease in the demand for *A* will lead to a decrease in the equilibrium price of *B*.

___ **13** If a 3 per cent decrease in price induces a 9 per cent decrease in quantity supplied, then the supply curve is elastic.

___ **14** Supply will generally be more inelastic in the long run than in the short run.

___ **15** If a decrease in supply causes revenue to decrease, then demand must be inelastic.

___ **16** For a linear demand curve, demand is more elastic at higher price ranges than at lower price ranges.

___ **17** If a 10 per cent increase in the price of good *A* causes a 6 per cent decrease in the quantity of good *B* demanded, the cross elasticity of demand between *A* and *B* is 0.6.

___ **18** If a 9 per cent increase in price leads to a 5 per cent decrease in quantity demanded, total revenue has decreased.

MULTIPLE-CHOICE

1 Two points on the demand curve for volleyballs are shown in Table 5.1.

Table 5.1

Price per volleyball (pounds)	Quantity demanded
19	55
21	45

What is the elasticity of demand between these two points?
a 2.5
b 2.0
c 0.5
d 0.4
e none of the above

2 The fact that butter has margarine as a close substitute in consumption
a makes the supply of butter more elastic.
b makes the supply of butter less elastic.
c makes the demand for butter more elastic.
d makes the demand for butter less elastic.
e does not affect butter's elasticity of supply or demand.

3 If the price elasticity of demand is 2, then a 1 per cent decrease in price will
a double the quantity demanded.
b reduce the quantity demanded by half.
c increase the quantity demanded by 2 per cent.
d reduce the quantity demanded by 2 per cent.
e increase the quantity demanded by 0.5 per cent.

4 A good will have a more price inelastic demand
a the higher its price.
b the larger the percentage of income spent on it.
c the longer the time elapsed.
d if it is a luxury good.
e if it has no close substitutes.

5 If the demand for frozen orange juice is price elastic, then a severe frost which destroys large quantities of oranges will probably

a reduce the equilibrium price of juice but increase total consumer spending on it.

b reduce the equilibrium quantity of juice as well as total consumer spending on it.

c reduce both the equilibrium quantity and the price of juice.

d increase the equilibrium price of juice as well as total consumer spending on it.

e increase the equilibrium price of juice but leave total consumer spending on it constant.

6 If a 4 per cent rise in the price of peanut butter causes the total revenue from peanut butter sales to fall by 8 per cent, then demand for peanut butter

a is elastic.

b is inelastic.

c is unit elastic.

d has an elasticity of $\frac{1}{2}$.

e has an elasticity of 2.

7 Tina and Brian work for the same recording company. Tina claims that they would be better off by increasing the price of their tapes while Brian claims that they would be better off by decreasing the price. It can be concluded that

a Tina thinks the demand for tapes has price elasticity of zero and Brian thinks price elasticity equals one.

b Tina thinks the demand for tapes has price elasticity equal to one and Brian thinks price elasticity equals zero.

c Tina thinks the demand for tapes is price elastic and Brian thinks it is price inelastic.

d Tina thinks the demand for tapes is price inelastic and Brian thinks it is price elastic.

e Tina and Brian should stick to singing and forget about economics.

8 Given the relationship shown in Fig. 5.1 between total revenue from the sale of a good and the quantity of the good sold, then

a this is an inferior good.

b this is a normal good.

c the elasticity of demand is zero.

d the elasticity of demand is infinity.

e the elasticity of demand is one.

9 If an increase in price causes a decrease in total revenue then price elasticity of demand is

a negative.

b zero.

c greater than zero but less than one.

d equal to one.

e greater than one.

Figure 5.1

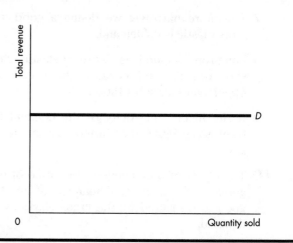

10 If a 4 per cent decrease in income (at a constant price) causes a 2 per cent decrease in the consumption of books then

a the income elasticity of demand for books is negative.

b books are a necessity and a normal good.

c books are a luxury and a normal good.

d books are an inferior good.

e **a** and **d** are true.

11 Luxury goods tend to have income elasticities of demand which are

a greater than one.

b greater than zero but less than one.

c positive.

d negative.

e first positive and then negative as income increases.

12 If a 10 per cent increase in income causes a 5 per cent increase in quantity demanded (at a constant price), what is the income elasticity of demand?

a 0.5

b −0.5

c 2.0

d −2.0

e none of the above

13 The cross elasticity of the demand for white tennis balls with respect to the price of yellow tennis balls is probably
  a negative and high.
  b negative and low.
  c positive and high.
  d positive and low.
  e zero.

14 A decrease in the price of X from £6 to £4 causes an increase in the quantity of Y demanded (at the current price of Y) from 900 to 1,100 units. What is the cross elasticity of demand between X and Y?
  a 0.5
  b −0.5
  c 2
  d −2
  e **a** or **b**, depending on whether X and Y are substitutes or complements

15 When price goes from £1.50 to £2.50, quantity supplied increases from 9,000 to 11,000 units. What is the price elasticity of supply?
  a 0.4
  b 0.8
  c 2.5
  d 4.0
  e none of the above

16 The magnitude of *both* the elasticity of demand and the elasticity of supply depend on
  a the ease of substitution between goods.
  b the proportion of income spent on a good.
  c the time elapsed since the price change.
  d the technological conditions of production.
  e none of the above factors.

17 The long-run supply curve is likely to be
  a more elastic than momentary supply but less elastic than short-run supply.
  b less elastic than momentary supply but more elastic than short-run supply.
  c less elastic than both momentary and short-run supply curves.
  d more elastic than both momentary and short-run supply curves.
  e vertical.

SHORT ANSWER

1 In each of the following, compare the price elasti-city of demand for each pair of goods and explain why the demand for one of the goods is more elastic than demand for the other.
  a IBM personal computers before the development of other 'clone' personal computers versus IBM personal computers after the production of such clones
  b Television sets versus matches
  c Electricity just after an increase in its price versus electricity two years after the price increase

2 Why does demand tend to be more elastic in the long run?

3 Why does supply tend to be more elastic in the long run?

4 Which demand curve in Fig. 5.2 (D_A or D_B) is more elastic in the price range P_1 to P_2? Explain why. [*Hint*: use the formula for price elasticity of demand.]

Figure 5.2

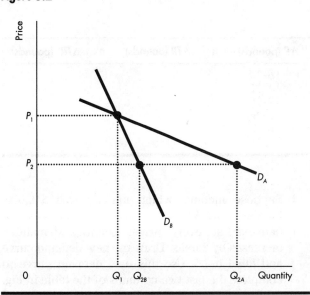

PROBLEMS

1 a Given the demand curve in Fig. 5.3, complete the second and third columns of the table in this figure: η (the price elasticity of demand) and *TR* (the change in total revenue) as the price falls from the higher price to the lower price. Describe the relationship between elasticity and change in total revenue as price falls (moving down the demand curve).

Figure 5.3

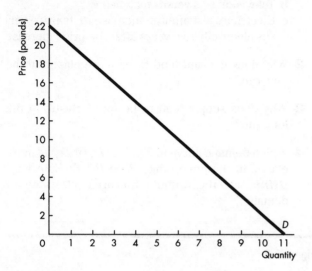

ΔP (pounds)	η	ΔTR (pounds)	η	ΔTR' (pounds)
16–14				
14–12				
12–10				
10–8				
8–6				

b Suppose income, which initially was £10,000, increases to £14,000, causing an increase in demand: at every price, quantity demanded increases by 2 units. Draw the new demand curve and label it D'. Use this new demand curve to complete the last two columns of the table in Fig. 5.3 for η (the new price elasticity of demand) and TR'(the new change in total revenue).

c Using the price range between £16 and £14, explain why D' is more inelastic than D.

d Calculate the income elasticity of demand, assuming the price remains constant at £12. Is this a normal or inferior good? Explain why you could have answered the question even without calculating the income elasticity of demand.

2 Table 5.2 gives the demand schedules for good A when the price of good B (P_B) is £8 and when the price of good B is £12. Complete the last column of the table by computing the cross elasticity of demand between goods A and B for each of the three prices of A. Are A and B complements or substitutes?

Table 5.2 Demand Schedules for Good A

	$P_B = £8$	$P_B = £12$	
P_A	Q_A	Q'_A	η_X
8	2,000	4,000	
7	4,000	6,000	
6	6,000	8,000	

DATA QUESTIONS

High tax weapon in smoking battle

Higher taxation is likely to reduce smoking, Mrs Joy Townsend, a research scientist at Northwick Park Hospital, Harrow, told the Association. In 1981, the then Chancellor Sir Geoffrey Howe, imposed one of the largest post-war increases in tobacco tax, putting up the price by 20 per cent. Since then the tax has increased in line with inflation.

In the past four years, cigarette prices had risen by 26 per cent in real terms and consumption had fallen by 20 per cent, providing an extra £425 million. Tax was therefore working as an ally of preventative medicine and health education.

Source: Adapted from an AEB A-level question set in June 1988.

1 a Use the figures in the article to calculate the price elasticity of demand during 'the last four years'.
b Why might this figure not provide a measure of the responsiveness of the demand for cigarettes to change in price?

2 Explain and illustrate, using a demand and supply diagram, the likely effect of the change in cigarette prices upon the price of cigarettes.

ANSWERS

CONCEPT REVIEW

1 price elasticity

2 quantity demanded; price

3 inelastic; elastic; unit elastic

4 elastic; inelastic

5 elastic

6 decrease

7 income elasticity

8 quantity demanded; income

9 negative

10 cross elasticity

11 positive; negative

12 quantity supplied; price

13 momentary; long-run

14 elastic; elastic

TRUE OR FALSE

1 F It measures the responsiveness of quantity to changes in price.

2 F Definition.

3 F Elasticity increases as time passes.

4 F More substitutes lead to greater elasticity.

5 F Revenue increases when price rises when demand is elastic.

6 T The smaller the proportion of income spent on a good, the lower the elasticity.

7 T Narrow definitions are associated with more substitutes.

8 F In the long run more substitutes will be produced.

9 F For inferior goods, as income increases less is demanded.

10 T Definition.

11 F Cross elasticity is positive for substitutes.

12 T Follows from definition.

13 T When percentage change in quantity is greater than percentage change in price, demand is elastic.

14 F Supply becomes more elastic in the long run.

15 F Fall in supply leads to an increase in total revenue, so demand is inelastic.

16 T Elasticity changes along a straight line.

17 F Cross elasticity is *minus* 0.6.

18 F Percentage increase in price is greater than the percentage fall in quantity, so total revenue increases.

MULTIPLE-CHOICE

1 b $(-10/50)/(2/20) = 2$

2 c Closer substitutes lead to more elastic demand.

3 c Q and P are always inversely related on demand curve.

4 e **a** and **d** irrelevant, elasticity falls with smaller proportion of income spent on a good and shorter elapsed time.

5 b Supply curve will shift to the left; the rise in price will lead to a bigger fall in demand.

6 a If increase in price leads to a fall in total revenue, elasticity must be greater than one.

7 d Better off means increased total revenue. If demand is elastic a price cut will increase revenue.

8 e Note total revenue on y-axis. Since total revenue is constant as quantity increases (and presumably price falls), elasticity = 1.

9 e Definition.

10 b Income elasticity > 0, so normal good. Necessities tend to have income elasticity < 1.

11 a See previous answer. **c** is correct, but **a** is best answer.

12 a Positive, because income and price move in same direction.

13 c Close substitutes, so cross elasticity is positive and high.

14 b Substituting into formula gives $(200/1,000)/(-2/5) = 0.5$

15 a Substituting into formula gives $(2,000/10,000)/(1/2) = 0.4$.

16 c **a** and **b** affect price elasticity only; **d** affects supply elasticity only.

17 d Definition. Momentary supply curve most vertical.

SHORT ANSWER

1 a The demand for IBM personal computers will be more elastic after the production of clone personal computers since there would then be more readily available substitutes.

b The demand for television sets will be more elastic since they will generally take a larger proportion of consumer income.

c The demand for electricity after the passage of two years will be more elastic since consumers will have more time to find substitutes for electricity (for example, a gas stove).

2 Demand is more responsive to price changes (more elastic) in the long run because more substitutes become available to consumers. Not only are new goods invented but consumers also learn about and begin to use new substitutes.

3 Supply is more elastic in the long run because the passage of time allows producers to find better (more efficient) ways of producing that are not available in the short run. The responsiveness of production to an increase in price will increase as firms have time to discover and implement new technologies or to increase the scale of operation.

4 D_A is more elastic than D_B. To see why, look at the formula for price elasticity of demand:

$$\eta = \left| \frac{\% \Delta \text{ quantity demanded}}{\% \Delta \text{ price}} \right|$$

The percentage change in price is the same for the two demand curves. But the percentage change in quantity is greater for D_A. At P_1, the initial quantity demanded is the same for both demand curves (Q_1). With the fall in price to P_2, the increase in quantity demanded is greater for D_A (to Q_{2A}) than for D_B (to Q_{2B}). Therefore, D_A is more elastic than D_B. (See Fig. 5.4.)

PROBLEMS

1 a The completed columns of the table attached to Fig. 5.3 are shown here in Table 5.3. The second and third columns of the table show that as price falls, total revenue increases when demand is elastic; total revenue remains constant when demand is unit elastic; total revenue falls when demand is inelastic.

Figure 5.4

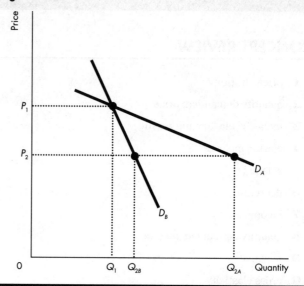

Table 5.3

ΔP (pounds)	η	Δ*TR* (pounds)	η	Δ*TR′* (pounds)
16–14	2.14	+8	1.36	+4
14–12	1.44	+4	1.00	0
12–10	1.00	0	0.73	−4
10–8	0.69	−4	0.53	−8
8–6	4.67	−8	0.37	−12

Figure 5.5

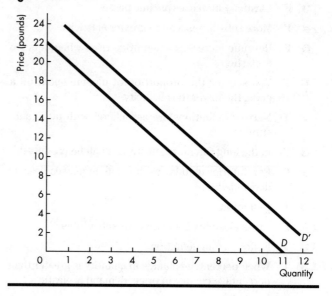

b The new demand curve is labelled D' (Fig. 5.5). The last two columns of the table have been completed on the basis of the new demand curve.

c Since they are parallel, D' and D have exactly the same slope. Thus, we know that for a given change in price, the change in quantity demanded will be the same for the two curves. However, elasticity is determined by *percentage* changes, and the percentage change in quantity demanded is different for the two curves (although the percentage change in price will be the same). For a given percentage change in price, the percentage change in quantity demanded will always be less for D'. For example, as the price falls from £16 to £14 (a 13 per cent change), the quantity demanded increases from 5 to 6 units along D' but from 3 to 4 along D. The percentage change in quantity demanded is only 18 per cent along D' and 29 per cent along D. Since the percentage change in price is the same for both curves, D' is more inelastic than D.

d Income increases from £10,000 to £14,000. At a constant price of £12, the increase in income, which shifts out the demand curve to D', increases the quantity consumers will demand from 5 units to 7 units. Substituting these numbers into the formula for the income elasticity of demand yields:

$$\eta_Y = \left(\frac{\Delta Q}{Q_{ave}}\right) \Big/ \left(\frac{\Delta Y}{Y_{ave}}\right)$$

$$= \left(\frac{2}{6}\right) \Big/ \left(\frac{4,000}{12,000}\right) = +1$$

The income elasticity of demand is a positive number, since both Q and Y are positive. Therefore, this is a normal good. We already knew that from the information in part **b**, which stated that the demand curve shifted out to the right with an increase in income. If this were an inferior good, the increase in income would have shifted the demand curve in to the left, and the income elasticity of demand would have been negative.

2 The cross elasticities of demand between A and B are listed in Table 5.4. Since the cross elasticities are positive, we know that A and B are substitutes.

Table 5.4 Demand Schedules for Good A

	$P_B = £8$	$P_B = £12$	
P_A	Q_A	Q'_A	η_X
8	2,000	4,000	1.67
7	4,000	6,000	1.00
6	6,000	8,000	0.71

DATA QUESTIONS

The answer given below is the author's solution to the question on p. 48 and should not be taken as being the definitive answer required by the AEB.

1 a Price elasticity = 20% / 26% = 0.77
  b Elasticity changes over time because variables change; for example, health education may affect people's desire to smoke.

2 So far as firms are concerned, a tax is similar to a rise in raw material costs so that firms are willing to supply fewer cigarettes at every price. Hence the supply curve shifts to the left as shown in Fig. 5.6. The result is a fall in the number of cigarettes bought and sold, and a rise in price.

Figure 5.6

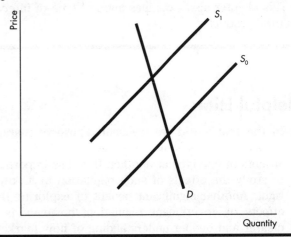

Chapter 6   **Markets in Action**

Chapter in Perspective, Text Pages 133–151

This chapter extends the theory of demand and supply by focusing on markets in action. In particular, it examines various types of government intervention in the economy. This can take several forms. Governments intervene in markets such as housing and labour because they believe that markets fail. Hence they introduce schemes such as minimum wage legislation to help low-paid workers. They intervene on a huge scale by imposing taxes on goods and services, and to a smaller extent by giving subsidies. Governments also affect markets by prohibiting some products, particularly drugs, and this chapter examines the effect that this has on the quantity and price of such products.

This chapter also examines another type of intervention; that of the European Union in the market for agricultural products.

Helpful Hints

1 In the real world we frequently observe market regulation by governments in the form of price constraints of one type or another. It is thus important to study the effects of such regulation in its own right. Another significant benefit of exploring the effects of government regulation, however, is a clearer and deeper understanding of how markets work when, by contrast, the government does *not* affect the normal operation of markets.

Whenever something happens to disturb an equilibrium in an unregulated (free) market, the desires of buyers and sellers are brought back into balance by price movements. If prices are controlled by government regulation, however, the price mechanism can no longer serve this purpose. Thus, 'balance'

must be restored in some other way. In the case of price ceilings, black markets are likely to arise. If black markets cannot develop because of strict enforcement of the price ceiling, then demanders will be forced to bear the costs of increased search activity, waiting in queues, or something else.

2 In any market with a legal price ceiling set below the market-clearing price, we will observe excess quantity demanded, because the price cannot increase to eliminate it. As a consequence, the value of the last unit of the good available will exceed the controlled price, and therefore demanders are willing to engage in costly activities up to the value of that last unit (for example, search activity, queuing and black market activity) in order to obtain the good.

Furthermore, if the price is allowed to increase in response to a decrease in supply or an increase in demand, there are incentive effects for suppliers to produce more and demanders to purchase less (that is, movements along the supply and demand curves). Indeed it is the response to these incentives that restores equilibrium in markets with freely adjusting prices. If, however, the price cannot adjust, these price-induced incentive effects do not have a chance to operate.

Key Figures

Figure 6.1 The San Francisco Housing Market in 1906, text page 136

In 1906, San Francisco was hit by a devastating earthquake that destroyed more than half the existing housing. Figure 6.1 illustrates the response of the unregulated housing market in San Francisco. Part (a) gives the equilibrium situation before the earthquake. The short-run response of the market is illustrated in part (b). After the earthquake, the short-run supply of housing decreases and the short-run supply curve shifts from SS to SS_A. At the old equilibrium rent of $110 per month, there is a large shortage of housing, which drives rent up to the new equilibrium level of $120 per month. As the rent rises, the shortage is eliminated because existing housing is used more intensively (reflected in the movements along the D and SS_A curves). The increase in rent to $120 also provides a profit incentive to build more housing units. Since the current rent of $120 is higher than the long-run supply price of housing, new units will be built. This shifts the SS_A curve to the right until the rent has fallen back to $110 per month, as indicated in part (c).

Figure 6.2 A Rent Ceiling, text page 137

This illustrates what would have happened in the San Francisco housing market after the 1906 earthquake if a rent ceiling of $110 per month had been imposed. Since rent could not rise to clear the market, there would be no incentive to use existing housing more intensively or to construct additional housing in the long run.

Figure 6.3 A Market for Unskilled Labour, text page 139

This illustrates the consequences of a decrease in the demand for labour in an unregulated market for unskilled labour. Part (a) illustrates the market in an initial equilibrium. Then a labour-saving machine is invented which shifts the demand for labour curve to the left; from D to D_A in part (b). If the wage rate is allowed to adjust freely, wages and employment will fall in the short run. At the lower wage, some workers have the incentive to leave the unskilled labour market to seek training that qualifies them for higher paying jobs. This causes the short-run supply curve of labour to shift to the left; from SS to SS_A in part (c). As a result, the wage rate begins to rise while employment falls.

Figure 6.4 Minimum Wages and Unemployment, text page 141

Like Fig. 6.3, this figure examines the consequences of a decrease in the demand for unskilled labour, but now a minimum wage is imposed. In this case, the wage rate is not able to fall to clear the market. The result is an increase in unemployment.

Figure 6.7 An *Ad Valorem* Tax on Expenditure, text page 145

To producers, the imposition of an expenditure tax is similar to the effect of a rise in the price of raw materials; it causes less to be supplied at each price. This causes the supply curve to shift to the left leading to a fall in quantity and a rise in price.

Figure 6.11 The EU's Common Agricultural Policy, text page 153

The demand curve in this figure is the familiar downward sloping line marked D. Without any EU intervention, food would be supplied to the European Union from all over the world, and the supply curve would be horizontal. The CAP imposes a tariff which shifts the supply curve to $S + tariff$. This leads to a higher price, causing EU farmers to increase their supply. The result is a surplus since consumers are not willing to buy all the food supplies at this higher price.

Figure 6.12 The Market for an Illegal Drug, text page 159

This shows that *selling* an illegal drug adds costs so that supply falls to $S + CBL$, resulting in a lower quantity consumed and a higher price. If *buying* drugs becomes illegal, demand will fall, resulting in a lower quantity and price.

SELF-TEST

CONCEPT REVIEW

1 In an unregulated housing market, a sudden decrease in the supply of housing would cause rent to _____ in the short run and thus create an incentive for the construction of new housing to _____ in the long run.

2 A(n) _____ _____ is a regulation making it illegal to charge a rent higher than a specified level.

3 If a price ceiling is below the market clearing price, an excess quantity _____ of the relevant good will exist. In such a situation two mechanisms will tend to arise in order to achieve equilibrium. We will observe an increase in _____ activity as demanders spend more time trying to find a seller. In addition, illegal markets, called _____ markets may arise in order to satisfy demand.

4 The invention of a new labour-saving technology will cause the demand curve for unskilled labour to shift to the _____ . If the labour market is unregulated, the wage rate will _____ .

5 Unemployment will be created if a legal minimum wage is established, which is _____ the market clearing wage rate.

6 A tax on expenditure will lead to a(n) _____ in price and a(n) _____ in quantity .

7 A subsidy will lead to a(n) _____ in price and a(n) _____ in quantity.

TRUE OR FALSE

1 In an unregulated housing market, higher rents will result in an increase in the quantity of housing supplied.

2 When rents in an unregulated housing market rise due to a decrease in supply, people who are unable to pay the higher rents will not get housing.

3 In a housing market with rent ceilings, there will be a strong incentive to construct new housing.

4 If a rent ceiling exceeds people's willingness to pay, search activity and black markets will arise.

5 Search activity will tend to be greater in unregulated markets than in markets with price ceilings.

6 The black market price of a good is usually below the regulated price.

7 An increase in the minimum wage will reduce the number of workers employed.

8 In an unregulated labour market a decline in the demand for labour causes the wage rate to increase.

9 The impact of minimum wage laws on unemployment among young workers tends to be about the same as it is for older workers.

10 A specific tax is set as a fixed amount per unit of the commodity.

11 Taxes on goods such as cigarettes and alcohol are examples of *ad valorem* taxes.

12 The imposition of an expenditure tax shifts the supply curve upward by the amount of the tax.

13 The CAP shifts income from consumers to farmers.

14 If penalties are imposed on both sellers and buyers in a market for prohibited goods, the price remains constant and the quantity bought decreases.

MULTIPLE-CHOICE

1 The short-run supply curve for rental housing is positively sloped because
a the supply of housing is fixed in the short run.

b the current stock of buildings will be used more intensively as rents rise.

c the cost of constructing a new building increases as the number of buildings increases.

d the cost of constructing a new building is about the same regardless of the number of buildings in existence.

e new buildings will be constructed as rents rise.

2 Rent ceilings imposed by governments

  a keep rental prices below the unregulated market price.

  b keep rental prices above the unregulated market price.

  c keep rental prices equal to the unregulated market price.

  d increase the stock of rental housing.

  e increase the intensity of use of the current stock of rental housing.

3 Which of the following is *not* a likely outcome of rent ceilings?

  a a black market for rent-controlled housing

  b long waiting lists of potential renters of rent-controlled housing

  c a short-run shortage of housing

  d black market prices below the rent ceiling prices

  e increased search activity for rent-controlled housing

4 In an unregulated market which of the following is *not* a likely result of the sudden destruction of a large proportion of the stock of housing?

  a higher rental prices

  b a shortage of rental housing

  c more basement flats offered for rent

  d more families sharing living quarters

  e the construction of new rental housing

5 A price ceiling set below the equilibrium price will result in

  a excess supply.

  b excess demand.

  c the equilibrium price.

  d an increase in supply.

  e a decrease in demand.

6 A price floor set below the equilibrium price results in

  a excess supply.

  b excess demand.

c the equilibrium price.

d an increase in supply.

e a decrease in demand.

7 If the minimum wage is set at £2 per hour in Fig. 6.1, what is the level of unemployment in millions of hours?

  a 50

  b 40

  c 20

  d 10

  e 0

Figure 6.1

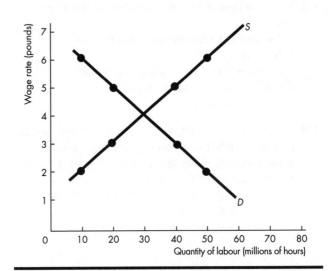

---

8 In Fig. 6.1, if the minimum wage is set at £6 per hour, what is the level of unemployment in millions of hours?

  a 50

  b 40

  c 20

  d 10

  e 0

9 Which of the following types of labour would be most significantly affected by an increase in the legal minimum wage?

  a professional athletes

  b young, unskilled labour

c skilled union workers
d university professors
e self-employed labour

10 A minimum wage law creates
a gainers
b losers
c gainers and losers
d a decrease in supply
e an increase in hours worked

11 The burden of an expenditure tax falls on
a consumers
b governments
c consumers and governments
d producers
e consumers and producers

12 The Common Agricultural Policy of the European Union
a forces the Union to buy surplus food
b increases farm incomes
c increases the price paid by consumers
d sets a common external tariff
e all of the above

13 Which of the following combinations would generally yield the greatest price fluctuations?
a large supply shifts and inelastic demand
b large supply shifts and elastic demand
c large supply shifts and perfectly elastic demand
d small supply shifts and inelastic demand
e small supply shifts and elastic demand

SHORT ANSWER

1 a Suppose there is a significant reduction in the supply of petrol. Explain how an unregulated market adjusts.
b What is it that induces consumers willingly to reduce their consumption of petrol?

2 Explain the effects of the imposition of a minimum wage.

3 Explain what happens when the government imposes an expenditure tax.

4 Suppose the Nudist party wins the next election and they pass a law making clothes illegal. Unfortunately for the Nudists, the police don't take the law seriously and put little effort into enforcement. Use a diagram to explain why the black market price of now illegal clothes will be close to the unregulated equilibrium price.

PROBLEMS

1 Suppose that the market for rental housing is initially in long-run equilibrium. Use graphs to answer the following:
a Explain how an unregulated market for rental housing would adjust if there is a sudden significant increase in demand. Consider what will happen to rent and the quantity of units rented in the short run and in the long run. Be sure to discuss the effect on incentives (in both the short run and the long run) as the market-determined price (rent) changes.
b Now explain how the market would adjust to the increase in demand if rent ceilings are established at the level of the initial equilibrium rent. What has happened to supplier incentives in this case?

2 Answer the following, given the information about the demand for and supply of petrol in Table 6.1.
a What is the equilibrium price of petrol and the equilibrium quantity of petrol traded?

Table 6.1

Price (pounds per litre)	Quantity demanded (millions of litres per day)	Quantity supplied
1.40	8	24
1.30	10	22
1.20	12	20
1.10	14	18
1.00	16	16
0.90	18	14

b Suppose that the quantity of petrol supplied suddenly declines by 8 million litres per day at every price. Construct a new table of price, quantity demanded and quantity supplied, and draw a graph of the demand curve and the initial and new supply curves. Assuming that the market for petrol is unregulated, use either your table or your graph to find the new equilibrium price of petrol and the new equilibrium quantity of petrol traded.

c How has the change in price affected the behaviour of demanders? the behaviour of suppliers?

d Suppose that the government imposes a price ceiling of £1 per litre of petrol at the same time as the decrease in supply reported in part **b**.

   i What is the quantity of petrol demanded?

   ii What is the quantity of petrol supplied?

   iii What is the quantity of petrol actually sold?

   iv What is the excess quantity of petrol demanded?

   v What is the highest price demanders are willing to pay for the last litre of petrol available?

   vi Consider someone who values petrol as in **d v**. How long would that consumer be willing to queue to buy 10 litres of petrol if the best alternative was to work at a wage rate of £8 per hour?

DATA QUESTIONS

The cost of the CAP

The costs of the Common Agricultural Policy are considerable and include:

◆ The cost of buying and storing surplus produce
◆ Payments to farmers for structural improvements
◆ Transfers from consumers in the form of higher prices

It is not possible to make precise calculations of these costs because these depend in part on the effect of EU surpluses on the world price of food. These surpluses are sold on the world market and force down the world price of many commodities. Thus one result is that there is a fall in the incomes of Third World farmers.

Within the European Union, the costs and benefits are not distributed evenly since large farmers benefit much more than those with only small farms.

1 What are the aims of the CAP?

2 Draw a diagram to show the effect of EU food exports on the world price of food.

3 Who benefits and who loses from the CAP system?

4 How can the surpluses be eliminated?

ANSWERS

CONCEPT REVIEW

1 increase; increase

2 rent ceiling

3 demanded; search; black

4 left; fall

5 above

6 rise; fall

7 fall; rise

TRUE OR FALSE

1 T Movement up supply curve unobstructed by ceiling.

2 T At equilibrium, all who can afford housing get it, but not necessarily all who need it.

3 F Returns on investment in housing will be low.

4 F The rent ceiling will have little effect.

5 F Because people will search for bargains.

6 F Black market prices are higher.

7 **T** Increase in minimum wage leads to a fall in quantity demanded.

8 **F** Wage will fall.

9 **F** Greater impact on young workers because they have lower wages.

10 **T** Definition.

11 **F** They are excise duties on quantities.

12 **T** Taxes reduce supply since they are similar to an increase in raw material prices.

13 **T** Consumers face higher prices, farmers receive more than the equilibrium price.

14 **F** Supply shifts to the right.

MULTIPLE-CHOICE

1 **b** **c, d**, and **e** refer to the long run.

2 **a** Definition **d** and **e** result of increase in rent in unregulated market.

3 **d** Black markets cause shortages and lead to prices above the official price.

4 **b** Price would rise and stimulate supply as after San Francisco earthquake.

5 **b** Draw a graph. No change in *ceteris paribus* assumptions so no shift in supply or demand.

6 **c** A price floor below the equilibrium will have no effect.

7 **e** Floor below equilibrium price does not prevent market from reaching equilibrium.

8 **b** Quantity supplied (50) > quantity demanded (10).

9 **b** Lowest wage labour.

10 **c** Some will gain from higher wages, some will not find employment at higher wage.

11 **e** Both consumers and producers bear tax burden depending on elasticity.

12 **e** These are the effects of intervention.

13 **a** Draw graph to see.

SHORT ANSWER

1 **a** If the market for petrol is initially in equilibrium and there is a significant reduction in the supply of petrol, there will be excess quantity demanded at the existing price. As a result, the price of petrol will rise, which will cause movements along the new supply curve and the demand curve. As the price rises there will be a price-induced increase in quantity supplied and a price-induced decrease in quantity demanded. The price will continue to rise until the excess quantity demanded is eliminated.

b It is the price increase that causes consumers to reduce their desired consumption of petrol.

2 Minimum wage legislation stops employers paying their workers wages lower than a minimum set by government. The result is that some people benefit and others lose. Employers lose because they have to pay higher wages. Other losers include those who cannot find work since the higher wages cause firms to reduce their demand for labour. The main benefit accrues to those low-paid workers who receive higher wages as a result of the pay increase. The exact results will depend on the level at which the minimum wage is set and on the elasticity of demand and supply of labour. If these are both inelastic, the result will be only a small fall in employment. If they are elastic, there will be a considerable fall in employment.

3 An expenditure tax results in a rise in prices and a fall in the quantity of goods bought and sold. This is illustrated in Fig. 6.2.

Figure 6.2

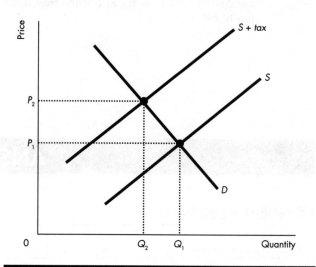

The tax will shift the supply curve to the left (the vertical distance between the supply curves measures the extent of the tax). The result is a rise in price from P_1 to P_2 and a fall in quantity from Q_1 to Q_2. The extent of these changes depends on the shape of the demand curve, that is, on its elasticity.

Figure 6.3

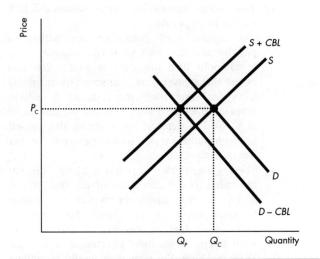

Figure 6.4

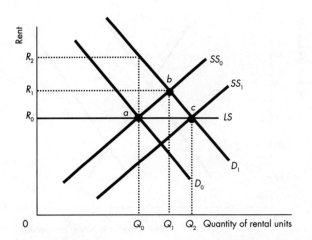

4 The clothing market is illustrated in Fig. 6.3. The demand curve is D and the supply curve is S. Since police enforcement is lax, the cost of breaking the law *(CBL)* is small for both buyers and sellers, so the demand and supply curves move only a short distance and the effect is small.

PROBLEMS

1 a Figure 6.4 corresponds to an unregulated market for rental housing. The initial demand, short-run supply, and long-run supply curves are D_0, SS_0, and LS respectively. The market is initially in long-run equilibrium at point a corresponding to rent R_0 and quantity of rental units Q_0. Demand then increases to D_1, creating excess quantity demanded of $Q_2 - Q_0$ at the initial rent. In the short run, in an unregulated market, rent will rise to R_1 to clear the market and the equilibrium quantity of housing rented is Q_1 (point b). Note that as the rent rises, the quantity of rental housing supplied increases (a movement from point a to point b along supply curve SS_0) as the existing stock of housing is used more intensively. Also the quantity of housing demanded decreases (a movement from point c to point b along demand curve D_1). Together, these movements eliminate the excess quantity demanded. The

higher rent also provides an incentive to construct new housing in the long run. This is illustrated by the shift in the supply curve from SS_0 to SS_1. Finally, a new long-run equilibrium is achieved at point c, with rent restored to its original level and the number of units rented equal to Q_2.

b We now use the graph in Fig. 6.4 to discuss the behaviour of a market with a rent ceiling set at R_0. Again we start in the same long-run equilibrium at point a. Once again we observe an increase in demand from D_0 to D_1. In this case, however, the rent cannot rise to restore equilibrium. There will be no incentive to use the existing stock of housing more intensively in the short run or to construct new housing in the long run. The quantity of rental housing supplied will remain at Q_0. Since the last unit of rental housing is valued at R_2, but rent is fixed at R_0, demanders of rental housing will be willing to bear additional costs up to $R_2 - R_0$ (in the form of additional search activity or illegal payments) in order to obtain rental housing.

2 a The equilibrium price of petrol is £1 per litre since, at that price, the quantity of petrol demanded is equal to the quantity supplied (16 million litres per day). The equilibrium quantity of petrol traded is 16 million litres of petrol per day.

b The new table and graph are shown in Table 6.2 and Fig. 6.5.

Figure 6.5

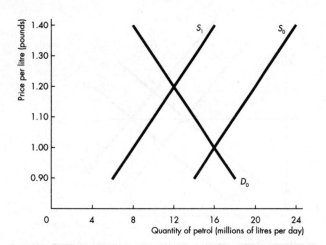

Table 6.2

Price (pounds per litre)	Quantity demanded (millions of litres per day)	Quantity supplied
1.40	8	16
1.30	10	14
1.20	12	12
1.10	14	10
1.00	16	8
0.90	18	6

The new equilibrium price is £1.20 per litre since, at that price, the quantity of petrol demanded equals the new quantity supplied (12 million litres per day). The new equilibrium quantity traded is 12 million litres of petrol per day.

   c The increase in price has caused the quantity of petrol demanded to decrease by 4 million litres per day (from 16 to 12 million). Given the new supply curve S_1, the increase in price from £1 to £1.20 per litre increases the quantity of petrol supplied by 4 million litres per day (from 8 to 12 million).

   d **i** At the ceiling price of £1, the quantity demanded is 16 million litres per day.

     ii The quantity supplied is 8 million litres per day.

     iii The quantity of petrol actually sold is 8 million litres per day. When, at a given price, quantity demanded and quantity supplied differ, whichever quantity is the *lesser* will determine the quantity actually sold.

     iv The excess quantity of petrol demanded is 8 million litres per day.

     v The highest price consumers are willing to pay for the last unit of petrol supplied (the 8 millionth litre per day) is £1.40. You can obtain this answer from your graph by imagining a vertical line from the quantity 8 million litres up to where it intersects the demand curve at £1.40. The demand curve shows the highest price consumers would be willing to pay for that last litre supplied.

     vi The regulated price of petrol is £1 per litre but the value to the consumer of the last litre is £1.40, so the consumer would be willing to bear costs of £4 above the regulated price of petrol to obtain 10 litres (£0.40 × 10 litres). If the best alternative is to earn £8.00 per hour, the consumer would be willing to spend up to half an hour queuing to buy the 10 litres.

DATA QUESTIONS

   1 The objectives of the CAP are to increase agricultural productivity, to increase farm incomes, to stabilize prices and to ensure reasonable prices for agricultural products.

Figure 6.6

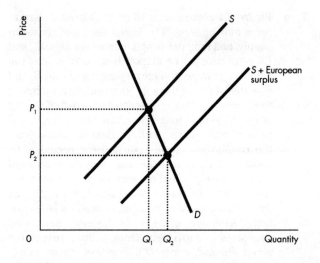

2 The effect of the EU's food surpluses on the world market are shown in Fig. 6.6. The result is a fall in world prices and an increase in quantity.

3 Large farmers in particular benefit. The biggest losers are consumers and Third World farmers who cannot compete with subsidized EU exports.

4 Several measures can be used to reduce surpluses. These include cutting the price at which the Union buys agricultural products, selling surpluses abroad at low prices, imposing quotas that limit the quantity of food which farmers are allowed to produce, and paying farmers to 'set aside' land, that is, to let land lie fallow.

Chapter 7 **Utility and Demand**

Chapter in Perspective, Text Pages 170–191

The fundamental economic concept of demand was introduced in Chapter 4. There we assumed that as the price of a good rises, the quantity demanded will decline. Assuming this law of demand allowed us to draw a number of useful conclusions and make predictions about the behaviour of prices and quantity traded. Our confidence in these results would be enhanced if it were not necessary to assume the law of demand – if this could be derived as a prediction of a more fundamental theory. This is the major task of this chapter. Not only is the law of demand derived as a prediction of the marginal utility theory, but other results that had previously been assumed (for example, a change in income causes a shift in demand) also turn out to be predictions.

This chapter and the next greatly deepen our understanding of the forces underlying the law of demand and associated concepts.

Helpful Hints

1 The concept of utility is an extremely useful abstract device which allows us to think more clearly about consumer choice. Marginal utility theory assumes that an individual is able to judge whether the additional satisfaction per pound spent on good X is greater or less than the additional satisfaction per pound spend on Y. If it is greater, then the decision is to consume an additional unit of X. How much greater is irrelevant for the decision.

2 The marginal utility per pound spent on good X can be written as MU_X/P_X where MU_X is the marginal utility of the last unit of X consumed and P_X is the price of a unit of good X. The consumer equilibrium (utility-maximizing) condition for goods X and Y can thus be written:

$$\frac{MU_X}{P_X} = \frac{MU_Y}{P_Y}$$

This implies that, in consumer equilibrium, the ratio of marginal utilities will equal the ratio of prices of the two goods:

$$\frac{MU_X}{MU_Y} = \frac{P_X}{P_Y}$$

3 If an individual is not in consumer equilibrium, then the equation above is not satisfied. For example, consider spending all of one's income on a consumption plan where:

$$\frac{MU_X}{P_X} > \frac{MU_Y}{P_Y}$$

or, equivalently

$$\frac{MU_X}{MU_Y} > \frac{P_X}{P_Y}$$

Since P_X and P_Y are given, this means that MU_X is 'too large' and MU_Y is 'too small'. Utility can be increased by increasing consumption of X (and thereby decreasing MU_X owing to the principle of diminishing marginal utility) and decreasing consumption of Y (and thereby increasing MU_Y owing to diminishing marginal utility).

4 Table 7.7 in the text on page 184 is a good review device.

Key Figures and Table

Figure 7.1 Individual and Market Demand Curves, text page 172

The market demand curve is obtained by adding the quantities demanded at each price by each individual. This figure illustrates this in a market with two individuals. At each price, quantity demanded in the market is equal to the quantity demanded by Katie plus the quantity demanded by Paul. This is illustrated graphically and in a table.

Figure 7.3 Total Utility and Marginal Utility, text page 175

This shows (a) the total utility Katie derives from consumption of pizzas as well as (b) the marginal (additional) utility resulting from each additional pizza. The table shows that, as Katie eats additional pizzas, her total utility increases but the marginal utility resulting from each additional pizza is less than the marginal utility of the previous pizza. Because of diminishing marginal utility, as Katie eats additional pizzas, her total utility increases but at a diminishing rate. There is an explicit relationship between the increase in total utility in part (a) and marginal utility

in part (b): between any two quantities, the slope of the total utility curve is equal to marginal utility. For example, between quantities 0 and 1, the slope of the total utility curve is 50/1, which is equal to the marginal utility in moving from 0 to 1 units consumed.

Figure 7.4 Equalising Marginal Utility Per Pound Spent, text page 177

This shows that as more of a good is consumed its utility will fall and rational consumers will therefore consume more of other goods.

Figure 7.5 A Fall in the Price of Pizzas, text page 179

When the price of a pizza falls, Katie buys more pizzas and this is shown in part (a) by a movement along the demand curve. Since, for Katie, pizzas and wine are substitutes, the fall in the price of pizzas causes a shift in her demand for wine, and this is shown in part (b).

Figure 7.6 A Rise in the Price of Wine, text page 180

The increase in the price of wine will cause a movement along the demand curve for wine, and also a shift in the demand curve for pizzas so that more pizzas are demanded.

Figure 7.7 Consumer Surplus, text page 185

Consumer surplus is the difference between the most a person is willing to pay for a good (its value to that person) and its price (the amount actually paid). This figure illustrates the calculation of consumer surplus by examining Katie's demand for pizzas. If the price of a pizza is £3, Katie will eat 5 pizzas per month. While the value of the fifth pizza is £3 to Katie, the values of the first to fourth pizzas are higher. Thus Katie enjoys some consumer surplus. The value of the first pizza is £7, but since the actual price is £3, Katie receives consumer surplus of £4 on it. Similarly, she receives £3 on the second, £2 on the third, and £1 on the fourth pizza. Thus, her total consumer surplus is the sum of these: £10.

Table 7.7 Marginal Utility Theory, text page 184

This summarizes the assumptions, implications and predictions of marginal utility theory. Note particularly that the first prediction is the law of demand.

SELF-TEST

CONCEPT REVIEW

1 The _____ demand curve is the sum of the quantities demanded by each individual at each _____ .

2 The benefit or satisfaction a person receives from the consumption of a good or a service is called _____ .

3 The additional utility a person receives from consuming one more unit of a good is called _____ _____ .

4 As consumption increases, marginal utility _____ . This is called the principle of _____ marginal utility.

5 We assume that a household will choose quantities to consume so as to _____ utility subject to its income and the prices it faces.

6 The marginal utility per pound spent is the marginal utility of the last unit of a good consumed divided by its _____ .

7 Utility will be maximized if the marginal utility per pound spent is _____ for all goods.

8 Marginal utility theory predicts that if the price of one good rises, _____ of it will be consumed and _____ of other goods will be consumed.

9 Marginal utility theory predicts that the higher household income is, the _____ is the quantity consumed of all normal goods.

10 The difference between the value of a good and its price is called _____ .

TRUE OR FALSE

___ **1** Market demand is the sum of all individual demands.

___ **2** Total utility equals the sum of the marginal utilities for all units consumed.

___ **3** The principle of diminishing marginal utility means that as consumption of a good increases, total utility declines.

___ **4** The principle of diminishing marginal utility means that as consumption of a good increases, total utility increases but at a decreasing rate.

___ **5** A consumer equilibrium exists when a consumer has allocated his/her income in a way that maximizes total utility.

___ **6** A household will be maximizing utility if the marginal utility per pound spent is equal for all goods and all its income is spent.

___ **7** When the price of good X rises, the marginal utility from the consumption of X decreases.

___ **8** If the marginal utilities from consuming two goods are not equal, then the consumer cannot be in equilibrium.

___ **9** If the marginal utility per pound spent on good X exceeds the marginal utility per pound spent on good Y, total utility will increase by increasing consumption of X and decreasing consumption of Y.

___ **10** Marginal utility theory predicts that if the price of a good falls, consumption of substitute goods will rise.

___ **11** Utility cannot be observed or measured.

___ **12** The value of a good is always the price of the good.

___ **13** The principle of diminishing marginal utility guarantees that consumers will always make some consumer surplus.

___ **14** Consumer surplus is the difference between the value of a good and its price.

___ **15** If a shift in supply decreases the price of a good, consumer surplus increases.

___ **16** The diamond–water paradox illustrates that relative prices actually reflect total utility rather than marginal utility.

MULTIPLE-CHOICE

1 Marginal utility equals
  a total utility divided by price.
  b total utility divided by the total number of units consumed.
  c the slope of the total utility curve.
  d the inverse of total utility.
  e the area below the demand curve but above market price.

2 If Ms Petersen is maximizing her utility in the consumption of goods A and B, which of the following statements must be true?
  a $MU_A = MU_B$
  b $\dfrac{MU_A}{P_A} = \dfrac{MU_B}{P_B}$
  c $\dfrac{MU_A}{P_B} = \dfrac{MU_B}{P_A}$
  d $TU_A = TU_B$
  e $\dfrac{TU_A}{P_A} = \dfrac{TU_B}{P_B}$

3 If a consumer is in equilibrium, then
  a total utility is maximized given the consumer's income and the prices of goods.
  b marginal utility is maximized given the consumer's income and the prices of goods.
  c marginal utility per pound spent is maximized given the consumer's income and the prices of goods.
  d the marginal utility of the last unit of each good will be the same.
  e none of the above is true.

4 If Renata is maximizing her utility and two goods have the same marginal utility then
  a she will buy only one of them.
  b she will buy equal quantities of them.
  c she will be willing to pay the same price for each of them.
  d she will get the same total utility from each of them.
  e none of the above is true.

5 Shelley is maximizing her utility in her consumption of mink coats and Porsches. If the marginal utility of her last purchased mink coat is twice the marginal utility of her last purchased Porsche, then we do not know with certainty that
  a Shelley buys twice as many mink coats as Porsches.
  b Shelley buys twice as many Porsches as mink coats.
  c Shelley buys more Porsches than mink coats, but we do not know how many more.
  d the price of a mink coat is twice the price of a Porsche.
  e the price of a Porsche is twice the price of a mink coat.

6 Total utility equals
  a the sum of the marginal utilities of each unit consumed.
  b the area below the demand curve but above the market price.
  c the slope of the marginal utility curve.
  d the marginal utility of the last unit divided by price.
  e the marginal utility of the last unit consumed multiplied by the total number of units consumed.

7 Samir consumes apples and bananas and is in consumer equilibrium. The marginal utility of the last apple is 10 and the marginal utility of the last banana is 5. If the price of an apple is £0.50, then what is the price of a banana?
  a £0.05
  b £0.10
  c £0.25
  d £0.50
  e £1.00

8 The value of a good is defined as the
  a market price.
  b average price paid by individuals in a market.
  c cost of producing the good.
  d highest price an individual is willing to pay.
  e total utility to an individual of all units of the good.

9 The difference between the value of a good and its price is known as
  a excess demand.
  b excess supply.
  c consumer surplus.
  d consumer excess.
  e marginal utility.

10 The demand schedule for marbles is shown in Table 7.1.

Table 7.1 Demand Schedule for Marbles

Price per marble (pounds)	Quantity demanded
10	1
9	2
8	3
7	4
6	5

If the actual price is £7, what is total consumer surplus?

a £3
b £4
c £6
d £12
e £27

11 The high price of diamonds relative to the price of water reflects the fact that at typical levels of consumption

a the total utility of water is relatively low.
b the total utility of diamonds is relatively high.
c the marginal utility of water is relatively high.
d the marginal utility of diamonds is relatively low.
e none of the above is true.

SHORT ANSWER

1 A consumer is initially maximizing his utility in the consumption of goods A and B so that:

$$\frac{MU_A}{P_A} = \frac{MU_B}{P_B}$$

The price of A then rises as a result of the shift in supply shown in Fig. 7.1. Use the above condition for utility maximization to explain how the consumer will move to a new utility-maximizing equilibrium. Show the connection between your explanation and the change on the diagram.

2 Explain why the consumer equilibrium condition and the principle of diminishing marginal utility imply the law of demand.

Figure 7.1

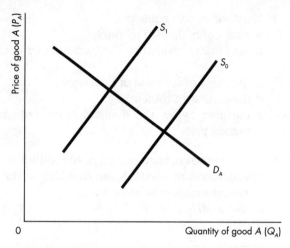

3 How does marginal utility theory resolve the diamond–water paradox of value?

PROBLEMS

1 Table 7.2 gives the demand schedules for broccoli for three individuals: Tom, Jana and Ted.

Table 7.2 Individual Demand for Broccoli

Price per kilogram (pounds)	Quantity demanded (kilograms per week)		
	Tom	Jana	Ted
£0.50	10	4	10
£0.75	9	2	7
£1.00	8	0	4
£1.25	7	0	1

a Calculate the market demand schedule.
b On a single diagram, draw the individual demand curves for Tom, Jana and Ted, as well as the market demand curve.

2 Suppose that a student spends his entire income of £8 on tennis rackets and books. The price of a tennis racket is £2 and the price of a book is £4. The marginal utility of each good, shown in Table 7.3, is independent of the amount consumed of the other good.

Table 7.3

	Marginal utility	
Quantity	Books	Rackets
1	20	36
2	18	32
3	16	20
4	8	16

a If the student is maximizing his utility, how many units of each good should he purchase?

b If the student's income rises to £24, how many units of each good should he purchase?

c Using the information in Table 7.3, calculate the student's income elasticity of demand for books.

3 Andy's weekly demand schedule for pizzas is shown in Table 7.4.

Table 7.4 Demand Schedule for Pizzas

Price per pizza (pounds)	Quantity demanded
15	1
12	2
10	3
9	4
8	5

If the price of a pizza is £9, what is Andy's consumer surplus for the following number of pizzas that he buys at that price?

a first pizza
b second pizza
c total number of pizzas

DATA QUESTIONS

Music, love and utility

Duke Orsino 'If music be the food of love, play on;
Give me excess of it, that, surfeiting,
The appetite may sicken, and so die.
… Enough! no more:
'Tis not so sweet now as it was before.'

Source: Shakespeare, *Twelfth Night*, Scene 1.

1 Explain the effect of music on love in terms of utility theory.

2 In the play Orsino wants his love to die because his love for Olivia is not returned. What would be the effect on the utility of music for him if she also loved him?

ANSWERS

CONCEPT REVIEW

1 market; price

2 utility

3 marginal utility

4 decreases; diminishing

5 maximize

6 price

7 equal

8 less; more

9 greater

10 consumer surplus

TRUE OR FALSE

1 T Definition.

2 T Definition.

3 F *Marginal* utility falls as more is consumed.

4 T Because marginal utility is positive but diminishing.

5 T Because any change would reduce utility.

6 T Definition.

7 F Rise in price leads to a fall in quantity and hence a rise in marginal utility.

8 F If prices are unequal, then marginal utilities must be unequal for consumers to be in equilibrium.

9 T Because it moves the ratio of marginal utility/price towards equality.

10 **F** More of the good will be consumed and less of substitute goods.

11 **T** Utility is an abstract concept.

12 **F** Price can be greater or less than value.

13 **T** Willingness to pay is greater than price for all units consumed except the last.

14 **T** Definition.

15 **T** The shift in supply leads to an increase in quantity consumed, so there are more units where consumers are willing to pay more than the price.

16 **F** Relative prices reflect marginal utility.

MULTIPLE-CHOICE

1 **c** Definition.

2 **b** Definition.

3 **a** Consumers maximize total utility. **c** and **d** wrong because MU/P equal for total utility maximization.

4 **c** From maximum condition of equal MU/P. There is no necessary relation between MU and quantity or total utility.

5 **d** From maximum condition of equal MU/P. No necessary relation between MU and quantity.

6 **a** **b** is consumer surplus. For **c**, MU = slope of the total utility curve. **d** and **e** are nonsense.

7 **c** Solve $10/0.5 = 5/P_b$ for P_b.

8 **d** Definition.

9 **c** Definition.

10 **c** For 4 marbles consumed, consumer surplus = $ (10 − 7) + (9 − 7) + (8 − 7) + (7 − 7)$.

11 **e** For diamonds: TU is relatively low, MU relatively high. For water: TU is relatively high, MU relatively low.

SHORT ANSWER

1 When the price of A rises, *ceteris paribus*:

$$\frac{MU_A}{P_A} = \frac{MU_B}{P_B}$$

The consumer is no longer in equilibrium. In order to restore the equality in the equilibrium condition, the consumer must change his consumption to make MU_A rise and MU_B fall. (The consumer cannot change the prices of A and B.) Since marginal utility diminishes with increases in quantity consumed, the consumer must decrease consumption of A and increase consumption of B. Decreased consumption of A moves the

consumer up to the left on the demand curve, from the initial intersection of D and S_0 to the new intersection of D and S_1. In the new consumer equilibrium, equality will be restored in the equilibrium condition.

2 Suppose we observe an individual in consumer equilibrium consuming X_0 units of good X and Y_0 units of good Y with the prices of X and Y given by P_X and P_Y respectively. This means that at consumption levels X_0 and Y_0, the marginal utility per pound spent on X equals the marginal utility per pound spent on Y. Now let the price of X increase to P_X^1. This increase implies that the marginal utility per pound spent on X declines and thus is now less than the marginal utility per pound spent on Y. Thus, to restore equilibrium, our consumer must increase the marginal utility of X and decrease the marginal utility of Y. From the principle of diminishing marginal utility we know that the only way to do this is to decrease the consumption of X and increase the consumption of Y. This demonstrates the law of demand since an increase in the price of X has been shown to require a decrease in the consumption of X to restore consumer equilibrium.

3 The paradox of value is resolved by recognizing that while the total utility from consumption of water is large, the marginal utility from the last unit of water is small. Likewise, the total utility from the consumption of diamonds is small, but the marginal utility of the last unit of diamonds is large. If consumers are in equilibrium, then the requirement that the marginal utility per pound spent be the same for water and diamonds means that the price of water must be low and the price of diamonds must be high.

PROBLEMS

1 **a** The market demand schedule (Table 7.5) is obtained by adding the quantities demanded by Tom, Jana and Ted at each price.

Table 7.5 Market Demand Schedule for Broccoli

Price per kilogram (pounds)	Quantity demanded (kilograms per week)
0.50	24
0.75	18
1.00	12
1.25	8

b Figure 7.2 illustrates the individual demand curves for Tom, Jana and Ted as well as the market demand curve.

2 a The utility-maximizing combination of goods is shown in Table 7.6.

Table 7.6

	MU/P	
Quantity	Books	Rackets
1	10	9
2	9	8
3	8	5
4	4	4

Figure 7.2

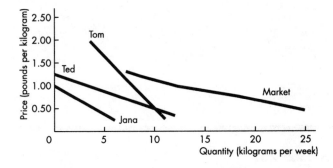

The student should purchase 2 books and 1 racket. He spends all of his income (£8) and the marginal utility per pound spent is the same for books and rackets (9).

b He should purchase 4 books and 4 rackets. He spends all of his income (£24) and the marginal utility per pound spent is the same for books and rackets (4).

c The income elasticity of demand for books is:

$$\eta_y = \frac{\Delta Q/Q_{ave}}{\Delta Y/Y_{ave}}$$

3 a The most Andy would be willing to pay for the first pizza is £15, but the price is only £9. Therefore, his consumer surplus is £6 (£15–£9).

b Andy's consumer surplus on the second pizza is the difference between the most he would be willing to pay (£12) and the price (£9). His consumer surplus is £3.

c At a price of £9, Andy will buy 4 pizzas. He will receive consumer surplus on the first three pizzas in the amount of £6, £3 and £1, respectively. Thus, his total consumer surplus is £10.

DATA QUESTIONS

1 If we eat too many cakes the marginal utility of cakes will fall, and eventually we will be surfeited – turned off cakes altogether. Orsino hopes this will also be the case with the effect of music on love. More music means an increase in love, but eventually the marginal utility of love will diminish and become zero. Hence he will no longer want love.

2 If Olivia falls in love with Orsino, the position will change (just as a drink may change the utility of another cake). Now, he will want love – and music, but not too much. He will choose additional amounts of music until the satisfaction he gets from love is maximized. Note that this assumes that the music is free. If he were paying for the music, he would buy more music until the cost of the music equalled the benefit he obtained from it.

Chapter 8

Possibilities, Preferences and Choices

Chapter in Perspective, Text Pages 192–217

This chapter provides an alternative analysis of consumer choice and the law of demand that complements the marginal utility analysis of Chapter 7. Here, the analysis uses a model of consumer behaviour based on a budget equation which represents *possible choices* given a consumer's income and an indifference curve representation of *preferences*.

The model allows more systematic analysis of what happens to quantity demanded when the price of a good changes and when income changes, as well as more insight into the distinction between normal and inferior goods. Compared with the marginal utility analysis, the budget equation/indifference curve model has the advantage that it does not depend on the abstract notion of utility. None the less, the two analyses of consumer choice have close parallels which are outlined in the appendix to the chapter on text pages 215–217.

Helpful Hints

1 The consumer's problem is to do the best given the constraints faced. These constraints, which limit the range of possible choices, depend on income and the prices of goods and are represented graphically by the budget line. 'Doing the best' means finding the most preferred outcome consistent with those constraints. In this chapter, preferences are represented graphically by indifference curves. Thus, graphically, the consumer problem is to find the highest indifference curve attainable given the budget line. To make graphical analysis feasible, we restrict ourselves to choices between only two goods, but the same principles apply in the real world where the array of choices is much broader.

2 Each of the two endpoints (the intercepts) of a budget line is just income divided by the price of the good on that axis. Connecting those endpoints with a straight line yields the budget line. The slope of the budget line provides additional information relevant for the consumer's choice between goods. The magnitude (absolute value) of the slope equals the relative price (or opportunity cost) of pizzas in terms of wine. To put it in different words, the magnitude of the slope equals the number of units of wine it takes to buy one pizza. More generally, the magnitude of the slope of the budget line (P_X/P_Y) equals the relative price (or opportunity cost) of the good on the horizontal x-axis in terms of the good on the vertical y-axis; or the number of units of vertical-axis goods it takes to buy one unit of the horizontal-axis good. See also the discussion of Table 8.1 under *Key Figures and Tables* on page 72.

3 The marginal rate of substitution *(MRS)* is the rate at which a consumer gives up good Y for an additional unit of good X and still remains indifferent. The *MRS* equals the magnitude of the slope of the indifference curve, Q_Y/Q_X.

Because indifference curves are bowed toward the origin (convex), the magnitude of the slope and hence the *MRS* diminish as we move down an indifference curve. The diminishing *MRS* means that the consumer is willing to give up less of good Y for each additional unit of good X. As the consumer moves down an indifference curve, the consumer is coming to value good Y more and value good X less. This is easily explained by the principle of diminishing marginal utility, which underlies the following equation from the appendix to the chapter:

$$\text{Marginal rate of substitution} = \frac{MU_X}{MU_Y}$$

At the top of the indifference curve, the consumer is consuming little X and much Y, so the marginal utility of X *(MU_X)* is high and the marginal utility of Y *(MU_Y)* is low. Moving down the curve, as the quantity of X consumed increases, MU_X decreases; and as the quantity of Y consumed decreases, MU_Y increases. Thus, the principle of diminishing marginal utility provides an intuitive understanding of why the *MRS* diminishes as we move down an indifference curve.

4 At the consumer's best affordable point, the budget line is just tangent to the highest affordable indifference curve, so the magnitude of the slope of the budget line equals the magnitude of the slope of the indifference curve.

5 Understanding the distinction between the income and substitution effects of a change in the price of a good is sometimes a challenge for students. Consider a decrease in the price of good A. This has two effects which will influence the consumption of A. First, the decrease in the price of A will reduce the relative price of A and, second, it will increase real income. The substitution effect is the answer to the question: how much would the consumption of A change as a result of the relative price decline if we also (hypothetically) reduce income by enough to leave the consumer indifferent between the new and original situations? The income effect is the answer to the following question: how much more would the consumption of A change if we (hypothetically) restore the consumer's real income but leave relative prices at the new level?

Key Figures and Table

Figure 8.1 The Budget Line, text page 194

Household consumption is limited by the level of household income and the prices of goods and services. A budget line graphically represents those limits to consumption choices. Figure 8.1 illustrates a budget line faced by Katie who has a monthly income of £30 to be allocated between two goods: wine and pizzas. The price of a pizza is £6 and the price of wine is £3. The table indicates six possible allocations of Katie's income, given these prices. The budget line simply represents these points graphically. To locate the budget line, find the endpoints by asking how many pizzas could be purchased if all income is spent on pizzas (the x-intercept) and how much wine bought could be bought if all income is spent on wine (the y-intercept). Then draw a straight line between the endpoints.

Figure 8.3 Mapping Preferences, text page 197

An indifference curve shows all the combinations of two goods among which an individual is indifferent. An indifference curve is thus a boundary between two areas: **(1)** combinations of the two goods that are preferred to any combination on the indifference curve, and **(2)** combinations that are inferior and so not preferred.

Katie is indifferent as to the choices along the indifference curve. For example, between 6 bottles of wine and 2 pizzas at point c or 6 pizzas and 2 bottles of wine at point g.

She would prefer to be in the preferred area because she would have more of at least one good, but this is not possible because of the budget constraint.

Figure 8.4 A Preference Map, text page 198

A preference map is a series of indifference curves for the same individual. This figure illustrates three indifference curves in Katie's preference map. Along each indifference curve, Katie is indifferent among the alternative consumption combinations; each would make her equally happy. However, points on a higher indifference curve are preferred to points on a lower indifference curve.

Figure 8.7 The Best Affordable Point, text page 201

Points along the budget line represent maximum affordable combinations of consumption goods. Higher indifference curves represent more preferred consumption points. The objective of the consumer is to obtain the best (most preferred) affordable consumption point possible. Graphically, this means that a consumer will choose the consumption point that is on the budget line and also on the highest indifference

curve possible. The best affordable point will always be a point where the budget line is just tangent to (that is, touches at one point only) the highest indifference curve possible. In this figure, this occurs at consumption point c. This is the best affordable consumption point because all other affordable points (on the budget line) intersect lower indifference curves. On the other hand, all points on higher indifference curves are not affordable.

Table 8.1 Calculating the Budget Equation, text page 195

This table derives the equation of Katie's budget line, given her income and the prices of wine and pizzas. In the first part of the table, symbols are defined (on the left) and specific values for income and price for the example in the text are given (on the right). The second part of the table gives the general expression of the budget equation. It simply says that the amount spent on pizzas ($P_p \times Q_p$) plus the amount spent on wine ($P_w \times Q_w$) is equal to income (y). The third part of the table shows how to derive the budget equation from the consumer's budget.

SELF-TEST

CONCEPT REVIEW

1 A _____ line describes the maximum amounts of consumption a household can undertake given its income and the prices of the goods it buys.

2 Real income is income expressed in units of _____ .

3 The price of one good divided by the price of another is called a(n) _____ price.

4 If the quantity of good A consumed is measured on the horizontal axis and the quantity of good B consumed is measured on the vertical axis, an increase in the price of good A will make the budget line _____ . An increase in income will shift the budget line _____ .

5 A(n) _____ curve shows all combinations of goods that would leave a consumer indifferent.

6 Suppose we measure good A on the horizontal axis and good B on the vertical axis. The rate at which a person would give up good B to obtain more of good A is called the _____ rate of _____ . As the consumer increases consumption of good A (and decreases consumption of good B so as to remain indifferent), this rate _____ .

7 The best affordable consumption point will be on both the _____ line and the highest attainable _____ curve.

8 If the price of good A rises, the _____ effect will always imply that less of A will be consumed, while the _____ effect reinforces this only if A is a normal good.

9 If a decrease in income causes an increase in the consumption of good B, then B is a(n) _____ good.

10 As the wage rate rises, the substitution effect encourages _____ leisure and the income effect encourages _____ leisure.

TRUE OR FALSE

___ **1** At any point on the budget line, all income is spent.

___ **2** An increase in the price of the good measured on the horizontal axis will make the budget line flatter.

___ **3** *Ceteris paribus*, an increase in the price of goods means that real income falls.

___ **4** An increase in income will cause an inward parallel shift of the budget line.

___ **5** Preferences depend on income and the prices of goods.

___ **6** We assume that more of any good is preferred to less of the good.

___ **7** An indifference curve shows all combinations of two goods which the consumer can afford.

___ **8** It is logically possible for indifference curves to intersect each other.

___ **9** The principle of the diminishing marginal rate of substitution explains why indifference curves are bowed toward the origin.

___ **10** The magnitude of the slope of an indifference curve is equal to the marginal rate of substitution.

___ **11** The marginal rate of substitution falls as consumption of the good measured on the y-axis falls and consumption of the good measured on the x-axis rises.

___ **12** At the best affordable consumption point, the slope of the budget line is equal to the slope of the indifference curve.

___ **13** When the relative price of a good falls, the substitution effect leads to less consumption of the good if it is inferior.

MULTIPLE-CHOICE

1 Which of the following statements best describes a consumer's budget line?
   a the amount of each good a consumer can purchase
   b the limits to a consumer's set of affordable consumption choices
   c the desired level of consumption for the consumer
   d the consumption choices made by a consumer
   e the set of all affordable consumption choices

2 If the price of the good measured on the vertical axis increases, the budget line will
   a become steeper.
   b become flatter.
   c shift inward but parallel to the original budget line.
   d shift outward but parallel to the original budget line.
   e shift inward and become steeper.

3 If income increases, the budget line will
   a become steeper.
   b become flatter.
   c shift inward but parallel to the original budget line.
   d shift outward but parallel to the original budget line.
   e shift parallel but outward or inward depending on whether a good is normal or inferior.

4 A change in income changes which aspect(s) of the budget equation?
   a slope and y-intercept
   b slope and x-intercept
   c x- and y-intercepts but not slope
   d slope only
   e none of the above

5 Bill consumes apples and bananas. Suppose Bill's income doubles and the prices of apples and bananas also double. Bill's budget line will
   a shift in but not change slope.
   b remain unchanged.
   c shift out but not change slope.
   d shift out and become steeper.
   e shift out and become flatter.

6 Suppose good X is measured on the horizontal axis and good Y on the vertical axis. The marginal rate of substitution is best defined as the a relative price of good X in terms of good Y.

b relative price of good Y in terms of good X.

c rate at which a consumer will give up good Y in order to obtain more of good X and remain indifferent.

d rate at which a consumer will give up good X in order to obtain more of good Y and remain indifferent.

e slope of the budget line.

7 In general, as a consumer moves down an indifference curve, increasing consumption of good X (measured on the horizontal axis),

a more of Y must be given up for each additional unit of X.

b a constant amount of Y must be given up for each additional unit of X.

c less of Y must be given up for each additional unit of X.

d the relative price of Y increases.

e the relative price of Y decreases.

8 Consider the budget line and indifference curve in Fig. 8.1. If the price of good X is £2, what is the price of good Y?

a £0.37

b £0.67

c £1.50

d £2.67

e impossible to calculate without additional information

Figure 8.1

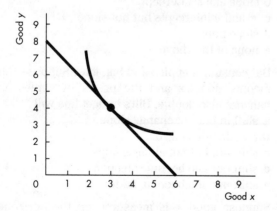

9 When the price of a good changes, the change in consumption that leaves the consumer indifferent is called the

a utility effect.

b substitution effect.

c income effect.

d price effect.

e Giffen effect.

10 When the price of a normal good rises, the income effect

a increases consumption of the good and the substitution effect decreases consumption.

b decreases consumption of the good and the substitution effect increases consumption.

c and the substitution effect both increase consumption of the good.

d and the substitution effect both decrease consumption of the good.

e is always larger than the substitution effect.

11 If the price of good X (measured on the horizontal axis) falls, the substitution effect is represented by a movement to a

a higher indifference curve.

b lower indifference curve.

c steeper part of the same indifference curve.

d flatter part of the same indifference curve.

e flatter part of a higher indifference curve.

12 The initial budget line labelled RS in Fig. 8.2 would shift to RT as a result of

a an increase in the price of good X.

b a decrease in the price of good X.

c a decrease in preferences for good X.

d an increase in the price of good Y.

e an increase in real income.

13 When the initial budget line labelled RS in Fig. 8.2 shifts to RT, the substitution effect is illustrated by the move from point

a a to b.

b a to c.

c a to d.

d b to d.

e d to c.

14 When the initial budget line labelled RS in Fig. 8.2 shifts to RT, the income effect is illustrated by the move from point

a a to b.

b a to c.

c a to d.

d *b* to *c*.

e *b* to *d*.

Figure 8.2

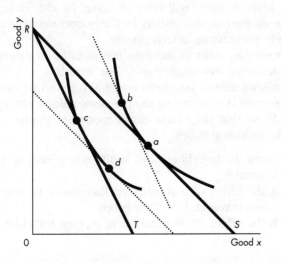

15 Over the last 100 years, the quantity of labour supplied has fallen as wages have increased. This indicates that the income effect

a and the substitution effect have both discouraged leisure.

b and the substitution effect have both encouraged leisure.

c discouraging leisure has been dominated by the substitution effect encouraging leisure.

d encouraging leisure has dominated the substitution effect discouraging leisure.

e has not affected the labour–leisure choice.

SHORT ANSWER

1 Why is an indifference curve negatively sloped?

2 The appendix to Chapter 8 on text pages 215 – 217 establishes that the

$$\text{Marginal rate} \atop \text{of substitution} = \frac{\text{Marginal utility of pizzas}}{\text{Marginal utility of wine}}$$

As we move down an indifference curve, use the principle of diminishing marginal utility to explain why the marginal rate of substitution diminishes.

3 Suppose the price of a normal good falls. Without the use of graphs, distinguish between the income and substitution effects of this price decline.

PROBLEMS

1 Jan and Dan both like bread and peanut butter and have the same income. Since they each face the same prices, they have identical budget lines. Currently, Jan and Dan consume exactly the same quantities of bread and peanut butter; they have the same best affordable consumption point. Jan, however, views bread and peanut butter as close (though not perfect) substitutes, while Dan considers bread and peanut butter to be quite (but not perfectly) complementary.

a On the same diagram, draw a budget line and representative indifference curves for Jan and Dan. (Measure the quantity of bread on the horizontal axis.)

b Now, suppose the price of bread declines. Graphically represent the substitution effects for Jan and Dan. For whom is the substitution effect greater?

2 Kurt consumes both coffee and whisky. The initial price of coffee is £1 per unit and the price of whisky is £1.50 per unit. Kurt's initial income is £12.

a What is the relative price of coffee?

b Derive Kurt's budget equation and draw his budget line on a graph. (Measure coffee on the horizontal axis.)

c On your graph, draw an indifference curve so that the best affordable point corresponds to 6 units of coffee and 4 units of whisky.

d What is the marginal rate of substitution of coffee for whisky at this point?

e Show that any other point on the budget line is inferior.

3 Given the initial situation described in Problem 2, suppose Kurt's income now increases.

a Illustrate graphically how the consumption of coffee and whisky are affected if both goods are normal. (Numerical answers are not necessary. Just show whether consumption increases or decreases.)

b Draw a graph showing the effect of an increase in Kurt's income if whisky is an inferior good.

4 Return to the initial circumstances described in Problem 2. Now, suppose the price of coffee doubles to £2 a unit while the price of whisky remains at £1.50 per unit and income remains at £12.

a Draw the new budget line.

b Why is the initial best affordable point (label it point *r*) no longer the best affordable point?

c Using your graph, show the new best affordable point and label it *t*. What has happened to the consumption of coffee?

d Decompose the effect on the consumption of *X* into the substitution effect and the income effect. On your graph, indicate the substitution effect as movement from point *r* to point *s* (which you must locate) and indicate the income effect as movement from point *s* to point *t*.

DATA QUESTION

Age and mobility

Look at almost any bus. The passengers will not be a cross-section of the public as a whole because those with high incomes will tend to travel by car. Hence those on the bus will usually be the poorer sections of society, particularly elderly people.

Those who want to increase the mobility of elderly people make two suggestions. The first is a subsidy that allows elderly people to travel at a reduced price. The second is to increase the pensions paid to elderly people so that they have more money to spend on goods, including buses.

1 Draw budget lines and indifference curves to illustrate:

a the effect of a subsidy on the choice between bus travel and all other goods.

b the effect of an increase in income for elderly people.

ANSWERS

CONCEPT REVIEW

1 budget

2 goods

3 relative

4 steeper; out

5 indifference

6 marginal; substitution; diminishes

7 budget; indifference

8 substitution; income

9 inferior

10 less; more

TRUE OR FALSE

1 **T** Definition.

2 **F** The budget line will move to the left.

3 **T** Real income = income/price of goods.

4 **F** Parallel shift to the right.

5 **F** Definition.

6 **T** One of three fundamental assumptions about preferences.

7 **F** Definition of budget line.

8 **F** Logically impossible.

9 **T** Definition.

10 **T** Definition.

11 **T** Describes movements down along indifference curve.

12 **T** Budget line tangent to indifference curve.

13 **F** Fall in price leads to more consumption for inferior goods.

MULTIPLE-CHOICE

1 **b** **a** should be combinations of goods, **c** about indifference curves, **d** about best affordable point, **e** includes area inside budget line.

2 **b** *y*-intercept shifts down, *x*-intercept is unchanged.

3 d Increase in income does not change slope, but increase in x and y intercepts.

4 c Change in income does not change slope but does change intercepts.

5 b Numerators and denominators of both intercepts double, so intercepts do not change.

6 c Definition. **a** and **b** relate to the slope of the budget line. $MRS = $ **e** only at best affordable point.

7 c Due to diminishing MRS. **d** and **e** are wrong since relative price relates to budget line, not indifference curve.

8 c Income = £12 (£2 × 6 units X) so price of Y = £12/8 units Y.

9 b Definition.

10 d Both work in same direction. Rise in price leads to fall in consumption.

11 d New budget line is flatter and drawn tangent to same indifference curve.

12 b With the same income there is a fall in quantity of X that can be purchased.

13 a Budget line with new prices tangent to original indifference curve.

14 d Hypothetically restore original income (reverse increase in real income), but keep prices constant at new level.

15 d Substitution effect always discourages leisure. But rise in wages leads to rise in income and an increase in leisure (since leisure is a normal good).

SHORT ANSWER

1 An indifference curve tells us how much the consumption of one good must change as the consumption of another good decreases in order to leave the consumer indifferent (no better or worse off). It is negatively sloped because the goods we measure on the axes are both desirable. This means that as we *decrease* the consumption of one good, in order not to be made worse off, consumption of the other good must *increase*. This implies a negative slope.

2 As we move down an indifference curve we change the combination of goods consumed by increasing the quantity of one good consumed and decreasing the quantity of the other good consumed. As consumption of a good increases its marginal utility falls because of the principle of diminishing marginal utility. Thus the value of the numerator on the right-hand side of the following equation decreases:

$$\text{Marginal rate of substitution} = \frac{\text{Marginal utility of } X}{\text{Marginal utility of } Y}$$

As consumption of Y decreases, each previous X consumed yields higher marginal utility. Thus, the value of the denominator on the right-hand side of the equation increases. The effect of both a decrease in the numerator and an increase in the denominator is that the ratio MU_X/MU_Y falls as we move down an indifference curve, corresponding to a diminishing marginal rate of substitution on the left-hand side of the equation.

3 A decrease in the price of a good will have two effects on the consumption of the good. First, if all other prices remain constant, when the price of one good falls, real income increases. The substitution effect is the increase in consumption of the good resulting from the fall in its relative price accompanied by a hypothetical reduction in real income which leaves the consumer indifferent between the new and initial situations. The income effect for a normal good is the further increase in consumption of the good when we hypothetically restore the consumer's real income but leave relative prices unchanged at the new level.

PROBLEMS

1 a Initially, Jan and Dan are at point c on the budget line labelled AB in Fig. 8.3. Jan's indifference curve is illustrated by I_J. Note that her indifference curve is close to a straight line reflecting the fact that bread and peanut butter are close substitutes. On the other hand, since Dan considers bread and peanut butter to be complementary, his indifference curve, I_D, is more tightly curved.

b If the price of bread declines, the budget line will become flatter, such as the line labelled AD in Fig. 8.3. In order to measure the substitution effect we find the point on the original indifference curve that has the same slope as the new budget line. Since Dan's indifference curve is more sharply curved, it becomes flatter quite rapidly as we move away from point c. Thus the substitution effect is quite small: from c to point e. Since Jan's indifference curve is almost a straight line, the substitution effect must be much larger: from c to point f.

2 a The relative price of coffee is the price of coffee divided by the price of whisky:

$$\frac{£1}{£1.50} = \frac{2}{3}$$

Figure 8.3

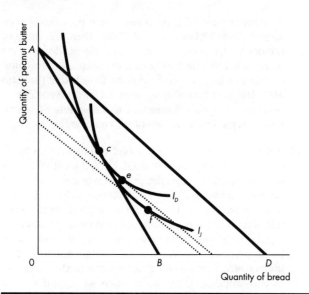

Figure 8.4

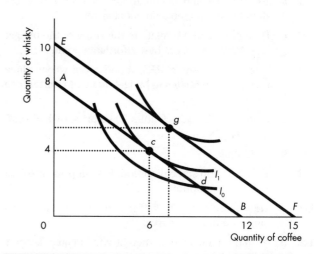

b Let P_c be the price of coffee, P_w be the price of whisky, Q_c the quantity of coffee, Q_w the quantity of whisky, and y be income. The budget equation, in general form, is:

$$Q_w = \frac{y}{P_w} = \frac{P_c}{P_w}Q_c$$

Since $P_c = £1$, $P_w = £1.50$, and $y = £12$, Kurt's budget equation is specifically given by:

$$Q_w = 8 - \tfrac{2}{3}Q_c$$

The graph of this budget equation, the budget line, is given by the line labelled AB in Fig. 8.4.

c If the best affordable point corresponds to 6 units of coffee and 4 units of whisky, then the relevant indifference curve must be tangent to (just touch) the budget line AB at c which is indifference curve I_1.

d The marginal rate of substitution is given by the magnitude of the slope of the indifference curve at point c. We do not know the slope of the indifference curve directly but we can easily compute the slope of the budget line. Since, at point c, the indifference curve and the budget line have the same slope, we can obtain the marginal rate of substitution of coffee for whisky. Since the slope of the budget line is $-2/3$, the marginal rate of substitution is $2/3$. For example, Kurt is willing to give up 2 units of whisky in order to receive 3 additional units of coffee and still remain indifferent.

e Since indifference curves cannot intersect each other and since indifference curve I_1 lies everywhere above

the budget line (except at point c), we know that every other point on the budget line is on a lower indifference curve. For example, point d lies on indifference curve I_0. Thus every other point on the budget line is inferior to point c.

3 a An increase in income will cause a parallel outward shift of the budget line, for example, to EF in Fig. 8.4. If both coffee and whisky are normal goods, Kurt will move to a point like g at which the consumption of both goods has increased.

b If whisky is an inferior good, then its consumption will fall as income rises. This is illustrated in Fig. 8.5. Once again the budget line shifts from AB to EF, but Kurt's preferences are such that his new consumption point is given by a point like g' where the consumption of whisky has actually declined.

4 a Kurt's initial budget line is given by AB and the initial best affordable point by r in Fig. 8.6. The new budget line following an increase in the price of coffee to £2 (income remains at £12) is represented by AH.

b After the price increase, point r is no longer the best affordable point since it is no longer even affordable.

c The new best affordable point (labelled t in Fig. 8.6) indicates a decrease in the consumption of coffee.

d The substitution effect of the increase in the price of coffee is indicated by the movement from r to s in Fig. 8.6. This gives the effect of the change in relative prices while keeping Kurt on the same indifference curve. The income effect is indicated by movement from s to t.

Figure 8.5

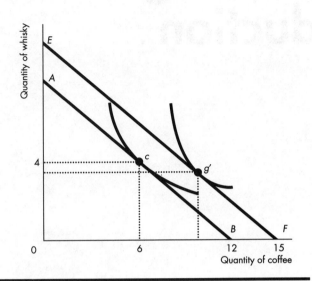

Figure 8.6

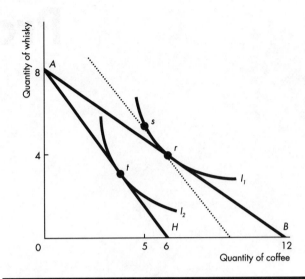

DATA QUESTION

1 a Elderly people's original budget line is *AB* in Fig. 8.7, and they will maximize satisfaction at point *x* on indifference curve I_1. A subsidy for bus travel will shift the budget line to *CB* and satisfaction will be maximized at point *y* on I_2. They will consume considerably more bus travel and a little more of other goods.

b An increase in income will shift the entire budget line from *AB* to *CD* as shown in Fig. 8.8. However, since bus travel is an inferior good, they will move along budget line *CD* to position *y* on indifference curve I_2. The result will be a fall in the consumption of bus travel and an increase in the consumption of other goods such as taxis and private motoring.

Figure 8.7

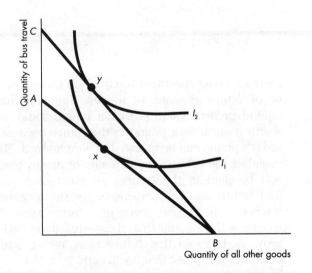

Figure 8.8

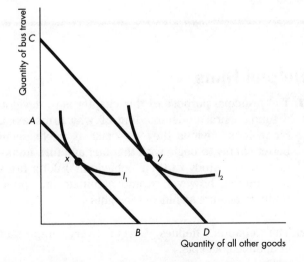

Chapter 9

Organizing Production

<hr>

Chapter in Perspective, Text Pages 218–239

This chapter begins the analysis of firm choice and the principles underlying supply. The analysis here focuses on key differences that exist in how firms organize production.

The first difference relates to types of firms. While there are common characteristics shared by all firms, there are different forms of business organization, each with pros and cons. The second difference relates to types of business finance. Concepts you read about every day in the business press – bonds, shares, present value, price–earnings ratios – are examined, as well as a difference between the accountant's and the economist's concepts of cost that depend crucially on opportunity cost. The third difference relates to the concepts of technological versus economic efficiency and the concepts of firm versus market coordination. The efficiency of firms (as institutions) make them a primary coordinating mechanism through which market economies tackle the problem of scarcity.

<hr>

Helpful Hints

1 The principal purpose of this chapter is to develop a fundamental understanding of why firms exist. Since it is obvious they do exist, it might seem better simply to begin with that fact and turn immediately to a study of their behaviour. Taking firms for granted, however, would eliminate an opportunity to acquire significant insights.

2 The chapter defines several very important economic concepts.

   a The concept of present value is fundamental in

thinking about the value today of an investment or of future amounts of money. The intuition behind present value is that a pound today is worth more than a pound in the future because today's pound can be invested to earn interest. To calculate the value *today* of a sum of money that will be paid in the future, we must discount that future sum to compensate for the forgone interest. The *present value* of a future sum of money is the amount that, if invested today, will grow as large as that future sum, taking into account the interest that it will earn.

   b In this chapter, we again meet our old friend

opportunity cost. Here we look at the costs firms face with a special emphasis on the differences between historical cost measures used by accountants and opportunity cost measures used by economists. Historical cost includes only explicit, out-of-pocket costs. Opportunity cost, which is the concept of cost relevant for economic decisions, includes *explicit costs and imputed costs*. Important examples of imputed costs include the owner's/investor's forgone interest, forgone rent and forgone income. These differences in cost measures between accountants and economists lead to differences in profit measures as well, as outlined here.

Accountants
Historical costs = Explicit costs
Accounting profits = Revenues − Explicit costs

Economists
Opportunity costs = Explicit costs +
                         Imputed costs

Economic profits = Revenues − (Explicit costs +
                              Imputed costs)

Imputed costs, which economists include but accountants exclude, are the key difference between accountants' and economists' measures of cost and profit.

c It is important to distinguish between technological efficiency and economic efficiency. The difference is critical since economic decisions will be made only on the basis of economic efficiency. Technological efficiency is an engineering concept and occurs when it is not possible to increase output without increasing inputs. There is no consideration of input costs. Economic efficiency occurs when the *cost* of producing a given output is at a minimum. All technologically efficient production methods are not economically efficient. But all economically efficient methods are also technologically efficient.

Key Tables

Table 9.1 The Pros and Cons of Different Types of Firms, text page 224
There are three main types of business organization: sole proprietorship, partnership and company. This table presents some of the characteristics of these types of firms in the form of lists of advantages and disadvantages of each.

Table 9.2 Dawson's Mountain Bikes' Revenue, Cost and Profit Statement, text page 229
Accounting costs and opportunity costs are usually *not* equal. As a result, accounting profit and economic profit will not be equal. This table illustrates the differences using the example of Dawson's Mountain Bikes.

Table 9.4 Costs of Four Ways of Making 10 TV Sets per Day, text page 231
There are generally many technological methods available to produce a given quantity of a particular good, each of them using a different combination of inputs. The firm must choose which of these input combinations it will use. For a given set of input prices, a profit-maximizing firm will choose the method (input combination) that has least cost. It will choose the economically efficient method. This table gives the costs associated with four different methods of producing 10 TV sets a day. Remember that the economically efficient method depends critically on input prices. Note that when input prices change, the economically efficient method can change.

SELF-TEST

CONCEPT REVIEW

1 An institution that organizes resources it has purchased or hired to produce and sell goods and services is called a(n) _____ .

2 There are three main forms of business organization. The two simpler forms are a(n) _____ (which has a single owner) and a(n) _____ . In these two forms owners face _____ liability. The third more

complicated form is a(n) _____ in which owners face _____ liability.

3 Firms can raise money by selling _____ which are legal obligations to pay specified amounts at specified future dates. Companies can also raise money by issuing _____ .

4 An agent is a person or firm hired by a _____ to do a specified job.

5 In assessing costs, accountants measure _____ cost, which values resources at the prices originally paid for them. Economists measure _____ cost.

6 The change in the market price of a durable input over a given period is called economic _____ .

7 _____ efficiency is achieved when the cost of producing a given output is as low as possible. _____ efficiency is achieved when no more output can be produced without increasing inputs.

8 Firms coordinate economic activity when they can do so more efficiently than _____ .

9 The costs associated with finding a buyer, reaching agreement about exchange, and ensuring the fulfilment of the agreement are _____ costs.

10 _____ of _____ exist when the cost of producing a unit of output falls as we produce more.

TRUE OR FALSE

___ **1** A firm purchases or hires factors of production and organizes production of goods and services.

___ **2** A partnership has joint unlimited liability.

___ **3** The residual claimants of a company are its bondholders.

___ **4** The perpetual 'life' of a company is an advantage over other forms of business organization when it comes to raising large sums of money.

___ **5** A cooperative is a firm that has equal total costs and total revenue.

___ **6** Historical cost is more likely to be the same as opportunity cost when firms use their own funds rather than borrowing.

___ **7** In general, opportunity cost will be greater than historical cost.

___ **8** When a firm produces using a machine it owns, its opportunity cost is lower than if it had rented the machine.

___ **9** The opportunity cost of using inventories is the current replacement cost.

___ **10** A production process that is economically efficient may become economically inefficient if the relative prices of inputs change.

___ **11** Firms will coordinate economic activity in situations where there are economies of team production.

___ **12** Markets will coordinate economic activity in situations where there are economies of scale.

MULTIPLE-CHOICE

1 Which of the following statements is *not* true of firms?
   a Firms are like markets in that they are institutions for coordinating economic activity.
   b Firms organize factors of production in order to produce goods and services.
   c Firms sell goods and services.
   d Technologically efficient firms can eliminate scarcity.
   e Firms include Crown corporations.

2 What is a firm called that has two or more owners with joint unlimited liability?
   a a proprietorship
   b a partnership
   c a conglomerate
   d a company
   e none of the above

3 What is a *disadvantage of a company* relative to a proprietorship or partnership?
   a Owners have unlimited liability.
   b Profits are taxed as corporate profits and as dividend income to shareholders.

c There is difficulty in raising money.
d Perpetual life.
e None of the above.

4 The owner's stake in a business is called
a present value.
b redemption value.
c historical cost.
d equity capital.
e preferred stock.

5 Historical cost calculates the value of resources at the
a original purchase price.
b original purchase price minus depreciation.
c original purchase price minus economic depreciation.
d current market price.
e value of the best forgone alternative.

6 The construction cost of a building is £100,000. The conventional depreciation allowance is 5 per cent per year. At the end of the first year the market value of the building is £80,000. For the first year, the depreciation cost is
a £20,000 to an accountant or an economist.
b £5,000 to an accountant or an economist.
c £5,000 to an accountant but £20,000 to an economist.
d £20,000 to an accountant but £5,000 to an economist.
e none of the above.

7 John operates his own business and pays himself a salary of £20,000 per year. He was offered a job that pays £30,000 per year. What is the opportunity cost of John's time in the business?
a £10,000
b £20,000
c £30,000
d £50,000
e zero

8 The rate of interest is 10 per cent per year. If you invest £50,000 of your own money in a business and earn *accounting* profits of £20,000 after one year, what are your *economic* profits?
a £20,000
b £15,000
c £5,000
d £2,000
e –£15,000

9 Which of the following statements is *true*?

a All technologically efficient methods are also economically efficient.
b All economically efficient methods are also technologically efficient.
c Technological efficiency changes with changes in relative input prices.
d Technologically efficient firms will be more likely to survive than economically efficient firms.
e None of the above statements is true.

10 Firms will be more efficient than the market as a coordinator of economic activity when firms have
a lower transactions costs.
b lower monitoring costs.
c economies of scale.
d economies of team production.
e all of the above.

11 Economies of scale exist when
a transactions costs are high.
b transactions costs are low.
c hiring additional inputs does not increase the price of inputs.
d the cost of producing a unit of output falls as the output rate increases.
e the firm is too large and too diversified.

SHORT ANSWER

1 Compare the historical cost and opportunity cost approaches in each of the following cases:
a depreciation cost
b the firm borrows money to finance its operation
c the firm uses its own funds rather than borrowing

2 Distinguish between technological efficiency and economic efficiency.

3 Markets and firms are alternative ways of co-ordinating economic activity that arises because of scarcity. Why is it that both firms and markets exist?

PROBLEMS

1 Your roommate has said that it is always more economically efficient to produce wheat using some machinery than using only labour. Suppose that there are two technologically efficient methods of producing a tonne of wheat.

Method 1 requires 20 machine hours plus 20 human hours.

Method 2 requires 100 human hours.

Country *A* has a highly developed industrial economy, while country *B* is less developed. In country *A* the price of an hour of human labour (the wage rate) is £8, while the wage rate in country *B* is £4. The price of a machine hour is £20 in both countries. Which method is economically efficient in country *A*? in country *B*? Explain.

2 Consider countries *A* and *B* described in Problem 1.
   a What wage rate in country *B* would make the two methods equally efficient in country *B*?
   b What price of a machine hour would make the two methods be equally efficient in country *A*?

DATA QUESTIONS

Firms and markets
No one knows who invented firms – or even markets –

but both play crucial roles in the modern economy. In addition to conventional privately owned 'firms', there are many kinds of formal organizations which play a part in the economic life of the country, for example, charities such as War on Want, educational institutions such as schools and other bodies such as athletics clubs. All have economic influences. Nevertheless, it is true that firms have a profound effect on the economy. Many of these are small – in 1990 in the United Kingdom there were 143,000 businesses and of these 129,000 employed fewer than 100 people. At the other extreme, 135 huge businesses employed more than 50,000 people.

In some circumstances, firms will be used to allocate resources. That will occur when they represent a more efficient method of organizing production. In other circumstances, markets will be used to allocate resources.

1 List some economic agents that are not firms.

2 Comment on the variation in the sizes of firms given in the text.

3 When will firms 'represent a more efficient method of organizing production'?

4 When will markets be used to allocate resources?

ANSWERS

CONCEPT REVIEW

1 firm

2 proprietorship; partnership; unlimited; company; limited

3 bonds; shares

4 principal

5 historical; opportunity

6 depreciation

7 Economic; Technological

8 markets

9 transactions

10 Economies; scale

TRUE OR FALSE

1 T Definition
2 T This is the legal status
3 F Bondholders have priority status.
4 T The legal status gives confidence to lenders.
5 F A cooperative is a form of organization where owners have equal shares.
6 F More likely to be different.
7 T Usually true, but it depends on the existence of imputed costs.

8 F Opportunity cost is equal whether or not the machine is owned or rented.

9 T Definition of opportunity cost

10 T Economic efficiency depends on prices; if these change so does the efficiency of the process.

11 T Because this will reduce costs.

12 F Firms are more efficient where there are economies of scale.

MULTIPLE-CHOICE

1 d Scarcity can never be eliminated.

2 b Definition.

3 b **d** is an advantage; **a**, **c** are disadvantages of proprietorship and partnership.

4 d Definition.

5 a Definition.

6 c Accountant's depreciation = (5 per cent) × £100,000. Economist's depreciation = change in market value.

7 c Forgone income.

8 b Economic profits = accounting profits – imputed costs = £20,000 – (0.10 × £50,000).

9 b **c** is true for economic efficiency; the reverse of **d** is true.

10 e Definition.

11 d Definition.

SHORT ANSWER

1 a From the historical cost approach, depreciation cost is computed as a prespecified percentage of the original purchase price of the capital good, with no reference to current market value. The opportunity cost approach measures economic depreciation cost as the change in the market value of the capital good over the period in question.

b If a firm borrows money, the historical and opportunity cost approaches will be the same; both will include the explicit interest payments.

c If a firm uses its own funds rather than borrowing, the historical and opportunity cost approaches will again differ. The historical cost will be zero since there are no explicit interest payments. The opportunity cost approach recognizes that those funds could have been loaned out and thus the (imputed) interest income forgone is the opportunity cost.

2 A method is technologically efficient if it is not possible to increase output without increasing inputs. A method

is economically efficient if the cost of producing a given level of output is as low as possible. Technological efficiency is independent of prices while economic efficiency depends on the prices of inputs. An economically efficient method of production is always technologically efficient, but a technologically efficient method is not necessarily economically efficient.

3 As we saw in the text example on page 233, car repair can be coordinated by the market or by a firm. The institution (market or firm) which actually coordinates in any given case will be the one which is more efficient. In cases where there are significant transaction costs, economies of scale, or economies of team production, firms are likely to be more efficient, and we will see firms dominate the coordination of economic activity. But the efficiency of firms is limited and there are many circumstances in which we observe market coordination of economic activity because it is more efficient.

PROBLEMS

1 Both production methods are technologically efficient. To find the economically efficient production method we want to know which of the methods has the lower cost of producing a tonne of wheat. In country A, the price of an hour of labour is £8 and the price of a machine hour is £20. Thus, the cost of producing a tonne of wheat is £560 using method 1 and £800 using method 2. Therefore method 1 is economically efficient for country A.

The price of an hour of labour is £4 in country B and thus it will face different costs of producing a tonne of wheat. Under method 1, the cost will be £480 but under method 2 which uses only labour, the cost will be £400. So method 2 is economically efficient for country B.

The reason for this difference is that economic efficiency means producing at lowest cost. If the relative prices of inputs are different in two countries, there will be differences in the relative costs of production using alternative methods. Therefore, your roommate is wrong.

2 a If the wage rate in country B were to increase to £5 an hour, then production of a tonne of wheat would be £500 under either method. How did we obtain this answer? Express the cost under method 1 (C_1) and the cost under method 2 (C_2) as follows:

$$C_1 = 20\,P_m + 20\,P_h$$
$$C_2 = 100\,P_h$$

where P_m is the price of a machine hour and P_h is the price of a human hour (the wage rate). We are given that $P_m = £20$ and asked to find the value of P_h that makes the two methods equally efficient; the value of P_h that makes $C_1 = C_2$. Thus, we solve the following equation for P_h:

$$20P_m + 20P_h = 100P_h$$
$$20(£20) + 20P_h = 100P_h$$
$$£400 = 80P_h$$
$$£5 = P_h$$

b If the price of a machine hour is £32, production of a tonne of wheat would be £800 under either method in country A. This question asks: given the wage rate of £8 (P_h) in country A, what value of P_m makes $C_1 = C_2$? Thus we solve the following equation for P_m:

$$20P_m + 20P_h = 100P_h$$
$$20P_m + 20(£8) = 100(£8)$$
$$20P_m = £640$$
$$P_m = £32$$

DATA QUESTIONS

1 Other economic agents include cooperatives, nationalized industries and government departments.

2 In some industries there are economies of scale. These exist when the cost of producing a unit of output falls as the quantity produced increases. Hence in industries such as car production firms tend to be large. When the product does not permit economies of scale – for example in hairdressing or plumbing – the enterprise remains small.

3 Firms achieve lower transaction costs, economies of scale and economies of team production.

4 Markets are used to allocate resources when firms do not provide an optimal solution.

Chapter 10 **Output and Costs**

Chapter In Perspective, Text Pages 240–267

In a modern market economy, goods and services are produced primarily by firms. In Chapter 9 we saw that firms exist because they provide economically efficient ways of organizing factors of production for producing and selling goods and services. In this chapter we begin to analyse the production and cost constraints that firms face, and thus how efficiency is pursued.

What kinds of costs do firms face? How do these costs change as a firm's planning horizon changes? How will a firm, motivated by the desire to maximize profit, decide how much output to produce? When will a firm hire more labour? When will it increase its plant size? This chapter begins to answer these questions.

Helpful Hints

1 There is a simple and fundamental relationship between production functions and cost functions.

The chapter begins with the short-run production function and the concepts of total product, marginal product and average product. This is followed by the short-run cost function and the concepts of total cost, marginal cost, average variable cost and average total cost.

All of these seemingly disparate concepts are related to the law of diminishing returns. The law states that as a firm uses additional units of a variable input, while holding constant the quantity of fixed inputs, the marginal product of the variable input will eventually diminish. This law explains why the marginal product and average product curves eventually fall, and why the total product curve becomes flatter. When productivity falls,

costs increase, and the law explains the eventual upward slope of the marginal cost curve. The marginal cost curve, in turn, explains the U-shape of the average variable cost and average total cost curves. When the marginal cost curve is below the average variable (or total) cost curve, the average variable (or total) cost curve is falling. When marginal cost is above the average variable (or total) cost curve, the average variable (or total) cost curve is rising. The marginal cost curve intersects the average variable (or total) cost curve at the minimum point on the average variable (or total) cost curve.

Use the law of diminishing returns as the key to understanding the relationships between the many short-run concepts and graphs in the chapter. Pay most attention to the unit cost concepts and graphs – especially marginal cost, average variable cost and average total cost – because these will be used the most in later chapters to analyse the behaviour of firms. Be sure to thoroughly understand text Fig. 10.4(b) on page 251. It is the most important figure in the entire chapter.

2 You will probably draw the unit cost graph with the marginal cost, average variable cost and average total cost curves many times in this course. Here are some hints on drawing the graph quickly and easily.

a Be sure to label the axes; quantity of output *(Q)* on the horizontal axis and average cost on the vertical axis.

b Draw a shallow U-shaped curve (see Fig. 10.1) and mark its minimum point. Then pick a second point above and to the right of that first minimum point. Draw another shallow U-shaped curve whose minimum point passes through your second point. Draw an upward-sloping marginal cost curve which passes through the two minimum points. The marginal cost curve can have a small downward-sloping section at first, but this is not important for subsequent analysis. Finally, label the curves.

c Any time a test question asks about these curves, *draw a graph* before you answer.

Figure 10.1

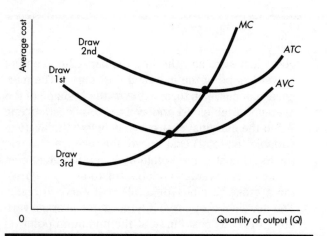

3 Be sure to understand how economists use the terms *short run* and *long run*. These terms do not refer to any notion of calendar time. They are better thought of as planning horizons. The short run is a planning horizon short enough that while some inputs are variable, at least one input cannot be varied but is fixed. The long run refers to a planning

horizon that is long enough that all inputs can be varied.

4 The later sections of the chapter explain the long-run production function and cost function when plant size is variable. While diminishing returns are the key for understanding short-run costs, the concept of returns to scale is the key for understanding long-run costs. Returns to scale are the increase in output relative to the increase in inputs when *all inputs* are increased by the same percentage. Returns to scale can be increasing, constant, or decreasing, and correspond to the downward-sloping, horizontal and upward-sloping sections of the long-run average cost curve.

Key Figures and Tables

Figure 10.2 Total Product and Marginal Product, text page 245

This illustrates how to calculate marginal product from total product. Marginal product of labour is the increase in total product resulting from the use of an additional unit of labour. Part (a) illustrates the total product curve and indicates the addition to total product associated with each additional unit of labour. Notice that the slope of the total product curve, *TP/L*, is equal to marginal product. Thus, if you know the total product curve, you can always derive the marginal product curve.

When graphing the marginal product curve, as in part (b), notice that marginal product is plotted midway between the corresponding units of labour, emphasizing that marginal product is the result of *changing* inputs. For example, the marginal product of changing from 0 to 1 worker is 4 sweaters, and the value 4 is plotted midway between 0 and 1 workers.

Figure 10.3 Total Product, Marginal Product and Average Product, text page 246

This uses the same data as Fig. 10.2, and simply adds the calculation of average product. Average product is defined as *TP/L*, and is computed in the table. As the quantity of labour increases, notice that the slope of the line from the origin to the corresponding point on the total product curve first increases, reaches a maximum and then decreases.

Part (b) simply represents the average product graphically. Notice the relationship between the average product and marginal product curves. The marginal product curve is above the average product curve when average product is increasing and below the average product curve when average product is decreasing. The marginal product curve intersects the average product curve when average product is at a maximum.

Figure 10.4 Short-run Costs, text page 251

In the short run, total cost *(TC)* is divided into total fixed cost *(TFC)* and total variable cost *(TVC)*. The left half of the table lists these costs for Knitters. Part (a) illustrates graphically the corresponding total cost, total fixed cost and total variable cost curves. Since *TC = TFC + TVC*, the vertical distance between the *TC* and *TVC* curves is equal to *TFC*, which by definition is constant (fixed).

The graph in part (b) is one of the most important graphs in all of microeconomics, and you must understand it thoroughly. The curves for average total cost *(ATC)*, average fixed cost *(AFC)* and average variable cost *(AVC)* are derived by taking the values for *TC*, *TFC* and *TVC* and dividing by quantity of output. Since these are average values for a fixed quantity of output, they are plotted directly above the corresponding units of output. On the other hand, marginal cost *(MC)* is the *change* in total cost (or equivalently, in total variable cost) resulting from a one-unit increase in output. It is plotted in the graph in part (b) midway between the corresponding units of output. The *ATC*, *AVC* and *MC* curves are crucially important. The *ATC* and *AVC* curves are both U-shaped. The *MC* curve is also U-shaped and intersects the *ATC* and *AVC* curves at their minimum points. The *MC* curve is below the *ATC* and *AVC* curves when *ATC* and *AVC* are falling, and above the *ATC* and *AVC* curves when they are rising. The less important *AFC* curve falls continuously as output increases. See Helpful Hint 2 for tips on how to draw the crucially important curves.

Figure 10.6 Short-run and Long-run Costs, text page 257

In the short run, capital inputs are fixed while in the long run all inputs are variable. This figure illustrates the relationship between short-run and long-run costs for Knitters. Four different plants are considered: one for each of the four units of capital (knitting machines). Given a choice of plant, Knitters is then in the short run. In the long run, Knitters will choose the plant which minimizes the *ATC* of producing the desired level of output. The construction of the long-run average cost *(LRAC)* curve is illustrated in Fig. 10.7. The *LRAC* traces the lowest *ATC* for each level of output.

Figure 10.8 Returns to Scale, text page 260

This figure uses the *LRAC* curve from Fig. 10.7 on text page 257 to illustrate the ranges over which the *LRAC* curve exhibits alternative returns to scale. When the *LRAC* curve is negatively sloped (for example, up to an output of 15 sweaters per day), there are increasing returns to scale or economies of scale. When the *LRAC* curve is positively sloped (for example, output levels above 15 sweaters per day), there are decreasing returns to scale or diseconomies of scale.

Table 10.2 A Compact Glossary on Product, text page 248

Numerous new total, average and marginal concepts of product are introduced in this chapter. This table brings them together in a convenient summary form, and is an excellent study tool.

Table 10.3 A Compact Glossary on Cost, text page 252

This handy table summarizes the relationships between various definitions of cost.

SELF-TEST

CONCEPT REVIEW

1 The profits of a firm are limited by two types of constraints: _____ constraints, which are conditions under which the firm can buy its inputs and sell its output, and _____ constraints, which limit the feasible ways in which inputs can be converted into output.

2 A production process that uses large amounts of capital relative to labour is called a(n) _____ - _____ technique while a(n) _____ - _____ technique uses a large amount of labour relative to capital.

3 The term economists use for a period of time in which the quantities of some inputs are fixed while others can be varied is the _____ _____ . The period of time in which all inputs are variable is the _____ _____ .

4 The total product curve is a graph of the maximum output attainable at each level of a _____ input, given the amount of fixed inputs. The change in total product resulting from a one-unit increase in labour input, holding the quantity of capital constant, is called the _____ . _____ of labour. The average product of labour is _____ _____ divided by the units of _____ .

5 If marginal product is greater than average product, then average product must be _____ . Marginal product _____ average product when average product reaches a maximum.

6 The shape of the marginal product curve can be described as follows: it first _____ , reaches a _____ and then _____ as labour inputs increase.

7 Increasing marginal returns occur when the marginal product of an additional worker is _____ than the marginal product of the previous workers. As more of a variable input is used, holding other inputs fixed, the marginal product of the variable input begins to decline. This is a statement of the law of _____ _____ .

8 $TC = FC +$ _____ .

9 Marginal cost is the increase in total cost resulting from a one-unit increase in _____ .

10 If the average variable cost curve is decreasing, then the marginal cost curve must be _____ the average variable cost.

11 If output increases by 20 per cent when all inputs are increased by 10 per cent, the production process is said to display _____ _____ to _____ .

12 If a firm is experiencing constant returns to scale, a 10 per cent increase in inputs will result in a ———————— per cent ———————— in

output. When the long-run average cost curve rises, there are _____ returns to scale.

13 A technological advance will tend to _____ product curves and _____ cost curves.

TRUE OR FALSE

— **1** All economically efficient production methods are also technologically efficient.

— **2** The short run is a time period in which there is at least one fixed input and at least one variable input.

— **3** All inputs are fixed in the long run.

— **4** Marginal product is given by the slope of the total product curve.

— **5** Average product can be measured as the slope of a line drawn from the origin to a point on the total product curve.

— **6** The average product curve cuts the marginal product curve from above at the maximum point on the marginal product curve.

— **7** Average total cost, average variable cost and average fixed cost are all U-shaped.

— **8** Average variable cost reaches its minimum at the same level of output at which average product is a maximum.

— **9** In the real world, marginal cost curves are rarely upward sloping.

— **10** A firm producing on the downward-sloping part of its average total cost curve is said to have excess capacity.

— **11** By capacity, economists mean the physical limits of production.

— **12** If average total cost is greater than marginal cost, then average total cost must be increasing.

— **13** Increasing returns to scale means that the long-run average cost curve is negatively sloped.

— **14** In the long run, the total cost and total variable cost curves are the same.

___ **15** If the price of inputs falls, the average variable cost and average total cost curves will shift up.

___ **16** A firm facing highly variable demand for its output would want to increase plant size only if it were persistently operating on the upward-sloping part of its short-run average total cost curve.

MULTIPLE-CHOICE

1 In economics, the short run is a time period
  a of one year or less.
  b in which all inputs are variable.
  c in which all inputs are fixed.
  d in which there is at least one fixed input and at least one variable input.
  e in which all inputs are variable but the technology is fixed.

2 The average product of labour can be measured as the
  a slope of a straight line from the origin to a point on the total product curve.
  b slope of the total product curve.
  c slope of a straight line from the origin to a point on the marginal product curve.
  d slope of the marginal product curve.
  e change in output divided by the change in labour input.

3 A field of ripe corn is waiting to be harvested. Labour is the only variable input, and the total product (in bushels) of various numbers of labourers is given in Table 10.1.

Table 10.1

Number of labourers	Total product
0	0
1	3
2	7
3	10
4	12

Diminishing returns *begin* when you add which labourer?
  a 1st labourer
  b 2nd labourer
  c 3rd labourer
  d 4th labourer
  e there are no diminishing returns since total product always rises

4 When the marginal product of labour is less than the average product of labour
  a the average product of labour is increasing.
  b the marginal product of labour is increasing.
  c the total product curve is negatively sloped.
  d the firm is experiencing diminishing returns.
  e none of the above is true.

5 The vertical distance between the TC and TVC curves is
  a decreasing as output increases.
  b increasing as output increases.
  c equal to AFC.
  d equal to TFC.
  e equal to MC.

6 The marginal cost (MC) curve intersects the
  a ATC, AVC and AFC curves at their minimum points.
  b ATC and AFC curves at their minimum points.
  c AVC and AFC curves at their minimum points.
  d ATC and AVC curves at their minimum points.
  e TC and TVC curves at their minimum points.

7 Marginal cost is the amount that
  a total cost increases when one more labourer is hired.
  b fixed cost increases when one more labourer is hired.
  c variable cost increases when one more labourer is hired.
  d total cost increases when one more unit of output is produced.
  e fixed cost increases when one more unit of output is produced.

8 A firm's fixed costs are £100. If total costs are £200 for one unit of output and £310 for two units, what is the marginal cost of the second unit?
  a £100
  b £110
  c £200
  d £210
  e £310

9 If ATC is falling then MC must be
  a rising.
  b falling.

    c equal to *ATC*.
    d above *ATC*.
    e below *ATC*.

10 In the long run
    a only the scale of plant is fixed.
    b all inputs are variable.
    c all inputs are fixed.
    d a firm must experience decreasing returns to scale.
    e none of the above is true.

11 The marginal cost curve slopes upward because of
    a diminishing marginal utility.
    b diminishing returns.
    c technological inefficiency.
    d economic inefficiency.
    e none of the above statements.

12 Constant returns to scale means that as all inputs are increased
    a total output remains constant.
    b average total cost remains constant.
    c average total cost increases at the same rate as inputs.
    d long-run average cost remains constant.
    e long-run average cost rises at the same rate as inputs.

13 The long-run average cost curve
    a shifts up when fixed costs increase.
    b shifts down when fixed costs increase.
    c is the short-run average total cost curve with the lowest cost.
    d traces the minimum points on all the short-run average total cost curves for each scale of plant.
    e traces the minimum short-run average total cost for each output.

14 A firm will want to increase its scale of plant if
    a it persistently produces on the upward-sloping part of its short-run average total cost curve.
    b it persistently produces on the downward-sloping part of its short-run average total cost curve.
    c it is producing below capacity.
    d marginal cost is below average total cost.
    e marginal cost is below average variable cost.

15 The average variable cost curve will shift up if
    a there is an increase in fixed costs.
    b there is a technological advance.

    c the price of variable inputs decreases.
    d the price of output increases.
    e none of the above occurs.

SHORT ANSWER

1 What market constraints does a firm face on its ability to make profits?

2 Why does a steeper slope of the total product curve imply a higher level of the marginal product curve?

3 Why is it the case that the marginal product curve must intersect the average product curve at its maximum point?

4 What is the difference, if any, between diminishing returns and decreasing returns to scale?

PROBLEMS

1 For a given scale of plant, Table 10.2 gives the total monthly output of golf carts attainable using varying quantities of labour.

Table 10.2   Monthly Golf Cart Production

Labourers (per month)	Output (units per month)	Marginal product	Average product
0	0		
1	1		
2	3		
3	6		
4	12		
5	17		
6	20		
7	22		
8	23		

    a Complete the table for the marginal product and average product of labour. (Note that marginal product should be entered midway between rows to emphasize that it is the result of *changing* inputs – moving from one row to the next. Average product corresponds to a *fixed* quantity of labour and should be entered on the appropriate row.)
    b Label the axes and draw a graph of the total product curve *(TP)*.

c On a separate piece of paper, label the axes and draw a graph of both marginal product *(MP)* and average product *(AP)*. (Marginal product should be plotted midway between the corresponding units of labour, as in text Fig. 10.2 on page 245, while average product should be plotted directly above the corresponding units of labour, as in text Fig. 10.3(b) on page 246.)

2 Now let's examine the short-run costs of golf cart production. The first two columns of Table 10.2 are reproduced in the first two columns of Table 10.3. The cost of 1 labourer (the only variable input) is £2,000 per month. Total fixed cost is £2,000 per month.

Table 10.3 Short-run Costs

Labourers (per month)	Output (units per month)	TFC (£)	TVC (£)	TC (£)	MC (£)	AFC (£)	AVC (£)	ATC (£)
0	0	2,000						
1	1							
2	3							
3	6							
4	12							
5	17							
6	20							
7	22							
8	23							

a Given this information, complete Table 10.3 by computing total fixed cost *(TFC)*, total variable cost *(TVC)*, total cost *(TC)*, marginal cost *(MC)*, average fixed cost *(AFC)*, average variable cost *(AVC)* and average total cost *(ATC)*. Your completed table should look like the table in text Fig. 10.4 on page 251, with marginal cost entered midway between the rows.

b Label the axes and draw the *TC*, *TVC* and *TFC* curves on a single graph.

c Label the axes and draw the *MC*, *ATC*, *AVC* and *AFC* curves on a single graph. Be sure to plot *MC* midway between the corresponding units of output.

d Now suppose that the price of a labourer increases to £2,500 per month. Construct a table for the new *MC* and *ATC* curves (output, *MC*, *ATC*). Label the axes and draw a graph of the new *MC* and *ATC* curves. What is the effect of the increase in the price of the variable input on these curves?

3 Figure 10.2 gives a sequence of short-run *ATC* curves numbered 1 to 7 corresponding to seven different factory sizes.

Figure 10.2

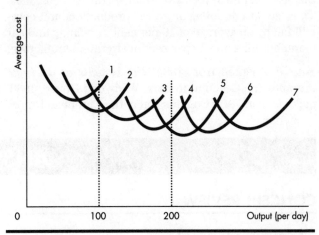

a Draw the long-run average cost curve on Fig. 10.2.

b If the desired level of output is 100 units per day, what is the best factory size? (Give the number of the associated short-run *ATC* curve.)

c If the desired level of output is 200 units per day, what is the best factory size?

DATA QUESTIONS

Economies of scale in the European Union
Increased trade and sharper competition triggered by market integration will enable firms to make savings linked to larger scale production. Empirical studies show that the bigger the market, the greater the move towards the size needed to achieve the necessary economies of scale to complete.

There are three complicating factors:
a Potential gains vary significantly by industry: the fall in costs resulting from economies of scale are of the order of 1 per cent for sectors like petroleum products, but reach 3–6 per cent for heavy electrical equipment and means of transport other than cars.

b In addition to economies in the production process, firms may realize economies in research, marketing and finance.

c These economies of scale take time to achieve.

Taking just manufacturing undustries, the total cost savings to be had from economies of scale for production would be about 60 billion ecus. In addition, there would be substantial economies in other sectors, particularly services. Moreover, learning 'on the job' means that as larger quantities are produced the unit cost falls. Thus, given a doubling of overall production, unit costs will fall by an average of 10 per cent in refining and car manufacturing and 20 per cent in aircraft manufacture.

Source: Adapted from 1992: *The benefits of a single market* (The Cecchini Report) Wildwood House, 1988, pages 77 and 78. © Commission of the European Union.

1 Explain what is meant by 'economies of scale'.

2 Why do you think some industries benefit more from economies of scale than others?

3 Draw points on average cost curves for (a) cars, and (b) aircraft manufacture.

4 If large firms benefit from substantial economies of scale, why are not all industries made up of enormous firms?

ANSWERS

CONCEPT REVIEW

1 market; technological

2 capital-intensive; labour-intensive

3 short run; long run

4 variable; marginal product; total product (output); labour

5 rising; equals

6 increases; maximum; decreases

7 greater; diminishing returns

8 VC

9 output

10 below

11 increasing returns; scale

12 10; increase; decreasing

13 raise; lower

TRUE OR FALSE

1 T Definition.

2 T Definition.

3 F All inputs are variable in the long run.

4 T Change in *TP*/Change in *L*.

5 T Geometrical relationship.

6 F This would be true if the terms 'average product' and 'marginal product' were switched.

7 F See cost curve diagrams.

8 T $AVC = TVC/Q = WL/Q = W/(Q/L) = W/AP$

9 F Marginal costs sometimes fall, sometimes rise.

10 T Could increase output up to capacity (quantity associated with minimum *ATC*).

11 F Capacity = capacity associated with minimum *ATC*.

12 F Draw curves to check.

13 T Definition.

14 T All costs are variable in the long run.

15 F The curves will shift down.

16 T If it were on the downward part of the short run average cost curve it could increase production and cut costs without any new plant.

MULTIPLE-CHOICE

1 d Definition.

2 a Equals *TP/L*.

3 c *MP* 1st = 3. *MP* 2nd = 4. *MP* 3rd = 3.

4 d When *MP* < *AP*, *MP* is falling (diminishing returns), *AP* is falling and *TP* is positively sloped.

5 d *TC* = *TFC* + *TVC*. Distance is constant.

6 d *AFC* always falls, *TC* and *TVC* always rise.

7 d Definition.

8 b Fixed costs are irrelevant. Change in *TC*/Change in quantity = (£310 – £200) / (2 – 1).

9 e *MC* could be rising or falling below *ATC* when *ATC* is falling.

10 b Definition. All returns to scale possible in long run.

11 b Diminishing returns will cause marginal costs to rise.

12 d *LRAC* is horizontal.

13 e Definition. **d** is Jacob Viner's mistake (see *Our Advancing Knowledge* text page 258). **a** and **b** apply to the short run since fixed costs.

14 a **b** and **c** plant too big. **d** and **e** relate to short run.

15 e **a** and **d** don't affect *AVC*. **b** and **c** shift *AVC* down.

SHORT ANSWER

1 Every firm is constrained by the supply of inputs it uses and by the demand for the output it produces. Because of the law of supply, firms, in general, can obtain more inputs only if they are willing to pay more for them. On the other hand, given the law of demand, firms, in general, sell more of their output only if they are willing to drop the price.

2 Marginal product is equal to the slope of the total product curve since it is defined as the change in total product resulting from an increase in the variable input. Since a steeper slope means a larger slope, it also means a higher marginal product.

3 Since the average product curve first rises and then falls, when average product is rising, marginal product must be greater than average product, and when average product is falling, marginal product must be lower than average product. If this is the case, then the marginal product curve intersects the average product curve at its maximum point. In order for average product to increase, it must have been *pulled up* by a larger increase in product from the last unit of input. Therefore, the marginal product is higher than average product. Similarly, when average product is falling, it must be that it has been *pulled down* by a lower marginal product. When average product is at its maximum, it is neither rising nor falling, so marginal product cannot be higher or lower than average product. Therefore, the marginal product must be equal to average product.

4 The law of diminishing returns states that as a firm uses additional units of a variable input, *while holding constant the quantity of fixed inputs*, the marginal product of the variable input will eventually diminish. Decreasing returns to scale occur when a firm increases *all of its inputs by an equal percentage*, and this results in a lower percentage increase in output. Diminishing (marginal) returns is a short-run concept since there must be a fixed input. Decreasing returns to scale is a long-run concept since all inputs must be variable.

PROBLEMS

1 a The completed table is shown as Table 10.4.

Table 10.4 Monthly Golf Cart Production

Labourers (per month)	Output (units per month)	Marginal product	Average product
0	0		0
		...1	
1	1		1.00
		...2	
2	3		1.50
		...3	
3	6		2.00
		...6	
4	12		3.00
		...5	
5	17		3.40
		...3	
6	20		3.33
		...2	
7	22		3.14
		...1	
8	23		2.88

b Figure 10.3 gives the graph of the total product curve.

c Figure 10.4 gives the graphs of marginal product and average product.

Figure 10.3

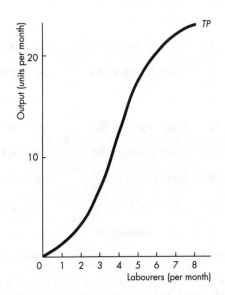

Figure 10.4

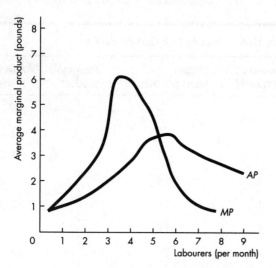

Figure 10.5

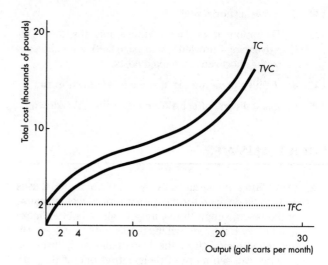

2 a The completed table is given as Table 10.5.

Table 10.5 Short-run Costs (Monthly)

Labourers (per month)	Output (units per month)	TFC (£)	TVC (£)	TC (£)	MC (£)	AFC (£)	AVC (£)	ATC (£)
0	0	2,000	0	2,000				
					2,000			
1	1	2,000	2,000	4,000		2,000	2,000	4,000
					1,000			
2	3	2,000	4,000	6,000		667	1,333	2,000
					667			
3	6	2,000	6,000	8,000		333	1,000	1,333
					333			
4	12	2,000	8,000	10,000		167	667	833
					400			
5	17	2,000	10,000	12,000		118	588	706
					667			
6	20	2,000	12,000	14,000		100	600	700
					1,000			
7	22	2,000	14,000	16,000		91	636	727
					2,000			
8	3	2,000	8,000	18,000		87	696	783

b The TC, TVC and TFC curves are graphed in Fig. 10.5.
c The MC, ATC, AVC and AFC curves are graphed in Fig. 10.6.

d The new MC and ATC curves (and the associated table) are given in Fig. 10.7. The original curves, MC_1 and ATC_1, are indicated for reference. The new curves are labelled MC_2 and ATC_2. Both curves have shifted up as a result of an increase in the price of labour.

Figure 10.6

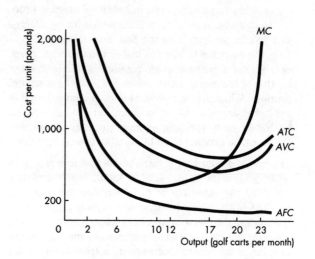

Figure 10.7

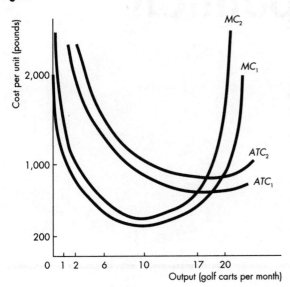

Figure 10.8

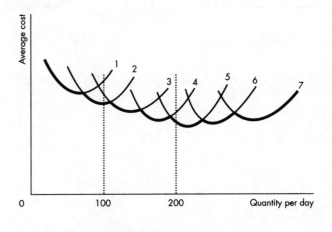

Output	MC (£)	ATC (£)
0	...2,500	0
1	...1,250	4,500
3	833	2,333
6	417	1,583
12	500	1,000
17	833	853
20	...1,250	850
22	...2,500	886
23		957

4 a The long-run average cost curve is indicated in Fig. 10.8 by the heavy line tracing out the lowest short-run average total cost of producing each level of output.

b If the desired level of output is 100 units, the best plant size is the one associated with short-run average total cost curve 2.

c If the desired level of output is 200 units, the best plant size is the one associated with short-run average total cost curve 5.

DATA QUESTIONS

1 Economies of scale exist when the cost of producing a unit of a good falls as the level of output increases.

2 Some industries (such as car manufacture) enjoy considerable economies of scale, but in other industries (such

Figure 10.9

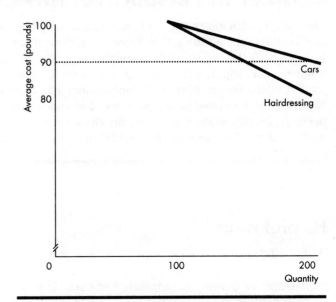

as hairdressing and other personal services) there are few economies of scale.

3 The cost curves are shown in Fig. 10.9.

4 There are two main reasons why the economy is not completely dominated by large firms. In the first place, there are often substantial diseconomies of scale so that growth may mean less efficiency. This is discussed in the text on page 255. Second, there is only a small market for some products so firms in these industries are inevitably small.

Chapter 11 **Competition**

Chapter In Perspective, Text Pages 279–310

This chapter combines the cost information of Chapters 9 and 10 with new revenue information in order to analyse the profit-maximization decisions of firms in a perfectly competitive market. The analysis includes derivations of both the individual firm supply curve and the industry supply curve. While we have previously simply assumed that supply curves are upward sloping, this chapter derives upward-sloping supply curves as a prediction of the theory of perfect competition. The theory also allows us to make precise predictions about the behaviour of firms and their responses to changes in market conditions. Although perfect competition does not occur frequently in the real world, the theory allows us to isolate the effects of competitive forces which are at work in *all* markets, even in those which do not match the assumptions of the theory of perfect competition.

Helpful Hints

1 Although perfectly competitive markets are quite rare in the real world, there are three important reasons to develop a thorough understanding of their behaviour.

First, many markets quite closely approximate perfectly competitive markets. Thus, the analysis developed in this chapter gives direct and useful insights into the behaviour of these markets.

Second, the theory of perfect competition allows us to isolate the effects of competitive forces which are at work in *all* markets, even in those which do not match the assumptions of perfect competition.

Third, the perfectly competitive model serves as a useful benchmark against which to evaluate relative allocative efficiency.

2 In the short run, a perfectly competitive firm cannot change the scale of its plant – it has fixed inputs. The firm also is a price taker; it always sells at the market price which it cannot influence. Thus, the only variable that the firm controls is its level of output. The short-run condition for profit maximization is to choose the level of output at which marginal revenue equals marginal cost. This is a general condition which, as we will see in subsequent chapters, applies to other market structures such as monopoly and monopolistic competition. Since for the perfectly competitive firm, marginal revenue is equal to price, this profit-maximizing condition takes a particular form; choose the level of output at which price is equal to marginal cost $(P = MC)$.

3 Many students have trouble understanding why a firm continues to operate at the break-even point, where economic profits are zero. The key to understanding lies in the definition of which costs are included in the average total cost curve. Recall from Chapter 9 that a firm's total costs are defined by the economist as *opportunity costs*, which include both explicit costs and *imputed costs*.

Imputed costs include the owners'/investors' forgone interest, forgone rent and forgone income. Therefore, at the break-even point where total revenue equals total cost (or, equivalently, average revenue equals average total cost), the owners/investors of the firm are earning a return on their investment which is equal to the best return that they could earn elsewhere. That is the definition of opportunity cost – the best alternative forgone. Economists sometimes refer to these imputed costs or best alternative return on investment as 'normal profits'. As the phrase implies, these are profits that could normally be earned in any other industry. At the break-even point, the firm is earning 'normal profits' even though its economic profits (sometimes called 'extra-normal profits') are zero. In earning 'normal profits,' the firm is earning just as much profit as it could anywhere else, and is therefore totally content to continue producing in this industry.

4 When the price of output falls below the break-even point, but is above the shutdown point, the firm will continue to produce even though it is making economic losses. In order to switch industries, the firm would have to shut down, which entails losing its total fixed costs.

As long as the price is above the shutdown point (minimum average variable cost), however, a firm will decide to produce since it will be covering total variable cost and part of total fixed cost. Thus its loss will be less if it continues to produce at the output where $P = MC$ than if it shuts down.

If the price falls below the shutdown point, a firm which produces output will lose not only its total fixed costs, but it will also lose additional money on every unit of output produced, since average revenue is less than average variable cost. Thus, when the price is less than average variable cost, the firm will choose to minimize its loss by shutting down.

5 In the long run, fixed costs disappear and the firm

can switch between industries and change scale of plant without cost. Economic profits serve as the signal for the movement or reallocation of firm resources until long-run equilibrium is achieved. Firms will move out of industries with negative economic profits and into industries with positive economic profits. Only when economic profits are zero will there be no tendency for firms to exit or enter industries.

The fact that there are no restrictions on entry into the industry is what assures that economic profits will be zero and that firms will be producing at the minimum of their long-run average cost curves in long-run equilibrium.

6 In long-run equilibrium, three conditions are satisfied for each firm in a competitive industry:
   a $MR = P = MC$. This implies that profits are maximized for each firm.
   b $P = ATC$. This implies that economic profits are zero and each firm is earning just 'normal profits'.
   c $P = $ minimum $LRAC$. This implies that production takes place at the point of minimum long-run average cost.

Key Figures

Figure 11.2 Total Revenue, Total Cost and Profit, text page 285

Profit is defined as total revenue minus total cost. In part (a) of this figure, the total revenue and total cost curves are both illustrated. Profit (or loss) is the vertical distance between them. In part (b), profit and loss are plotted against output as the profit curve in the graph. In the example, profit is a maximum when 9 metres are produced.

Figure 11.3 Marginal Revenue, Marginal Cost and Profit-maximizing Output, text page 286

This illustrates the alternative profit-maximizing condition: marginal revenue *(MR)* equals marginal cost *(MC)*. Producing and selling one more unit of a good (metres of linen in the example) add both to revenue and to cost. If the addition to revenue *(MR)* is greater than the addition to cost *(MC)*, then profit will increase and the additional unit should be produced.

If, on the other hand, marginal revenue is less than marginal cost, profit will decrease and the additional unit should not be produced. Therefore, a profit-maximizing firm should produce each unit up to the point at which marginal revenue equals marginal cost.

This is illustrated with a table and corresponding graph for the example of Linentex. Producing each of the first up to the ninth metre adds to profit (*MR > MC*) but the tenth sweater decreases profit (*MR < MC*). Nine sweaters is the profit-maximizing output at which the profit-maximizing condition, *MR = MC*, holds. Since, for a perfectly competitive firm, *MR = P*, the profit-maximizing condition can also be expressed as the output at which *P = MC*.

Figure 11.5 Linentex's Supply Curve, text page 290

Part (a) derives Linentex's supply curve by asking: how much will Linentex, a profit-maximizing firm, produce at given prices? This, of course, is exactly what a supply curve tells us.

Since the profit-maximizing condition is *P = MC*, Linentex's supply curve is the same as its marginal cost curve as long as the price is above minimum average variable cost.

The most important section of the supply curve is the upward-sloping section corresponding to the portion of the marginal cost curve above minimum average variable cost.

Figure 11.6 Firm and Industry Supply Curves, text page 292

The industry supply curve is obtained by summing horizontally the individual supply curves of all of the firms in the industry. For a given price, this means moving horizontally to each individual firm's supply curve, reading off the quantity supplied, and summing these quantities.

Figure 11.13 Long-run Price and Quantity Changes, text page 300

This illustrates three alternative relationships between price and quantity supplied in the long run. Starting in long-run equilibrium, suppose there is an increase in demand. In the long run, does the price of the good rise, fall, or remain the same? In industries where costs increase as output increases (external diseconomies), the long-run price will be higher. In industries where costs decrease as output increases (external economies), the long-run price will be lower. And in industries where costs remain unchanged as output increases (no external economies or diseconomies), the long-run price will remain unchanged.

Figure 11.15 Allocative Efficiency, text page 303

Allocative efficiency is achieved when marginal social benefit (*MSB*) equals marginal social cost (*MSC*). Additional output adds to both social benefit and social cost.

If the addition to social benefit (*MSB*) is greater than the addition to social cost (*MSC*), the additional unit should be produced.

If the marginal social benefit of an additional unit of output is less than the marginal social cost, it should not be produced. Allocative efficiency occurs at output *Q**, where *MSB = MSC*.

If there are no external costs or benefits, the perfectly competitive industry supply curve is the marginal social cost curve and the industry demand curve is the marginal social benefit curve. Thus the competitive market equilibrium will achieve allocative efficiency.

SELF-TEST

CONCEPT REVIEW

1 Perfect competition occurs in a market under the following conditions.
   a There are _____ firms, each selling a(n) _____ product.
   b There are _____ buyers.
   c There are no restrictions on _____ into the industry.

2 A firm in a perfectly competitive market is said to be a price _____ since it cannot influence the price of the good it produces. Such a firm faces a demand curve that is perfectly _____ .

3 We assume that the firm's single objective is to maximize its _____ .

4 Total revenue divided by the total quantity sold is called _____ _____ .

The change in revenue resulting from a one-unit increase in the quantity sold is called _____ _____ .

5 In the case of perfect competition, average revenue and marginal revenue are both equal to _____ .

6 An output at which total cost equals total revenue is called a _____ - _____ point. The point at which a firm's maximum profit (minimum loss) is the same regardless of whether the firm produces any output or not is called the _____ point.

7 Profit is maximized when marginal revenue equals _____ _____ .

8 Market price is determined by _____ demand and _____ supply.

9 In the range of prices greater than the minimum average variable cost, a perfectly competitive firm's supply curve is the same as its _____ _____ curve. At prices below minimum average variable cost, the firm will produce _____ and make a loss equal to its_____ _____ _____ .

10 New firms will enter a perfectly competitive industry if firms in the industry are making economic _____. As new firms enter the industry, the price will _____ . If economic_____ are being made, firms will tend to exit the industry.

11 Long-run equilibrium occurs in a perfectly competitive industry when economic profits are _____ . Each firm will also be producing at the _____ point of its long-run average cost curve.

12 Factors beyond the control of an individual firm that lower its cost as industry output increases are called _____ _____. Factors beyond the control of an individual firm that raise its costs as industry output increases are called _____ _____ .

13 _____ _____ occurs when no one can be made better off without making someone else worse off.

14 Costs that are not borne by the producer but are borne by other members of society are called _____ _____ . Benefits which accrue to people other than the buyer of a good are called _____ _____ .

TRUE OR FALSE

___ 1 In a perfectly competitive industry no single firm can exert a significant effect on the market price of a good.

___ 2 In a perfectly competitive industry there are no restrictions on entry into the industry.

___ 3 The industry demand curve in a perfectly competitive industry is horizontal.

___ 4 The objective of firms in a competitive industry is to maximize revenue.

___ 5 If marginal revenue is greater than marginal cost, a firm can increase profit by decreasing output.

___ 6 A firm is breaking even if its economic profit is zero.

___ 7 If the price is below the minimum average total cost, a firm will shut down.

___ 8 All firms in a competitive market will be maximizing profit in short-run equilibrium.

___ 9 The short-run industry supply curve is obtained as the horizontal sum of the supply curves of the individual firms.

___ 10 In long-run equilibrium, each firm in a perfectly competitive industry will be making zero economic profit.

___ 11 The entry of new firms into an industry will increase the price and increase the profit of each firm.

___ 12 In long-run equilibrium, each firm in a perfectly competitive industry will choose the scale of plant associated with the minimum long-run average cost.

___ 13 If, in a competitive industry, there are external economies, the long-run industry supply curve will be positively sloped.

___ 14 Suppose a competitive industry is in long-run equilibrium when there is a substantial

____ **15** If a firm is economically efficient, then it must be allocatively efficient.

____ **16** A firm is economically efficient if it is maximizing profit.

____ **17** Allocative efficiency occurs when marginal social benefit is greater than marginal social cost.

____ **18** A perfectly competitive industry will achieve allocative efficiency if there are no external costs or external benefits.

MULTIPLE-CHOICE

1 If a firm faces a perfectly elastic demand for its product, then
  a it is not a price taker.
  b it will want to lower its price to increase sales.
  c it will want to raise its price to increase total revenue.
  d its marginal revenue curve is equal to the price of the product.
  e it will always earn zero economic profits.

2 A perfectly competitive firm is maximizing profit if
  a marginal cost equals price and price is above minimum average variable cost.
  b marginal cost equals price and price is above minimum average fixed cost.
  c total revenue is at a maximum.
  d average variable cost is at a minimum.
  e average total cost is at a minimum.

3 In which of the following situations will a perfectly competitive firm earn economic profits?
  a $MR > AVC$
  b $MR > ATC$
  c $ATC > MC$
  d $ATC > AR$
  e $AR > AVC$

4 The maximum loss a firm will experience in the short run is equal to
  a zero.
  b total costs.
  c total variable costs.

  d total fixed costs.
  e none of the above.

5 The short-run industry supply curve is
  a the horizontal sum of the individual firms' supply curves .
  b the vertical sum of the individual firms' supply curves.
  c vertical at the total level of output being produced by all firms.
  d horizontal at the current market price.
  e none of the above.

6 If a perfectly competitive firm in the short run is able to pay its variable costs and part, but not all, of its fixed costs, then it is operating in the range on its marginal cost curve that is
  a above the break-even point.
  b below the break-even point.
  c above the shutdown point.
  d below the shutdown point.
  e between the shutdown and break-even points.

7 In a perfectly competitive industry, the market price is £10. An individual firm is producing the output at which $MC = ATC = £15$. AVC at that output is £10. What should the firm do to maximize its short-run profits?
  a shut down
  b expand output
  c contract output
  d leave output unchanged
  e insufficient information to answer

8 In a perfectly competitive industry, the market price is £5. An individual firm is producing the level of output at which marginal cost is £5 and is increasing, and average total cost is £25. What should the firm do to maximize its short-run profits?
  a shut down
  b expand output
  c contract output
  d leave output unchanged
  e insufficient information to answer

9 The maximum loss a firm will experience in long-run equilibrium is
  a zero.
  b its total cost.
  c its total variable cost.
  d its average total cost.
  e none of the above.

10 The long-run competitive industry supply curve will be positively sloped if there are
   a external economies.
   b external diseconomies.
   c no external economies or diseconomies.
   d external costs.
   e external benefits.

11 Which of the following is *not* true of a new long-run equilibrium resulting from a new technology in a perfectly competitive industry?
   a Price will be lower.
   b Industry output will be greater.
   c Firm profits will be greater.
   d All firms in the industry will be using the new technology.
   e Average total cost will be lower.

12 If an industry experiences external economies as the industry expands in the long run, the long-run industry supply curve will
   a be perfectly inelastic.
   b be perfectly elastic.
   c have a positive slope.
   d have a negative slope.
   e have allocative inefficiency.

SHORT ANSWER

1 Why will a firm in a perfectly competitive industry choose not to charge a price either above or below the market price?

2 Why is the perfectly competitive firm's supply curve the same as the marginal cost curve above minimum average variable cost?

3 Why will economic profits be zero in long-run equilibrium in a perfectly competitive industry?

4 Suppose output is at a level such that marginal social benefit is greater than marginal social cost. Explain why this level of output is allocatively *inefficient*.

PROBLEMS

1 a Table 11.1 gives the total cost structure for one of many identical firms in a perfectly competitive industry. Complete the table by computing total variable cost, average total cost, average variable cost and marginal cost at each level of output. (Remember, as in the problems in *Study Guide* Chapter 10, marginal cost should be entered midway between rows.)

Table 11.1

Quantity (units per day)	Total cost (pounds)	Total variable cost (pounds)	Average total cost (pounds)	Average variable cost (pounds)	Marginal cost (pounds)
0	12				
1	24				
2	32				
3	42				
4	54				
5	68				
6	84				

b Complete Table 11.2 by computing the profit (per day) for the firm at each level of output if the price of output is £9, £11, or £15.

Table 11.2

Quantity (units per day)	Profit P = £9	Profit P = £11	Profit P = £15
0			
1			
2			
3			
4			
5			
6			

c Consider the profit-maximizing output decision of the firm at alternative prices. How much will the firm produce if the price of output is £9? £11? £15? Explain each of your answers.

2 A firm will maximize profit if it produces every unit of output for which marginal revenue exceeds marginal cost. This is sometimes called the marginal approach to profit maximization. Using the marginal approach, determine the profit-maximizing level of output for the firm of Problem 1 when the price of output is £15. How does your answer here compare with your answer in 1c?

3 a Consider a perfectly competitive industry in long-run equilibrium. All the firms in the industry are identical. Draw a two-part graph illustrating the long-run equilibrium for the industry (part (a) on the left) and for the typical firm (part (b) on the right). The graph of the firm should include the *MC, ATC, MR* and *LRAC* curves.

Assume that the *LRAC* curve is U-shaped as it is in text Fig. 11.10 on page 296. Label the equilibrium price P_0, the equilibrium industry quantity traded Q_0, and the output of the firm q_0.

b Now, suppose there is a decline in industry demand. Using your graphs from part (a)

i show what happens to market price, firm output, firm profits and industry quantity traded in the short run (assume that the shutdown point is not reached).

ii show what happens to market price, firm output, firm profits and industry quantity traded in the long run (assume that there are no external economies or diseconomies). What has happened to the number of firms?

DATA QUESTIONS

Perfect competition in the lead mining industry – a nineteenth century case study

The structure of the lead mining industry has changed enormously over the last couple of centuries and today large firms account for great proportions of output. But the price at which they sell their product is still determined by market forces, and the producers have little control over the price of their product and are therefore price takers.

The Snailbeach Company worked a vein of ore in Shropshire. It took a lease in 1783 and continued to produce lead until 1912. Before analysing the firm it is worth while to outline the features of lead mining which made for a perfect market.

Firstly, there were a large number of firms; in the early years of the eighteenth century most mines were worked as partnerships and needed only small amounts of capital to work what were, in effect, little more than shallow holes in the ground. The fixed costs of the company were therefore very small.

The normal method of sale was for the company to put a sample of their ore into the market and buyers would inspect this and then make an offer for the whole lot. The price of lead was therefore determined by the market, thus satisfying the condition of perfect competition which requires that the firm has no control over the price of the product it sells. In times of scarcity the price of lead was high, and in times of surplus or demand deficiency it fell. In consequence the price of lead exerted an enormous influence over the whole structure of the industry, determining profits, wages and the opening up and closing down of enterprises.

During the 1860s demand increased to such an extent that a shortage of ore occurred. However, it was only a matter of time before the bubble burst. In the early 1870s lead ore was selling at between £13 and £14 a ton, but by 1890 the price had fallen to £7 a ton. The reason for the fall was an increased supply from overseas sources in Australia and America. With falling prices it was impossible for many firms to stay profitable, and many companies went out of business.

Source: Adapted from F. Brook,'Perfect competition in the lead mining industry – a nineteenth century case study', *Economics*, Journal of the Economics Association, Autumn 1970, **8**(5), No. 35, 240–555.

1 Outline the characteristic features of perfect competition. To what extent did the lead mining industry of the period satisfy the criteria needed for perfect competition?

2 Draw diagrams to show the effect on the industry and the firm of an increase in demand for lead.

3 Draw diagrams for the industry and the firm to show why prices fell between 1880 and 1890.

ANSWERS

CONCEPT REVIEW

1 many; identical; many; entry

2 taker; elastic

3 profit

4 average revenue; marginal revenue

5 price

6 break-even; shutdown

7 marginal cost

8 industry; industry

9 marginal cost; nothing; total fixed cost

10 profits; fall; losses

11 zero; minimum

12 external economies; external diseconomies

13 Allocative efficiency

14 external costs; external benefits

TRUE OR FALSE

1 T Each firm is a price taker.

2 T Definition.

3 F The individual firm's demand curve is horizontal. The industry demand curve is downward sloping.

4 F Firm aims to maximize total profit.

5 F Profits will increase if it increases output since each additional unit's revenue is greater than its cost.

6 T Definition.

7 F It would be true if $P <$ minimum AVC.

8 T Otherwise they would be making losses.

9 T Definition.

10 T Otherwise new firms would enter and bring down profits till they reached zero.

11 F New firms will lead to lower prices and profits.

12 T Otherwise the firm would be driven out of busness by lower cost firms.

13 F Negatively sloped.

14 T ATC will rise with no change in marginal cost. This will lead to losses and some firms will go bust.

15 F It is true if there are no external costs or benefits, otherwise it is false.

16 T Maximizing profit means minimizing costs.

17 F Allocative efficiency occurs when marginal social benefit equals marginal social cost.

18 T The 'invisible hand' will lead to economic efficiency and consumer efficiency.

MULTIPLE-CHOICE

1 d Firm can increase quantity without changing price, so MR from additional quantity = price.

2 a AFC is irrelevant. Maximizing profit does not equal maximizing revenue. **d, e** might be true, depending on P.

3 b Since $MR = AR$, $AR > ATC$. Multiply by Q gives $TR > TC$, so economic profits.

4 d Equals shutdown cost. Any potentially greater loss, firm will shut down.

5 a Definition. **c** is momentary supply curve. **d** is demand curve facing individual firm.

6 e If couldn't pay variable costs → below shutdown. If paying all variable and fixed costs → break even.

7 c Draw a graph. Firm should choose lower Q where $P = MC$. If AVC at current $Q = £10$, minimum AVC must be $< £10$, so new $Q >$ minimum AVC.

8 e Firm is at Q where $P = MC$, but is losing money since $AR < ATC$. Need AVC information to determine if **a** or **d** is correct.

9 a Definition. Long-run equilibrium leads to zero economic profits.

10 b Rise in costs as industry quantity increases.

11 c In long-run equilibrium, economic profits are zero.

12 d Because fall in costs as industry Q rises.

SHORT ANSWER

1 If a firm in a perfectly competitive industry charged a price even slightly higher than the market price, it would lose all of its sales. Thus, it will not charge a price above the market price. Since it can sell all it wants at the market price, it would not be able to increase sales by lowering its price. Thus, it would not charge a price below the market price since this would decrease total revenue and hence profits.

2 A perfectly competitive firm will want to supply the quantity that will maximize profit. This is done by equating marginal revenue and marginal cost. Since marginal revenue is equal to price for a perfectly competitive firm, the firm will produce the level of output at which price equals marginal cost. Since this is true for each price above minimum AVC, the firm's supply curve is the same as its marginal cost curve above minimum AVC. For prices below minimum AVC, the firm will maximize profit (actually minimize loss) by shutting down. The loss from shutting down will be equal to total fixed cost. If the firm continued to produce at a price below minimum *AVC*, its loss would exceed total fixed cost.

3 In a perfectly competitive industry, the existence of positive economic profits will attract the entry of new firms, which will shift the industry supply curve to the right, causing the market price to fall and firm profits to decline. This tendency will exist so long as there are positive economic profits. Similarly, the existence of economic losses will cause firms to exit from the industry, which will shift the industry supply curve to the left, causing the market price to rise and firm profits to rise (losses to decline). This tendency will exist as long as losses are being made. Thus, the only point of rest in the long run (the only equilibrium) is one in which economic profits are zero.

4 A level of output at which marginal social benefit is greater than marginal social cost is allocatively inefficient, because some people can be made better off without making anyone worse off if more is produced. Since the production of an additional unit of output will add more to social benefit than to social cost, those who bear the additional costs can be compensated out of the additional benefits (and thus be left no worse off) with some additional benefits left over (making those who receive the additional benefits better off).

PROBLEMS

1 a The completed Table 11.1 is shown here as Table 11.3.

Table 11.3

Quantity (units per day)	Total cost (pounds)	Total variable cost (pounds)	Average total cost (pounds)	Average variable cost (pounds)	Marginal cost (pounds)
0	12	0	–	–	
1	24	12	24.00	12.00	...12
2	32	20	16.00	10.00	...8
3	42	30	14.00	10.00	...10
4	54	42	13.50	10.50	...12
5	68	56	13.60	11.20	...14
6	84	72	14.00	12.00	...16

b The completed Table 11.2 is given here as Table 11.4. The values for profit are computed as total revenue minus total cost, where total revenue is price times quantity and total cost is given in Table 11.1.

Table 11.4

Quantity (units per day)	Profit P = £9	Profit P = £11	Profit P = £15
0	-12	-12	-12
1	-15	-13	-9
2	-14	-10	-2
3	-15	-9	3
4	-18	-10	6
5	-23	-13	7
6	-30	-18	6

c If the price is £9, profit is maximized (actually loss is minimized) when the firm shuts down and produces zero units. If the firm chooses to produce, its loss will be at least £14, which is greater than the fixed cost loss of £12. Therefore the firm will minimize losses by shutting down. If the price is £11, the firm is still unable to make a positive economic profit. The loss is minimized (at £9) if the firm produces 3 units. At this price all of variable cost and part of fixed cost can be recovered. At a price of £15, the firm will maximize profit (at £7) at an output of 5 units per day.

2 The marginal approach to profit maximization states that the firm should produce all units of output for which marginal revenue exceeds marginal cost. For a perfectly competitive firm, marginal revenue equals price, so the approach states (equivalently) that the firm should produce every unit for which price exceeds marginal cost. If the price of output is £15, we can see from Table 11.3 that the firm should produce 5 units. Since the marginal cost of moving from the 4th to the 5th unit (£14) is less than price (£15), the 5th unit should be produced. The marginal cost of moving to the 6th unit (£16), however, is greater than price. It should not be produced. The answer obtained here is the same as the answer obtained in **1c**.

3 a A long-run equilibrium in a perfectly competitive industry is illustrated in Fig. 11.1.

Part (a) illustrates industry equilibrium at the intersection of industry demand (D_0) and industry supply (S_0): point *a*. The equilibrium industry quantity traded is labelled Q_0 and the equilibrium market price is labelled P_0.

Part (b) illustrates the situation for a single firm in long-run equilibrium. The firm is at point *a'*, the minimum point of both the short-run average total cost

Figure 11.1

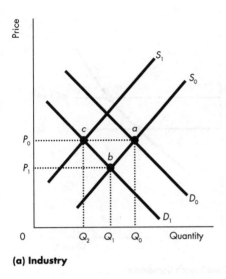

(a) Industry

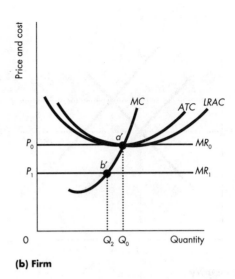

(b) Firm

curve *(ATC)* and the long-run average cost curve *(LRAC)*. The firm is producing the output labelled Q_0 and earning zero economic profit.

b i The new short-run equilibrium is also illustrated in Fig. 11.1. The decrease in demand shifts the market demand curve to the left, from D_0 to D_1. The new market equilibrium is at point *b*. The price has fallen from P_0 to P_1 and the industry quantity traded has fallen from Q_0 to Q_1. The fall in price induces firms to reduce output as shown by the move from point *a'* to point *b'* on the *MC* curve in part (b). Since P_1 is less than minimum *ATC*, firms are making losses in the new short-run equilibrium.

ii The new long-run equilibrium is also illustrated in Fig. 11.1. Since losses are experienced in short-run equilibrium, firms will exit from the industry in the long run.

This will cause the industry supply curve to shift to the left causing the price to rise and thus reducing losses. Firms will continue to leave until the industry supply curve has shifted enough to eliminate losses, from S_0 to S_1. This gives a new long-run industry equilibrium at point *c* and the price has returned to its initial level, P_0, but industry quantity traded has fallen to Q_2. As firms exit and the market price rises, remaining firms will increase their output (moving up the *MC* curve from point *b'* to point *a'*) and their losses will be reduced. When sufficient firms have left the industry, the price will have risen (returned) to P_0 and firms will have returned to point *a'* in part (b). At this point, each firm is again earning zero economic profit and firm output has

returned to Q_0. But, since there are now fewer firms, industry quantity traded is less.

DATA QUESTIONS

1 The characteristic features of perfect competition are: many firms, identical product, many buyers, easy entry and that existing firms have no advantage over new entrants, and perfect knowledge. The lead industry in the nineteenth century satisfied many of these criteria, but we do not know that those involved had perfect knowledge about the product and the industry.

Moreover, the product was not identical – different samples of lead ore differed in quality. However, it is safe to conclude that the industry exhibited many of the characteristics of perfect competition.

2 The position is shown in Fig. 11.2.

In this figure the demand curve for the firm is horizontal because the Snailbeach Company has to take the price determined by the supply and demand for lead in the industry as a whole. It can then sell all the lead ore it wants at this price because it is only a small firm in a large industry. The original equilibrium is at price P_0 and quantity Q_0. The increase in demand will cause the demand curve to shift and a new equilibrium at price P_1 and quantity Q_1.

3 Prices fell because there was a large increase in supply from overseas firms. This caused the supply curve to shift and the result was that price fell from P_0 to P_1 while quantity rose from Q_0 to Q_1 as shown in Fig. 11.3.

Figure 11.2

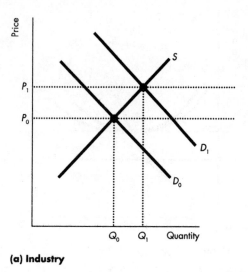

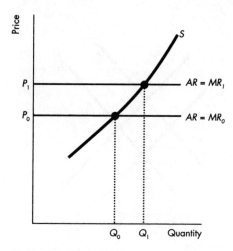

(a) Industry

(b) Snailbeach Company

Figure 11.3

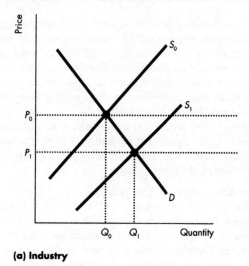

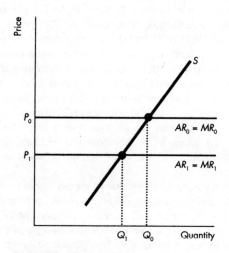

(a) Industry

(b) Snailbeach Company

Chapter 12   **Monopoly**

Chapter In Perspective, Text Pages 311–339

The perfectly competitive firms of Chapter 11 are price takers. At the opposite extreme are industries in which there is a single firm, a monopoly. Unlike a perfectly competitive firm, a monopoly's output decision has a direct effect on price; it cannot sell more output unless it drops its price.

This chapter pursues the answers to numerous questions about monopoly: Why does monopoly exist? How does a monopoly choose how much to produce? What constraints on behaviour does a monopoly face? How much profit will a monopoly make? When will a monopoly charge different prices to different customers for the same good or service? How does a monopoly compare with perfect competition in terms of efficiency? Is monopoly always 'bad'?

Helpful Hints

1 A monopoly is a single firm with the ability to set both quantity and price. Because there is only one firm, the industry demand curve is also the firm demand curve. In order to sell additional output, the monopoly must lower the price. A single-price monopoly must lower the price on all units of output, not just the additional unit. As the following explanation for Fig. 12.1 states, this means that marginal revenue is less than price. Combining this new revenue situation with our familiar cost curves from Chapter 10 yields the important diagram shown in Fig. 12.1.

Notice the following:

a The rule for profit maximization is to find the quantity of output where $MR = MC$. This is the same rule that applies to a perfectly competitive firm.

Figure 12.1

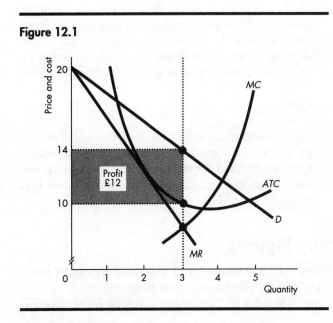

For a perfectly competitive firm *MR* is also equal to price, so the intersection of *MR* and *MC* yields the profit-maximizing output and price. That is not true for the monopolist. *MR* is not equal to price, and once the profit-maximizing output is identified, the monopolist still has to set the price.

b To find the profit-maximizing price, draw an imaginary vertical line up to the demand curve from the intersection of *MR* and *MC*. Then draw an imaginary horizontal line to the price axis to read the price.

c Understanding what the vertical and horizontal distances of the total profit area represent will make you less likely to make mistakes in drawing that area. The vertical distance is between the demand (or average revenue) curve and the average total cost curve. That distance measures average revenue minus average total cost, which equals average profit, or profit per unit. The horizontal distance is just the number of units produced. So the area of the rectangle (vertical distance × horizontal distance) = profit per unit × number of units = total profit. Do *not* make the mistake of drawing the vertical distance down to the intersection of *MC* and *MR*. That intersection has no economic meaning for the calculation of total profit.

2 There is an easy trick for drawing the marginal revenue curve corresponding to any linear demand curve. The price intercept (where $Q = 0$) is the same as for the demand curve, and the quantity intercept (where $P = 0$) is exactly *half* of the output of the demand curve. The marginal revenue curve is, therefore, a downward-sloping straight line whose slope is twice as steep as the slope of the demand curve.

3 Price discrimination can be profitable for a monopoly only if different groups have different elasticities of demand for the good. The monopolist can then treat each group as a separate market and produce where *MR* = *MC* for each group.

Key Figures

Figure 12.1 Demand and Marginal Revenue for a Single-price Monopoly, text page 315

This illustrates the relationship between the demand and marginal revenue curves for a single-price monopolist using the example of Jackie's hairdressing salon. If the firm wants to sell one more unit of output, it must lower its price. This has two effects on revenue. First, the sale of an additional unit will increase revenue by the amount of the price. However, since the firm must also *drop the price on previous units*, revenue on these will decrease. The net change in revenue, the marginal revenue, will thus be less than price and the marginal revenue curve will lie below the demand curve.

Figure 12.2 A Single-price Monopoly's Revenue Curves, text page 316

This illustrates the relationship between a single-price monopolist's revenue curves and the elasticity of demand. Recall that in the elastic range of the demand curve, a drop in price will increase total revenue, so marginal revenue will be positive. When the demand curve is unit elastic, a drop in price will leave total revenue unchanged so marginal revenue will be zero. In the inelastic range of the demand curve, a drop in price will decrease total revenue so marginal revenue will be negative. These relationships are combined and shown graphically in part (a). The corresponding ranges of increasing total revenue, maximum total revenue and decreasing total revenue are shown in part (b).

Figure 12.3 The Monopoly's Output and Price, text page 317

The table associated with this figure reports the revenues and costs for Jackie's hairdressing salon. This information is used to illustrate how a single-price monopoly will choose the profit-maximizing output and price.

Part (a) shows the total revenue and total cost curves facing the firm. Profit is a maximum when the vertical amount by which total revenue exceeds total cost is a maximum. For Jackie's hairdressing salon, this turns out to be 3 haircuts per hour.

Part (b) shows the total profit curve itself; it is derived from part (a) by taking the difference between total revenue and total cost at each level of output. Profit is maximized when this curve reaches its maximum. Part (c) shows that profit is a maximum at the quantity where marginal revenue is equal to marginal cost. In the case of Jackie's hairdressing salon, the profit-maximizing output is 3 haircuts per hour, the price is $7 per haircut, and total profit is $6 per hour. The diagram of marginal cost and marginal revenue in part (c) is the most important and useful of the three diagrams.

Figure 12.7 Monopoly and Competition Compared, text page 328

This compares the price and quantity results in a monopoly industry with the price and quantity results if the same industry were competitive.

A competitive industry will produce at the intersection of the industry supply and demand curves (labelled S and D). Thus, a competitive industry will produce the quantity C and charge the price P_C.

If the same industry became a single-price monopoly, its marginal cost curve would be the supply curve of the competitive industry. A profit-maximizing single-price monopoly will produce the output level at which marginal revenue equals marginal cost. Thus the monopoly will produce the quantity M and charge the price P_M. The single-price monopoly output is lower than for a competitive industry and the price is higher than the competitive price. A perfectly price-discriminating monopoly produces the competitive output C and charges a different price (all above P_C) for each unit sold.

SELF-TEST

CONCEPT REVIEW

1 A firm that is the single supplier of a good in an industry is called a(n) _____ . The key feature of such an industry is the existence of _____ preventing the entry of new firms.

2 A monopoly that charges the same price for every unit of output it sells is called a(n) _____ - _____ monopoly.

3 The demand curve facing a monopoly firm is the _____ demand curve.

4 For a monopoly charging a single price, the average revenue curve is the _____ curve and the marginal revenue curve is _____ the average revenue curve.

5 The output range over which total revenue is rising is the same as that over which marginal revenue is _____ . This is the same range of input over which the (price) elasticity of demand is _____ than 1. If elasticity of demand is _____ than 1, marginal revenue is _____ . This implies that a profit-maximizing monopoly will never produce an output in the _____ range of its demand curve.

6 Unlike a perfectly competitive firm, a monopoly's decision to produce more or less of a good will affect the _____ of the good.

7 A profit-maximizing monopoly will want to produce less if, at the current level of output, marginal _____ is greater than marginal _____ .

8 Unlike a perfectly competitive firm, a monopoly can be making positive economic _____ in the long run.

9 The practice of charging some customers a higher price than others for exactly the same good is called _____ _____ . This kind of pricing policy can be seen as an attempt by the monopoly to capture all or part of the consumer _____ .

10 Charging different prices to different groups of customers will increase the profits of a monopoly only if the groups of customers have different _____ of demand for the product. A monopoly that charges different prices to different groups of customers will produce _____ than will a monopoly that charges a single price.

11 If a perfectly competitive industry is taken over by a single monopoly firm, output will _____ and the price will _____ . The reduction in consumer and producer surplus resulting from this new monopoly is called the _____ loss.

12 The activity of creating monopoly is called _____ _____ . If there are no barriers to such activity, the value of the resources used up in the process will, in equilibrium, be _____ _____ the monopoly's profit.

13 A firm that has a decrease in average total cost when it increases the number of different goods it produces is said to have economies of _____ .

TRUE OR FALSE

___ **1** Natural monopoly can arise because of economies of scale.

___ **2** For a single-price monopoly, average revenue always equals price.

___ **3** Over the output range where total revenue is decreasing, marginal revenue is positive.

___ **4** The marginal revenue curve lies below the demand curve for a single-price monopoly because, when the price is lowered to sell additional units of output, it must be lowered on all units of output.

___ **5** A profit-maximizing single-price monopoly will produce only in the elastic range of its demand curve.

___ **6** The supply curve of a monopoly firm is its marginal cost curve.

___ **7** A monopoly will always make economic profits.

___ **8** Price discrimination occurs when a firm charges one group of customers more than another or when a firm gives quantity discounts.

___ **9** A monopoly can acquire all of the consumer surplus for itself if it practises perfect price discrimination.

___ **10** Price discrimination is an attempt by a monopolist to capture the producer surplus.

___ **11** For a perfect price-discriminating monopolist, the demand curve is also the marginal revenue curve.

___ **12** Price discrimination works only for goods that can be readily resold.

___ **13** In moving from perfect competition to single-price monopoly, all of the surplus lost by consumers is captured by the monopoly.

___ **14** No deadweight loss results from a perfect price-discriminating monopoly because the monopoly gains everything the consumer loses.

___ **15** Because of the existence of rent seeking, the social cost of monopoly is smaller than the deadweight loss.

___ **16** A monopoly industry with large economies of scale and scope may produce more output and charge a lower price than does a perfectly competitive industry.

MULTIPLE-CHOICE

1 Which of the following is a natural barrier to the entry of new firms in an industry?
  a licensing of professions
  b economies of scale
  c issuing a patent
  d a public franchise
  e all of the above

2 In order to increase sales from 7 units to 8 units, a single-price monopolist must drop the price from £7 per unit to £6 per unit. What is marginal revenue in this range?
  a £48
  b £6
  c £1
  d −£1
  e none of the above

3 A single-price monopolist will maximize profits if it produces the output where
  a price equals marginal cost.
  b price equals marginal revenue.
  c marginal revenue equals marginal cost.
  d average revenue equals marginal cost.
  e average revenue equals marginal revenue.

4 If a profit-maximizing monopoly is producing at an output at which marginal cost exceeds marginal revenue, it
  a should raise price and lower output.
  b should lower price and raise output.
  c should lower price and lower output.
  d is making losses.
  e is maximizing profit.

5 A single-price monopoly never operates
  a on an elastic portion of the demand curve.
  b on a portion of the demand curve that is unit elastic.

c on an inelastic portion of the demand curve.

d at a quantity where marginal revenue is positive since total revenue is not at a maximum.

e under any of the above conditions.

6 For the single-price monopoly depicted in Fig. 12.2, when profit is maximized quantity is

a 3 and price is £3.

b 3 and price is £6.

c 4 and price is £4.

d 4 and price is £5.

e 5 and price is £4.

Figure 12.2

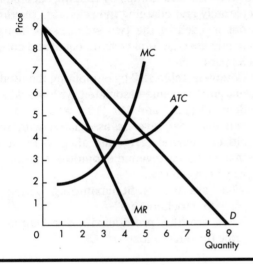

7 If the monopoly depicted in Fig. 12.2 is maximizing profit, what is the total profit?

a £3

b £4

c £6

d £9

e none of the above

8 A perfect price-discriminating monopoly

a has a demand curve which is also its average revenue curve.

b will maximize revenue.

c is assured of making a profit.

d will produce the quantity at which the marginal cost curve intersects the demand curve.

e will be allocatively inefficient.

9 Table 12.1 lists marginal costs for the XYZ firm. If XYZ sells 3 units at a price of £6 each, what is its producer surplus?

a £2

b £6

c £7

d £9

e £12

Table 12.1

Quantity	Marginal cost
1	2
2	3
3	4
4	5

10 Consider the industry demand curve in Fig. 12.3. Which area in the figure indicates the deadweight loss from a single-price monopoly?

a *eacf*

b *acd*

c *abd*

d *bcd*

e none of the above

Figure 12.3

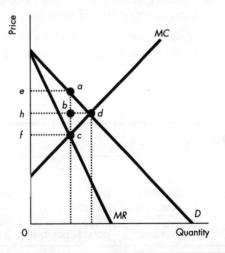

11 Which area in Fig. 12.3 indicates the deadweight loss from a perfect price-discriminating monopoly?

a *eacf*

b *acd*

c *abd*

d *bcd*

e none of the above

12 Why is the quantity of output produced by a single-price monopolist allocatively inefficient?
a Average social cost exceeds average social benefit.
b Marginal social cost exceeds marginal social benefit.
c Average social benefit exceeds average social cost.
d Marginal social benefit exceeds marginal social cost.
e None of the above.

13 Activity for the purpose of creating monopoly is
a called rent seeking.
b illegal in the United Kingdom.
c called price discrimination.
d called legal monopoly.
e costless.

SHORT ANSWER

1 Does a single-price monopoly produce in the elastic or inelastic range of its demand curve? Why?

2 Explain why the output of a competitive industry will always be greater than the output of the *same* industry under single-price monopoly.

3 Under what circumstances would a monopoly be more efficient than a large number of competitive firms? Illustrate graphically such a situation where a monopoly produces more and charges a lower price than would be the case if the industry consisted of a large number of perfectly competitive firms.

PROBLEMS

1 Keith's Lunch has two kinds of customers for lunch: stockbrokers and retired senior citizens. The demand schedules for lunches for the two groups are given in Table 12.2.

Keith has decided to price discriminate between the two groups by treating each demand separately and charging the price that maximizes profit in each of the two submarkets. Marginal cost and average total cost are equal and constant at £2 per lunch.

a Complete Table 12.2 by computing the total and marginal revenue associated with stockbroker demand (TR_{SB} and MR_{SB}) as well as the total and marginal revenue associated with senior citizen demand (TR_{SC} and MR_{SC}). (Remember that marginal revenue should be entered midway between rows.)
b What are the profit-maximizing output and price for stockbrokers?
c What are the profit-maximizing output and price for senior citizens?

Table 12.2

	Stockbrokers			Senior citizens		
Price (P) (pounds)	Quantity demanded (Q_D) (lunches)	Total revenue (TR_{SB}) (pounds per lunch)	Marginal revenue (MR_{SB}) (pounds per lunch)	Quantity demanded (Q_D) (lunches)	Total revenue (TR_{SC}) (pounds per lunch)	Marginal revenue (MR_{SC}) (pounds per lunch)
8	0			0		
7	1			0		
6	2			0		
5	3			1		
4	4			2		
3	5			3		
2	6			4		
1	7			5		
0	8			6		

d What is total profit?

e Show that the total profit in part **d** is the maximum by comparing it with total profit if instead Keith served

i 1 additional lunch *each* to stockbrokers and senior citizens.

ii 1 less lunch *each* to stockbrokers and senior citizens.

2 Figure 12.4 gives the demand, marginal revenue and marginal cost curves for a certain industry. In this problem we consider how consumer and producer surplus are distributed under each of four ways of organizing the industry. In each case redraw any relevant part of Fig. 12.4 and then: **(1)** indicate the region of the graph corresponding to consumer surplus by drawing horizontal lines through it; **(2)** indicate the region corresponding to producer surplus by drawing vertical lines through it; and **(3)** indicate the region (if any) corresponding to deadweight loss by putting dots in the area.

a The industry consists of many perfectly competitive firms.

b The industry is a single-price monopoly.

c The industry is a price-discriminating monopoly charging two prices: P_1 and P_3.

d The industry is a perfect price-discriminating monopoly.

DATA QUESTIONS

Price discrimination in the car industry
The following passage is adapted from an article by Professor Garel Rhys.

Price discrimination will tend to occur when firms have some market power and control over their prices, where demand conditions are different in different segments of the market, and where these segments can be kept separate with no resale from one to the other. Within the United Kingdom price discrimination is practised between the private motorists' market and that for fleet and company buyers. Fleet and company buyers tend to receive price discounts unrelated to any variation in the costs of manufacture and distribution. The fleet and company market consists of sophisticated buyers more interested in initial sale, resale value and running costs of what is a 'tool for the job', than in, say, the style or advertising of a car. The other major form of price discrimination in the vehicle market involves charging different ex-works prices at home and abroad. A vehicle firm can enjoy a degree of protection in one market but much more competitive conditions in the other. This enables vehicle makers to charge a higher price in the home market, though this is not always what happens. An illustration of price discrimination of this kind is shown in Table 12.3.

1 Explain how the conditions required for successful price discrimination apply to the private motorists' market and the market for fleet cars in the United Kingdom.

2 Explain why the manufacturer benefits from charging a higher price to the private motorist than to the fleet and company buyer.

3 Describe the changes in the degree of price discrimination which have occurred between the United Kingdom and European car markets over the period 1975 to 1984.

Source: Adapted from Associated Examining Board GCE 'A' level question November 1988.

Figure 12.4

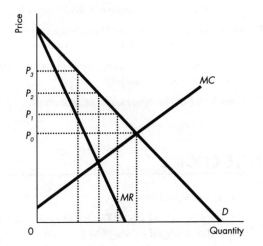

Table 12.3   Index of Comparative Car Prices in the EC (UK = 100)

	UK	W. Germany	France	Italy	Netherlands	Belgium	Ireland	Denmark
1975	100	97.8	101.3	103.4	93.4	90.2	93.1	86.4
1980	100	80.7	80.3	87.0	74.1	76.7	82.0	64.7
1981	100	72.0	71.7	—	65.6	65.2	83.3	53.3
1982	100	75.1	72.4	77.2	71.9	61.4	93.3	55.0
1983	100	83.0	81.0	87.0	—	72.0	—	—
1984	100	85.0	88.0	93.0	—	77.0	—	—

Source: 1975–82 Commission's Twelfth Report on Competition Policy (1975 and 1980 Eurostat Survey; 1981 and 1982 BEUC survey). © Philip Allan Publishers Ltd.

ANSWERS

CONCEPT REVIEW

1 monopoly; barriers

2 single-price

3 industry

4 demand; below

5 positive; greater; less; negative; inelastic

6 price

7 cost; revenue

8 profits

9 price discrimination; surplus

10 elasticities; more

11 decrease; increase; deadweight

12 rent seeking; equal to

13 scope

TRUE OR FALSE

1 **T**   Natural monopolies have high fixed costs.

2 **T**   Average of all (equal) prices of a product = price.

3 **F**   *MR* is negative.

4 **T**   Draw curves to verify this.

5 **T**   If it produced in the inelastic range it would increase profits by increasing price.

6 **F**   Monopolist has no supply curve.

7 **F**   Monopoly gives no guarantee of profits if consumers are unwilling to buy the product.

8 **T**   Definition.

9 **T**   Definition.

10 **F**   It is an attempt to capture consumer surplus.

11 **T**   Demand curve gives revenue for each successive unit.

12 **F**   Cannot be readily sold – otherwise those buying at low price would resell to high price purchasers.

13 **F**   Some lost consumer surplus is deadweight loss.

14 **T**   True for perfect price-discriminating monopoly (though not for other kinds of monopolies).

15 **F**   Social cost is greater because resources are used in rent seeking cost to society.

16 **T**   This is one of the advantages of monopoly.

MULTIPLE-CHOICE

1 **b**   Others are legal barriers.

2 **d** TR ($P = £7$) = $£7 \times 7 = £49$. TR ($P = £6$) = $£6 \times 8 = £48$, MR = change in TR = $£48 - £49$.

3 **c**   All firms will maximize profits if they produce where $MR = MC$.

4 a Draw graph. If *MC* exceeds *MR* firm should cut production, so increasing *MR* and cutting *MC*.

5 c Since *TR* falls needlessly, *MR* must always be > 0 to intersect (positive) *MC*.

6 b Profit is maximized where *MR* = *MC*.

7 c $(AR - ATC) \times Q = (\pounds 6 - \pounds 4) \times 3$

8 d Same outcome as perfectly competitive industry, so **e** wrong. *D* = *MR* so **a** wrong. Profit maximizing, so **b** wrong.

9 d Sum of $(P - MC)$ for each unit of output.

10 b Sum of lost producer *(bcd)* and consumer *(abd)* surplus compared to competitive outcome.

11 e Deadweight loss is zero.

12 d *MSB* measured on demand curve, *MSC* on *MC* curve.

13 a Definition. Activity has costs.

Figure 12.5

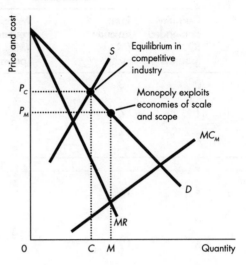

SHORT ANSWER

1 A single-price monopoly will always produce in the elastic range of the demand curve. The reason is straight-forward. Marginal cost is always positive. Thus the profit-maximizing condition that marginal cost equals marginal revenue must be satisfied over the range of output for which marginal revenue is positive, the elastic range.

2 A competitive industry will produce the level of output at which the industry marginal cost curve intersects the demand curve facing the industry. A single-price mono-poly will produce at the level of output at which the industry marginal cost curve intersects the monopoly marginal revenue curve. Since the marginal revenue curve lies below the demand curve, this implies a lower level of output in the monopoly industry.

3 A monopoly is more efficient than perfect competition if the monopoly has sufficient economies of scale and/or scope. Those economies must be large enough that the monopoly produces more than the competitive industry and sells it at a lower price. Figure 12.5 illustrates such a situation. The important feature is that the marginal cost curve for the monopoly must not only be lower than the supply curve of the competitive industry, but it must also be sufficiently lower so that it intersects the *MR* curve at an output greater than *C* (the competitive output). Such a situation could arise if there are extensive economies of scale and/or scope.

PROBLEMS

1 a The completed table is given in Table 12.4.
For stockbrokers, equilibrium output occurs where $MC = MR = 2$, $Q_{SB} = 3$, $P_{SB} = 5$.
For senior citizens, equilibrium output occurs where $MC = MR = 2$, $Q_{SC} = 2$, $P_{SC} = 4$.

b The profit-maximizing output for stockbrokers occurs when $MC = \pounds 2 = MR_{SB}$. This is at 3 lunches and the price is £5 per lunch to stockbrokers.

c The profit-maximizing output for senior citizens occurs when $MC = \pounds 2 = MR_{SC}$. This occurs at 2 lunches and the price to senior citizens is £4 per lunch.

d Since average total cost is also £2 per lunch, the total cost is $£2 \times 5$ lunches = £10. Total revenue is £15 from stockbrokers and £8 from senior citizens, or £23. Thus total profit is £13.

e i If Keith served 1 additional lunch each to stock-brokers and senior citizens, that would make 4 lunches for stock brokers (at £4 per lunch) and 3 lunches for senior citizens (at £3 per lunch). Since average total cost is £2 per lunch, the total cost is £2 × 7 lunches = £14. Total revenue is £16 from stock-brokers and £9 from senior citizens, or £25. Thus total profit is £11, less than the £13 in part **d**.

ii If Keith served 1 less lunch each to stockbrokers and senior citizens, that would make 2 lunches for stock-brokers (at £6 per lunch) and 1 lunch for senior

Table 12.4

Price (P) (lunches)	Stockbrokers				Senior citizens		
	Quantity demanded (Q_D) (pounds per lunch)	Total revenue (TR_SB) (pounds per lunch)	Marginal revenue (MR_SB) (pounds per lunch)		Quantity demanded (Q_D) (lunches)	Total revenue (TR_SC) (pounds per lunch)	Marginal revenue (MR_SC) (pounds per lunch)
8	0	0			0	0	
			...7				...0
7	1	7			0	0	
			...5				...0
6	2	12			0	0	
			3				...0
5	3	15			1	5	
			1				3
4	4	16			2	8	
			−1				1
3	5	15			3	9	
			3				−1
2	6	12			4	8	
			−5				−3
1	7	7			5	5	
			−7				−5
0	8	0			6	0	

citizens (at £5 per lunch). Since average total cost is £2 per lunch, the total cost is £2 × 3 lunches = £6. Total revenue is £12 from stockbrokers and £5 from senior citizens, or £17. Thus total profit is £11, less than the £13 in part **d**.

2 a Under perfect competition, price equals marginal cost. The amount of consumer surplus is given by the area under the demand curve but above the price (P_0) while the amount of producer surplus is given by the area above the MC curve but below the price. See Fig. 12.6(a).
b If the industry is a single-price monopoly, price will be greater than MC and output will be less than under competition. Consumer surplus is still given by the area under the demand curve but above the price (P_2), while producer surplus is given by the area above the MC curve but below the price up to the monopoly level of output. The remaining part of the large triangle is a deadweight loss since it is the amount of surplus under competition that is lost under a single-price monopoly. See Fig. 12.6(b).
c Similar reasoning allows us to establish regions in Fig. 12.6(c) corresponding to consumer surplus, producer surplus and deadweight loss.
d Under perfect price discrimination, all of the potential surplus is captured by the producer and there is no deadweight loss (or consumer surplus). See Fig. 12.6(d).

DATA QUESTIONS

The answer given below is the author's solution to the questions on p. 115 and should not be taken as being the definitive answer required by the AEB.

1 Price discrimination is the practice of charging a higher price to some customers than to others for an identical item or charging an individual customer a higher price on a small purchase than on a large one. It can be practised only when it is impossible for a buyer to sell the good and when customers have different elasticities. In the case of cars, fleet buyers receive a discount for bulk purchase because their demand is elastic and because they will not resell the new car since their transactions costs are high. The table suggests that demand for cars by private buyers in the United Kingdom is relatively inelastic since manufacturers can charge a higher price for the same car in the United Kingdom than in other countries.

2 The manufacturer benefits by obtaining a higher revenue (price × quantity) by charging a higher price when demand is inelastic and a lower price when demand is elastic.

3 In almost all cases the degree of price discrimination increased in the period 1975–84.

Figure 12.6

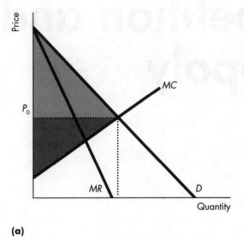

(a)

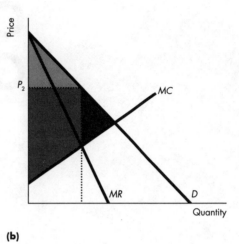

(b)

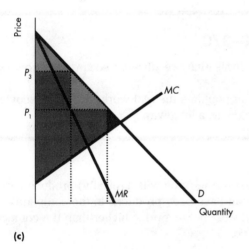

(c)

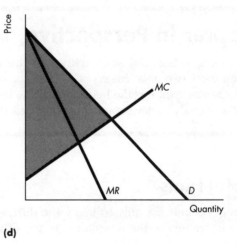

(d)

Chapter 13 Monopolistic Competition and Oligopoly

Chapter In Perspective, Text Pages 340–370

Perfect competition and strict monopoly are quite rare. Most firms that we observe seem to lie somewhere between these two polar cases.

This chapter explores the behaviour of the in-between firms that populate the real world. We will discover that the tools of analysis developed in the previous two chapters will take us a long way.

Helpful Hints

1 It is important not only to know the different key characteristics of the alternative forms of market structure (see text Table 13.2 on page 345 for a review) but also to understand how these characteristics explain differences in firm behaviour.

2 We continue to assume that all firms are profit maximizers. In spite of this common objective, the equilibrium price and level of output will be different for each of the market structures. This is because of differences in the nature of constraints faced by firms in each of the four types of market structure. For example, except in the case of perfect competition, firms face downward-sloping demand curves and thus have some control over the price of the good they sell. In these cases, profit-

maximizing firms will (typically) produce less than would have been produced in the competitive case and will charge a price higher than the competitive price.

3 In graphing a monopolistically competitive firm in long-run equilibrium, be sure that the *ATC* curve is tangent to the demand curve at the same level of output at which the *MC* and *MR* curves intersect. Also be sure that the *MC* curve intersects the *ATC* curve at the minimum point on the *ATC* curve.

4 This chapter explains the use of elementary game theory to help understand oligopoly. Be sure to understand the prisoners' dilemma game because it illustrates, simply, the most important game theory concepts (rules, strategies and payoffs) which are then used in more complex game theory models like those of repeated games.

Understand the incentives faced by the players and why a particular outcome is an equilibrium. The key to finding the equilibrium of a simple game is to construct and examine the payoff matrix carefully.

Key Figures and Tables

Figure 13.2 Monopolistic Competition, text page 346

This illustrates the output and pricing decisions of a monopolistically competitive firm in both the short run and the long run. In the short run, the firm can make either a positive profit, as illustrated in part (a), or a loss. When firms are making profits, new firms will enter, causing the demand curves of existing firms to shift to the left. Prices and firm profits will fall. Similarly, if firms are making losses in the short run, some will leave the industry, which will increase prices and profits (that is, reduce losses).

In long-run equilibrium, part (b), firms will be making zero profits and there will be no more tendency for firms to either exit or enter the industry.

Figure 13.5 Costs and Demand, text page 355

If there are no barriers to entry, an industry will be characterized by duopoly if costs and industry demand are such that only two firms can survive in the long run. This figure illustrates such an industry using the example of two firms: Trick and Gear.

The firms have identical costs, which are shown in part (a). The minimum *ATC* of £6,000 occurs at the quantity of 3,000 switchgears per firm per week. Since, at a price of £6,000, the total quantity demanded in the industry is 6,000 switchgears per week, only two firms can survive in the long run.

Figure 13.6 Colluding to Make Monopoly Profits, text page 356

The two firms of a duopoly industry obtain maximum total profit by colluding. This is illustrated in this figure once again using the example of Trick and Gear.

In order to maximize total profit, the firms will, together, behave as a single monopolist by producing the output at which *industry* marginal cost is equal to *industry* marginal revenue.

The firms will produce the quantity at which the *MC* and *MR* curves intersect (4,000 units) and charge the

monopoly price obtained from the industry demand curve (£9,000). The firms then divide the production and the profits. As seen in part (a), each firm produces 2,000 switchgears per week and earns a profit of £2 million per week.

Figure 13.8 Both Firms Cheat, text page 359

After the firms of a duopoly enter into a collusive agreement, each firm can either abide by the agreement or cheat by increasing output and reducing price.

Each firm has an incentive to cheat since it can increase its profit (at the expense of the non-cheating firm) by doing so. The case of both firms cheating is illustrated for Trick and Gear in this figure. The limit to the breakdown of the agreement is the competitive equilibrium. The limit for each firm is shown in part (a) and for the industry in part (b).

Once the collusive agreement has broken down by the cheating of the firms, successively lower prices will result until the price has fallen to the competitive level and both firms are making zero profit as seen in part (a). The industry output and price will be those associated with the competitive equilibrium, at the intersection of the industry marginal cost curve and the industry demand curve.

Table 13.2 Market Structure, text page 345

This summarizes the characteristics of the four market structures that have been discussed in this and previous chapters. These are, from most competitive to least competitive: perfect competition, monopolistic competition, oligopoly and monopoly. These are compared on the basis of the number of firms in the industry, the kind of product, the nature of any barriers to entry, the firm's control over price and the concentration ratio. The table also provides examples of each market structure. This table is an excellent study tool.

Table 13.4 Duopoly Payoff Matrix, text page 360

One way to analyse the interactive behaviour of firms in an oligopoly is to use game theory and construct a payoff matrix. A payoff matrix indicates the payoffs associated with the alternative strategy combinations of the players of the game. The payoff matrix for Trick and Gear is illustrated in this table. It indicates the profit for each firm which results from each of the four possible strategy pairs. Each firm then chooses its best strategy.

For example, Trick will consider its best strategy under each choice that Gear might make. If Gear cheats, Trick is better off by cheating (zero profit is better than a £1 million loss). If Gear complies, Trick is also better off by cheating (a £4.5 million profit is better than a £2 million profit). Thus Trick's dominant strategy is to cheat. The same analysis leads Gear to decide also to cheat. The result is a Nash equilibrium in which both firms cheat.

SELF-TEST

CONCEPT REVIEW

1 The most commonly used measure of concentration is called the five-firm _____ _____ . This is the percentage of _____ accounted for by the largest five firms in the industry.

2 The market structure characterized by a large number of firms that compete with each other by making similar but slightly different products is called _____ _____ . The market structure characterized by a small number of producers competing with each other is called _____ .

3 When profits are being made in a monopolistically competitive industry, firms will _____ . If losses are being made, firms will _____ . As a result, in a monopolistically competitive industry, in long-run equilibrium, each firm will make a(n) _____ economic profit and will have _____ capacity.

4 The modern approach to understanding oligopoly uses _____ theory, a method of analysing strategic interaction invented by John von Neumann. In such a theory all the possible actions of each player are called _____ and the score of each player is called the _____ .

5 A market structure in which only two producers of a commodity compete with each other is called _____ .

6 The table that shows the payoffs for every possible action by each player for every possible action by the other player is called a(n) _____ _____ .

7 The equilibrium of a game like the prisoners' dilemma is called a(n) _____ equilibrium. A special case of such an equilibrium occurs when the best strategy for each player is the same regardless of the action taken by the other player. This is called a(n) _____ _____ equilibrium.

8 A group of firms that has entered into a collusive agreement to restrict output and increase price and profits is called a(n) _____ . Each firm in the group can pursue one of two strategies: it can either comply or _____ .

9 In a repeated game, the strategy in which a player begins by cooperating and then cheats only if the other player cheated the previous time the game was played is called a(n) _____ - _____ - _____ strategy.

10 In a repeated game, the strategy in which a player cooperates if the other player cooperates, but plays the Nash equilibrium strategy forever thereafter if the other player cheats is called a _____ _____ .

11 The equilibrium which results from each player responding rationally to a credible threat of a heavy penalty from the other player if the agreement is broken is called a(n) _____ equilibrium.

TRUE OR FALSE

___ **1** A low concentration ratio indicates a low degree of competition.

___ **2** In a monopolistically competitive industry, each firm faces a downward-sloping demand curve.

___ **3** Product differentiation is what gives a monopolistically competitive firm some monopoly power.

___ **4** A critical difference between monopoly and monopolistic competition is that in the latter case there is free entry.

___ **5** If firms in a monopolistically competitive industry are making profits, we can expect to see their demand curves shift to the left as new firms enter.

___ **6** In long-run equilibrium, a monopolistically competitive firm will produce more output than that associated with the minimum point on its average total cost curve.

___ **7** An oligopolist will consider the reaction of other firms before it decides to cut its price.

___ **8** A Nash equilibrium occurs when A takes the best possible action given the action of B and B takes the best possible action given the action of A.

___ **9** If two players in a game face the same choices, there cannot be a dominant strategy equilibrium.

___ **10** If duopolists agree to collude, they can (jointly) make as much profit as a single monopoly.

___ **11** A member of a cartel could increase its profit if it increased its output and all other members of the cartel produced their agreed level of output.

___ **12** In the case of colluding duopolists in a non-repeated game, the dominant strategy equilibrium is for both firms to cheat.

MULTIPLE-CHOICE

1 The five-firm concentration ratio measures the share of the largest five firms in total industry
  a profits.
  b sales.
  c cost.
  d capital.
  e none of the above.

2 Under monopolistic competition, long-run economic profits tend toward zero *because of*

  a product differentiation.
  b the lack of barriers to entry.
  c excess capacity.
  d inefficiency.
  e the downward-sloping demand curve facing each firm.

3 In the long run, the firm in monopolistic competition will
  a face a perfectly elastic demand curve.
  b produce more than the quantity that minimizes ATC.
  c produce less than the quantity that minimizes ATC.
  d produce the quantity that minimizes ATC.
  e earn economic profits.

4 Figure 13.1 represents a monopolistically competitive firm in short-run equilibrium. What is the firm's level of output?
  a Q_1
  b Q_2
  c Q_3
  d Q_4
  e zero

Figure 13.1

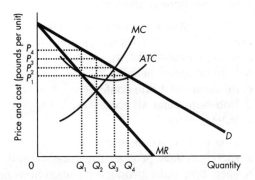

5 What will be the price charged by the monopolistic competitor of Fig. 13.1?
  a P_1
  b P_2
  c P_3
  d P_4
  e zero, since the firm has shut down.

6 Refer again to the short-run situation illustrated in Fig. 13.1. We know that in the long run,

  a there will be entry of new firms and each existing firm's demand will shift to the left.

  b there will be entry of new firms and each existing firm's demand will shift to the right.

  c existing firms will leave and each remaining firm's demand will shift to the left.

  d existing firms will leave and each remaining firm's demand will shift to the right.

  e there will be no change from the short run.

7 Which of the following is true for perfect competition, monopolistic competition and single-price monopoly?

  a homogeneous product

  b zero long-run economic profits

  c short-run profit maximizing quantity where $MC = MR$

  d easy entry and exit

  e none of the above

8 The kinked demand curve theory

  a suggests that price will remain constant even with fluctuations in demand.

  b suggests how the current price is determined.

  c assumes that marginal revenue sometimes increases with output.

  d assumes that competitors will match price cuts and ignore price increases.

  e suggests none of the above.

9 In the prisoners' dilemma with players Alf and Bob, the dominant strategy equilibrium is

  a both prisoners confess.

  b both prisoners deny.

  c Alf denies and Bob confesses.

  d Bob denies and Alf confesses.

  e indeterminate.

10 If a duopoly with collusion maximizes profit,

  a each firm must produce the same amount.

  b each firm must produce its maximum output possible.

  c industry marginal revenue must equal industry marginal cost at the level of total output.

  d industry demand must equal industry marginal cost at the level of total output.

  e total output will be greater than without collusion.

11 The firms Trick and Gear form a cartel to collude to maximize profit. If this game is non-repeated, the dominant strategy equilibrium is

  a both firms cheat on the agreement.

  b both firms comply with the agreement.

  c Trick cheats while Gear complies with the agreement.

  d Gear cheats while Trick complies with the agreement.

  e indeterminate.

12 Consider the same cartel consisting of Trick and Gear. Now, however, the game is repeated indefinitely and each firm employs a tit-for-tat strategy. The equilibrium is

  a both firms cheat on the agreement.

  b both firms comply with the agreement.

  c Trick cheats while Gear complies with the agreement.

  d Gear cheats while Trick complies with the agreement.

  e indeterminate.

13 The equilibrium in Question 12 is called a

  a credible strategy equilibrium.

  b dominant player equilibrium.

  c duopoly equilibrium.

  d trigger strategy equilibrium.

  e cooperative equilibrium.

SHORT ANSWER

1 a Considering the geographical scope of markets, how might concentration ratios *understate* the degree of competitiveness in an industry?

  b How might they *overstate* the degree of competitiveness in an industry?

2 Why will a firm in a monopolistically competitive industry always have excess capacity in long-run equilibrium?

3 Compare the advantages and disadvantages of perfect competition and monopolistic competition in terms of allocative efficiency.

4 Consider the case of two colluding duopolists in a non-repeated game. Why will both firms cheat on the agreement in equilibrium?

PROBLEMS

1 Consider a single firm in a monopolistically competitive industry in the short run. On a grid similar to the grid shown in Fig. 13.2, draw a new graph for each of the following situations.

Figure 13.2

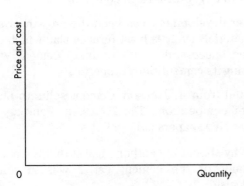

Figure 13.3

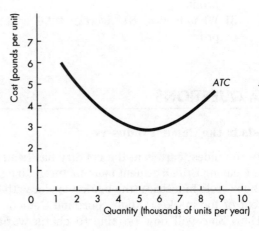

(a)

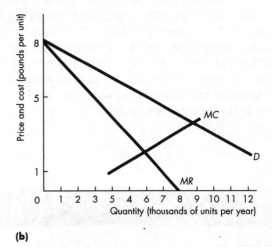

(b)

a The firm is making a profit.
b The firm is making a loss that will cause shut-down.
c The firm is making a loss but is still producing.
d Starting from the situation in **c**, explain what will happen in this industry and how your graph in **c** will be affected. (No new graph required.)
e The firm is in long-run equilibrium.

2 A duopoly industry with no collusion consists of firms *A* and *B* which are essentially identical. Currently, neither firm is advertising and each is making a profit of £5 million per year. If *A* advertises and *B* does not, *A* will make an annual profit of £12 million while *B* will make a loss of £5 million.

On the other hand, if *B* advertises and *A* does not, *B* will make a £12 million profit and *A* will make a loss of £5 million. If both advertise, each will make a zero profit.
a Represent this duopoly as a game by identifying the players, strategies and possible outcomes.
b Construct the payoff matrix.
c What is the equilibrium outcome? Explain.

3 Use the graphs given in Fig. 13.3 to answer this question. Figure 13.3(a) gives the average total cost *(ATC)* curve for each of two identical firms (call them *A* and *B*) in a duopoly. Figure 13.3(b) gives the market demand curve and the firms' joint marginal cost curve. Suppose these firms collude to maximize profit and agree to divide output equally *for a single year*.

a How much will each firm produce by the agreement and what price will they charge?
b What is each firm's average total cost and profit?
c Now suppose that firm *B* convinces *A* that demand has decreased and they must reduce their price by £1 per unit in order to sell their agreed-upon quantity. Of course, demand has *not* decreased but *A* produces its agreed amount and charges £1 less per unit. Firm *B*, the cheater, also charges £1 less than the original agreement price but increases output sufficiently to satisfy the rest of the demand at this price.

    i How much does *B* produce?
    ii What is firm *A*'s average total cost and profit?
    iii What is firm *B*'s average total cost and profit?

DATA QUESTIONS

Cartels in the Cement Industry

One of the oldest cartels in the country has been disbanded leaving British cement manufacturers to fight it out. Blue Circle Industries (the market leader with 56.5 per cent of the market), Rugby Portland Cement and Rio Tinto Zinc will now be able to charge variable prices throughout the country. This was a reluctant decision on the part of the cartel.

    The common price agreement has been in exist-ence since 1934, the firms maintaining that it was in the public interest for cement prices to be fixed countrywide. However, faced with a declining market after the construction industry peak in 1973, the major cement manufacturers were vulnerable. A major reason for the decline in the construction industry was cuts in public expenditure causing construction industry output to fall by 15 per cent in the period 1973–1985. By the late 1970s excess capacity in Britain was accompanied by a surplus in the rest of the world. The British market became a target for foreign companies.

Another development has been the growth of substitute materials such as blast furnace slag which can be blended successfully with ordinary cement without impairing its cementitious properties.

(Adapted from A. Jackson 'Cement splits to face the frost of competition', *The Times*, 13 February 1987. © Times Newspapers Ltd., 1987.)

1 Why should the author suggest that the abandonment of the cement cartel was 'a reluctant decision'?

2 How might cement manufacturers have argued that the cartel was in the public interest?

3 Using appropriate diagram(s), analyse the factors which caused cement manufacturers to become 'vulnerable' after 1973.

Source: University of London Schools Examination Board GCE A-level question, January 1990. © University of London Examinations and Assessment Council.

ANSWERS

CONCEPT REVIEW

1 concentration ratio; sales
2 monopolistic competition; oligopoly
3 enter; leave; zero; excess
4 game; strategies; payoff
5 duopoly
6 payoff matrix
7 Nash; dominant strategy
8 cartel; cheat
9 tit-for-tat
10 trigger strategy
11 cooperative

TRUE OR FALSE

1 **F** Low concentration ratio = high degree of competition.
2 **T** Firm will have to cut price to sell more.
3 **T** Creates a downward-sloping demand curve.
4 **T** Definition.
5 **T** Increase in supply moves curve to left.
6 **F** Profits would fall if it produced beyond the minimum point.
7 **T** Oligopoly involves strategic behaviour.
8 **T** Definition.
9 **F** Prisoners' dilemma players face same choices leading to dominant strategy equilibrium.

10 T With collusion they act like a monopoly.

11 T So long as its MR > MC.

12 T True for non-repeated game, but may be false for repeated game.

MULTIPLE-CHOICE

1 b Definition.

2 b **a** and **e** lead to possible profits, **c** and **d** are outcomes.

3 c Excess capacity at Q where demand is tangent to downward slope *ATC*.

4 b Where $MR = MC$.

5 c Highest possible price to sell Q_2.

6 a Since firm is making profits, new firms will enter so each firm will sell less.

7 c **b** and **d** false for monopoly, **a** false for monopolistic competition.

8 d **a** is true if there are fluctuations in *MC*. **c** is false because *MR* always falls as quantity rises.

9 a Outcome of game.

10 c See textbook, Figure 13.6.

11 a Similar to prisoners' dilemma outcome.

12 b Cooperative equilibrium; each player responds rationally to credible threat of the other.

13 e Definition.

SHORT ANSWER

1 a Since concentration ratios are calculated from a national perspective, if the actual geographical scope of the market is not national, the concentration ratio is likely to mis-state the degree of competitiveness in an industry. For example, if the actual market is global, the concentration ratio will understate the degree of competitiveness, and it will be too high. It is possible for a firm to have a concentration ratio of 100 because it is the only producer in the nation, but face a great deal of international competition.

b Similarly, when the scope of the market is regional, the degree of competitiveness is likely to be less than would be indicated by the simple concentration ratio.

2 A firm is defined to have excess capacity if it is producing in the negatively-sloped portion of its average total cost curve. At the long-run equilibrium level of output (sales) in a monopolistically competitive industry, each firm will be earning zero profit and its average total cost curve will be tangent to its demand curve. Since the demand curve of a monopolistic competitor is downward sloping, so is the average total cost curve at that level of output. Therefore, the monopolistically competitive firm will have excess capacity in long-run equilibrium.

3 The advantage of perfect competition is that it leads to production at minimum average total cost, while monopolistic competition leads to a higher average total cost with reduced output.

The advantage of monopolistic competition is that it leads to greater product variety, which consumers value, while in a perfectly competitive industry there is a single, identical product produced by all firms. Thus, the loss in allocative efficiency (higher *ATC*) that occurs in monopolistic competition has to be weighed against the gain of greater product variety.

4 Each firm's best strategy is to cheat regardless of the strategy of the other firm. Call the firms *A* and *B*. Firm *A* knows that if firm *B* follows the collusive agreement, *A* can increase its profit by cheating. If firm *B* cheats, then firm *A* knows that it must also cheat to minimize its loss of profit. Thus cheating is the dominant strategy for firm *A*. Accordingly, it is also the dominant strategy for firm *B*.

PROBLEMS

1 a Figure 13.4(a) illustrates a monopolistically competitive firm making a profit in the short run. The important feature of the graph is that at the profit-maximizing output, price is greater than average total cost. Profit is given by the shaded area in the graph.

b Figure 13.4(b) illustrates a firm that will shut down in the short run since price is less than average variable cost at the profit-maximizing (loss-minimizing) level of output.

c Figure 13.4(c) illustrates a firm making a loss but continuing to produce. The loss is given by the shaded area in the graph. Note that, at the profit-maximizing output, price is less than *ATC* but greater than *AVC*.

d Since firms are typically experiencing a loss, firms will leave the industry. This means that the demand curves facing each of the remaining firms will begin to shift out as they each attract some of the customers of the departing firms. As the firm demand curves shift out, losses are reduced. Firms will continue to have an incentive to leave until losses have

Figure 13.4

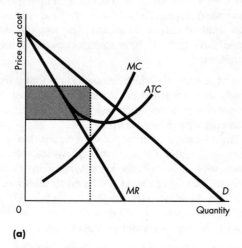

(a)

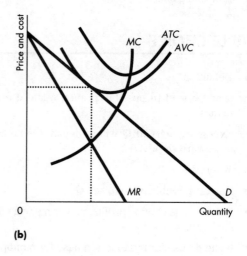

(b)

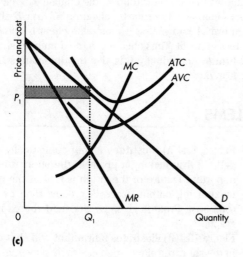

(c)

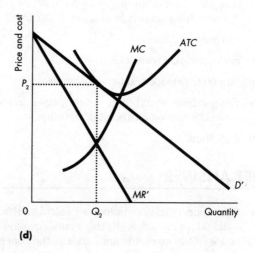

(d)

been eliminated. Thus, firm demand curves will continue to shift out until they are tangent to the *ATC* curve.

e Figure 13.4(d) illustrates a typical monopolistically competitive firm in long-run equilibrium. The key feature is that the demand curve facing the firm is tangent to the *ATC* curve at the profit-maximizing output. Thus the firm is making a zero profit.

2 a The players are firms *A* and *B*. Each firm has two strategies: to advertise or not to advertise. There are four possible outcomes: (1) both firms advertise, (2) firm *A* advertises but firm *B* does not, (3) firm *B* advertises but firm *A* does not, and (4) neither firm advertises.

b The payoff matrix is given in Table 13.1. The entries give the profit earned by firms *A* and *B* under each of the four possible outcomes.

Table 13.1

		Firm **B**	
		Advertise	Not advertise
Firm A	**Advertise**	A: 0 B: 0	A: £12 million B: −£15 million
	Not Advertise	A: −£5 million B: £12 million	A: £5 million B: £5 million

c First consider how firm *A* decides which strategy to pursue. If *B* advertises, *A* can advertise and make zero profit or not advertise and make a £5 million loss. Thus firm *A* will want to advertise if firm *B* does.

If *B* does not advertise, *A* can advertise and make a £12 million profit or not advertise and make a £5 million profit. Therefore, firm *A* will want to advertise whether firm *B* advertises or not. *B* will come to the same conclusion. Thus, the dominant strategy equilibrium is that both firms advertise.

3 a The firms will agree to produce 3,000 units each and sell at a price of £5 per unit. We determine this by noticing (Fig. 13.3b) that the profit-maximizing (monopoly) output is 6,000 units for the industry (*MR* = *MC* at 6,000) at a price of £5. Since the firms have agreed to divide output equally, each will produce 3,000 units.

b From Fig. 13.3(a) we determine that, at 3,000 units, each firm's average total cost is £4 per unit. Since price is £5, profit will be £3,000 for each firm.

c **i** At the new price of £4 the total quantity demanded is 8,000 units. Since *A* continues to produce 3,000 units this means that firm *B* will produce the remaining 5,000 units demanded.

ii Since firm *A* continues to produce 3,000 units, its average total cost continues to be £4 per unit. With the new price also at £4, firm *A* will make a zero profit.

iii Firm *B* has increased output to 5,000 units, which implies average total cost of £3 per unit. Thus, given a price of £4, firm *B*'s profit will be £5,000.

DATA QUESTIONS

The University of London Examination and Assessment Council accepts no responsibility whatsoever for the accuracy or method of working in the answers given.

1 The decision was reluctant because a cartel can give substantial advantages to their members. They are a special form of oligopoly and, as shown in Fig. 13.6 in the main text, can lead to higher prices and profits. They can also give a comforting stability to the market.

2 The arguments which can be put forward in favour of restrictive practices such as price agreements are discussed in detail in Chapter 20. For the present it is sufficient to say that some customers would benefit from charging the same price for cement throughout the country, irrespective of differences in the costs of production.

3 The position faced by UK cement manufacturers was very similar to that faced by OPEC members when a fall in oil prices forced them to abandon their price agreements. In the case of cement there was a fall in demand and an increase in supply and, as shown in Fig. 13.5, this caused price to fall from *a*, where the original demand and supply curves intersect, to a new equilibrium at *b*. This fall in price caused firms to 'cheat' in order to try to obtain the best for their particular firm.

Figure 13.5

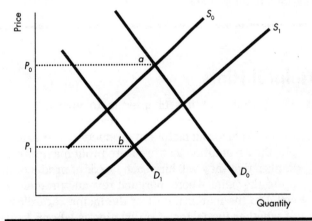

Chapter 14

Pricing and Allocating Factors of Production

Chapter In Perspective, Text Pages 374–403

This chapter explains how factor prices are determined. As with the prices of outputs of goods and services, the prices of productive inputs are determined in markets – markets for factors of production. These markets have many of the same characteristics as the markets for goods and services we examined in Chapters 11 to 13. Here we take a broad first look at markets for factors of production, leaving more detailed discussion of specific markets to later chapters.

Helpful Hints

1 The purpose of this chapter is to give a broad overview of the characteristics that are common to the markets for all factors of production. For example, the assumption that firms are profit maximizers implies that they will hire each factor of production up to the point where marginal revenue product is equal to the marginal cost of the factor, regardless of whether the factor of production is labour, land or capital.

2 Be sure to distinguish carefully between the marginal revenue product of a factor of production and the marginal revenue of a unit of output. As noted in the text, the marginal revenue product of a factor of production can be calculated by multiplying mar-

ginal revenue and marginal product ($MRP = MR \times MP$). We can think of this intuitively as follows: marginal product tells us how much more output we receive from using more of a factor, and marginal revenue tells us how much more revenue we receive from each unit of that additional output. Therefore, MP times MR tells us how much more revenue we receive from using more of the factor (the MRP).

Key Figures and Tables

Figure 14.1 Demand and Supply in a Factor Market, text page 376
This depicts the market for a factor of production. The quantity of a factor demanded decreases as the price

of the factor increases and the quantity of a factor supplied increases as the price of the factor increases.

Equilibrium occurs at the intersection of the demand and supply curves. The amount of total factor income is given by the area of the blue rectangle which is the price of a unit of the factor *(PF)* times the quantity of factors hired *(QF)*.

Figure 14.4 Marginal Revenue Product and the Demand for Labour at Wendy's Wash 'n' Wax, text page 382

A firm's demand for labour curve is the same as its marginal revenue product curve of labour. This is illustrated in the figure using the example of Wendy's Wash 'n' Wax.

Part (a) shows the average revenue product curve *(ARP)* and the corresponding marginal revenue product curve *(MRP)*. These curves plot the values reported in Table 14.1 on text page 380.

Notice that the values for *MRP* are plotted midway between the labour inputs used in their calculation. For example, the *MRP* of moving from 0 to 1 labourer is 20, so the value of 20 on the *MRP* curve is plotted midway between 0 and 1 labourers.

Part (b) constructs Wendy's demand for labour by asking how much labour Wendy would be willing to hire at alternative wage rates. Since Wendy is a profit maximizer, she will want to hire labour up to the point where the marginal revenue product of labour is equal to the wage rate. For example, if the wage rate is £10 per hour, Wendy will hire 3 workers since marginal revenue product is £10 when 3 workers are hired. Other points on the labour demand curve can be obtained in similar fashion. The result, as seen in part (b), is that the labour demand curve is the same as the *MRP* curve.

Figure 14.8 Labour Market Equilibrium, text page 391

This shows equilibrium in two different labour markets. Part (a) illustrates the labour market for footballers. Footballers are portrayed as having a very high marginal revenue product (as indicated by the height of the demand curve). Since the supply of talented footballers is low, the equilibrium wage rate for footballers is very high (£4,000 per game).

Part (b) illustrates the labour market for fast-food servers. The marginal revenue product of fast-food servers is relatively low and the supply is large. As a result, the wage rate for fast-food servers is quite low (£2 an hour).

Figure 14.10 Land Market Equilibrium, text page 393

This illustrates factors that determine whether equilibrium rent in specific land markets will be high or low. Part (a) illustrates a market in which the marginal revenue product of land is high but there is a very limited fixed supply (note that the quantity of land is measured in square metres). This market is for well-located urban land such as London's West End. The result is a very high land rent of £2,000 per square metre. Part (b) illustrates a market in which the marginal revenue product of land is not so high and the fixed supply is large (note that the quantity of land is measured in hectares). This is the market for Scottish farmland. The resulting equilibrium annual land rent is rather low: £300 per hectare.

Figure 14.11 Economic Rent and Transfer Earnings, text page 396

Total income received by the owners of a factor of production can be divided into two components: economic rent and transfer earnings. This figure illustrates the division. It shows the demand and supply curves for a factor of production. The total income received by the factor owners is given by the price of the factor *(PF)* times the quantity of the factor hired *(QF)*, which is the area of the green and yellow rectangle in the figure.

Transfer earnings are the part of income that is required to induce the supply of the factor. They are measured by the part of the income rectangle that lies below the supply curve, shown in yellow in the figure. Economic rent is the part of factor income that exceeds transfer earnings, shown in green in the figure.

Table 14.2 A Compact Glossary of Factor Market Terms, text page 381

While this chapter discusses a variety of specific factor markets, there are some important general terms that are used when discussing any factor markets. These terms are reviewed in this table, providing a handy resource for reference and review.

Table 14.3 Two Conditions for Maximum Profit, text page 383

In previous chapters we learned that a profit-maximizing firm will choose the level of output at which marginal revenue equals marginal cost *(MR = MC)*. In this chapter, we have seen that a profit-maximizing firm will hire a factor up to the level at which marginal revenue product equals the price of the factor *(MRP = PF)*. This table demonstrates that these two profit-maximization conditions are equivalent.

Table 14.4 A Firm's Demand for Labour, text page 384

This summarizes the law of demand as it applies to labour. The quantity of labour demanded is negatively related to the price of labour (the wage rate) along a given demand for labour curve. The table also indicates the *ceteris paribus* assumptions that, if changed, cause the demand for labour curve to shift.

SELF-TEST

CONCEPT REVIEW

1 Owners of factors of production receive income from firms for the use of those factors of production. The payment for labour is called _____ , the payment for capital is called _____ and the payment for land is called _____ .

2 An increase in the demand for a factor of production will _____ that factor's income. If the supply curve for a factor of production is very elastic, the resulting change in quantity traded will be _____ and the change in price will be _____ .

3 The demand for a factor as an input in the productive process rather than for its own sake is called a(n) _____ demand.

4 The change in total revenue resulting from _____ an additional unit of _____ is called the marginal revenue product of labour. If a profit-maximizing firm finds that the marginal revenue product of labour exceeds the wage, the firm should _____ the quantity of labour it hires.

5 The law of diminishing returns implies that the marginal revenue product curve will be _____ sloped. A firm's demand for labour curve will be based on its _____ _____ _____ curve.

6 If the price of the good produced by firm *A* increases, the demand curve for labour hired by firm *A* will shift to the _____ . A technological change that increases the marginal product of labour will shift the demand curve for labour to the _____ .

7 Other things being equal, the higher the elasticity of demand for a product, the _____ is the elasticity of demand for the labour that produces it. The more readily capital can be substituted for labour in production, the _____ elastic is the long-run elasticity of demand for labour.

8 The lowest wage for which a household will supply labour to the market is called its _____ wage.

9 An increase in the wage will have two effects on the quantity of labour supplied by a household. The income effect will lead to a(n) _____ in the quantity of labour supplied and the substitution effect will lead to a(n) _____ in the quantity of labour supplied.

10 The income received by the owner of a factor of production which exceeds the amount just necessary to induce the owner to offer the factor for use is called _____ _____ . The income required to induce the supply of the factor is called _____ earnings.

TRUE OR FALSE

— 1 When the elasticity of demand for labour is greater than 1, an increase in the supply of labour will lead to a decrease in labour income.

— 2 As long as the labour supply curve is positively sloped, an increase in the demand for labour will increase total labour income.

— 3 A profit-maximizing firm will hire the quantity of a factor of production for which the marginal revenue product equals the marginal cost of the factor.

— 4 The firm's demand for labour curve is the same as the average revenue product curve.

___ **5** The market demand curve for labour is the horizontal sum of the individual firms' marginal revenue product of labour curves.

___ **6** When discussing the short-run demand for labour, labour is considered to be the only variable input.

___ **7** If the production of good *A* is labour intensive, the demand for labour used in the production of good *A* is likely to be rather inelastic.

___ **8** The steeper the marginal product curve for labour, the less elastic is the firm's demand for labour.

___ **9** The short-run elasticity of demand for labour depends on the substitutability of capital for labour in the production process.

___ **10** If the wage rate increases, the substitution effect results in the household's increasing the time spent in market activities and decreasing the time spent in non-market activities.

___ **11** If the wage rate increases, the income effect results in the household's increasing its demand for leisure.

___ **12** The household supply curve for capital shows the relationship between the interest rate and the quantity of capital supplied.

___ **13** The market supply of a particular piece of land is perfectly elastic.

___ **14** In the long run, the equilibrium interest rate on capital will be the same in all industries.

___ **15** If the supply of a factor of production is perfectly inelastic, its entire income is transfer earnings.

MULTIPLE-CHOICE

1 The income received by owners of factors of production are wages paid for labour,
- **a** profit paid for capital and interest paid for money.
- **b** dividends paid for capital and interest paid for money.
- **c** dividends paid for capital and rent paid for land.
- **d** interest paid for capital and rent paid for land.
- **e** profit paid for capital and rent paid for land.

2 An increase in the supply of a factor of production will
- **a** increase the factor's income if the elasticity of factor demand is less than 1.
- **b** decrease the factor's income if the elasticity of factor demand is less than 1.
- **c** increase the factor's income if the elasticity of factor supply is less than 1.
- **d** decrease the factor's income if the elasticity of factor supply is less than 1.
- **e** always decrease the factor's income.

3 The change in total revenue resulting from employing an additional unit of capital is the
- **a** marginal product of capital.
- **b** marginal revenue of capital.
- **c** marginal revenue cost of capital.
- **d** marginal revenue product of capital.
- **e** average revenue product of capital.

4 When a firm is a price taker in the labour market, its marginal revenue product of labour curve is also its
- **a** marginal cost curve for labour.
- **b** demand curve for labour.
- **c** supply curve of labour.
- **d** supply curve of output.
- **e** average revenue curve.

5 A profit-maximizing firm will continue to hire units of a variable factor of production until the
- **a** marginal cost of the factor equals its marginal product.
- **b** marginal cost of the factor equals its average revenue product.
- **c** average cost of the factor equals its marginal revenue product.
- **d** marginal cost of the factor equals its marginal revenue product.
- **e** factor's marginal revenue product equals zero.

6 Suppose a profit-maximizing firm hires labour in a competitive labour market. If the marginal revenue product of labour is greater than the wage, the firm should
- **a** increase the wage rate.
- **b** decrease the wage rate.
- **c** increase the quantity of labour it hires.
- **d** decrease the quantity of labour it hires.
- **e** shift to a more labour-intensive production process.

7 The demand curve for a factor of production will shift to the right as a result of
a a decrease in the price of the factor.
b an increase in the price of the factor.
c a decrease in the price of a substitute factor.
d an increase in the price of a substitute factor.
e a decrease in the price of output.

8 A technological change that causes an increase in the marginal product of labour will shift
a the labour demand curve to the left.
b the labour demand curve to the right.
c the labour supply curve to the left.
d the labour supply curve to the right.
e **b** and **d**.

9 Other things being equal, the larger the proportion of total cost coming from labour, the
a more elastic is the demand for labour.
b less elastic is the demand for labour.
c more elastic is the supply of labour.
d less elastic is the supply of labour.
e lower is the demand for labour.

10 If the wage rate increases, the *substitution* effect will give a household an incentive to
a raise its reservation wage.
b increase its non-market activity and decrease its market activity.
c increase its market activity and decrease its non-market activity.
d increase both market and non-market activity.
e decrease both market and non-market activity.

11 If the wage rate increases, the *income* effect will give a household an incentive to
a raise its reservation wage.
b increase its non-market activity and decrease its market activity.
c increase its market activity and decrease its non-market activity.
d increase both market and non-market activity.
e decrease both market and non-market activity.

12 As the wage rate continues to rise, a household will have a backward-bending supply of labour curve if
a the income effect is in the same direction as the substitution effect.
b the wage rate rises above the reservation wage.
c the substitution effect dominates the income effect.
d the income effect dominates the substitution effect.
e leisure is an inferior good.

13 In the short run, a firm faces a supply of capital that is
a perfectly elastic.
b perfectly inelastic.
c positively sloped.
d negatively sloped.
e backward bending.

14 If the desire for leisure increased, the wage rate would
a rise and the quantity of labour hired would fall.
b rise and the quantity of labour hired would rise.
c fall and the quantity of labour hired would fall.
d fall and the quantity of labour hired would rise.
e fall and the quantity of labour demanded would rise.

15 Economic rent is the
a price paid for the use of a hectare of land.
b price paid for the use of a unit of capital.
c income required to induce a given quantity of a factor of production to be supplied.
d income received that is above the amount required to induce a given quantity of a factor of production to be supplied.
e transfer earnings of a factor of production.

16 Consider the supply schedule of a factor of production given in Table 14.1. If 4 units of the factor are supplied at a price of £8 per unit, what are the transfer earnings?
a £8
b £12
c £20
d £32
e none of the above

Table 14.1

Price of a factor (pounds)	Quantity of factor supplied
2	1
4	2
6	3
8	4
10	5

17 Consider the supply schedule of a factor of production given in Table 14.1. If 4 units of the factor are supplied at a price of £8 per unit, what is the economic rent?

a £8
b £12
c £20
d £32
e none of the above

SHORT ANSWER

1 Why will an increase in the supply of a factor of production result in an increase in income if the demand for the factor has elasticity greater than 1, and result in a decrease in income if the elasticity of demand for the factor is less than 1?

2 Why is the demand for a factor of production given by its marginal revenue product curve?

3 Discuss the substitution and income effects on the quantity of labour supplied if the wage rate *decreases*.

4 Why do younger households tend to save less than older households?

5 Are prices of retail goods in central London high because rents are high, or are rents high because prices are high? Explain.

PROBLEMS

1 Table 14.2 gives the total and marginal product schedules for a firm that sells its output in a competitive market and buys labour in a competitive market. Initially the price at which the firm can sell any level of output is £5 per unit and the wage rate at which it can purchase any quantity of labour is £15 per unit.

a Complete the first two blank columns in Table 14.2 by computing the TR and MRP_L corresponding to price of output = £5.

b The text informs us that the values obtained for the marginal revenue product of labour (MRP_L) are the same when they are computed by either of the following formulas:

$$MRP_L = \Delta TR / \Delta L$$

$$MRP_L = MR \times MP_L$$

where ΔTR = the change in total revenue, ΔL = the change in labour, MR = marginal revenue, and MP_L = marginal product of labour. Show

that these two formulas are equivalent for the case when the quantity of labour changes from 1 to 2 units.

Table 14.2

Quantity of labour (L) (workers)	Output (Q) (units per hour)	Marginal product of labour $(MP_l = \Delta Q/\Delta L)$ (units per worker)	Total revenue $(TR = £5 \times Q)$ (pounds per hour)	Marginal revenue product $(MRP = \Delta TR/L)$ (pounds per worker)	Total revenue $(TR = £3 \times Q)$ (pounds per hour)	Marginal revenue product $(MRP_l = TR/L)$ (pounds per worker)
0	0					
		...12				
1	12					
		...10				
2	22					
		...8				
3	30					
		...6				
4	36					
		...4				
5	40					
		...2				
6	42					

c If the firm maximizes profit, what quantity of labour will it hire? How much output will it produce?

d If total fixed cost is £125, what is the amount of profit?

e What is its profit if the firm hires one more unit of labour than the profit-maximizing quantity? One less unit of labour than the profit-maximizing quantity?

f Draw a graph of the demand for labour and the supply of labour and illustrate labour market equilibrium.

2 Now, suppose that the market demand for the output of the firm in Problem 1 decreases, causing the price of output to decrease to £3 per unit. The total and marginal product schedules remain unchanged.

a Complete the last two blank columns in Table 14.2 by computing the TR and MRP_L corresponding to price of output = £3.

b If the wage remains at £15 per unit of labour, what is the profit-maximizing quantity of labour that the firm will hire? How much output will it produce?

c Total fixed cost continues to be £125. What is the amount of profit?

d Will the firm shut down in the short run? Explain.

e Draw a new graph of the new labour market equilibrium.

3 The price of output for the firm in Problem 2 remains at £3 but the wage now rises to £21 per unit of labour. The total and marginal product schedules remain unchanged.

a What happens to the demand curve for labour (the *MRP* of labour curve)?

b Under these circumstances, what is the profit-maximizing quantity of labour that the firm will hire? How much output will it produce?

c Total fixed cost continues to be £125. What is the amount of profit?

d Draw a graph of the labour market equilibrium.

DATA QUESTIONS

The Market for Coal Miners

Figure 14.1 shows coal output in the United Kingdom in the period 1966–1990. One reason for the fall in output was that many British households installed central heating so that there was less demand for coal. Moreover, imports of coal increased as foreign producers exploited rich seams of coal that could be extracted at lower cost than in the United Kingdom. British Coal responded to the challenge by using new technology to improve productivity as shown in Fig. 14.2.

1 Explain the effect of falling demand for coal on the market for coal miners in the United Kingdom.

2 Explain the effect of improved productivity on the market for miners.

Figure 14.1

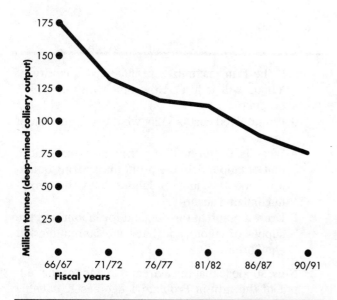

Fiscal years

Figure 14.2

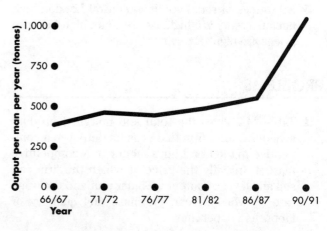

Source of figures: BCC Reports and Accounts 1989–1990.

ANSWERS

CONCEPT REVIEW

1 wages; interest; rent

2 increase; large; small

3 derived

4 hiring; labour; increase

5 negatively; marginal revenue product

6 right; right

7 higher; more

8 reservation

9 decrease; increase

10 economic rent; transfer

TRUE OR FALSE

1 F Fall in price leads to rise in income.

2 T Income is price times quantity.

3 T A specific example of the *MR = MC* rule.

4 F Same as *MRP* curve.

5 T The *MRP* curve is the firm's demand for labour curve.

6 T Definition.

7 F Tends to be elastic.

8 T Steep *MRP* curve means inelastic demand.

9 F Short-run elasticity of demand for labour depends on elasticity of demand for the product, labour intensity and slope of marginal product curve – capital cannot be substituted in short run.

10 T People will substitute work for leisure.

11 T Definition. Leisure is a normal good.

12 T Definition.

13 F Perfectly inelastic.

14 T Capital moves out of low-return industries to high-return industries, so equalizing returns.

15 F Entire income is economic rent.

MULTIPLE-CHOICE

1 d Definition.

2 b Increase in factor of production with inelastic demand leads to increase in ($PF \times QF$).

3 d Revenue from selling marginal product of capital.

4 b Shows quantity of labour hired at each wage rate.

5 d Where supply curve of factor to firm *(MC)* intersects with demand curve for factor *(MRP)*.

6 c Hiring more labour leads to more profit since *MRP > MC*. Firm cannot change wage.

7 d Firm demands more of the now relatively cheaper factor. **a** and **b** move along curve, **e** shifts curve left.

8 b Definition.

9 a Increase in wage leads to greater increase in total costs and increase in price of product. This leads to greater fall in sales and labour hired.

10 c Substitute work for leisure.

11 b Consume more normal goods including leisure, which entails working less.

12 d Income and substitution effects opposite for labour.

13 b Fixed in specific capital equipment.

14 a Labour supply would shift left.

15 d Definition. Price paid for land use is rent.

16 c £2 + £4 + £6 + £8.

17 b Total income (£32 = 4 × £8) minus transfer earnings (£20).

SHORT ANSWER

1 An increase in the supply of a factor of production will cause the price of the factor to decrease and the quantity of the factor hired to increase. Income received by the factor is equal to the price of the factor times the quantity hired. If the percentage increase in the quantity hired is greater than the percentage decrease in price (if the elasticity of demand for the factor is greater than 1), income will increase. Similarly, if the percentage increase in the quantity hired is less than the percentage decrease in price (if the elasticity of demand for the factor is less than 1), income will decrease.

2 The marginal revenue product curve for a factor of production gives its demand curve because firms are profit maximizers. As a consequence, they will hire an additional unit of a factor of production until the marginal cost of the factor (its price) is equal to the additional revenue from its use (its *MRP*). Thus, the quantity of the factor demanded at each price (the demand curve) is given by the *MRP* curve.

3 If the wage rate decreases, households will have a tendency to shift from work to leisure (the substitution effect), thus reducing the quantity of labour supplied. The lower wage also decreases the household's income and, thus, causes the household to reduce its demand for leisure and other normal goods (the income effect) thereby increasing the quantity of labour supplied.

4 Households will tend to save less when current income is low relative to expected future income and save more when current income is high relative to expected future income. Younger households are largely in this first situation while older households are largely in the second.

5 Rents are high because prices are high. Land in central London has a perfectly inelastic supply, so the price of land (its rent) is determined entirely by demand for the land.

Demand is high because shop owners know that the prime retail location will allow them to charge higher prices and potentially earn higher profits than in other locations.

PROBLEMS

1 a The completed columns for *TR* and MRP_L corresponding to price of output = £5 are shown in Table 14.3. The values for *TR* are obtained by multiplying the quantity of output by the price of output (£5). The values for MRP_L between any two quantities of labour are obtained by dividing the change in *TR* by the change in quantity of labour.

Table 14.3

Quantity of labour (L) (workers)	Output (Q) (units per hour)	Marginal product of labour $(MP_L = \Delta Q/\Delta L)$ (units per worker)	Total revenue $(TR = £5 \times Q)$ (pounds per hour)	Marginal revenue product $(MRP = \Delta TR/L)$ (pounds per worker)	Total revenue $(TR = £3 \times Q)$ (pounds per hour)	Marginal revenue product $(MRP_L = TR/L)$ (pounds per worker)
0	0		0		0	
		...12		...60		...36
1	12		60		36	
		...10		...50		...30
2	22		110		66	
		...8		...40		...24
3	30		150		90	
		...6		...30		...18
4	36		180		108	
		...4		...20		...12
5	40		200		120	
		...2		...10		...6
6	42		210		126	

b From **a**, the formula $MRP_L = TR/L$ yields a marginal revenue product of labour of 60 when the quantity of labour changes from 1 to 2 units. To confirm that the second formula ($MRP_L = MR \times MP_L$) gives the same answer when the quantity of labour changes from 1 to 2 units, substitute in the values for *MR* (£5, the price of an additional unit of output) and MP_L (12 units of output). This yields the same marginal revenue product of labour as above: £5 × 12 units = £60.

c The firm maximizes profit by hiring labour up to the point where the *MRP* of labour is equal to the marginal

cost of labour (the wage rate). That point occurs at 5 units of labour. The *MRP* of moving from 4 to 5 units of labour is 20, and the *MRP* of moving from 5 to 6 units of labour is 10. Thus, by interpolation, the *MRP* at exactly 5 units of labour is 15 (midway between 20 and 10). So when 5 units of labour are hired, the *MRP* of labour is equal to the wage rate (£15). Given that 5 units of labour are hired, the profit-maximizing output will be 40 units (from Table 14.3).

d To calculate profit, we must first calculate total revenue and then subtract total cost. Total revenue is £200 (40 units of output times £5 per unit) and total cost is also £200 – the sum of total variable (labour) cost of £75 (5 units of labour times £15 per unit) and total fixed cost of £125. Thus profit is zero.

e If the firm hires one more unit of labour (6 units), total revenue will be £210 (42 units of output times the £5 price). Total cost will be the £125 fixed cost plus £90 in total variable cost (6 units of labour times the £15 wage rate) or £215. Thus profit will be a negative £5 (a £5 loss).

If the firm hires one less unit of labour (4 units), total revenue will be £180 (36 units of output times the £5 price). Total cost will be the £125 fixed cost plus £60 in total variable cost (4 units of labour times the £15 wage rate) or £185. Thus profit will be a negative £5 (a £5 loss).

f The graph of labour market equilibrium appears in Fig. 14.3. The demand for labour is given by the firm's MRP_L curve which is labelled D_0 (D_1 will be discussed in Problem 2).

Notice that the values for *MRP* are plotted midway between the corresponding quantities of labour. For example, *MRP* of 60 is plotted midway between 0 and 1 units of labour.

Since the firm purchases labour in a perfectly competitive labour market, the supply of labour to the firm is perfectly elastic at the market wage rate. The labour supply curve is labelled *W* = £15. The equilibrium is at the intersection of these curves, and corresponds to a wage rate of £15 and a quantity of labour hired of 5 units.

2 a The completed columns for *TR* and MRP_L corresponding to price of output = £3 are shown above in Table 14.3. The values for *TR* are obtained by multiplying the quantity of output by the price of output (£3). The values for MRP_L between any two quantities of labour are obtained by dividing the change in *TR* by the change in quantity of labour.

b If the wage rate remains at £15, the profit-maximizing quantity of labour will fall to 4 units since MRP_L equals the wage rate at 4 units of labour. The *MRP* of moving from 3 to 4 units of labour is 18, and the *MRP* of moving from 4 to 5 units of labour is 12. Thus, by interpolation, the *MRP* at exactly 4 units of labour is 15 (midway between 18 and 12). Given that 4 units of labour are employed, the profit-maximizing output will be 36 units (from Table 14.3).

Figure 14.3

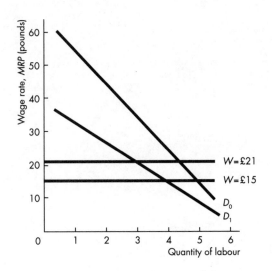

c Profit equals total revenue minus total cost. Total revenue is £108 (36 units of output times £3 per unit) and total cost is £185 – the sum of total variable (labour) cost of £60 (4 units of labour times £15 per unit) and total fixed cost of £125. Thus profit is –£77, or a loss of £77.

d The firm will not shut down since total revenue (£108) is enough to cover total variable cost (£60) and part of fixed cost. If the firm decided to shut down, it would lose the £125 of fixed cost rather than just £77.

e The graph of labour market equilibrium appears in Fig. 14.3. The new demand for labour is given by the firm's new MRP_L curve, which is labelled D_1. The supply of labour has not changed; it continues to be horizontal at £15, the competitive market wage. The new equilibrium is at the intersection of these curves, and corresponds to a wage rate of £15 and a quantity of labour hired of 4 units.

3 a Since marginal revenue and the marginal product of labour are unaffected by a change in the wage rate, the demand curve for labour (the MRP of labour) will remain at D_1.

b If the wage rate rises to £21, the profit-maximizing quantity of labour will fall to 3 units since MRP_L equals the wage rate at 3 units of labour. Given that 3 units of labour are employed, the profit-maximizing output will be 30 units (from Table 14.3).

c Profit equals total revenue minus total cost. Total revenue is £90 (30 units of output times £3 per unit) and total cost is £188 – the sum of total variable (labour) cost of £63 (3 units of labour times £21 per unit) and total fixed cost of £125. Thus profit is –£98, or a loss of £98.

d See Fig. 14.3. The relevant demand for labour curve continues to be D_1, but the labour supply curve reflects the rise in the competitive wage rate; it is now horizontal at a wage rate of £21 (labelled $W = £21$). The equilibrium is at the intersection of these curves and corresponds to a wage rate of £21 and a quantity of labour hired of 3 units.

DATA QUESTIONS

1 The demand for a factor of production such as labour is derived from the demand for the product made by that factor. Hence, demand for coal miners is derived from the demand for coal. When this falls there will be a fall in the demand for miners and consequently a fall in their wages as shown in Fig. 14.4.

Figure 14.4

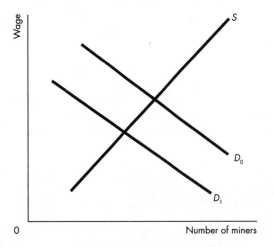

2 The demand for a factor depends on its MRP. An improvement in technology which increases labour productivity will lead to a rise in the MRP of miners and hence to a rise in the number of miners employed as shown in Fig. 14.5.

Figure 14.5

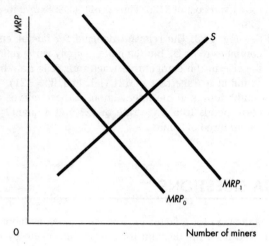

Chapter 15 Labour Markets

Chapter In Perspective, Text Pages 406–427

Labour markets play a very important role in the economic well-being of almost every household since household income is determined largely by the operation of these markets. This chapter looks more carefully at labour markets to explain how wage rates and employment levels are determined. We investigate why some groups earn more than other groups: why skilled workers earn more than unskilled workers; why union workers earn more than non-union workers; and why, on average, men earn more than women. We also examine why some people are paid by the hour and others on performance criteria.

Helpful Hints

1 This chapter introduces the concept of a monopsonist, a firm that is the only buyer in a market, such as labour. The monopsonist faces an upward-sloping supply curve of labour and, as a result, its marginal cost of labour curve (*MCL*) is different from the labour supply curve.

The monopolist, as the only seller in an output market, faces a downward-sloping demand curve. The marginal revenue from the sale of an additional unit of output is *less* than the selling price because the monopolist must *lower* the price on all previous units as well. Thus, the *MR* curve lies *below* the demand curve for the monopolist. For the monopsonist in a labour market, the marginal cost of hiring an additional unit of labour is *higher* than the wage because the monopsonist must *raise* the wage on all 'previous' units of labour as well. Thus, the *MCL* curve lies *above* the supply of labour curve for the monopsonist.

2 A particular labour market may *not* establish a wage rate and a level of employment in the simple sense of the intersection of demand and supply curves. The broader notion of labour market equilibrium includes determination of quantity and of the type of compensation scheme, of which time rates of pay (wage rates) are only one possibility. Equilibrium occurs when the market is at rest in the sense that no worker or firm has an incentive to change.

Key Figures and Table

Figure 15.1 Skill Differentials, text page 407
Different workers receive different wages depending on their level of skill. This figure shows how differences in wages can be explained using the model of competitive labour markets. Part (a) shows that the demand for skilled labour is higher than the demand for unskilled labour because skilled labour has a

higher marginal revenue product. The vertical distance between the two demand curves gives the difference in marginal revenue product, which is the marginal revenue product of the skill.

Part (b) gives the supply curves for skilled and unskilled labour. It illustrates that the supply curve for skilled labour lies above the supply curve for unskilled labour because skills are costly to obtain. As a result, skilled labour must receive a higher wage in order to induce workers to obtain the skill. The vertical distance between the two labour supply curves gives the required additional wage.

Part (c) puts together the demand and supply curves from parts (a) and (b) in order to look at the equilibrium wage rate for each type of labour. Not surprisingly, the equilibrium wage rate for skilled workers is higher than for unskilled workers.

Figure 15.3   A Union Restricting Supply in a Competitive Labour Market, text page 411

Competitive equilibrium occurs where the demand curve D_C cuts the supply curve S_C. If a union restricts employment the supply curve will shift to S_U and wages rise from £5 to £8 an hour. If the union can increase demand for the product made by the workers, the result will be a new demand curve, higher wages and more jobs.

Figure 15.4 A Union Demanding a Wage Increase in a Competitive Labour Market, text page 412

Original equilibrium is 1,000 hours at a wage of £5. If the union prevents its members working at less than £5 an hour the result is a new supply curve of labour S_U. This increases the wages, but cuts the number of hours. As in Fig. 15.3, an increase in demand for the product raises both wages and employment.

Figure 15.5 A Monopsony Labour Market, text page 415

A monopsonist is the only buyer of a product or factor of production. Profit is maximized when the marginal

cost of labour curve *MCL* equals the marginal revenue product curve *MRP*.

Figure 15.6 Minimum Wage in Monopsony, text page 415

A firm wishing to maximize profit will hire labour until the *MRP* of labour equals its marginal cost. In this case equilibrium will be at £5 an hour and 50 hours will be employed. If the government forces the firm to pay a minimum wage of £7 an hour, the result is a new kinked supply curve S' because the firm has to pay more than £7 if it wishes to employ more than 70 hours of labour. In this case the firm would employ 70 hours. Part (b) shows the effect of higher wages.

Figure 15.8 Discrimination, text page 418

This illustrates how discrimination affects wage rates and employment. Part (a) shows that discrimination against a particular group of workers (in this case, life insurance saleswomen) will reduce wages and employment below what they would have been without discrimination. The prejudice of customers makes the marginal revenue product of the workers who are discriminated against (MRP_{DA}) lower than the marginal revenue product without discrimination (MRP).

Part (b) shows that customer prejudice in favour of a particular group (in this case, life insurance salesmen) makes the marginal revenue product of the workers who are discriminated in favour of (MRP_{DF}) higher than the marginal revenue product without discrimination. This will raise wages and employment above what they would have been without discrimination.

Table 15.1 A Compact Glossary on Unions, text page 409

This conveniently brings together much of the terminology associated with labour unions. It provides definitions of terms used frequently in analysing the operation of unions in the economy.

SELF-TEST

CONCEPT REVIEW

1 The demand curve for skilled labour lies _____ the demand curve for unskilled labour, because the marginal revenue product of

skilled workers is _____ than that of unskilled workers. The supply curve for skilled labour lies _____ the supply curve for unskilled labour, because skills are costly to acquire.

2 Education and training can be viewed as investments in _____ capital. The value of that capital is the _____ _____ of the extra future earnings that result from the increased education or training.

3 A market in which there is only one buyer is called _____ . If there is only one firm that buys labour, the wage rate will be _____ than the marginal cost of labour. A situation in which a single seller of labour, such as a union, faces a single buyer of labour is called _____ monopoly.

4 Three possible explanations of wage differentials between the sexes are discussed in Chapter 15. The first explanation is discrimination. The second explanation is that the two groups have differences in _____ capital. The third explanation is that there are differences in the degree of _____ in market and non-market activities.

5 Often, either worker effort or worker output is difficult, if not impossible, to observe. An individual who sets a rule for compensating workers, which motivates the worker to choose activities advantageous to the individual, is called a(n) _____ . Each worker in such a situation is called a(n) _____ .

TRUE OR FALSE

__ **1** The marginal revenue product of unskilled workers is lower than that of skilled workers.

__ **2** The vertical distance between the labour supply curves for skilled and unskilled workers is the marginal revenue product of the skill.

__ **3** The larger the marginal revenue product of the skill and the more costly it is to acquire, the smaller is the wage differential between skilled and unskilled workers.

__ **4** Unions support minimum wage laws in part because they increase the cost of unskilled labour, a substitute for skilled union labour.

__ **5** A firm that is a monopsonist in the labour market must compete with other firms for the labour it hires.

__ **6** The more elastic is labour supply, the less opportunity a monopsonist has to make an economic profit.

__ **7** In a monopsonistic labour market, the introduction of a minimum wage that is above the current wage will raise the wage but reduce employment.

__ **8** The evidence suggests that, after allowing for the effects of skill differentials, union workers earn no more than non-union workers.

__ **9** Economic theory tells us that discrimination in employment will result in wage differentials.

__ **10** If males on average earn more than females, we can conclude that there must be discrimination.

MULTIPLE-CHOICE

1 Which of the following is *not* a reason why the wage of skilled workers exceeds the wage of unskilled workers?
  a The market for skilled workers is more competitive than the market for unskilled labour.
  b The marginal revenue product of skilled workers is greater than that of unskilled workers.
  c The cost of training skilled workers is greater than the cost of training unskilled workers.
  d Skilled workers have acquired more human capital than unskilled workers.
  e The demand curve for skilled workers lies to the right of the demand curve for unskilled workers.

2 The economic value of the increase in human capital owing to additional education is
  a the money cost of the additional education.
  b the money cost of the additional education plus forgone earnings.
  c the present value of all expected future earnings.
  d the present value of all extra expected future earnings that are the result of the additional education.
  e none of the above.

3 Which of the following would unions be *least* likely to support?

a increasing the legal minimum wage
b restricting immigration
c encouraging imports
d increasing demand for the goods their workers produce
e increasing the marginal product of union labour

4 The most important way in which unions increase wages is by
  a increasing the marginal (physical) product of labour.
  b increasing the marginal revenue product of labour.
  c increasing the demand for labour.
  d decreasing the supply of labour.
  e increasing the marginal cost of labour.

5 Figure 15.1 illustrates a monopsonist in the labour market (*MCL* = marginal cost of labour). The profit-maximizing wage rate and quantity of labour hired will be
  a £4 per hour and 800 hours of labour.
  b £4 per hour and 400 hours of labour.
  c £7 per hour and 600 hours of labour.
  d £9 per hour and 400 hours of labour.
  e none of the above.

Figure 15.1

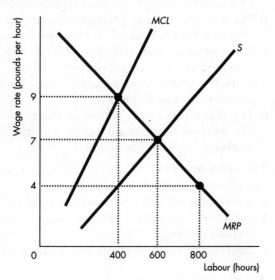

6 If the labour market illustrated in Fig. 15.1 became competitive, the equilibrium wage rate and quantity of labour hired would be
  a £4 per hour and 800 hours of labour.
  b £4 per hour and 400 hours of labour.

c £7 per hour and 600 hours of labour.
d £9 per hour and 400 hours of labour.
e none of the above.

7 Wage differentials between males and females can be explained by
  a occupational differences.
  b human capital differences.
  c degree of specialization differences.
  d discrimination.
  e all of the above.

8 Which of the following cases is most likely to be characterized by a time rate of pay?
  a Individual effort is readily observed but individual contribution to output is not.
  b Individual effort is not readily observed but individual contribution to output is.
  c Neither individual effort nor individual contribution to output is readily observable.
  d Monitoring costs are very high.
  e None of the above statements is most likely.

SHORT ANSWER

1 Members of trade unions earn wages well above the minimum wage. Even so, why is it in the interest of a union to support increases in the legal minimum wage?

2 Bob and Sue form a household. They have decided that Sue will fully specialize in market activity and Bob will pursue activities both in the job market and in the household. If most households are like Bob and Sue, why would the result be a difference between the earnings of men and women, even if there is no discrimination?

3 In a principal–agent model, what is the objective of the principal?

4 Many large firms are owned by a group of stockholders who hire managers to run the firm. Why is profit sharing a good compensation scheme for top management in such a firm?

PROBLEMS

1 Figure 15.2 shows the demand for and supply of skilled and unskilled labour. S_U and S_S are the supply curves for unskilled and skilled workers, respectively, and D_U and D_S are the demand curves for unskilled and skilled workers, respectively.

Figure 15.2

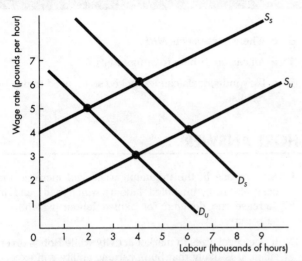

Figure 15.3

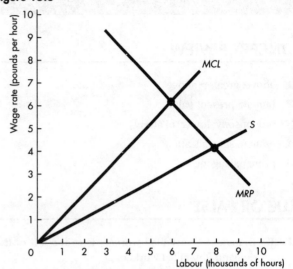

a What is the marginal revenue product of skill if 5,000 hours of each kind of labour are hired?

b What is the amount of extra compensation per hour required to induce the acquisition of skill at the same level of hiring?

c What are the equilibrium wage and quantity of labour in the market for skilled labour?

d What are the equilibrium wage and quantity of labour in the market for unskilled labour?

2 Yuri has an opportunity to increase his human capital by taking a training course that will raise his income by £100 every year for the rest of his life. Assume that there are no other benefits of the course. The cost of the course is £1,200 and Yuri's best alternative investment pays an interest rate of 10 per cent per year for the rest of his life. Should Yuri pay the £1,200 and take the course? Explain.

3 Figure 15.3 illustrates a profit-maximizing monopsonist in the labour market.

a What wage rate will the monopsonist pay and how much labour will be employed? What is the value of labour's marginal revenue product at this level of employment?

b If this were a competitive labour market with the same marginal revenue product curve, what would the equilibrium wage rate and the level of employment be?

c Suppose the government imposes a minimum wage of £4 per hour. What wage rate will the monopsonist pay and how much labour will be employed now?

DATA QUESTIONS

Table 15.1 Wages in Non-agricultural Activities: Earnings Per Hour (National Currencies)

		1985	1987	1989	1991
Denmark	M	87	102	112	121
	F	73	83	93	101
France	M	39	42	45	–
	F	32	34	36	–
Germany	M	17	19	20	22
	F	13	13	15	17
Netherlands	M	20	18	19	20
	F	16	14	14	15
United Kingdom	M	3.7	4.2	4.8	5.7
	F	2.6	2.9	3.4	4.0

Source: *Yearbook of Labour Statistics 1993*, International Labour Organisation, Geneva. Reproduced courtesy of Datastream International.

1 Analyse these statistics and comment on your results, noting in particular:

a In which countries is the difference between male and female pay

i the greatest?

ii the least?

b What reasons do you think explain these differences?

2 Why, on average, do men earn more than women?

ANSWERS

CONCEPT REVIEW

1 above; greater; above

2 human; present value

3 monopsony; lower; bilateral

4 human; specialization

5 principal; agent

TRUE OR FALSE

1 **T** Demand for unskilled workers is to the left of the demand for skilled workers.

2 **F** Vertical distance is compensation for cost of acquiring skill.

3 **F** The larger the wage differential.

4 **T** Increase in the price of a substitute leads to rise in demand for union labour.

5 **F** Definition. Monopsonist is sole buyer.

6 **T** Draw diagram to verify this.

7 **F** True for competitive market.

8 **F** Union members earn more than non-union members with similar skills.

9 **T** Discrimination means that those discriminated against earn less.

10 **F** Differences may be due to discrimination, human capital differences and/or specialization.

MULTIPLE-CHOICE

1 **a** Wage differences not due to competitive differences. In any case, an increase in competitiveness would lead to a fall in skilled wages.

2 **d** Return on investment in additional education.

3 **c** Increase in imports would lead to a fall in sales of domestic products and hence in demand for domestic labour.

4 **d** **a, b** and **c** are indirect ways.

5 **b** Quantity of labour is where *MCL* intersects *MRP*. Then the lowest wage required for labour to supply that quantity (on supply curve).

6 **c** Where *S* intersects *MRP*.

7 **e** All can contribute to differentials.

8 **a** Lazy individuals can be sacked so no need to pay by results.

SHORT ANSWER

1 An increase in the minimum wage will increase the cost of hiring unskilled labour, which will tend to increase the demand for skilled labour which is a substitute.

2 If Sue specializes in market activity while Bob is diversified, it is likely that Sue's earning ability will exceed Bob's owing to the gains from her specialization. If most households followed this pattern of specialization, the income of women would exceed that of men even without discrimination.

3 The principal wants to set a compensation rule that motivates the agent to make choices that are to the best advantage of the principal.

4 In this case the owners (stockholders) are the principals and the top managers are the agents. Neither the effort nor the output of the managers can be easily monitored. But since the decisions of managers have a direct and significant bearing on the profit of the firm, their incentive is to make decisions that maximize profit if they share in any increase in profit through a profit-sharing compensation scheme.

PROBLEMS

1 **a** The marginal revenue product of skill is the difference between the marginal revenue products of skilled versus unskilled labour; the vertical distance between the demand curves for skilled and unskilled labour. In Fig. 15.2, the marginal revenue product of skill is £3 per hour when 5,000 hours of each kind of labour are employed.

b Since labour supply curves give the minimum compensation workers are willing to accept in return for supplying a given quantity of labour, the extra compensation for skill is the vertical distance between the supply curves of skilled and unskilled labour. At 5,000 hours of employment for both kinds of labour, this is £3 per hour.

c In equilibrium in the market for skilled labour, the wage rate will be £6 per hour and employment will be 4,000 hours of labour. This occurs at the intersection of the D_S and S_S curves.

d In equilibrium in the market for unskilled labour, the wage rate will be £3 per hour and employment will be 4,000 hours of labour. This occurs at the intersection of the D_U and S_U curves.

2 Yuri should take the course only if the value of the course exceeds the cost of the course. The cost of the course is £1,200 while the value of the course is the present value of the extra £100 in income Yuri can expect to receive each year for the rest of his life. The present value of this income stream is the amount of money which, if invested today at 10 per cent (Yuri's best alternative return) would yield an equivalent stream of income. Thus the present value of the extra income is £1,000. Since this is less than the cost of the training course, Yuri should not take it.

3 a The profit-maximizing monopsonist will hire additional labour up to the point where the marginal cost of labour *(MCL)* equals the marginal revenue product of labour *(MRP)*. Referring to Fig. 15.3, this means that the monopsonist will hire 6,000 hours of labour. The wage rate is given by the labour supply curve *S* and, for 6,000 hours of labour, will be £3 per hour. This is less than the £6 per hour marginal revenue product of labour.

b In a competitive market, the wage rate would be £4 per hour and 8,000 hours of labour would be employed.

c If the government establishes a minimum wage at £4 per hour, the marginal cost of labour to the monopsonist becomes constant at £4 per hour (up to 8,000 hours of labour). Thus, equating the marginal cost of labour and the marginal revenue product of labour leads to a wage rate of £4 and 8,000 hours of labour employed.

DATA QUESTIONS

1 a The overwhelming fact is that in all countries men earn significantly more than women, and that this difference is persistent, despite equal pay legislation.
  i The difference (at the end of the period) is greatest in the United Kingdom.
  ii Denmark is the country with the least difference.

b There are many possible reasons, but one is that Denmark (and to a lesser extent other continental countries) have social legislation which not only reduces discrimination but also encourages women to obtain human capital and to specialize in occupations which are well paid. The United Kingdom has a very high percentage of women workers, but many of these are in low paying occupations.

2 The explanations for the lower pay earned by women are: discrimination, differences in human capital and in degree of specialization. These are discussed in detail in the main text, pages 416–421, and there is no need to repeat the arguments here.

Chapter 16 Capital and Natural Resource Markets

Chapter In Perspective, Text Pages 428–456

This chapter continues a more detailed examination of markets for specific factors of production and we expand our understanding of capital and natural resource markets. What determines interest rates and share prices? How are the prices of natural resources determined? Can we rely on market forces to regulate the use of exhaustible resources? These and related issues are discussed in this chapter.

Helpful Hints

1 A profit-maximizing firm will hire an additional unit of a factor as long as the factor's use adds more to revenue than to cost; in other words, as long as its marginal revenue product *(MRP)* is greater than its marginal cost *(MC)*. The profit-maximizing quantity will be the quantity at which the marginal revenue product of a factor is just equal to its marginal cost. Since, in a competitive market, the marginal cost is the price of the factor (P_F), this profit-maximizing condition becomes $MRP = P_F$ in a competitive factor market. This implies that the demand curve for a factor is given by its *MRP* curve.

2 The profit-maximizing condition given in Helpful Hint 1 is easy to apply in the case of capital markets in which capital is rented. The profit-maximizing

firm will rent capital up to the point at which the marginal revenue product per rental period is equal to the rental price.

If, however, a firm considers purchasing capital rather than renting it, we must be careful in applying the profit-maximizing condition. The reason is that capital is generally operated over more than one period and will generate marginal revenue products that are distributed over time. The purchase price, however, must be paid now. Therefore, in order to compare the purchase price (P_F) with the stream of marginal revenue products, we must compute the present value of that stream.

In the case of capital that will be used over more than one period, the profit-maximizing condition becomes: hire an additional unit of capital until the present value of the stream of marginal revenue products is equal to the price of the unit of capital. Since the net present value is defined as the difference between the present value of the stream of marginal revenue products and the price of the unit of capital, an equivalent condition is: the net present value of the last unit of capital is zero.

3 Note that financial analysts equate a *rise* in bond prices with a *fall* in interest rates.

Key Figures and Tables

Figure 16.1 Capital Market Flows, text page 433
This shows the major participants in capital markets and indicates the directions of interactions among them.

Figure 16.5 Capital Market Equilibrium, text page 443
Equilibrium in the capital market is achieved at the interest rate at which the quantity of capital demanded is equal to the quantity of capital supplied. For the example in this figure, the equilibrium interest rate is 6 per cent and the equilibrium quantity of capital traded is £120 billion.

Table 16.1 Balance Sheet of Dawson's Mountain Bikes on 1 January 1994, text page 430
A balance sheet is a list of assets and liabilities. This table illustrates the concept of a balance sheet by reporting the assets and liabilities of the firm Dawson's Mountain Bikes. The firm's assets (items owned by the firm) are listed on the left-hand side of the table, and the firm's liabilities (money the firm owes – to the bank and to Dawson) are listed on the right. Note that the two sides of the balance sheet balance because total assets equal total liabilities.

Table 16.2 Financial Assets and Physical Assets of Dawson's Mountain Bikes on 1 January 1994, text page 430
This uses the same information contained in the balance sheet of Table 16.1, but distinguishes between financial assets and physical assets. For this firm, net financial assets are –£225,000 since financial liabilities exceed financial assets.

The bottom part of the table lists the firm's physical assets, which consist of its inventory of bikes and fixtures and fittings. Total capital is £225,000.

Table 16.5 The Balance Sheet for the United Kingdom's Personal Sector on 31 December 1993, text page 434
This shows the assets of the UK's personal sector. Financial assets exceed liabilities.

Table 16.6 Net Present Value of an Investment by Taxsave, text page 436
A firm will decide to purchase an additional unit of capital if the net present value of the investment is positive; if the present value of the marginal revenue product of the investment is greater than the cost of the unit of capital. The calculation of net present value is illustrated in this table using the example of Anne's decision to purchase a new computer for her firm, Taxsave.

Part (a) of the table reports the information necessary to compute the net present value of the investment: the price of the computer, the life of the computer, the marginal revenue product in each year and the interest rate.

Part (b) uses this information to compute the present value of the flow of marginal revenue product.

In part (c), the cost of the computer is subtracted from the present value of the marginal revenue product of the computer to obtain the net present value of the investment. Since the net present value is positive, it pays Anne to buy the computer.

SELF-TEST

CONCEPT REVIEW

1 There are two broad classes of assets. Those that are paper claims against a household, firm, or the government are called _____ assets, and physical capital like buildings, factories and machinery are called _____ assets.

2 A firm maximizes its net worth when the _____ _____ of the marginal revenue product of capital is equal to the price of capital. Thus, an increase in the interest rate means that the quantity of capital demanded will _____ .

3 The quantity of capital supplied depends on the _____ decisions of households. As the interest rate increases, the substitution effect causes a(n) _____ in the quantity of capital supplied by the household; the income effect causes a(n) _____ in the quantity of capital supplied if the household is a net borrower. If the proportion of young people in the population increases, we would expect to see the capital supply curve shift to the _____ .

4 A takeover occurs when the stock market value of a firm is _____ than the present value of expected future profits from operating the firm. A merger occurs when the two firms involved think that by combining their assets, their combined stock market value will _____ .

5 Natural resources that can be used only once and not replaced are called _____ natural resources. According to the Hotelling Principle, the market for the stock of such a resource will be in equilibrium when the price of the resource is expected to rise over time, at a rate equal to the _____ _____ .

6 The price at which it no longer pays to use a natural resource is called its _____ price.

7 The higher the interest rate, the _____ will be the current price of a natural resource. The higher the marginal revenue product of a natural resource, the _____ will be its current price. The larger is the initial stock of a natural resource, the _____ will be its current price.

TRUE OR FALSE

___ 1 If we add depreciation to net investment, we have gross investment.

___ 2 Portfolio decisions determine a person's wealth.

___ 3 The quantity of capital is an example of a flow.

___ 4 If the price of a unit of capital exceeds the present value of its marginal revenue product, a profit-maximizing firm should buy it.

___ 5 If the net present value of an investment is positive, a profit-maximizing firm will buy the item.

___ 6 A new machine that is expected to last one year and, at the end of the year, increase firm revenue by £1,050, sells at a price of £1,000. The firm should buy the machine if the interest rate is 6 per cent.

___ 7 In equilibrium, if financial asset A is riskier than financial asset B, it will have a higher rate of interest.

___ 8 To say that the price of a bond has risen is the same as saying that the yield on the bond has declined.

___ 9 If a cheap substitute for oil is developed, we would expect to see the choke price for oil decline.

___ 10 The higher the interest rate, the lower is the current price of a natural resource.

___ 11 The economic model of exhaustible natural resources implies that the market will provide an automatic incentive to conserve as the resource gets closer to being depleted.

MULTIPLE-CHOICE

1 Which of the following is a real asset?
a a shovel
b IBM shares
c money
d a General Motors bond
e all of the above

2 Which of the following is an example of a stock?
a investment
b depreciation
c capital
d income
e none of the above

3 The decline in the value of capital resulting from its use over time is given by
a the level of saving.
b investment.
c net investment.
d gross investment minus net investment.
e net present value.

4 Firms that are primarily engaged in taking deposits, making loans and buying securities are called
  a brokers.
  b financial intermediaries.
  c insurance companies.
  d monopsonists.
  e pension funds.

5 A profit-maximizing firm will choose to buy an extra unit of capital whenever
  a the present value of the flow of marginal revenue product is greater than zero.
  b the cost of capital exceeds the present value of the flow of marginal revenue product.
  c the cost of capital equals the present value of the flow of marginal revenue product.
  d net present value is greater than zero.
  e none of the above occurs.

6 Which of the following would cause the supply of capital curve to shift to the right?
  a an increase in the proportion of young households in the population
  b an increase in the interest rate
  c a decrease in the interest rate
  d an increase in average household income
  e an increase in the marginal revenue product of capital

7 A machine that costs £2,000 will generate marginal revenue product of £1,100 at the end of one year and the same amount at the end of two years. What is the net present value of the machine if the rate of interest is 10 per cent?
  a −£90.91
  b −£49.90
  c 0
  d £90.91
  e £1,909.09

8 Bond A is more risky than bond B. Then, in equilibrium,
  a the interest rate on A must be higher than that on B.
  b the interest rate on A must be lower than that on B.
  c the interest rate on A must be equal to the interest rate on B.
  d no one will want to buy bond A.
  e only those who prefer risk will buy bond A.

9 A *takeover* of a firm is likely to occur when
  a the stock market value of the firm is higher than expected future profit from operating the firm.
  b the stock market value of the firm is lower than expected future profit from operating the firm.
  c current firm profit is higher than expected future profit from operating the firm.
  d current firm profit is lower than expected future profit from operating the firm.
  e interest rates are low.

10 Which of the following is an exhaustible natural resource?
  a coal
  b land
  c water
  d trees
  e none of the above

11 The yield on a stock of a natural resource is the
  a rate of interest on the loan used to buy the resource.
  b marginal revenue product of the resource.
  c marginal revenue product of the resource divided by its price.
  d marginal revenue product of the resource multiplied by the market interest rate.
  e rate of change in the price of the resource.

12 The current price of a natural resource is higher when
  a its marginal revenue product is lower.
  b the stock of the resource remaining is larger.
  c the interest rate is lower.
  d the choke price is lower.
  e none of the above is true.

SHORT ANSWER

1 Why does the quantity of capital demanded increase when the interest rate falls?

2 Suppose firms A and B earned the same amount of profit per share in the most recent year but that the price of a share of stock in firm A is higher than for firm B.
  a What does this imply about the two firms' price–earnings ratios?
  b What does this reflect about expected future profits of the two firms?

3 Why will the market for the stock of an exhaustible natural resource be in equilibrium only if the price of the resource is expected to rise at a rate equal to the rate of interest?

4 Why does a higher interest rate imply a lower current price of an exhaustible resource?

PROBLEMS

1 Larry's Lawn Care began the year with a stock of capital equal to £100,000. The value of that stock of capital depreciated by 12 per cent during the year. Larry also bought £10,000 worth of new lawn care equipment during the year. What was Larry's gross investment during the year? Net investment?

2 Larry's Lawn Care is considering the purchase of additional lawn mowers. These lawn mowers have a life of 2 years and cost £120 each. Marginal revenue products for each year are given in Table 16.1

Table 16.1

Number of lawn mowers	MRP in first year (pounds)	MRP in second year (pounds)	NPV (r = 0.05) (pounds)	NPV (r = 0.10) (pounds)	NPV (r = 0.15) (pounds)
1	100	80			
2	80	64			
3	72	62			

a Complete Table 16.1 by computing net present values *(NPV)* if the interest rate is 5 per cent (*r* = 0.05), 10 per cent (*r* = 0.10), or 15 per cent (*r* = 0.15).
b How many lawn mowers will Larry's purchase if the interest rate is 15 per cent? 10 per cent? 5 per cent?
c Construct an approximate lawn mower demand curve for Larry by graphically representing the three points identified in **b** and drawing a curve through them.

3 Gunk is an exhaustible natural resource and we are running out of it. There are only 1,215 barrels of gunk remaining. Table 16.2 gives the marginal revenue product schedule for gunk.

Table 16.2

Barrels of gunk per year	Marginal revenue product (pounds)
0	14.64
133	13.31
254	12.10
364	11.00
464	10.00
555	9.09

a Draw a graph of the demand curve for gunk (as a flow).
b What is the choke price of gunk?
c Suppose that the interest rate is 10 per cent.
  i What is the current equilibrium price of a barrel of gunk? How did you determine this?
  ii If the current year is year 1, complete Table 16.3 for each year until the stock of gunk is exhausted.

Table 16.3

Year	Price (pounds per barrel of gunk)	Initial stock of gunk (barrels)	Final stock of gunk (barrels)
1		1,215	
2			
3			
4			
5			

DATA QUESTIONS

Controlling the Price of Copper
The price of copper is usually very sensitive to fluctuations in the business cycle because it is used extensively in industries such as electronics, construction and transport which are themselves subject to considerable fluctuations. About 70 per cent of world copper exports are controlled by a group of producers who, in 1967, formed an organization called Conseil Intergovernmental des Pays Exportateurs de Cuivre (CIPEC). CIPEC aims to coordinate the activities of its members in order to ensure 'continuous increase in the growth of real earnings of copper exports'. CIPEC faces considerable difficulties in achieving this goal.

1 Why is the price of copper 'usually very sensitive to fluctuations in the business cycle'?

2 Explain the factors which determine the price and the quantity of a natural resource such as copper.

3 What difficulties do you think face CIPEC in its attempt to achieve an increase in the real earnings of copper exports?

Source: Adapted from University of London Schools Examining Board GCE A-Level question, June 1989. © University of London Examinations and Assessment Council.

ANSWERS

CONCEPT REVIEW

1 financial; real

2 present value; decrease

3 savings; increase; decrease; left

4 lower; increase

5 exhaustible; interest rate

6 choke

7 lower; higher; lower

TRUE OR FALSE

1 **T** Net investment = gross investment – depreciation.

2 **F** Other factors also influence wealth.

3 **F** Quantity of capital is a stock.

4 **F** Reverse is true.

5 **T** Definition.

6 **F** Present value = £1,050/(1 + 0.06) = £990.56. NPV = £990.56 – £1,000 = –£9.44. Since NPV is negative, don't buy.

7 **T** Higher interest compensates for higher risk.

8 **T** Bond yield = (fixed earnings)/(price of bond).

9 **T** Less demand for oil so people would stop using it, even at a lower price.

10 **T** Inverse relationship.

11 **T** Because price will rise.

MULTIPLE-CHOICE

1 **a** Others are financial assets.

2 **c** Others are flows.

3 **d** Equals depreciation.

4 **b** Definition.

5 **d** When the present value of the flow of the marginal product exceeds the cost of capital.

6 **d** **a** would cause a leftward shift, **b** and **c** movements along supply curve, **e** shifts demand curve.

7 **a** NPV = [£1,100/(1.1) + £1,100/(1.1)^2] – £2,000.

8 **a** Higher return is necessary to compensate for higher risk if investors are to hold the bond.

9 **b** Definition.

10 **a** Others are non-exhaustible natural resources.

11 **e** Definition.

12 **c** Reverse of **a** and **b** is true. No direct relation between current and choke prices.

SHORT ANSWER

1 Profit-maximizing firms will demand capital as long as the present value of the stream of future marginal revenue product from the new capital exceeds the price of the new capital; in other words, as long as its net present value is positive. Since a lower interest rate implies that the present value of any given future stream of marginal revenue product will be larger, the net present value will be positive for a larger number of additional capital and thus more capital will be purchased. Therefore, the quantity of capital demanded increases as the interest rate falls.

2 **a** The price–earnings ratio is the current price of a share of stock divided by the most recent profits per share. Thus, the price–earnings ratio of firm *A*'s stock is greater than the price–earnings ratio of firm *B*'s stock. This implies that, although the recent profits (per share) of the two firms may be the same, future profits (per share) for firm *A* are expected to be higher than for firm *B*.

b The price of a share of stock represents the present value of *expected* future profits, so a higher price implies higher expected future profits.

3 The yield on the stock of an exhaustible resource is the percentage rate of change in the price of the resource. In order for the market for the stock of the resource to be in equilibrium, there must be no incentive for movement into or out of the market. This will be the case only if the yield on the stock of the exhaustible resource is the same as the yield on other assets, which is given by the rate of interest.

4 In equilibrium, the current price of the resource will be the price which, if the price continues to increase at a rate equal to the interest rate, the choke price will be reached at the same time that the resource is depleted. A higher interest rate means that the price is expected to rise at a faster rate. Therefore, if it is to reach the choke price at the right time, it must start from a lower current price.

PROBLEMS

1 Gross investment is £10,000, the amount of the purchase of new capital. Net investment is –£2,000, the amount of gross investment minus depreciation of £12,000.

2 a The completed table is shown as Table 16.4. *NPV* is calculated as the present value of the stream of marginal revenue products resulting from an investment minus the cost of the investment. For lawn mowers with a 2-year life, the *NPV* is calculated using the following equation:

$$NPV = \frac{MRP_1}{1+r} + \frac{MRP_2}{(1+r)^2} - P_L$$

where MRP_1 and MRP_2 are the marginal revenue products in the first and second years, respectively, and P_L is the price of a lawn mower. The values of MRP_1 and MRP_2 are given in Table 16.1 for 1, 2 and 3 lawn mowers and P_L is given as £120. The values for *NPV* given in Table 16.4 are obtained by substituting these values into the above equation and evaluating the expression for the alternative values of r, the interest rate.

Table 16.4

Number of lawn mowers	MRP in first year (pounds)	MRP in second year (pounds)	NPV (r = 0.05) (pounds)	NPV (r = 0.10) (pounds)	NPV (r = 0.15) (pounds)
1	100	80	47.80	37.02	27.45
2	80	64	14.24	5.62	-2.04
3	72	62	4.81	-3.31	-10.51

b If the interest rate is 15 per cent, only 1 additional lawn mower will be purchased since the second lawn mower has negative net present value. If the rate of interest is 10 per cent, 2 lawn mowers will be purchased, and if the rate of interest is 5 per cent, 3 lawn mowers will be purchased.

c The approximate lawn mower demand curve is illustrated in Fig. 16.1. The curve indicates that, at an interest rate of 15 per cent, 1 lawn mower will be demanded. At an interest rate of 10 per cent, 2 lawn mowers will be demanded, and, at an interest rate of 5 per cent, 3 lawn mowers will be demanded.

Figure 16.1

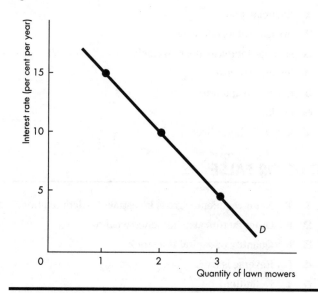

3 a The demand curve for gunk is given by the marginal revenue product curve. It is illustrated in Fig. 16.2.

b The choke price for gunk is £14.64. This is the price that is high enough that the resource will not be used at all.

c i If the interest rate is 10 per cent, the current price of a barrel of gunk is £10. We know that the current (equilibrium) price must be such that if the price of gunk is increasing at a rate of 10 per cent per year (equal to the rate of interest), the stock will be depleted just as the choke price is achieved. We can find the current price by noting that (1) the choke price is £14.64 and (2) the remaining stock is 1,215 barrels and working backwards.

Since the price of gunk is growing at the rate of 10 per cent per year, the price in the year before the choke price is reached must be £14.64 (the choke price) divided by 1.10 (1 + the 10 per cent growth

Figure 16.2

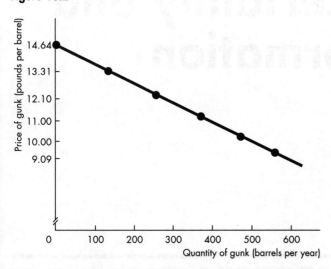

Table 16.5

Year	Price (pounds per barrel of gunk)	Initial stock of gunk (barrels)	Final stock of gunk barrels)
1	10.00	1,215	751
2	11.00	751	387
3	12.10	387	133
4	13.31	133	0
5	14.64	0	

rate of price) or £13.31. From Table 16.2 (and recognizing that gunk is just depleted as the £14.64 price is reached) we can infer that 133 barrels of gunk would be purchased in that year. Proceeding in a similar manner, working backwards until all 1,215 barrels of gunk have been purchased, we discover that the current equilibrium price must be £10.

ii Using the procedure outlined in **c**, Table 16.3 can be completed as shown in Table 16.5.

DATA QUESTIONS

1 a Demand for raw materials such as copper fluctuates very considerably over time. When the economy is booming demand rises very quickly; when the world economy is in recession demand for materials such as copper falls very considerably. One reason for this is that manufacturers increase their stocks when times are good, but cut them when depression occurs. The topic of fluctuations in investment is discussed in more detail in Chapter 25.

2 The factors which determine the price and the flow of a natural resource such as copper are the rate of interest, the demand for the flow and the stock of the resource remaining. These are discussed in detail in the text on pages 446–451.

3 The earnings of CIPEC members depend on the demand for and the supply of copper. The factors which affect demand are discussed in Questions 1 and 2; they are very difficult for any organization to control. CIPEC, like OPEC, attempts to control the price by restricting supply. However, individual members may break ranks to increase their own sales if they think it will benefit them. This is discussed in the main text on pages 341–366.

Chapter 17 Uncertainty and Information

Chapter In Perspective, Text Pages 457–478

This chapter explains how people make decisions when they are uncertain about the consequences, and why it pays to buy insurance and disseminate information. It also looks at a variety of markets in which uncertainty and information play important roles.

Helpful Hints

1 The existence of risk and uncertainty is an objective feature of reality. How decision makers cope with uncertainty, however, depends on their attitudes towards risk. Some people are more risk averse than others.

A utility of wealth schedule reflects a person's degree of risk aversion. Economists believe that most people's utility of wealth schedules exhibit diminishing marginal utility as wealth increases. However, for two people, for example, Alexis and Madeleine, Alexis's marginal utility of wealth may decrease at a faster rate than Madeleine's. Alexis would be more risk averse than Madeleine and less likely to undertake risky ventures that offer the possibility of a high return at the cost of a greater probability of loss. *Ceteris paribus*, Alexis will be less likely to undertake risky ventures because she will attach a relatively greater utility weight to the probable decrease in wealth from a loss than to the probable increase in wealth from a success. Because of these relative weights, a risk-averse person is also more likely to take out insurance against loss.

2 Two important concepts for analysing choice under uncertainty are expected wealth and expected utility. Expected wealth (sometimes called expected value) is the average wealth arising from all possible outcomes. It is computed as the weighted average of the wealth associated with each possible outcome, where the weights are the probabilities of each outcome. For example, if there are three possible outcomes yielding wealth of W_1, W_2, and W_3, and the probabilities associated with these outcomes are p_1, p_2, and p_3, respectively, then expected wealth equals

$$(W_1 \times p_1) + (W_2 \times p_2) + (W_3 \times p_3).$$

Expected utility is the average utility arising from all possible outcomes. It is calculated in the same way. If the utilities associated with each possible wealth outcome are U_1, U_2 and U_3, respectively, then expected utility equals

$$(U_1 \times p_1) + (U_2 \times p_2) + (U_3 \times p_3).$$

In analysing choice under uncertainty, we must first calculate expected wealth. But a decision is ultimately based on the expected utility associated with that expected wealth.

Key Figures

Figure 17.1 The Utility of Wealth, text page 461
This assumes that utility can be measured. Increasing wealth means taking more risks, so the utility of wealth curve flattens out.

Figure 17.2 Choice under Uncertainty, text page 461
The average utility arising from all possible outcomes is called *expected* utility. In the figure, extra risk is compensated for by extra expected wealth, leaving Tania indifferent between two alternatives.

Figure 17.5 Optimal-search Rule, text page 466
Finding things out costs time. It would be foolish to spend a week to find the cheapest packets of drawing pins in London – the cost would exceed the benefit.

In this figure, the marginal cost of search is constant – shown by a horizontal line. As the lowest price found declines, the marginal utility (expected benefits) of searching further also falls.

The optimum-search rule is to search until the reservation price (the highest price the buyer is willing to pay) is found and then to buy at the lowest price found.

SELF-TEST

CONCEPT REVIEW

1 Facing uncertainty, it is rational to maximize _____ _____, that is, the average utility for all possible events.

2 The utility of wealth schedule describes attitudes towards _____. Increased wealth leads to increased utility, but the _____ _____ of wealth declines.

3 People buy insurance to reduce _____. Insurance works by _____ risks. It is profitable because people are risk _____.

4 Buyers searching for the lowest price use the _____ search rule, that is they search until the expected _____ of search equal the marginal _____ of search, then buy.

5 Moral _____ arises when there is a post-agreement incentive to increase personal benefits at the expense of others who are uninformed.

6 Risk in financial markets can be lowered by _____ asset holdings (don't put all your eggs in one basket), buying in _____ markets and _____ markets (taking positions in forward markets without necessarily taking delivery of goods).

TRUE OR FALSE

1 Risk is a state in which more than one event may occur, but we don't know which one.

2 The more rapidly your marginal utility of wealth diminishes, the less risk averse you are.

3 A risk-neutral person has a constant marginal utility of wealth.

4 If Petro-Anglia drills in an uncharted region of the Atlantic Ocean without any idea of the likelihood of striking oil, Petro-Anglia faces uncertainty rather than risk.

5 Risk neutrality makes insurance possible and profitable.

6 Advertising increases the price of the goods advertised.

7 Advertising for search goods is designed mainly to inform rather than persuade.

8 If you are careless with matches because you know you have fire insurance, an adverse selection problem exists.

9 The rational expectation of price is the price at which expected demand equals expected supply.

___ **10** A forecast based on rational expectations will be correct.

___ **11** In an efficient market, the actual price is rarely equal to the expected future price.

___ **12** If prices in an efficient market are volatile, expectations about future prices must be volatile.

MULTIPLE-CHOICE

1 The more rapidly a person's marginal utility of wealth diminishes, the
   a more risk inclined the person is.
   b more risk neutral the person is.
   c more risk averse the person is.
   d more likely it is that the person has a moral hazard problem.
   e less likely the person is to take out insurance.

2 The expected value of a game that gives a 50 per cent chance of winning £60 and a 50 per cent chance of winning nothing is
   a £10.
   b £20.
   c £30.
   d £60.
   e none of the above.

3 On a normal utility of wealth curve diagram with wealth on the horizontal axis and utility on the vertical axis, the marginal utility of wealth is
   a a point on the horizontal axis.
   b a point on the vertical axis.
   c an area under the utility of wealth curve.
   d the slope of a line from the origin to a point on the utility of wealth curve.
   e the slope of the utility of wealth curve.

4 Goods whose quality can be assessed only after they are bought are called
   a private information goods.
   b search goods.
   c experience goods.
   d inferior goods.
   e lemons.

5 The buyer's reservation price is
   a the lowest price that the buyer is willing to pay.
   b the highest price that the buyer is willing to pay.
   c the price equating the expected marginal benefit and marginal cost of searching.

   d **a** and **c**.
   e **b** and **c**.

6 According to the utility of wealth schedules in Table 17.1,
   a Chloe is more risk averse than Esther.
   b Esther is more risk averse than Chloe.
   c Chloe is risk neutral, while Esther is risk averse.
   d Esther is risk neutral, while Chloe is risk averse.
   e it is impossible to calculate risk aversion and risk neutrality.

Table 17.1

Wealth (pounds)	Utility (units)	
	Chloe	Esther
0	0	0
20	45	60
40	80	90
60	110	100
80	130	105

7 Chloe's expected wealth from an investment opportunity that will pay either £40 or £80 with equal probability is
   a £60.
   b £105.
   c £120.
   d £210.
   e none of the above.

8 Which compensation scheme is most likely to be efficient in the case of a chief executive officer of a corporation?
   a commission on sales
   b share of total firm profits
   c salary based on years of employment
   d tournament-like prize
   e **b** and **d**

9 Which compensation scheme is most likely to be efficient in the case of a salesperson?
   a hourly wage rate
   b commission on sales
   c share of total firm profits
   d salary based on years of employment
   e none of the above

10 A rational expectation of a price is not
  a based on forecasts of expected demand *(ED)*.
  b based on forecasts of expected supply *(ES)*.
  c the price at which *ED = ES*.
  d necessarily equal to actual price.
  e a forecast that uses all relevant available information.

11 Mira must choose Option *A* or Option *B*. Option *A* guarantees her £10,000. Option *B* gives her £5,000 with probability 0.5 and £15,000 with probability 0.5. Having a normal utility of wealth curve, Mira will
  a prefer and choose *A*.
  b prefer and choose *B*.
  c prefer *A* but choose *B*.
  d prefer *B* but choose *A*.
  e be indifferent between *A* and *B*.

12 If there are three possible events and each has a probability of occurrence of one-third, then
  a neither uncertainty nor risk exists.
  b uncertainty exists, but not risk.
  c risk exists, but not uncertainty.
  d both uncertainty and risk exist.
  e there is not enough information to distinguish between uncertainty and risk.

13 In an efficient market, which of the following statements is false?
  a The current price is equal to the expected future price.
  b The current price embodies all available information.
  c No forecastable profit opportunities exist.
  d Prices are stable.
  e Expectations are subject to fluctuations.

14 An efficient compensation scheme
  a cannot incorporate the effects of luck.
  b will not be accepted by the agent.
  c splits revenues equally between the agent and principal.
  d maximizes the agent's expected income.
  e maximizes the principal's expected profit.

15 Optimizing buyers will devote additional resources searching for information when
  a expected marginal benefit is positive.
  b expected marginal benefit is less than the marginal cost of searching.
  c expected marginal benefit equals the marginal cost of searching.

  d marginal cost of searching is positive.
  e none of the above.

16 If buyers cannot assess the quality of used cars and there are no warranties,
  a only bad used cars will be sold.
  b only good used cars will be sold.
  c good cars will be sold at a higher price than bad cars.
  d there is a moral hazard problem.
  e there is no adverse selection problem.

17 In a forward market, a contract is made today for an exchange at a future date. The typical forward contract specifies
  a price but not quantity.
  b quantity but not price.
  c both price and quantity.
  d neither price nor quantity.
  e none of the above.

18 After purchasing theft insurance, you decide to spend less on home security devices. Your behaviour is an example of
  a adverse selection.
  b free riding.
  c insurance market signalling.
  d asymmetric information.
  e moral hazard.

19 Advertising
  a for search goods is designed to persuade.
  b for experience goods is designed to inform.
  c that is persuasive increases competition.
  d is costly.
  e is all of the above.

20 Stock market prices are volatile because
  a expectations are irrational.
  b expectations change frequently owing to new information.
  c stock markets are inefficient markets.
  d stockholders do not behave like inventory holders.
  e all of the above statements are true.

SHORT ANSWER

1 If you agree to pay the first £200 worth of damage (£200 excess), your car insurance premium might be £1,000 per year. But if you agree to a £500 excess, your insurance premium might be £800 per year. Why do insurance companies charge premiums that are related inversely to the total loss that the customer agrees to bear?

2 Many large firms are owned by a group of shareholders who hire managers to run the firm. Why is profit sharing a good compensation scheme for top management in such a firm?

3 Define a rational expectation and explain how to go about calculating the rational expectation of a future price.

4 What is meant by an efficient market? Explain why the current market price will always be equal to the expected future price in an efficient market.

PROBLEMS

1 Table 17.2 presents the utility of wealth schedules for Peter and Mary. Who is more risk averse, Peter or Mary? Explain.

Table 17.2

Wealth (pounds)	Utility (units)	
	Peter	Mary
0	0	0
20	100	60
40	150	110
60	175	150
80	187	180
100	193	200

2 Table 17.3 presents Leonard's utility of wealth schedule. Leonard is considering an investment project that will pay either zero or £20,000 with equal probability.

Table 17.3 Leonard's Utility of Wealth

Wealth (thousands of pounds)	Utility (units)
0	0
4	52
5	60
8	79
10	87
15	98
20	104

a What is Leonard's expected wealth from the project?
b What is Leonard's expected utility?
c What is Leonard's cost of risk?
d Is Leonard willing to undertake the project if it costs him £5,000?

3 Dylan owns some land on which he usually grows vegetables. This year he has accepted a job as a bartender and will not be able to tend the vegetable patch. Dylan is thinking of hiring Thomas, who has some gardening experience, to grow vegetables for him.

Thomas has been milking cows for a dairy farmer, and working very hard for £30 per day. From conversations with Thomas, Dylan gathers that Thomas places a value of £10 on relaxation – Thomas prefers to relax rather than to work, but a day of working for £10 or a day of relaxing are equally acceptable.

Dylan knows that total income from growing vegetables depends on how hard the cultivator works and on weather conditions. Table 17.4 gives the alternative total incomes from the possible combinations of work effort and weather conditions. There is a 50–50 chance of good or bad weather.

Table 17.4 Total Income from Vegetable Growing (pounds per day)

Weather	Worker's effort	
	Works hard	Relaxes
Good	£160	£80
Bad	£80	£80

Dylan is considering two alternative compensation schemes:

Scheme 1 Dylan pays Thomas £31 per day.
Scheme 2 Dylan pays Thomas £10 per day plus 26 per cent of the total income from vegetable growing.

Using this information, work out which compensation scheme Dylan should adopt. Remember that an efficient compensation scheme has two features. It must maximize profit for the principal and be acceptable to the agent (make the agent at least as well off as in the best alternative job).

4 The expected demand for and supply of wheat are given in Table 17.5.

Table 17.5

Price (£/bushel)	Expected quantity demanded	Expected quantity supplied
	(millions of bushels per year)	
4.00	140	350
3.50	180	320
3.00	220	290
2.50	260	260
2.00	300	230
1.50	340	200

a If nothing happens to change expectations, what is the rational expectation of the price of a bushel of wheat? Of the quantity of wheat traded?

b Suppose that actual demand is exactly as expected but that the weather turns out to be better than usual for growing wheat. Actual wheat production (momentary supply) is 40 million bushels greater than the quantity expected. What is the quantity of wheat actually traded? What is the actual price of a bushel of wheat?

c How much wheat would farmers have supplied if they had accurately forecast the price in **b**?

DATA QUESTION

There is no data question for this chapter.

ANSWERS

CONCEPT REVIEW

1 expected utility

2 risk; marginal utility

3 risk; pooling; averse

4 optimal; costs; benefits

5 hazard

6 diversifying; forward; futures

TRUE OR FALSE

1 F Definition uncertainty.

2 F More risk averse.

3 T Definition. Linear marginal utility of wealth curve.

4 T Risk means probabilities could be estimated.

5 F Risk aversion.

6 F Advertising is costly, but it may cut price through increased competition and greater economies of scale.

7 T Quality can be assessed before buying.

8 F Moral hazard problem.

9 T Definition.

10 F Will be correct on average.

11 F Actual price = expected future price.

12 T Definition.

MULTIPLE-CHOICE

1 c Moral hazard irrelevant. More likely to insure.

2 c $(\$60 \times 0.5) + (\$0 \times 0.5)$.

3 e Change in utility/change in wealth.

4 c Definition.

5 e Definition.

6 b Marginal utility of wealth diminishes more rapidly.

7 a $(\$40 \times 0.5) + (\$80 \times 0.5)$.

8 e Strong connection effort/competition and profit.

9 b Directly links unmonitored effort to outcome.

10 d Equals actual price on average.

11 a Expected value *A* and *B* equal, but *A* less risky, so preferable.

12 d Definitions. Risk is subset of uncertainty.

13 d Prices fluctuate with changes in expectations.

14 e Designed by principal and must be acceptable to agent.

15 e When expected marginal benefit > marginal cost.

16 a Opposite **d**, **e** true.

17 c Definition.

18 e Definition.

19 d **a**, **b** and **c** true if reverse persuade and inform.

20 b Only source of change in efficient market.

SHORT ANSWER

1 By allowing customers to pay lower premiums if they agree to bear a higher share of total damages, insurance companies alleviate the adverse selection problem. High-risk drivers know that they are accident prone and are willing to pay higher premiums for nearly full coverage, while low-risk drivers know that they seldom have accidents and will choose lower premiums with lower coverage. With excesses, the adverse selection problem of high-risk people driving low-risk people out of the market is less likely to occur. The insurance company can charge differential premiums that reflect the different risks that it is insuring.

2 The owners (shareholders) are the principals and the top managers are the agents. Neither the effort nor the output of the managers can be monitored easily. But since the decisions of managers have a direct and significant bearing on the profit of the firm, their incentive is to make decisions that maximize profit if they share in any increase in profit through a profit-sharing compensation scheme.

3 A rational expectation is the forecast that uses all of the relevant information available about past and present events and that has the least possible error. The rational expectation of a future price is the price at which expected quantity demanded equals expected quantity supplied. Thus, to calculate the rational expectation of a price, we must forecast, using all available and relevant information, the variables that determine the expected demand and expected supply curves.

The forecast of expected demand depends on the expected values of the prices of substitutes and complements in consumption, income, population and preferences. The forecast of expected supply depends on the expected values of the prices of substitutes and complements in production, the prices of resource inputs and technology.

4 An efficient market is one in which the actual price embodies all available relevant information. The price will thus be equal to the rational expectation of the future price and there will be no forecastable profit opportunities. The current market price will always be equal to the expected future price in an efficient market because any deviation would be eliminated immediately since it provides an expected profit opportunity.

PROBLEMS

1 To find out who is more risk averse, we must determine whose marginal utility of wealth decreases faster as wealth increases. Table 17.6 presents the total and marginal utility of wealth for Peter and Mary. Since Peter's marginal utility of wealth decreases faster than Mary's, Peter is the more risk averse.

Table 17.6

Wealth (pounds)	Peter			Mary	
	Total utility (units)	Marginal utility (units)		Total utility (units)	Marginal utility (units)
0	0			0	
		...100			...60
20	100			60	
		...50			...50
40	150			110	
		...25			...40
60	175			150	
		...12			...30
80	187			180	
		...6			...20
100	193			200	

2 a Leonard's expected wealth is (£0 × 0.5) + (£20,000 × 0.5) = £10,000.

b Leonard's expected utility is (0 × 0.5) + (104 × 0.5) = 52 units.

c Uncertain wealth of £0 or £20,000 yields expected wealth of £10,000 and expected utility of 52 units. From Table 17.3, we can see that certain (no-risk) wealth of £4,000 also yields utility of 52 units. The cost of risk is £6,000, the amount by which expected wealth must be increased beyond no-risk wealth to give the same utility as the no-risk situation (£10,000 – £4,000).

d For Leonard, the forgone utility of the £5,000 cost of investing in the project (60 units) is greater than the expected utility of the risky project (52 units). Leonard is not willing to undertake the project.

3 Total income depends on whether Thomas works hard or relaxes and whether there is good or bad weather. The probability of good or bad weather is 0.5.

If Thomas works hard, expected total income is ($160 × 0.5) + ($80 × 0.5) = $120.

If Thomas relaxes, expected total income is ($80 × 0.5) + ($80 × 0.5) = $80.

To see which compensation scheme is efficient, calculate the outcome of each scheme for the principal and the agent.

Scheme 1: Dylan (principal) pays Thomas (agent) $31 per day. Will Thomas work hard or relax? If Thomas relaxes, he receives $31. Since he does not have to exert himself, the value of relaxing is also $31. If Thomas works hard, he also receives $31, but since he has to exert himself, the value of working hard is $31 – $10 = $21. Thomas will choose to relax. Expected total income will be $80 per day, with $31 going to Thomas and $49 going to Dylan.

Scheme 2: Dylan (principal) pays Thomas (agent) $10 plus 26 per cent of the total income from vegetable growing. If Thomas relaxes, he receives $10 + (0.26 × $80) = $30.80. Since he does not have to exert himself, the value of relaxing is also $30.80. If Thomas works hard, he receives $10 + (0.26 × $120) = $41.20. Since he has to exert himself, the value of working hard is $41.20 – $10 = $31.20. Thomas will choose to work hard. Expected total income will be $120 per day, with $41.20 going to Thomas and $78.80 going to Dylan.

Both Dylan and Thomas are better off under compensation scheme 2. But is Thomas better off growing vegetables under compensation scheme 2 than he would be milking cows? If Thomas milks cows, he earns $30, but since he has to work hard, the value to him is $30 – $10 = $20. This is lower than the value he receives working hard growing vegetables under scheme 2. Therefore, compensation scheme 2 is more efficient.

4 a The rational expectation of the price of a bushel of wheat is $2.50 since, at that price, expected quantity demanded equals expected quantity supplied. The rational expectation of the quantity of wheat traded is 260 million bushels.

b The momentary supply turns out to be 300 million bushels, 40 million bushels more than the 260 million expected. Thus the quantity of wheat traded is 300 million bushels. To clear the market of the 300 million bushels (where momentary supply intersects demand), the actual price of a bushel of wheat must be $2.

c If farmers had accurately forecast the price of $2 per bushel, they would have produced 230 million bushels of wheat. Thus, farmers would regret having produced too much wheat (300 million bushels instead of 230 million).

Chapter 18

The Distribution of Income and Wealth

Chapter In Perspective, Text Pages 479–504

Income is the payment to owners of factors of production for the use of those resources. Individuals with more resources to sell or whose resources sell for a higher price will receive larger incomes. Thus, the distribution of income depends on the distribution of ownership of resources used in production and the market prices of those resources.

This chapter discusses the distribution of income and wealth in the United Kingdom, and addresses the following questions. How unequally are income and wealth actually distributed? What accounts for this inequality? What are the consequences of government policies intended to redistribute income or wealth? What are the major ideas that constitute a 'fair' distribution of income?

Helpful Hints

1 The major tool used by economists to picture the degree of inequality of income or wealth in an economy is the Lorenz curve.

2 A major message of this chapter is that statistics used to construct Lorenz curves do not always give an accurate picture of inequality.

For example, distribution of wealth which excludes the value of human capital will give a distorted picture relative to the distribution of income.

You should also understand why the distribution of annual (static) income will give a distorted picture relative to the distribution of lifetime (dynamic) income.

Finally, you should understand why the distribution of before-tax, before-transfer income will give a distorted picture relative to the distribution of after-tax, after-transfer income.

3 The issue of fairness discussed in this chapter is a normative issue. Note, however, that the trade-off between equity and economic efficiency (the so-called big trade-off) is a positive issue.

Key Figures

Figure 18.1 Lorenz Curves for Original Income and Wealth, text page 482

A Lorenz curve is a useful way to represent the distribution of income or wealth. It plots the cumulative percentage of income earned by a given cumulative percentage of families. This figure gives Lorenz curves for the United Kingdom.

Figure 18.3 Distribution of Income by Selected Household Characteristics, 1992, text page 487

This indicates the importance of certain characteristics in influencing a household's income. The most important characteristic influencing the incidence of low income is family type. Other important characteristics include the sex of the head of the household, whether the head is in or out of the labour force, the age of the head and the geographical region of the household.

Figure 18.5 Lorenz curves for Imaginary and Actual Economies, text page 491

This compares the United Kingdom with an imaginary economy where everyone has the same lifetime income and consumption.

SELF-TEST

CONCEPT REVIEW

1 Of the three basic factors of production, _____ earns the largest share of total income.

2 The diagram used by economists to illustrate the cumulative percentage of households ranked from the poorest to the richest is called a(n) _____ _____ . The straight line running through the middle of the diagram is called the line of _____ .

3 The most important factor in determining whether a person receives a high income or a low income is _____ .

4 An income tax system in which the marginal tax rate rises as income rises is called a(n) _____ income tax. A(n) _____ income tax is one in which the marginal tax rate falls with the level of income while for a(n) _____ income tax, the marginal tax rate is constant for all levels of income.

5 The distribution of income that would prevail in the absence of government policies is called the _____ distribution. The distribution that takes account of government policies is called the distribution after _____ and _____ .

6 A gift from one generation to the next is called a(n) _____ .

7 The tendency for people to marry within their own socio-economic class is called _____ _____ . This tendency contributes to a(n) _____ in the unequal distribution of wealth.

8 Theories of distributive justice that emphasize the equality of the outcomes of economic activity are called _____ - _____ theories while those emphasizing the equality of opportunity are called _____ theories.

9 The _____ theory states that the fairest outcome is the one that maximizes the sum of the utilities of all individuals in society.

10 According to the _____ theory, the fairest distribution of income gives the poorest member of society the largest income possible.

TRUE OR FALSE

____ **1** In the United Kingdom income is more unequally distributed than wealth.

____ **2** The further the Lorenz curve is from the line of equality, the more equal the distribution of income.

___ **3** Under a proportional income tax, the marginal tax rate does not change as income rises.

___ **4** A regressive income tax redistributes income from the rich to the poor.

___ **5** Compared to the market distribution of income, government benefits and taxes reduce the inequality of income distribution.

___ **6** Income is a stock of earnings received by an individual.

___ **7** Because it does not take into account the family's stage in the life cycle, the measured distribution of annual income will *understate* the degree of inequality.

___ **8** The existence of assortative mating tends to increase the inequality of the distribution of wealth.

___ **9** A normal distribution is bell-shaped and is symmetric around the average.

___ **10** The utilitarian theory is an example of an end-state theory of distributive justice.

MULTIPLE-CHOICE

1 Differences in the wage rates received by different individuals reflect differences in
a marginal product of labour.
b natural ability.
c human capital.
d all of the above.
e none of the above.

2 The inequality in the distribution of wealth is
a less than the inequality in the distribution of income.
b decreased by the existence of assortative mating.
c a better measure of the inequality in the distribution of economic resources than is the inequality in the distribution of income.
d even greater if we look at the distribution of wealth among the richest 1 per cent of all families.
e all of the above.

3 The wealthiest 1 per cent of UK families own what per cent of *total wealth*?

a 5 per cent
b 12 per cent
c 18 per cent
d 23 per cent
e 28 per cent

4 Consider the Lorenz curves in Fig. 18.1. Which Lorenz curve corresponds to the greatest income *inequality*?
a *A*
b *B*
c *C*
d *D*
e impossible to tell without additional information.

Figure 18.1

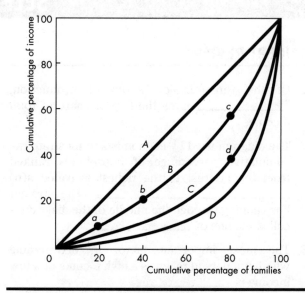

5 In Fig. 18.1, what is curve *A* (a straight line) called?
a market distribution line
b line of equality
c fairness line
d Okun trade-off curve
e none of the above

6 Which point in Fig. 18.1 indicates that the richest 20 per cent of families earn 40 per cent of the income?
a *a*
b *b*
c *c*

d *d*

e none of the above

7 If the marginal tax rate increases as income increases, the income tax is defined as
a progressive.
b proportional.
c negative.
d regressive.
e excessive.

8 The distribution of *annual income*
a understates the degree of inequality because it does not take into account the family's stage in its life cycle.
b understates the degree of inequality because it does not take into account the distribution of human capital.
c overstates the degree of inequality because it does not take into account the family's stage in its life cycle.
d overstates the degree of inequality because it does not take into account the distribution of human capital.
e is an accurate measure of the degree of inequality.

9 Which of the following *reduces* the inequality of income or wealth relative to the market distribution?
a government payments to poor people
b a regressive income tax
c large bequests
d assortative mating
e all of the above

10 According to the Rawlsian theory, income should be redistributed if the
a average person can be made better off.
b poorest person can be made better off.
c richest person can be made worse off.
d wage rate is greater than the marginal product of labour.
e wage rate is less than the marginal product of labour.

11 Which of the following is an example of an end-state theory of distributive justice?
a marginal product theory
b the theory of Robert Nozick
c the utilitarian theory
d the process theory
e none of the above

SHORT ANSWER

1 a What is a Lorenz curve?
b What does it illustrate?

2 Explain the differences and connections between the concepts of wealth and income.

3 a What are the two factors that determine a person's income?
b To what extent are these factors the result of forces beyond the control of the individual and to what extent are they the result of individual choice?

4 The two classes of theories of distributive justice are process theories and end-state theories.
a What is the principal characteristic of a process theory of distributive justice?
b Why is the utilitarian theory an end-state theory of distributive justice?

PROBLEMS

1 Table 18.1 gives information regarding the distribution of income in an economy which generates £100 billion in total annual income.

Table 18.1   Total Family Income

Percentage of families	Total income (billions of pounds)	Income share (per cent)	Cumulative percentage of families	Cumulative percentage of income
Poorest 20%	5			
Second 20%	10			
Third 20%	15			
Fourth 20%	20			
Richest 20%	50			

a Complete Table 18.1 by computing the entries in the last three columns.
b Draw the Lorenz curve for income in this economy and label it *A*.

2 Now suppose that a progressive income tax is levied on the economy. The distribution of after-tax income is given in Table 18.2. We have assumed that none of the revenue is redistributed to families in the economy. Note that total after-tax income is £71 billion.

Table 18.2   After-tax Family Income

Percentage of families	After-tax income (billions of pounds)	After-tax income share (per cent)	Cumulative percentage of families	Cumulative percentage of after-tax income
Poorest 20%	5			
Second 20%	9			
Third 20%	12			
Fourth 20%	15			
Richest 20%	30			

Table 18.3   After-transfer Family Income

Percentage of families	After-transfer income (billions of pounds)	After-transfer income share (per cent)	Cumulative percentage of families	Cumulative percentage of after-transfer income
Poorest 20%	15			
Second 20%	16			
Third 20%	18			
Fourth 20%	20			
Richest 20%	31			

Table 18.4

	Quintile groups of households ranked by equivalized disposable income					All house-holds
	Bottom fifth	Next fifth	Middle fifth	Next fifth	Top fifth	
Average per household (£ per year)						
Earnings of main earner	780	2,650	6,630	9,380	16,900	7,270
Earnings of others in the household	100	430	1,700	3,540	5,380	2,230
Occupational pensions, annuities	140	410	620	780	1,140	620
Investment income	140	260	400	630	1,810	650
Other income	80	110	120	180	240	140
Total original income						
+ Benefits in cash						
Contributory	1,480	1,560	990	630	430	1,020
Non-contributory	1,690	1,220	880	440	240	900
Gross income	4,400	6,630	11,340	15,580	26,140	12,820
− Income tax and NIC	150	620	1,760	2,920	5,770	2,250
− Domestic rates (gross)	430	440	480	510	620	500
Disposable income	3,810	5,570	9,100	12,150	19,740	10,070
Equivalized disposable income	3,730	5,370	7,450	10,230	18,540	9,060
− Indirect taxes	1,040	1,300	2,120	2,590	3,180	2,050
+ Benefits in kind						
Education	800	660	840	630	360	660
National Health Service	1,030	980	920	790	630	870
Housing subsidy	100	100	60	30	20	60
Travel subsidies	40	50	50	60	80	60
School meals and welfare milk	80	30	20	10	10	30
Final income	4,820	6,080	8,870	11,070	17,660	9,700
Average per household (numbers)						
Adults	1.7	1.7	2.1	2.1	2.0	1.9
Children	0.7	0.6	0.8	0.6	0.4	0.6
Economically active people	0.3	0.7	1.4	1.7	1.7	1.2
Retired people	0.7	0.7	0.4	0.2	0.2	0.4
Number of households in sample	1,479	1,479	1,480	1,479	1,479	7,396

Source: Social Trends. Central Statistical Office. Crown Copyright 1991. Reproduced by the permission of the Controller of HMSO and the Central Statistical Office.

a Complete Table 18.2.

b Draw the Lorenz curve for after-tax income on the same graph you used for **1b** and label it *B*.

c What effect has the progressive income tax had on inequality?

3 Finally, suppose that, in addition, the government redistributes all of the tax revenue so that the after-transfer (after-tax) income distribution is that given in Table 18.3. For example, those in the poorest group receive transfer income of £10 billion so that their after-transfer income becomes £15 billion.

a Complete Table 18.3.

b Draw the Lorenz curve for after-transfer income on the same graph you used for **1b** and **2b** and label it *C*.

c What effect has income redistribution through transfer payments had on inequality?

DATA QUESTIONS

The Redistribution of Income Through Taxes and Benefits in 1987

Table 18.4 shows how the wide range of household incomes is modified by the tax–benefit system in the United Kingdom. There are various measures of income used in the table, for example original income which shows income before benefits are received and taxes are deducted. Cash benefits can be either contributory (such as old-age pensions) or non-contributory (such as child benefit). Non-cash benefits such as free or subsidized education also affect the distribution of income.

1 a Use the data in the table to compare the distribution of original income with the distribution of final income.

b Account for the inequalities in original income which are shown in the table.

2 Compare the relative importance of the different categories of government expenditure and revenue as methods of reducing inequalities in the distribution of income.

3 Discuss the economic consequences of policies which result in a less equal distribution of income and wealth.

Source: Adapted from an Associated Examining Board Question GCE A-Level, June 1989.

ANSWERS

CONCEPT REVIEW

1 labour

2 Lorenz curve; equality

3 education

4 progressive; regressive; proportional

5 market; taxes; transfers

6 bequest

7 assortative mating; increase

8 end-state; process

9 utilitarian

10 Rawlsian

TRUE OR FALSE

1 **F** Wealth distribution is more unequal.

2 **F** Further away = more unequal.

3 **T** Definition.

4 **F** Regressive = from poor to rich.

5 **T** See Table 18.4 in Data Question.

6 **F** Income is a flow.

7 **F** Overstate inequality.

8 **T** Because rich men marry rich women.

9 **T** Definition.

10 **T** Sum of all individual utility outcomes maximized.

MULTIPLE-CHOICE

1 d All affect marginal revenue product of labour.

2 d The very rich are very rich!

3 c Fact. See text.

4 d Curve furthest from 45° line.

5 b Definition.

6 c Moving from 80 per cent to 100 per cent of families (richest 20 per cent) moves income from 60 per cent of total to 100 per cent (40 per cent).

7 a Definition.

8 c See text Fig. 18.5.

9 a Others increase inequality.

10 b Definition.

11 c Maximizes sum of utilities (end states) of individuals.

SHORT ANSWER

1 a The Lorenz curve gives a graphical representation of the distribution of income or wealth across some population.

b The horizontal axis measures the cumulative percentage of families ranked from the poorest to the richest. The vertical axis measures the cumulative percentages of income or wealth. The further the Lorenz curve is from the line of equality, the more unequal the distribution of income or wealth.

2 Wealth is the *stock* of assets owned by an individual while income is the *flow* of earnings received by an individual. The concepts are connected in that an individual's income is the earnings that flow from the person's stock of wealth.

3 a A person's income is determined by the market prices for productive resource services and the quantity of resource services the person is able and willing to sell at those prices.

b These two factors depend on a number of things, some of which are (at least partially) under the control of the individual and some of which are not.

   The price of labour services, the wage rate, is determined in the market for labour. But the wage rate will depend on the marginal product of labour which is affected by individual choices about training and education as well as personal inherent ability. The quantity of labour services supplied will also depend on personal choices about how to spend one's time. The quantity of other resource services supplied will also depend on personal choices as well as the individual's endowment of the factor.

4 a A process theory of distributive justice focuses on the fairness of the process or mechanisms by which results are achieved instead of focusing on the results themselves.

b The utilitarian theory suggests that the fairest system is one in which the sum of the utilities in the society is a maximum. Since the theory focuses on the outcome or the ends, it is an end-state theory of distributive justice.

PROBLEMS

1 a Table 18.1 is completed as Table 18.5. The income share for each group of families is the total income of that group as a percentage of total income in the economy (£100 billion). The cumulative percentage of income (last column) is obtained by adding the percentage income share of the group (from the third column) to the total percentage income share of all poorer groups of families.

Table 18.5   Total Family Income

Percentage of families	Total income (billions of pounds)	Income share (per cent)	Cumulative percentage of families	Cumulative percentage of income
Poorest 20%	5	5	20	5
Second 20%	10	10	40	15
Third 20%	15	15	60	30
Fourth 20%	20	20	80	50
Richest 20%	50	50	100	100

Figure 18.2

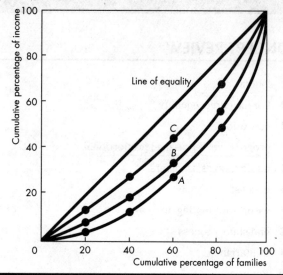

b The curve labelled A in Fig.18.2 is the Lorenz curve for total family income. This simply plots the values in the last two columns of Table 18.5.

2 a Table 18.2 is completed as Table 18.6.

b The curve labelled *B* in Fig. 18.2 is the Lorenz curve for after-tax family income.

c The progressive income tax has reduced inequality by taking a larger percentage of income from higher income groups.

Table 18.6   Solution After-tax Family Income

Percentage of families	After-tax income (billions of pounds)	After-tax income share (per cent)	Cumulative percentage of families	Cumulative percentage of after-tax income
Poorest 20%	5	7	20	7
Second 20%	9	13	40	20
Third 20%	12	17	60	37
Fourth 20%	15	21	80	58
Richest 20%	30	42	100	100

Table 18.7   After-transfer Family Income

Percentage of families	After-transfer income (billions of pounds)	After-transfer income share (per cent)	Cumulative percentage of families	Cumulative percentage of after-transfer income
Poorest 20%	15	15	20	15
Second 20%	16	16	40	31
Third 20%	18	18	60	49
Fourth 20%	20	20	80	69
Richest 20%	31	31	100	100

3 a Table 18.3 is completed as Table 18.7.

b The curve labelled *C* in Fig. 18.2 is the Lorenz curve for (after-tax) after-transfer family income.

c Income redistribution through transfer payments has reduced inequality.

DATA QUESTIONS

The answer given below is the author's solution to the questions on p. 169 and should not be taken as being the definitive answer required by the AEB.

1 a Final income is much more equally distributed than original income. For example, the bottom fifth saw their total income rise from £1,220 to £4,820 as a result of taxes and benefits. The income of the richest fifth fell from £25,470 to £17,660.

b The main cause is the difference in earned income. This is caused by factors such as differences in human capital which were discussed in Chapter 15. These differences are exacerbated by differences in invest-ment income.

2 Benefits in cash and kind play a substantial part in increasing the incomes of the poorest sections of the community. However, these are outweighed by the income removed from the richest fifth by income tax (£5,770 per household) and indirect taxes (£3,180 per household).

3 Policies which result in a less equal distribution of income and wealth will increase economic growth if they create incentives to work hard and to invest and if people respond to these incentives. However, less equal distribu-tions of income and wealth may mean that poor people suffer from ill-health and become less productive, while better-off people may find that their income rises so much that they do not need to work so hard. Hence the result may be a slower rate of economic growth.

Chapter 19 Market Failure and Public Choices

Chapter In Perspective, Text Pages 508–544

In this chapter we discover that there are circumstances in which markets fail to allocate goods and services efficiently. For example, if competitive markets are efficient, why is there so much pollution? As a result of such *market failure* to achieve efficiency, there are additional opportunities for government to improve allocation. This chapter begins a discussion of how an 'ideal' government might proceed to do so. In the next chapter we examine the behaviour of actual governments.

Helpful Hints

1 The criterion economists use to judge the success of the market is allocative efficiency. Allocative efficiency means that the economy is producing all goods and services up to the point at which the marginal cost is equal to the marginal benefit. In such a state, no one can be made better off without making someone else worse off.

   When the market fails to achieve this 'ideal' state of efficiency, we call it *market failure*. The market can fail by producing too little if the marginal benefit of the last unit exceeds the marginal cost. On the other hand, the market can fail by producing too much if the marginal cost of the last unit exceeds the marginal benefit.

2 All goods provided by the government are not necessarily public goods. A public good is defined by the characteristics of non-rivalry and non-excludability, not by whether or not it is publicly provided. For example, local authorities provide swimming pools and residential refuse collection but neither of these is a pure public good in spite of the fact that they may be provided by the government.

3 A private good is a rival in consumption. Therefore, to obtain the demand curve for the whole economy, we sum the individual marginal benefit (demand) curves *horizontally*. However, the economy's marginal benefit curve for a public good is obtained by summing the individual marginal benefit curves *vertically*. This is the relevant marginal benefit curve for evaluating the efficient provision level of the public good. (See the discussion of Key Figure 19.3.)

4 A competitive market will result in the quantity traded at which the marginal private cost is equal to the marginal private benefit. The efficient quantity is the quantity at which marginal social cost is equal to marginal social benefit.

The difference between *marginal social cost* and *marginal private cost* is external cost and the difference between *marginal social benefit* and *marginal private benefit* is external benefit.

When third parties are affected, there are external costs or benefits and competitive markets will not be efficient.

5 Competitive markets with externalities are not efficient because some of the costs or benefits are *external*. If those costs or benefits could be *internalized* somehow, then the market would be efficient. Two approaches to internalizing externalities are discussed in this chapter.

The first is to define clearly and to enforce strictly property rights. Then costs imposed on non-participants in a transaction can be recovered through the legal process and will thus be borne by those making the transaction decision: the costs will become internal (private).

The second approach to internalizing externalities is to tax activities that generate external costs and subsidize activities that generate external benefits. By charging a tax equal to the external cost, the entire cost becomes internal. Similarly, by paying a subsidy in the amount of external benefits, the entire benefit becomes internal.

6 Public choice theory provides a theory of the political marketplace that parallels the economic theory of the market for goods and services. In political markets the demanders are voters while in ordinary markets the demanders are consumers. In both cases, demanders are concerned about their own costs and benefits. The suppliers in political markets are politicians and bureaucrats, and again they are concerned about their own costs and benefits.

One way to analyse this market is to use the median voter theorem. This predicts that successful politicians will appeal to the median voter.

Key Figures

Figure 19.2   The Median Voter Theorem, text page 514

This explains the median voter theorem – that political parties will pursue policies that maximize the net benefit of the median voter.

Figure 19.3 Benefits of a Public Good, text page 517

If one person consumes a unit of a private good, that unit cannot be consumed by anyone else. However, the consumption of a public good by one person does not reduce the amount available for others. This implies that the economy's marginal benefit curve (demand curve) for a private good is obtained by summing the individual marginal benefit (demand) curves *horizontally* (see Chapter 7).

For a public good, however, the economy's marginal benefit curve is obtained by summing the individual marginal benefit curves *vertically*; by adding up the individual marginal benefits at each quantity. This is illustrated in the figure by considering an economy in which there are two individuals, Nicola and Robert, who receive benefits from acid-rain check satellites, a public good. Their total and marginal benefits are reported in the table. Their marginal benefit curves are given in parts (a) and (b) of the figure. The economy's marginal benefit curve is given in part (c) as the *vertical* sum of the marginal benefit curves of Nicola and Robert.

Figure 19.4 The Efficient Scale of Provision of a Public Good, text page 518

The efficient scale of provision of a public good is the amount that maximizes net benefit, which is total benefit minus total cost. Part (a) of this figure graphs the total cost (*TC*) and total benefit (*TB*) curves. Net benefit is given by the vertical distance between the two curves. We find that this distance (net benefit) is a maximum at a quantity of 2 satellites. Thus 2 satellites is the efficient scale of provision.

Part (b) illustrates an alternative way to find the same result. The efficient scale of provision is achieved if satellites are produced up to the level at which marginal benefit equals marginal cost. The marginal benefit (*MB*) and marginal cost (*MC*) curves are shown in part (b). Marginal benefit equals marginal cost at a quantity of 2 satellites.

Figure 19.5 Provision of a Public Good in a Political System, text page 520

This builds on Fig. 19.4 to show that given informed voters, competition between political parties will maximize the perceived net benefit accruing to voters. That is because provision will be at the level where the distance between total benefit curve *(TB)* and total cost curve *(TC)* is greatest.

Figure 19.6 Bureaucratic Overprovision, text page 521

If some voters are not well-informed, government may expand output above the level which maximizes net benefit.

Figure 19.7 The Efficient Scale of Production when External Costs Occur, text page 525

With no external costs Q_0 is the efficient level of output. However, there are external costs and these are shown by the difference between the $S = MPC$ curve and the marginal social cost curve *(MSC)*. Consequently, the efficient level of output is Q_1 where the marginal benefit to consumers of the last tonne of chemical equals the marginal social cost of providing it.

Figure 19.8 Taxing an External Cost, text page 527

If the production of a good or service produces external costs, a competitive market will result in a quantity which exceeds the allocatively efficient level. This figure illustrates that taxing the production of that good or service can induce the allocatively efficient quantity. The example used here is transport services, which produces external costs. The allocatively efficient quantity of transport services occurs at Q_1, the intersection of the $D = MB$ curve and the MSC curve. A competitive market, however, will result in the quantity at which the D and MPC curves intersect since producers take only private costs into account; market price will be P_0 and quantity will be Q_0, which is greater than the allocatively efficient quantity.

If, however, a tax is levied on producers in the amount of the external costs, the MSC curve becomes the new relevant marginal cost curve for producers. As a result, the market price will rise to P_1 and the quantity will fall to Q_1, and allocative efficiency is achieved.

SELF-TEST

CONCEPT REVIEW

1 If an unregulated market economy is unable to achieve allocative efficiency in all circumstances, we have _____ _____ .

2 There are two classes of economic theories of government behaviour. Public _____ theories predict that government will pursue actions that will achieve allocative efficiency. Public _____ theories study the behaviour of government as the outcome of individual choices made by voters, politicians and bureaucrats.

3 A good which, if consumed by one person, cannot be consumed by another is called a(n) _____ good. There are two important features of such a good. The fact that Bob's consumption of a good means that Sue cannot consume the same good illustrates the feature of _____ . If Sue has purchased a good, she owns it and can keep others from using it. This illustrates the feature of _____ .

4 A good which, if consumed by one person, is necessarily also consumed by everyone else is called a(n) _____ _____ good.

5 Someone who consumes a good without paying for it is called a(n) _____ _____ . When such individuals are prevalent in the consumption of a particular good, the amount of that good provided by the private market will be _____ than the allocatively efficient amount.

6 The maximum amount a person would be willing to pay for one more unit of public good is the _____ _____ of that good to the individual.

7 A cost or a benefit arising from a transaction which affects someone other than the direct parties in the transaction is called a(n) _____ . When a chemical firm dumps its waste into the river, it kills a large number of fish downstream. This is an example of an external _____ . When a neighbour plants flowers on the property line, you benefit. This is an example of an external _____ .

8 A legally established title to the sole ownership of a resource is a(n) _____ _____ _____ .

9 The marginal cost borne directly by the producer of a good is called the marginal _____ cost. This marginal cost together with the marginal external cost is the marginal _____ cost.

10 If there are external costs in the production of steel (for example pollution), the output of steel produced by the market will be _____ than the allocatively efficient level.

11 The _____ voter theorem predicts that successful political parties will pursue policies that maximize the net _____ of the _____ voter.

12 The marginal rate of _____ shows how much of one product we can get if we sacrifice a little of the other.

TRUE OR FALSE

___ **1** Restriction of output by monopolies is an example of market failure.

___ **2** According to the public choice theory of government behaviour, not only is there the possibility of market failure, but there is also the possibility of 'government failure'.

___ **3** The existence of public goods gives rise to the free-rider problem.

___ **4** Any good made available by the government is a public good.

___ **5** The economy's marginal benefit curve for a public good is obtained by adding the marginal benefits of each individual at each quantity of provision.

___ **6** The private market will produce much less than the efficient quantity of pure public goods.

___ **7** If the production of a good involves no external cost, then marginal social cost is equal to marginal private cost.

___ **8** If, at the current level of production of good *A*, marginal social benefit is less than marginal social cost, then output of good *A* should increase to achieve allocative efficiency.

___ **9** The existence of external benefits means that marginal social cost is less than marginal private cost.

___ **10** Externalities exist because someone is wilfully trying to harm others.

___ **11** The government can enhance allocative efficiency by subsidizing the production of goods that generate external benefits and taxing the production of goods that generate external costs.

___ **12** The public choice theory of government behaviour assumes that politicians and bureaucrats are motivated primarily by concern for the public interest.

___ **13** In order to be elected, a politician will tend to choose policies that appeal to the median voter.

___ **14** It is irrational for voters to be uninformed about an issue as important as defence.

MULTIPLE-CHOICE

1 Which of the following is *not* a source of market failure?
   a the existence of public goods
   b external costs
   c external benefits
   d an unequal distribution of income
   e the existence of monopolies

2 A good that exhibits both rivalry and excludability is a(n)
   a private good.
   b public good.
   c government good.
   d mixed good.
   e external good.

3 Governments provide pure public goods like national defence because
   a governments are more efficient than private firms at producing such goods.
   b of the free-rider problems which result in underproduction by private markets.
   c people do not value national defence very highly.
   d of the potential that private firms will make excess profits.
   e of external costs.

4 Which of the following goods has the non-excludability feature?
a city bus
b toll-bridge
c lighthouse
d art museum
e all of the above

5 The economy's total demand curve for a public good is obtained by
a summing the individual marginal cost curves horizontally.
b summing the individual marginal cost curves vertically.
c summing the individual marginal benefit curves horizontally.
d summing the individual marginal benefit curves vertically.
e none of the above methods.

6 The total benefit of a given level of provision of a public good can be obtained by
a adding the marginal benefit of each level of provision up to the given level.
b adding the marginal benefit of each level of provision and then subtracting the marginal cost of each level of provision.
c adding the net benefit of each level of provision up to the given level.
d multiplying net benefit by the quantity of the public good provided.
e none of the above methods.

7 Which of the following illustrates the concept of external cost?
a Bad weather reduces the size of the wheat crop.
b A reduction in the size of the wheat crop causes the income of wheat farmers to fall.
c Smoking harms the health of the smoker.
d Smoking harms the health of non-smokers who are nearby.
e Public health services reduce the transmission of disease.

8 Figure 19.1 depicts the demand for good *A* as well as the marginal private cost (*MPC*) and marginal social cost (*MSC*) associated with the production of good *A*. Production of the sixth unit of output generates an external
a cost of £1.50.
b cost of £3.
c cost of £6.

d benefit of £3.
e benefit of £6.

Figure 19.1

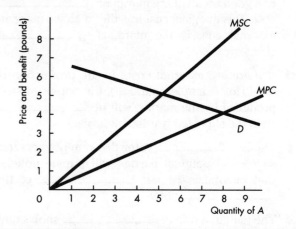

9 In Fig. 19.1, how many units of good *A* will be produced in an unregulated market?
a 0 units
b 5 units
c 6 units
d 8 units
e impossible to calculate without additional information

10 In Fig. 19.1, what is the allocatively efficient quantity of good *A*?
a 0 units
b 5 units
c 6 units
d 8 units
e impossible to calculate without additional information

11 Figure 19.2 depicts the demand curve for good *B* as well as the marginal social benefit (*MSB*) and marginal cost (*MC*) curves. How many units of good *B* will be produced and consumed in an unregulated market?
a 0 units
b 3 units
c 5 units
d 6 units
e 9 units

12 In Fig. 19.2, what is the allocatively efficient quantity of good *B*?
a 0 units

b 3 units

c 5 units

d 6 units

e 9 units

Figure 19.2

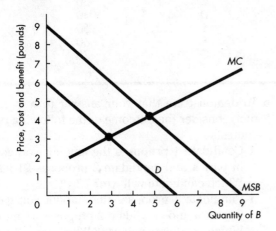

13 In Fig. 19.2, which of the following government policies would induce the market to achieve allocative efficiency?

a Tax the production of *B* in the amount of £3 per unit.

b Tax the production of *B* in the amount of £4 per unit.

c Subsidize the consumption of *B* in the amount of £1 per unit.

d Subsidize the consumption of *B* in the amount of £3 per unit.

e Subsidize the consumption of *B* in the amount of £4 per unit.

14 Public choice theory

a argues that government has a tendency to conduct policies that help the economy towards allocative efficiency.

b argues that politicians and bureaucrats tend to be more concerned about the public interest than individuals in the private sector.

c argues that the public choices of government maximize net benefits.

d applies economic tools used to analyse markets to the analysis of government behaviour.

e applies the tools of political analysis to the analysis of economic markets.

15 Competitors who make themselves identical to appeal to the maximum number of voters illustrate

a the principle of maximum differentiation.

b the principle of minimum differentiation.

c the principle of rational ignorance.

d non-rivalry.

e the Niskanen theory of bureaucratic behaviour.

16 Public choice theory assumes that those involved in the political process are generally motivated by

a self-interest.

b the desire to achieve allocative efficiency.

c dishonesty.

d public spirit.

e the desire for maximum profit.

17 Competition between two political parties will cause those parties to propose policies

a that are quite different.

b that are quite similar.

c of rational ignorance.

d that reduce the well-being of middle-income families and benefit rich people and poor people.

e that equate total benefits and total costs.

SHORT ANSWER

1 Explain the *non-rivalry* and *non-excludability* features of a pure public good.

2 What is the free-rider problem?

3 Governments provide education for free, or at least at a price (tuition) much less than cost. What is the economic argument that supports this policy?

4 Explain how a tax can be used to achieve efficiency in the face of external costs.

5 Briefly compare an equilibrium in a political market with an equilibrium in the market for goods and services.

PROBLEMS

1 The first two columns of Table 19.1 give the demand schedule for education while the third column gives the marginal private cost. Since education generates external benefits, marginal social benefit, given in the last column, is greater than marginal private benefit.

Table 19.1

Quantity (number of students)	Marginal private benefit (pounds)	Marginal private cost (pounds)	Marginal social benefit (pounds)
100	500	200	800
200	400	250	700
300	300	300	600
400	200	350	500
500	100	400	400
600	0	450	350

a Represent the data in Table 19.1 graphically.
b What equilibrium price and quantity would result if the market for education is unregulated?
c What is the allocatively efficient quantity of students?

2 In an attempt to address the inefficient level of education the government has decided to subsidize schooling.
  a The government offers £200 to each student who buys a year of education.
    i Draw the new marginal private benefit curve, which includes the subsidy, on your graph and label it MPB_1.
    ii What are the approximate new equilibrium price and quantity?
  b The government increases the subsidy to £400.
    i Draw another marginal private benefit curve, which includes the subsidy, on your graph and label it MPB_2.
    ii What are the approximate corresponding equilibrium price and quantity?
  c What level of subsidy will achieve the efficient quantity of education?

3 Two candidates are competing in an election for president of the Economics Club. The only issue dividing them is how much will be spent on the annual club party. The seven members of the club (A to G) have preferences as shown in Table 19.2 regarding how much should be spent on the party.
  a How much will each candidate propose to spend?

Table 19.2

Voting member	Proposed amount (pounds)
A	10
B	20
C	30
D	40
E	50
F	60
G	70

  b To demonstrate that your answer to a is correct, consider the outcome of the following two contests.
    i Candidate 1 proposes the amount you gave in part a and candidate 2 proposes £1 less. Which candidate will win? Why?
    ii Candidate 1 proposes the amount you gave in part a and candidate 2 proposes £1 more. Which candidate will win? Why?

DATA QUESTIONS

Car Ownership in Singapore

Singapore is a small densely populated island state which has experienced rapid economic growth. This has led to a rise in car ownership which the government is concerned to curtail because it believes the external costs of a rapidly expanding car population to be high. It has therefore used several ways to increase the cost of motoring.

The government has pushed up the showroom price of cars in three ways. First, by imposing an import duty; second, by requiring a registration fee; and third, by imposing a high Additional Registration Fee which now stands at 175 per cent of a car's dockside value.

Motorists have also had to pay higher running costs. They have suffered several large increases in parking fees as well as road and fuel taxes. Observers note that the tax increases raising motorists' fixed and variable costs are good revenue raisers. However, the Communications Ministry claims that the taxes are justifiable because: 'We cannot have more cars than our limited land and roads can bear. Otherwise paralysing traffic jams will increase travelling time for everybody, bringing adverse consequences for our economy'.

1 What 'external costs' are mentioned in the passage?

2 Define and give examples of fixed and variable costs facing a motorist in Singapore.

3 Suggest one policy not mentioned in the passage which might dissuade motorists from owning a car.

Source: Adapted from a University of London Schools Examination Board GCE A-Level question, June 1988. © University of London Examinations and Assessment Council.

ANSWERS

CONCEPT REVIEW

1 market failure
2 interest; choice
3 private; rivalry; excludability
4 pure public
5 free rider; less
6 marginal benefit
7 externality; cost; benefit
8 private property right
9 private; social
10 greater
11 median; benefit; marginal
12 transformation

TRUE OR FALSE

1 **T** Allocatively inefficient output.
2 **T** Believe government agents act in their own interest, not necessarily public interest.
3 **T** Non-excludability means no incentive to pay.
4 **F** 'Public good' has precise meaning.
5 **T** Definition.
6 **T** Because it ignores external benefits.
7 **T** $MSC = MPC$ + externality.
8 **F** Output should be cut.
9 **F** External benefits do not affect costs.
10 **F** No intention is implied.
11 **T** This will equalize MSC and MSB.

12 **F** The theory assumes that they are concerned for their own self-interest.
13 **T** Because this will maximize votes.
14 **F** There are costs involved in acquiring information, so it may be rational to stay ignorant.

MULTIPLE-CHOICE

1 **d** Any income distribution can be associated with allocative efficiency.
2 **a** Definition.
3 **b** Providing public goods would not be profitable for private firms.
4 **c** Can't exclude ships from seeing the light.
5 **d** See Figure 19.3 in text.
6 **a** **b–d** involve irrelevant costs.
7 **d** Cost falls on third party.
8 **b** Vertical distance between MSC and MPC at $Q = 6$.
9 **d** Where MPC intersects demand.
10 **b** Where MSC intersects demand.
11 **b** Where MC intersects demand.
12 **c** Where MC intersects MSB.
13 **d** Shift MC down by vertical distance between MSB and demand.
14 **d** Political marketplace.
15 **b** Definition.
16 **a** It assumes that people are motivated by self-interest.
17 **b** They will maximize their vote according to the principle of minimum differentiation.

SHORT ANSWER

1 A good has the non-rivalry feature if its consumption by one person does not reduce the amount available for others. The non-excludability feature means that if the good is produced and consumed by one person, others cannot be excluded from consuming it as well.

2 The free-rider problem is the problem of unregulated markets producing too little of a pure public good because there is little incentive for individuals to pay for the good. The reason is that the person's payment is likely to have no perceptible effect on the amount the person will be able to consume.

3 Government subsidizes education heavily. The economic argument is that education generates external benefits. In particular, when individuals are educated, society at large receives benefits beyond the private benefits that accrue to those choosing how much education to obtain.

4 The existence of external costs means that producers do not take into account all costs when deciding how much to produce. If a tax is levied that is exactly the amount of the external cost, the cost will no longer be external. As a result, the producer will take it into account and thus be induced to produce the efficient quantity.

5 In both cases, the equilibrium is a state of rest in the sense that no group has an incentive to change its choices. When a political market is in equilibrium neither demanders (voters) nor suppliers (politicians and bureaucrats) are able to make an alternative choice that will make them better off.

PROBLEMS

1 a Figure 19.3 is a graphical representation of the data in Table 19.1. The demand for education is given by the marginal private benefit curve (labelled *MPB*), the marginal private cost curve is labelled *MPC* and the marginal social benefit curve is labelled *MSB*.
b In an unregulated market, equilibrium price and quantity are determined by the intersection of the *MPB* and *MPC* curves. Thus, the equilibrium price would be £300 and the equilibrium quantity is 300 students.
c Since there are no external costs, the efficient quantity is determined by the intersection of the *MPC* and *MSB* curves. This implies that allocative efficiency is attained at a quantity of 500 students.

2 a i The subsidy increases the marginal private benefit to each student by the amount of the subsidy, £200. The new *MPB* curve, labelled MPB_1, is included in Fig. 19.3.

Figure 19.3

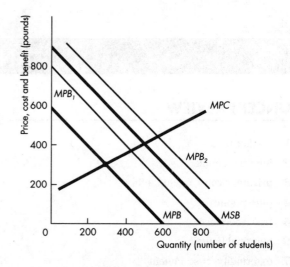

ii The new equilibrium after the £200 subsidy is at the intersection of the *MPC* and MPB_1 curves. The price of a unit of education will be approximately £370 (£366.67) and there will be approximately 430 (433.33) students.
b i With a subsidy of £400 per student, the *MPB* curve will shift to MPB_2 in Fig. 19.3.
ii With this subsidy the equilibrium will be at the intersection of the *MPC* and MPB_2 curves. The corresponding price of a unit of education will be approximately £430 (£433.33) and the number of students will be approximately 570 (566.67).
c In order to achieve an efficient outcome, the subsidy must make the *MPB* curve coincide with the *MSB* curve. This requires a subsidy of £300 per student.

3 a Each candidate will propose spending £40 since that is the preference of the median voter (voter *D*).
b i Candidate 1 will win because *D*, *E*, *F* and *G* will vote for that candidate because £40 comes closer to matching their preferences than the £39 proposed by candidate 2. Only *A*, *B* and *C* will vote for candidate 2.
ii Candidate 1 will win with the votes of *A*, *B*, *C* and *D*; only *E*, *F* and *G* will vote for candidate 2.

DATA QUESTIONS

The University of London Examinations and Assessment Council accepts no responsibility whatsoever for the accuracy or method of working in the answers given.

1 External costs include traffic jams and increased travelling time. Also 'limited land' implies parking difficulties.

2 A fixed cost is one that is independent of the level of output. In this case, import duties and the two registration fees increase costs irrespective of how much the car is used and so are fixed costs. A variable cost is one which changes with output; for a car the cost of fuel is a variable cost.

3 The policies mentioned above rely on financial penalties to reduce car ownership. Alternative methods could make use of physical rationing, such as a policy which stopped cars with even-numbered licence plates from being used on certain days.

Chapter 20   **Industry Policy**

Chapter In Perspective, Text Pages 545–574

This chapter examines government industrial policy. It focuses in particular on the economic aspects of public corporations and natural monopolies and examines how governments attempt to control such firms. This chapter also describes the competition policies adopted by the United Kingdom and the European Union and the reasons for regional policy.

Helpful Hints

1 Consider Fig. 20.1, which depicts revenue and marginal cost curves for an industry. Using this figure, it is helpful to think of regulation as determining how the potential total surplus (the area of triangle *abc*) is divided among consumer surplus, producer surplus and deadweight loss.

If the industry is perfectly competitive, then the quantity traded will be Q_c and the market price will be P_c. Total surplus is maximized and is given by the area of the triangle *abc*. Total surplus is equal to the sum of consumer surplus given by the area of triangle *dbc* and producer surplus given by the area of the triangle *adc*. There is no deadweight loss.

If the industry is a profit-maximizing monopoly, output will be Q_m and the price will be P_m. In this case, total surplus is represented by the area of trapezoid *abfg*. Because of monopoly restriction of output, total surplus under monopoly is less than under competition. The difference is the deadweight loss from monopoly, the amount of total surplus that is lost when we go from competition to

monopoly. The deadweight loss is given by the area of the triangle *gfc*. Total surplus can be divided into consumer surplus given by the area of triangle *ebf* and producer surplus given by the area of trapezoid *aefg*. Consumer surplus is quite small but producer surplus is at a maximum.

Figure 20.1

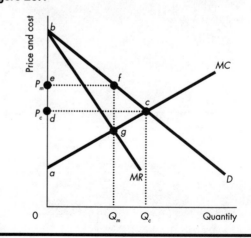

Of course, actual output may be between these bounds. As output moves from Q_c to Q_m, consumer surplus decreases while producer surplus and the deadweight loss both increase. If this industry is regulated, the public interest theory of intervention predicts that the result will be a level of output close to Q_c, while the capture theory of intervention predicts a level of output closer to Q_m.

Key Figures and Tables

Figure 20.1   Natural Monopoly: Marginal Cost Pricing, text page 552

Natural monopolies are heavily regulated. A natural monopoly has decreasing average total cost (*ATC*) over the entire range of market demand. Thus marginal cost (*MC*) is less than *ATC*. This figure illustrates a marginal cost pricing rule as applied to a natural monopoly. Setting the price at marginal cost maximizes total surplus.

Figure 20.2   Natural Monopoly: Average Cost Pricing, text page 554

This uses the same electricity supply example as Fig. 20.1 to illustrate an average cost pricing rule as applied to a natural monopoly. The price is set equal to average total cost – at the intersection of the *ATC* curve and the demand curve.

Average cost pricing gives a price of 4 pence per unit and results in 6 billion units per year. The electricity company is now breaking even, but consumer surplus is less than under marginal cost pricing and there is a deadweight loss generated equal to the area of the grey triangle. This is the outcome predicted by the public interest theory of intervention.

Figure 20.3 Natural Monopoly: Profit Maximization, text page 555

If a company is able to maximize profit, it will equate marginal cost (*MC*) and marginal revenue (*MR*). The resulting price will be above average total cost, and the company will now be making a profit. Consumer surplus (the area of the green triangle) has declined even further, and the deadweight loss has increased to the area of the grey triangle. This is the outcome predicted by the capture theory of intervention.

Figure 20.5 Collusive Oligopoly, text page 557

From Chapter 13, we know that an oligopoly industry can make monopoly profits if the firms in the industry form a cartel and enter into a collusive agreement. Because each firm has an incentive to cheat, however, it is difficult to enforce the cartel agreement. As a result, an oligopoly may 'demand' regulation which has the effect of having the government regulatory agency enforce the collusive agreement that generates monopoly profits for the industry. This is illustrated in the figure.

Figure 20.6 Public Enterprise, text page 560

This illustrates the operation of a public corporation. Part (a) shows that the public corporation will achieve allocative efficiency if it produces the output such that price equals marginal cost. Because that price is below average total cost, the corporation must receive a subsidy per unit equal to the difference between average total cost and price (marginal cost). That subsidy is collected by taxation in other areas, reducing the consumer surplus area in Fig. 20.1 by the total amount of the subsidy to yield the consumer surplus area in this figure. This outcome maximizes consumer surplus and achieves economic efficiency.

Part (b) illustrates the operation of the public corporation, if we assume that the corporation bureaucrats maximize their budget but still obey the marginal cost pricing rule. Output will remain at the economically efficient level but the bureaucrats pad costs up to a maximum level that completely exhausts the consumer surplus ($ATC_{(padded)}$). This outcome is efficient but maximizes the benefit of the producer by squeezing consumer surplus to zero.

Table 20.1 Regulatory Agencies Operating in the United Kingdom, text page 551

This lists the major regulatory agencies, together with a brief statement of their responsibilities.

Table 20.2   The Main UK Acts Promoting Competition, text page 563

This lists the main acts promoting competition in the United Kingdom.

Table 20.3   Gateways Which Can Be Used to Defend a Restrictive Practice, text page 565

UK law assumes that restrictive practices can sometimes be beneficial, and this table lists these 'gateways'.

SELF-TEST

CONCEPT REVIEW

1 There are three principal ways in which the government intervenes in monopolistic and oligopolistic markets. The first of these is, _____ which consists of rules administered by a government agency and intended to restrict the behaviour of firms. The second is _____ , which places a corporation under public ownership. The third is _____ _____ _____ , which legally prohibits certain kinds of monopoly practice.

2 The difference between the most that consumers are willing to pay and the amount they actually pay is called _____ _____ .
The difference between the revenue received by a producer and the opportunity cost of production is called _____ _____ . The sum of these is _____ _____ .

3 Allocative efficiency is achieved when total surplus is _____ .

4 The larger the consumer surplus per buyer resulting from intervention, the _____ is the demand for intervention by buyers. The larger the producer surplus per seller resulting from intervention, the _____ is the demand for intervention by sellers.

5 The _____ _____ theory of intervention claims that intervention is supplied in order to attain allocative efficiency. The _____ theory of intervention states that intervention is intended to maximize producer surplus.

6 The process of selling a publicly owned corporation to private shareholders is called _____ .

7 The pricing rule that maximizes total surplus and achieves allocative efficiency is the _____ _____ pricing rule.

8 When a regulatory agency sets the price of a regulated natural monopolist so that the regulated firm is able to earn a specified target percentage return on its capital, it is using _____ _____ _____ regulation. If the target rate of return is a normal rate of return, this form of regulation gives the same result as the _____ _____ pricing rule.

9 An efficient public corporation will produce an output such that price equals _____ _____ .

TRUE OR FALSE

___ 1 Regulation and privatization are the two main ways that the government intervenes in the operation of monopolistic and oligopolistic markets.

___ 2 In a monopoly industry, producer surplus is maximized at the profit-maximizing level of output.

___ 3 In a monopoly industry, total surplus is maximized at the profit-maximizing level of output.

___ 4 Intervention is supplied by politicians and bureaucrats.

___ 5 Evidence of higher-than-normal rates of return for regulated natural monopolies would match the predictions of the capture theory.

___ 6 According to the public interest theory of intervention, all government intervention will move the economy closer to allocative efficiency.

___ 7 A natural monopoly will always produce on the downward-sloping portion of its average total cost curve.

___ 8 For a natural monopoly, marginal cost will always be less than average total cost.

___ 9 An average cost pricing rule will achieve allocative efficiency.

___ 10 Under rate of return regulation, firms can get closer to maximizing producer surplus if they inflate their costs.

___ **11** According to the public interest theory, regulators will regulate a cartel to make sure that firms do not cheat on the collusive cartel agreement to restrict output.

MULTIPLE-CHOICE

1 The difference between the maximum amount consumers are willing to pay and the amount they actually do pay for a given quantity of a good is called
  a government surplus.
  b consumer surplus.
  c producer surplus.
  d total surplus.
  e deadweight surplus.

2 Total surplus is given by the sum of
  a the gain from trade accruing to consumers and the gain from trade accruing to producers.
  b the gain from regulation and the gain from anti-combination laws.
  c revenues received by firms and government subsidies.
  d consumer payments and producer profit.
  e none of the above.

3 Total surplus is maximized when
  a marginal cost equals marginal revenue.
  b marginal cost equals average total cost.
  c price equals marginal cost.
  d price equals average total cost.
  e price equals average variable cost.

4 A large demand for intervention by *producers* will result when there is a
  a small consumer surplus per buyer.
  b large consumer surplus per buyer.
  c large number of buyers.
  d small producer surplus per firm.
  e large producer surplus per firm.

5 Which of the following is consistent with the public interest theory of intervention?
  a regulation of a natural monopolist by setting price equal to marginal cost
  b regulation of a competitive industry in order to increase output
  c regulation of the airline industry by establishing minimum airfares
  d regulation of agriculture by establishing barriers to exit from the industry
  e none of the above

6 Which of the following is consistent with the capture theory of intervention?
  a regulation of a natural monopolist by setting price equal to marginal cost
  b regulation of a competitive industry in order to increase output
  c regulation of the airline industry by establishing minimum airfares
  d regulation of agriculture by establishing barriers to exit from the industry
  e none of the above

7 Figure 20.2 gives the revenue and cost curves for an industry. This industry will become a natural monopoly because
  a one firm can supply the entire market at a lower price than can two or more firms.
  b there are decreasing returns to scale over the entire range of demand.
  c there are diseconomies of scale over the entire range of demand.
  d even a single firm will be unable to earn a positive profit in this industry.
  e all of the above are true.

Figure 20.2

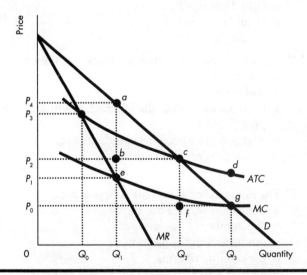

8 Consider the natural monopoly depicted in Fig. 20.2. If the firm is unregulated and operates as a private profit-maximizer, what output will it produce?
  a 0, because the firm suffers economic losses when $P = MC$.
  b Q_0

c Q_1
d Q_2
e Q_3

9 Consider the natural monopoly depicted in Fig. 20.2. If a regulatory agency sets a price just sufficient for the firm to earn normal profits, what output will it produce?
a 0, because the firm suffers economic losses when $P = MC$.
b Q_0
c Q_1
d Q_2
e Q_3

10 Consider the natural monopoly depicted in Fig. 20.2. Total surplus is a maximum when quantity is
a Q_0 and price is P_3.
b Q_1 and price is P_1.
c Q_1 and price is P_4.
d Q_2 and price is P_2.
e Q_3 and price is P_0.

11 Consider the natural monopoly depicted in Fig. 20.2. Producer surplus is a maximum when quantity is
a Q_0 and price is P_3.
b Q_1 and price is P_1.
c Q_1 and price is P_4.
d Q_2 and price is P_2.
e Q_3 and price is P_0.

12 A monopolist under rate of return regulation has an incentive to
a pad costs.
b produce more than the efficient quantity of output.
c charge a price equal to marginal cost.
d maximize consumer surplus.
e do both **a** and **b**.

13 The demand for intervention depends on
a consumer surplus per buyer.
b the number of buyers.
c producer surplus per firm.
d the number of firms.
e all of the above.

SHORT ANSWER

1 Regulation of monopoly is necessary because of the tension between the public interest and the producer's interest. Explain.

2 In the regulation of a natural monopoly, when would an average cost pricing rule be better than a marginal cost pricing rule?

3 Why is rate of return regulation equivalent to average cost pricing?

4 Explain the problem that the recent deregulation process poses for the capture theory of intervention.

PROBLEMS

1 a It has been suggested that government should eliminate monopoly profit by taxing each unit of monopoly output. What effect would such a policy have on the quantity a monopolist produces and the price it charges?
b What is the effect on economic efficiency?

2 The demand for Aerodiscs, a disc made from a unique material that flies a considerable distance when thrown, is given by this equation:

$$P = 10 - 0.01\, Q_D$$

The corresponding marginal revenue (*MR*) equation is

$$MR = 10 - 0.02\, Q$$

The Aerodisc Company is a natural monopoly. The firm's total fixed cost is £700 and the marginal cost is constant at £2 per disc. (*Note*: This implies that average variable cost is also constant at £2 per disc.) Suppose that the Aerodisc Company is not regulated.
a What will be the quantity sold and the price of an Aerodisc?
b How much is total profit or loss?
c How much is producer surplus?
d How much is consumer surplus?
e How much is total surplus?

3 Now suppose that the Aerodisc Company becomes regulated and that the regulator uses a marginal cost pricing rule.
a What will be the quantity sold and the price of an Aerodisc?
b How much is total profit or loss?
c How much is producer surplus?
d How much is consumer surplus?
e How much is total surplus?

4 Suppose that the regulator of the Aerodisc Company uses an average cost pricing rule.

    a What will be the price of an Aerodisc and how many will be sold?

    b How much is total profit or loss?

    c How much is producer surplus?

    d How much is consumer surplus?

    e How much is total surplus?

5 Figure 20.3 illustrates the industry demand, marginal revenue (*MR*) and marginal cost (*MC*) curves in an oligopoly industry. The industry is regulated.

    a What price and quantity will be predicted by the public interest theory of regulation? Why?

    b What price and quantity will be predicted by the capture theory of regulation? Why?

    c Can you explain why the firms in this industry might be demanders of regulation?

Figure 20.3

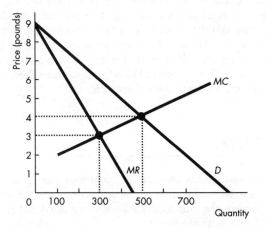

DATA QUESTIONS

The Nationalized Industries

The financial controls on the nationalized industries have been built on the arrangements which were set out in the 1978 White Paper 'The Nationalised Industries'. The control framework operates at a number of levels:

◆ Strategic objectives are agreed with each individual industry.

◆ Financial targets and performance aims. Financial targets, usually set for three-year periods, are the primary control on the industries.

◆ External financing limits are a short-term control on the amount of finance which an industry may raise during the financial year to supplement its income from trading.

◆ Investment appraisal and pricing principles. Most nationalized industries are required to aim at a rate of return on their new investment programmes of 5 per cent in real terms. This is intended to ensure proper return on investment and, at the same time, that the industries do not divert resources away from areas where they could be used more effectively.

◆ Monitoring plays an important part in stimulating and controlling the industries' performance in the interests of the taxpayer and consumer.

Source: Adapted from *The Government's Expenditure Plans 1989–1990 to 1991–1992.* Central Statistical Office. Crown Copyright 1992. Reproduced by the permission of the Controller of HMSO and the Central Statistical Office.

1 Explain what is meant by 'investment appraisal'.

2 Why should the government regulate the rate of return of the nationalized industries?

3 What disadvantages does this method have?

4 Explain the public interest theory of intervention.

ANSWERS

CONCEPT REVIEW

1 regulation; nationalization; general competition policy

2 consumer surplus; producer surplus; total surplus

3 maximized

4 larger; larger

5 public interest; capture

6 privatization

7 marginal cost

8 rate of return; average cost

9 marginal cost

TRUE OR FALSE

1 **F** Regulation but not privatization.

2 **T** Definition.

3 **F** True for competition.

4 **T** Definition.

5 **T** Regulators are captured and act in the interests of the monopoly.

6 **T** In this theory governments act in the public interest.

7 **T** To maximize profits.

8 **T** That's why *ATC* is always downward sloping.

9 **F** Marginal cost pricing will do this.

10 **T** Increased costs will allow them to increase profits.

11 **F** Regulators will prohibit collusive cartels.

MULTIPLE-CHOICE

1 **b** Definition.

2 **a** Consumer surplus plus producer surplus.

3 **c** Pricing rule for allocative efficiency.

4 **e** **b, c** lead to increased demand by buyers.

5 **a** This is the only option which will lead to increased efficiency.

6 **c** Helps airline firms, not consumers.

7 **a** Definition of natural monopoly.

8 **c** Where $MC = MR$.

9 **d** Where $P = ATC$.

10 **e** Where $P = MC$.

11 **c** Private monopoly outcome.

12 **a** Higher costs will allow higher profits.

13 **e** Definition.

SHORT ANSWER

1 It is in the public interest to achieve allocative efficiency; to expand output to the level that maximizes total surplus. On the other hand, it is in the interest of the monopoly producer to restrict output in order to maximize producer surplus and thus monopoly profit.

Since these interests are not the same, monopoly must be regulated in order to achieve allocative efficiency. The public interest theory of regulation suggests that this is the principle that guides regulation of monopoly industries.

2 An average cost pricing rule will create a deadweight loss but so will a marginal cost pricing rule, through the need to impose a tax.

Since, for a natural monopoly, marginal cost is less than average total cost, regulation by use of a marginal cost pricing rule requires the government to pay a subsidy in order for the firm to be willing to produce at all.

In order to pay that subsidy the government must levy a tax which will impose a deadweight loss on the economy. If the deadweight loss associated with the tax (for example, the deadweight loss of the marginal cost pricing rule with its attendant subsidy) is greater than the deadweight loss of an average cost pricing rule, the average cost pricing rule is superior.

3 The key here is to recall that economic cost includes a normal rate of return. Thus, because rate of return regulation sets a price that allows the firm to achieve a normal rate of return, it is setting the price equal to average total cost.

4 The capture theory predicts that producers will capture the regulatory process and use it to maximize producer surplus. But if the producer lobby was strong enough to achieve regulation, why have producers been unable to stop deregulation? A further question is: why do many producers *favour* deregulation? The capture theory has no good answers to these questions.

PROBLEMS

1 **a** Imposing a tax on each unit sold by a monopolist will increase marginal cost. As a consequence the profit-maximizing monopolist will raise the price and reduce the quantity produced.

b The tax will certainly reduce the profit of the monopolist and may even eliminate it, but the consequence will be to make the inefficiency due to monopoly even worse. This is illustrated in Fig. 20.4. The curve *MC* is the marginal cost curve before the tax. An unregulated monopolist will produce amount Q_2, while the economically efficient output is Q_3. The tax, however, causes the monopolist to reduce output from Q_1 to Q_2 which moves the market outcome farther away from efficiency.

2 Figure 20.5 will be helpful in answering questions about the Aerodisc market. It gives the relevant revenue and cost curves for the Aerodisc Company.

Figure 20.4

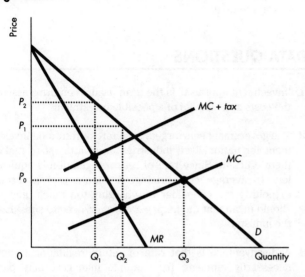

Figure 20.5

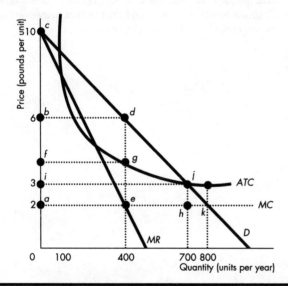

a In an unregulated market, the Aerodisc Company will choose output so as to maximize profit, where $MR = MC$. To calculate this output, set $MR = MC = 2$ and solve for Q:

$$10 - 0.02Q = 2$$
$$8 = 0.02Q$$
$$400 = Q$$

To calculate price, substitute $Q = 400$ into the demand equation:

$$P = 10 - 0.01Q_D$$
$$= 10 - 0.01\,(400)$$
$$= 10 - 4$$
$$= 6$$

400 Aerodiscs will be produced and sold at a price of £6 each.

b To determine total profit we first determine average total cost (ATC) when output (Q) is 400 units.

$$ATC = AFC + AVC$$
$$= (TFC/Q) + AVC$$
$$= (700/400) + 2$$
$$= 3.75.$$

Therefore, total profit is the difference between price (average revenue) and ATC times the quantity sold. This is equal to £90 and is represented in Fig. 20.5 by the region *fbdg*.

c Producer surplus is the difference between the producer's revenue and the opportunity cost of production. Total revenue is £2,400 (£6 × 400 units) and total opportunity cost is £800 (£2 × 400 units). Thus, producer surplus is £1,600. Graphically, producer surplus is the area of the rectangle *abde* in Fig. 20.5.

d Consumer surplus is readily obtained graphically as the area in the triangle denoted *bcd* in Fig. 20.5. The area of that triangle is £800.

e Total surplus is £2,400, the sum of producer and consumer surplus.

3 a Under a marginal cost pricing rule, the price of an Aerodisc will be equal to marginal cost or £2. To calculate the quantity sold, substitute the price into the demand equation:

$$P = 10 - 0.01Q_D$$
$$2 = 10 - 0.01Q_D$$
$$0.01Q_D = 8$$
$$Q_D = 800.$$

b To determine the amount of profit or loss, we must first determine ATC when output is 800. Using the procedure in the previous problem we find that at $Q = 800$, ATC is £2.875 which is greater than price by £0.875 (87.5 pence). Therefore, the Aerodisc Company will make a loss of £700 (£0.875 × 800). Alternatively, since MC is constant, if the price is set equal to MC which is equal to AVC, the total loss will be just TFC or £700.

c Producer surplus is zero.

d Consumer surplus is given by the area of the triangle *ach* in Fig. 20.5 which is £3,200.

e Total surplus is £3,200 (a maximum).

4 a Computation of ATC at various levels of output allows us to determine that the ATC curve crosses the demand curve when $Q = 700$ and $ATC = £3$. Thus, under an average cost pricing rule, the price of an Aerodisc will be £3 and 700 units will be sold.

b Since price is equal to average total cost, profit is zero.

c Producer surplus is £700, the area of the rectangle *aijh* in Fig. 20.5.

d Consumer surplus is £2,450, the area of the triangle *ijc* in Fig. 20.5.

e Total surplus is £3,150.

5 a The public interest theory predicts that regulators will set price and quantity so as to maximize total surplus. This means that they will choose quantity (and price) where *MC* is equal to demand. This corresponds to a quantity of 500 units and a price of £4 per unit.

b The capture theory predicts that the regulator will choose quantity and price so as to maximize the profit of the industry. This is the quantity that would be chosen by a profit-maximizing monopolist, 300 units, where *MC = MR*. The highest price that could be charged and still sell that quantity can be read from the demand curve: £6 per unit.

c Firms in the industry would be demanders of regulation if the regulation had the effect of increasing profit to the industry. As we discovered in Chapter 13, cartels are unstable because there is always an incentive to cheat on output restriction agreements and it is very difficult to enforce the agreements. If, however, the firms in an industry can get the government, through regulation, to enforce a cartel agreement, they will want to do it.

DATA QUESTIONS

1 'Investment appraisal' is the term used when firms assess the costs and benefits of a possible investment.

2 The government sets targets for a rate of return on investment for nationalized industries in an attempt to make them efficient. Since rate of return regulation is equivalent to average cost pricing, it should prevent firms exploiting the consumer by charging too much, and it should mean that the taxpayer does not need to subsidize the industry.

3 A disadvantage is that rate of return regulation is not necessarily efficient; for example managers may pad firms' costs.

4 The public interest theory of intervention suggests that the government should intervene in order to maximize total surplus. It predicts that the political process will eliminate deadweight loss and ensure that prices and output are close to their competitive levels.

Chapter 21

Unemployment, Inflation, Cycles and Deficits

Chapter In Perspective, Text Pages 579–606

With this chapter, we begin our study of macroeconomics, and so our attention turns to the economy as a whole. As a result, we will be interested in understanding the nature of many of the economic issues that dominate the daily headlines: unemployment, inflation, recession, government and balance of payments deficits. In this chapter, some of the basic concepts are introduced. Their causes and consequences are explored in the next several chapters.

Helpful Hints

1 The inflation rate is calculated as the percentage change in prices using the following formula:

$$\text{Inflation rate} = \frac{\substack{\text{Current year's} \\ \text{price level}} - \substack{\text{Last year's} \\ \text{price level}}}{\text{Last year's price level}} \times 100$$

When the problem of inflation is evaluated for an economy, it is crucial to know whether or not the inflation is *unanticipated* or *anticipated*. Unanticipated inflation creates problems by making it difficult to determine the value of money, and therefore to make certain decisions such as those about borrowing and saving.

Anticipated inflation does not share this problem, but it is still a problem because it continually reduces the value of money over time. This causes people to economize on the use of money, and results in too many transactions.

2 Note that to be unemployed, as officially measured in the United Kingdom, it is not enough to be without a job. One must also be 'actively' seeking a job and claiming job-seeker's allowance.

3 In a dynamic economy, not all unemployment is inefficient. Younger workers typically experience periods of unemployment as they try to find a job that matches their skills and interest.

The benefit to them of the resulting frictional unemployment is a much more satisfying and productive work life. Society benefits because the frictional unemployment that accompanies such a job-search process allows workers to find jobs in which they are more productive. As a result, the total production of goods and services in the economy rises.

4 When economists use the term 'full employment', it does not mean that everyone has a job. Rather, it means that the only unemployment is frictional unemployment. When the economy is at full employment, the rate of unemployment is called the natural rate of unemployment.

It is possible for the actual rate of unemployment to be less than the natural rate of unemployment. This is the same as saying that it is possible for the level of employment to exceed full employment. In these situations, people are spending too little time searching for jobs, and therefore less productive job matches are being made.

5 It is very important to understand the difference between real and nominal GDP. Nominal GDP is the value, in terms of current prices, of the output of final goods and services in the economy in a year. Real GDP evaluates those final goods and services in terms of the prices prevailing in a base year.

Nominal GDP can rise from one year to the next either because prices rise or because the output of goods and services rises. A rise in real GDP, however, means that the output of goods and services has risen.

Key Figures

Figure 21.1 UK Unemployment, 1900–1993, text page 581
The rate of unemployment has fluctuated considerably although the fluctuations seem to be generally smaller since the end of World War II. The worst period of unemployment was during the inter-war years.

Figure 21.3 The UK Price Level, 1900–1993, text page 587
This indicates the behaviour of the price level in the United Kingdom from 1900 to 1993. Over the entire period, there has been a general tendency for the price level to rise, although the rate of growth has not been steady.

Figure 21.5 Gross Domestic Product, 1968–1993, text page 594
Gross domestic product over the period 1968 to 1993 is given in this figure. Gross domestic product has grown steadily over this period, but most of the growth has been the result of increases in the growth rate of nominal GDP. On the other hand, real GDP (which is the increase in nominal GDP attributable to the increase in the volume of goods and services produced) has grown much more slowly.

Figure 21.6 UK Real GDP, 1900–1993, text page 594
The dominant feature here is the general tendency of real GDP to increase steadily. The growth rate has not been constant, however, and, in fact, real GDP has actually decreased in some periods.

Figure 21.8 The Business Cycle, 1978–1993, text page 597
The four phases of the business cycle are illustrated here by examining the behaviour of real GDP deviations from trend over the 1978–1993 period. The expansion ended with a peak in 1988.

Figure 21.9 Unemployment and the Business Cycle, 1900–1993, text page 598
The behaviour of real GDP relative to trend over the business cycle is mirrored by the behaviour of the unemployment rate. This is illustrated for the period between 1900 and 1993. Note that the scale of the unemployment rate measured on the right-hand side has been inverted so that an upward movement in the unemployment rate line indicates a decline in the unemployment rate. The important feature to notice is the fact that the two curves exhibit a strong tendency to move up and down together. This indicates the close association between the two measures of economic activity over business cycles.

SELF-TEST

CONCEPT REVIEW

1 An upward movement in the average level of prices is called _____. The average level of prices is called the price _____ and is measured by a price _____ .

2 The percentage change in the price level is called the _____ _____ . When the price level is rising, the value of money is _____ .

3 The rate at which the currency of one country exchanges for the currency of another is the _____ _____ rate.

4 An unanticipated _____ in the inflation rate benefits borrowers and hurts lenders, while an unanticipated _____ in the inflation rate hurts borrowers and benefits lenders.

5 _____ is a mechanism which automatically links payments made under a contract to the price level.

6 _____ is measured as the number of adult workers who have jobs. The unemployment rate is _____ expressed as a percentage of the _____ _____ .

7 People who do not have jobs and would like work but have stopped looking for a job are called _____ workers.

8 Unemployment that consists of (usually young) workers seeking their first or second job is called _____ unemployment. Unemployment that is caused by technological change is called _____ unemployment. When all unemployment is of these types, the economy is said to be at _____ employment and the unemployment rate is called the _____ rate of unemployment.

9 The value of all final goods and services produced in the economy is called _____ _____ _____ . This does not include _____ goods which are used as inputs in the production of other goods.

10 The value of final goods and services using current prices is called _____ GDP while the value of final goods and services using the prices that prevailed in some base period is called _____ GDP.

11 The periodic but irregular up and down movement in real GDP and other macroeconomic variables over time is called the _____ _____ . The part of this movement in which the pace of economic activity is slowing down is called a(n) _____ , while the period during which the pace of economic activity is speeding up is called a(n) _____ .

12 A downturn in economic activity in which real GDP falls for at least two successive quarters is called a(n) _____ .

13 The total expenditure of the government sector minus the total revenue it receives is called the government _____ .

14 The difference between the value of goods and services we sell to other countries and the value of goods and services other countries sell to us is called the _____ _____ _____ .

15 The three types of unemployment are _____ , _____ and _____ .

TRUE OR FALSE

___ **1** If the average level of prices doubles, the value of money is half of what it was.

___ **2** If the rate of inflation is higher in the United Kingdom than in Japan, we would expect to see the value of the pound fall in terms of the Japanese yen.

___ **3** If there is an unanticipated decrease in the rate of inflation, borrowers will be helped while lenders will be hurt.

___ **4** If the rate of inflation is expected to rise, people will want to hold less money on average.

__ **5** The labour force is the sum of the employed and the unemployed.

__ **6** In order to be at full employment, there must be no unemployment.

__ **7** Human capital tends to deteriorate when a worker is unemployed for a long period of time.

__ **8** When we measure GDP we do not include the value of intermediate goods and services produced.

__ **9** If nominal GDP is higher in year 2 than it was in year 1, we know that more goods and services were produced in year 2.

__ **10** In the contraction phase of a business cycle, the unemployment rate is rising.

__ **11** The behaviour of stock market prices is a very reliable leading indicator of business cycle turning points.

MULTIPLE-CHOICE

1 Price stability occurs when
  a all prices in the economy are constant.
  b the rate of inflation is zero.
  c the rate of inflation is constant.
  d the base period remains unchanged.
  e the price level increases at a steady rate.

2 A price index
  a is a technique used to link payments made under contract to the price level.
  b measures the rate of inflation in a base year.
  c measures the value of GDP in current pounds.
  d measures the average level of prices in one period as a percentage of their level in a base period.
  e measures the rate of change of prices.

3 If a price index was 128 at the end of 1993 and 136 at the end of 1994, what was the rate of inflation for 1994?
  a 4.2 per cent
  b 5.9 per cent
  c 6.25 per cent
  d 8 per cent
  e 9.4 per cent

4 If the rate of inflation is lower than anticipated,

  a lenders will gain at the expense of borrowers, and workers will gain at the expense of employers.
  b borrowers will gain at the expense of lenders, and workers will gain at the expense of employers.
  c lenders will gain at the expense of borrowers, and employers will gain at the expense of workers.
  d borrowers will gain at the expense of lenders, and employers will gain at the expense of workers.
  e lenders will gain at the expense of borrowers, and whether employers or workers gain or lose is uncertain.

5 A fully anticipated increase in the rate of inflation
  a is not costly because contracts can be adjusted.
  b benefits both workers and employers.
  c is costly because it reduces the opportunity cost of holding money.
  d is costly because it encourages an increase in the frequency of transactions that people undertake.
  e is costly because it redistributes from lender to borrower.

6 In a country with a population of 20 million, there are 9 million people employed and 1 million people unemployed. What is the labour force?
  a 20 million
  b 10 million
  c 9 million
  d 8 million
  e 1 million

7 In a country with a population of 20 million, there are 9 million people employed and 1 million people unemployed. What is the unemployment rate?
  a 11 per cent
  b 1 per cent
  c 8 per cent
  d 5 per cent
  e 10 per cent

8 Gross domestic product is defined as the value of all
  a goods produced in an economy in a year.
  b goods and services produced in an economy in a year.
  c final goods produced in an economy in a year.
  d final goods and services produced in an economy in a year.

e final goods and services produced in an economy in a year, controlling for the level of inflation.

9 Nominal GDP will increase
  a only if the average level of prices rises.
  b only if the quantity of goods and services produced increases.
  c only if the unemployment rate rises.
  d if the average level of prices rises and the quantity of goods and services produced increases.
  e if either the average level of prices rises or the quantity of goods and services produced increases.

10 Which of the following is *not* a reason for rising trend real GDP?
  a rising stock market prices
  b better educated workers
  c growing stock of capital equipment
  d growing population
  e advances in technology

11 Which of the following has consistently fluctuated closely with the deviation from trend in real GDP?
  a inflation rate
  b unemployment rate
  c government deficit
  e real stock prices
  e international deficit

SHORT ANSWER

1 a What is meant by the value of money?
  b Why does the value of money fall when there is inflation?

2 Consider borrowers and lenders. Who benefits and who is hurt when the rate of inflation is less than anticipated? Explain.

3 What is happening to the deviation from trend in real GDP and the unemployment rate during each of the four phases of the business cycle?

4 a What is the current account balance?
  b When is it in deficit?

PROBLEMS

1 When the rate of inflation is expected to be zero, Jennifer wants to lend money if the interest rate is at least 5 per cent, and Sean wants to borrow money if the interest rate is 5 per cent or less. Thus, they make a loan agreement at a 5 per cent rate of interest if they expect zero inflation.
  a If they both expect a rate of inflation of 4 per cent over the period of the loan, what interest rate will they agree to?
  b If they both expect a 2 per cent rate of deflation over the period of the loan, what interest rate will they agree to?
  c Suppose Jennifer expects the rate of inflation to be 4 per cent but Sean expects it to be 6 per cent. Will they be able to work out a loan agreement? If so, at what rate of interest?

2 Suppose nominal GDP rises by 75 per cent between year 1 and year 2.
  a If the average level of prices has also risen by 75 per cent between year 1 and year 2, what has happened to real GDP?
  b If the average level of prices has risen by less than 75 per cent between year 1 and year 2, has real GDP increased or decreased?

3 Consider the following information about an economy:

Population	25 million
Employment	10 million
Unemployment	1 million

  a What is the labour force in this economy?
  b What is the unemployment rate?
  c If 0.6 million of those unemployed are frictionally unemployed, what is the natural rate of unemployment?

DATA QUESTIONS

The Cost of Unemployment
The cost of unemployment to the individual worker is partially a monetary one. Most unemployed people are financially worse off than they were when employed. The difference is equal to the gap between their previous earnings and their current unemployment and social security benefits less net travel and related costs. In calculating net travel costs one has to take into account both the cost of travelling to work and the travel costs involved in searching for another job.

Non-monetary costs and benefits of being unemployed are more difficult to quantify. For many, a job is something which the individual enjoys. It also gives the person status and frequently is a source of friendship. On the other hand there are the potential benefits from having more leisure, although the ability to make best use of this leisure may be limited by financial constraints. In addition, there is now considerable evidence that unemployment can lead to increased stress both on the individual and the family, leading to an increase in ill health.

As well as the individual costs of being unemployed, there are also costs to society as a whole. Unemployment implies that the economy is inside the production possibility frontier so that fewer goods and services are produced than the economy would produce at full employment.

The government suffers a loss of income through taxation when unemployment is above the natural rate and equally sees an increase in its expenditure on unemployment benefits and social security payments. This drop in revenue and increase in expenditure will eventually affect those people in employment through increased taxes.

1 Explain what is meant by
  a 'production possibility frontier'
  b the 'natural rate of unemployment'.

2 Why do people in jobs lose from large-scale unemployment?

3 What are the benefits of unemployment?

ANSWERS

CONCEPT REVIEW

1 inflation; level; index
2 inflation rate; falling
3 foreign exchange
4 increase; decrease
5 indexing
6 Employment; unemployment; labour force
7 discouraged
8 frictional; structural; full; natural
9 gross domestic product; intermediate
10 nominal; real
11 business cycle; contraction; expansion
12 recession
13 deficit
14 current account balance
15 frictional; structural; cyclical

TRUE OR FALSE

1 T If prices double, each pound buys only half as much.
2 T Higher inflation means that the value of the pound falls as measured by the number of yen needed to buy one pound.

3 F Lenders will be helped since they will receive relatively more money from their loans.
4 T If inflation is anticipated people will realize that the value of money will fall and so will buy goods or other assets.
5 T Definition.
6 F There is frictional unemployment even at 'full' employment.
7 T Since unemployed people's knowledge becomes obsolete.
8 T If we did there would be double counting.
9 F There may be more goods produced, but it depends on the rate of inflation.
10 T As economy moves into recession, cyclical unemployment rises.
11 F Stock markets are sometimes a useful indicator, but not always.

MULTIPLE-CHOICE

1 b Definition.
2 d Definition.
3 c $6.25\% = [(136 - 128)/128] \times 100$
4 a Lenders will receive more than they expected and so will workers whose expected wage includes an amount for expected inflation.

5 d Higher inflation leads to a fall in the value of money causing people to reduce money holdings; hence more transactions.

6 b Labour force = employed people + unemployed people.

7 e Unemployment rate = unemployed/labour force = 1/10.

8 d Definition.

9 e Because nominal GDP includes both these factors.

10 a There is no relation between stock prices and trend GDP.

11 b The others are loosely related or not related to the business cycle.

SHORT ANSWER

1 a The value of money is the quantity of goods and services that can be purchased with one unit of money.

b Since inflation means that prices are rising on average, it means that one unit of money will buy less. Thus the value of money falls when there is inflation.

2 Because both borrowers and lenders realize that inflation reduces the value of money, loan agreements will specify a rate of interest that reflects the anticipated rate of inflation. In particular, if they expect a high rate of inflation, they will agree to a higher interest rate. If the rate of inflation turns out to be less than anticipated, borrowers are hurt and lenders benefit because the agreed upon interest rate, after adjusting for inflation, will be higher than expected.

3 During the contraction phase of the business cycle, the rate of growth of real GDP slows down and real GDP falls below its trend. During this phase the unemployment rate is rising.

During the trough phase, real GDP reaches its lowest point below trend and the unemployment rate is at its highest point over the cycle.

The trough is a turning point between the contraction phase and the expansion phase during which the rate of growth of real GDP increases and the unemployment rate falls.

At the end of an expansion, the economy reaches the peak phase of the business cycle. The peak is characterized by real GDP at its highest point above its trend and the rate of unemployment is at its lowest point over the business cycle.

4 a The current account balance is the difference between the value of all goods and services that we sell to other countries (exports) and the value of all the goods and services that we buy from other countries (imports).

b The current account is in deficit if we buy more from the rest of the world than we sell to the rest of the world, meaning that imports are greater than exports.

PROBLEMS

1 a Since both Jennifer and Sean expect the rate of inflation to be 4 per cent, they expect the value of money to decrease by 4 per cent. Thus, they will agree to a 9 per cent rate of interest to offset this, leaving a 5 per cent rate of interest really paid after accounting for inflation.

b If both Jennifer and Sean expect a rate of deflation of 2 per cent, they expect the value of money to increase by 2 per cent. By the same logic as above, they will agree to a 3 per cent rate of interest.

c If Jennifer expects a 4 per cent rate of inflation, she will want to loan only if the interest rate is at least 9 per cent. If Sean expects a 6 per cent rate of inflation, he will want to borrow if the rate of interest is 11 per cent or less. Thus Jennifer and Sean could agree on any interest rate between 9 and 11 per cent.

2 a Real GDP is unchanged. The increased value of goods and services is due only to increased prices.

b The fact that prices have risen less in proportion to the increase in nominal GDP means that real GDP has increased.

3 a The labour force is 11 million, the sum of employment and unemployment.

b The unemployment rate is 9.1 per cent, the number unemployed as a percentage of the labour force.

c The natural rate of unemployment is the rate of unemployment that would exist if the unemployment is frictional and structural. In our case, it is the rate of unemployment if unemployment were only 0.6 million. Thus the natural rate of unemployment is 5.45 per cent.

DATA QUESTIONS

1 a A production possibility frontier is the boundary between attainable and unattainable levels of production.

b The natural rate of unemployment is the rate of unemployment which exists when the economy is at full employment.

2 People in employment lose out when unemployment is high because they have to pay higher taxes to pay for the increased government expenditure and lower income which results from unemployment. There is also an opportunity cost – those in jobs cannot benefit from the goods and services which would have been produced if the unemployed people had been working.

3 Unemployment can impose large costs, but frictional unemployment is necessary and beneficial because it gives the labour market more flexibility and hence leads to a better allocation of resources.

Chapter 22

Measuring Output and the Price Level

Chapter In Perspective, Text Pages 607–636

How do we measure aggregate economic activity or the price level? In this chapter we address these questions in some detail.

The most widely used measure of economic activity is gross domestic product (GDP). Here we discuss what it is and how it is measured. We will also examine the Retail Prices Index and the GDP deflator, two measures of the price level. As indicated in Chapter 1, one of the components of any science is careful and systematic measurement. In this chapter, we will see how measurements of the behaviour of the aggregate economy are made. The concepts measured here will lay a foundation for our analysis of macroeconomic theory.

Helpful Hints

1 Be sure to distinguish carefully between intermediate goods and investment goods. Both are typically goods sold by one firm to another, but they differ in terms of their use. Intermediate goods are goods that are processed and then resold, while investment goods are final goods themselves. Also note that the national income accounts include purchases of residential housing as investment because housing, like business capital stock, provides a continuous stream of value over time.

2 Note the difference between government spending on goods and services *(G)* and government transfer payments. Both involve payments by the govern-

ment, but transfer payments are not payments for currently produced goods and services. Instead, they are simply a flow of money, just like taxes. Indeed it is often useful to think of transfer payments as negative taxes. Therefore, we define net taxes *(T)* as taxes minus transfer payments.

3 There are several key equations introduced in this chapter that are important for you to understand. The first four of these key equations can be understood by careful examination of the circular flow in Fig. 22.2 on text page 612. This figure shows a stylized view of the economy. The equations attempt to measure exactly the flows shown. As illustrated, gross domestic product can be measured in several different ways, all of which are equivalent:

i Income = Expenditure = Value of output (GDP)

This equation indicates that expenditures on final goods (in the goods markets) are received as income (in the factor markets), and that the value of the output (produced by firms) is reflected by the amount that is spent on goods and services. It gives rise to the three equivalent ways of computing GDP studied in this chapter:

ii $Y = C + I + G + EX - IM$

Equation **ii** reflects the expenditure approach to measuring GDP. It tells us that GDP is equal to the total amount of spending on domestic output in the economy by households, firms, government and foreigners. Spending on imports is subtracted to account for the fact that imports are not domestically produced.

iii $Y = C + S + T$

All income accrues to households that own the factors of production. Equation **iii** indicates that income must be spent on goods and services *(C)* or spent as net taxes *(T)* or saved *(S)*. Indeed, saving is defined as disposable income *(Y – T)* minus consumption expenditure *(C)*.

iv $I + G + EX = S + T + IM$

This equation follows from combining equations **ii** and **iii**. It indicates that injections into the circular flow *(I + G + EX)* equal leakages from the circular flow *(S + T + IM)*. This is necessary to create equilibrium.

v GDP deflator = (Nominal GDP/Real GDP) × 100

This is the definition of the GDP deflator.

4 A price index for the current year is computed as the ratio of the value of a basket of goods in the current year to the value of the *same* basket of goods in a base year, multiplied by 100. It therefore attempts to calculate the cost of purchasing the same choice of goods in two different years. Note that the basket of goods used to calculate the Retail Prices Index contains goods that are purchased by a typical household. The basket of goods used to calculate the GDP deflator, on the other hand, contains all goods and services included in GDP. It does, therefore, include capital goods.

Key Figures and Tables

Figure 22.1 The Circular Flow of Expenditure and Income between Households and Firms, text page 610

The circular flow diagram illustrates the relationships between households and firms which give rise to alternative measures of aggregate expenditures and output. Three types of money flows are illustrated by the coloured arrows.

The blue arrows show the payments (income) for the use of factors of production. The red arrows show the payments for the purchase and rental of final goods and services (expenditures). Finally, the green arrows show the flows of households' saving via financial markets to firms.

Figure 22.2 The Circular Flow Including Governments and the Rest of the World, text page 612

For purposes of simplicity, the circular flow illustrated in Fig. 22.1 ignored governments and foreign sectors. In this figure, these two sectors are added. Households pay taxes to governments and receive transfer payments from governments, with the resulting net flow of net taxes *(T)*. The governments also purchase goods and services from firms *(G)*. Firms sell goods and services to the rest of the world (exports = *EX*) and also buy goods and services from the rest of the world (imports = *IM*), with a resulting net flow of net exports *(NX)*.

This diagram illustrates the basic relationships in national income accounting. The flows from firms to factor markets illustrate the factor incomes approach, while the flows from goods markets to firms illustrate the expenditure approach.

Table 22.2 GDP: The Expenditure Approach, text page 615

The expenditure approach to measuring GDP divides the economy into four expenditure sectors and then adds together the spending of these sectors. GDP is obtained as the sum of consumers' expenditures *(C)*, gross private domestic investment *(I)*, government purchases of goods and services *(G)* and net exports *(NX)*.

This table illustrates the expenditure approach by reporting GDP for the different sectors in the United Kingdom.

Table 22.3 GDP: The Factor Incomes Approach, text page 617

GDP can also be measured using an income approach. All of the payments to households for the services of factors of production they hire are added together to obtain net national income at factor cost and then some adjustments are made. This approach to measuring GDP is illustrated using UK data. The percentage contribution to GDP for each of the entries is indicated in the final column of the table.

Table 22.4 GDP: The Output Approach, text page 619
The output approach to measuring GDP begins by summing the value added in each industry of the economy to obtain gross domestic product.

SELF-TEST

CONCEPT REVIEW

1 The aggregate expenditure by households on consumption goods and services is called _____ _____ . Total spending by firms on new plant, equipment and buildings, and additions to stocks is called _____ .

2 Payments from the government to households which are not payments for currently produced goods and services are called _____ _____ .

3 _____ is equal to disposable income minus consumers' expenditure. Disposable income equals aggregate income minus net _____ .

4 Investment, government spending on goods and services and exports are examples of _____ into the circular flow of income. Taxes, saving and imports are examples of _____ from the circular flow of income.

5 The method of measuring GDP which adds consumption expenditure, investment, government purchases of goods and services and net exports is called the _____ approach. The _____ _____ approach measures GDP by adding together all incomes paid to households by firms. The _____ approach measures GDP by adding together the value added by each firm in the economy.

6 The stock of raw materials, unfinished products and finished but unsold products held by a firm is called a(n) _____ .

7 A tax which is paid by consumers when they purchase goods and services from a firm is called a(n) _____ tax.

8 The amount by which the value of the capital stock is reduced from wear and tear and passage of time is called _____ . When we subtract this amount from gross investment we have _____ investment. Gross domestic product is equal to net domestic product plus _____ .

9 The value of the output of a firm minus the value of its inputs is called _____ _____ . We are double counting if we include expenditures on _____ goods as well as final goods in our calculation of GDP.

10 We refer to economic activity that is legal but not reported to the government as the _____ _____ .

11 The _____ _____ _____ is a measure of the average level of prices of consumers' goods and services purchased by a 'typical' urban household. The _____ _____ measures the average level of prices of all final goods and services produced in the economy.

TRUE OR FALSE

___ **1** In the aggregate economy, income is equal to expenditure and to GDP.

___ **2** The government pays High Flyer Aircraft Company for a military jet. This is an example of a transfer payment.

___ **3** Disposable income is equal to consumers' expenditure plus saving.

___ **4** Disposable income is equal to income plus transfer payments minus taxes.

___ **5** Imports is an example of an injection into the circular flow of income.

— **6** If there were only households and firms and no governments, market price and factor cost would be equal for any good.

— **7** In order to measure GDP using the factor incomes approach, we must subtract indirect taxes and add subsidies to net national income at factor cost.

— **8** Net domestic product equals gross domestic product minus depreciation.

— **9** If two economies have the same GDP, then the standard of living is the same in each economy.

10 The GDP deflator is calculated as real GDP divided by nominal GDP, multiplied by 100.

11 If you are interested in knowing whether the economy is producing a greater physical volume of output, you would want to look at real GDP rather than nominal GDP.

12 If the price of good *A* rises much more rapidly than the prices of other goods, then good *A* is responsible for high inflation.

MULTIPLE-CHOICE

1 Which of the following is *not* an example of investment in the expenditure approach to measuring GDP? Peugeot
   a buys a new auto stamping machine.
   b adds 500 new cars to stocks.
   c buys French government bonds.
   d builds another assembly plant.
   e replaces some worn-out stamping machines.

2 Which of the following is true for the aggregate economy? Income equals
   a expenditure, but these are not generally equal to GDP.
   b GDP, but expenditure is generally less than these.
   c expenditure equals GDP.
   d Income equals expenditure equals GDP only if there are no government or foreign sectors.
   e Income equals expenditure equals GDP only if there is no depreciation.

3 Saving can be measured as income minus
   a taxes.
   b transfer payments.
   c taxes minus consumers' expenditure.

   d net taxes minus consumers' expenditure.
   e net taxes plus subsidies.

4 Interest plus miscellaneous investment income is a component of which approach to measuring GDP?
   a factor incomes approach
   b expenditure approach
   c injections approach
   d output approach
   e opportunity cost approach

5 To obtain the factor cost of a good from its market price, one must
   a add indirect taxes and subtract subsidies.
   b subtract indirect taxes and add subsidies.
   c subtract both indirect taxes and subsidies.
   d add both indirect taxes and subsidies.
   e subtract depreciation.

6 Which of the following is an example of a leakage from the circular flow of income?
   a exports
   b investment
   c saving
   d subsidies
   e government purchases

7 The value of a firm's output minus the value of inputs purchased is
   a net exports.
   b value added.
   c net profit.
   d indirect production.
   e capital consumption allowance.

8 The existence of which of the following is *not* a reason for the fact that GDP gives an underestimate of the value of total output in the economy?
   a crime
   b non-market activities
   c the underground economy
   d capital consumption allowance
   e externalities such as pollution

Table 22.1

Item	Price (pounds) Base	Price (pounds) Current	Quantity Base	Quantity Current
Deck chairs	1.00	1.25	100	100
Beach towels	9.00	6.00	12	14

9 Table 22.1 gives price and quantity data for an economy with only two consumers' goods: deck chairs and beach towels. What is the Retail Prices Index for the current year?
 a 100
 b 112
 c 105.6
 d 100.5
 e 94.7

10 Refer to the data in Table 22.1. Between the base year and the current year the relative price of deck chairs
 a remained unchanged.
 b fell.
 c rose.
 d cannot be determined with the amount of information given.
 e depends on what happens to the Retail Prices Index.

11 If 1995 is the base year for the GDP deflator, we know that nominal GDP
 a equals real GDP in 1995.
 b is greater than real GDP in 1995.
 c is less than real GDP in 1995.
 d in 1996 will be greater than real GDP in 1995.
 e in 1996 will be greater than nominal GDP in 1995.

12 Consider the data in Table 22.2. What is the GDP deflator in 1994?
 a 160
 b 250
 c 200
 d 88.89
 e 125

c 220
d 336.22
e 110

SHORT ANSWER

1 In the aggregate economy, why does income equal expenditure?

2 In obtaining GDP we count expenditure only on final goods. Why do we *not* count expenditure on intermediate goods?

3 a What productive activities are not measured and thus are not included in GDP?
 b Is this a serious problem?

4 Does a 5 per cent increase in the RPI mean that the cost of living has increased by 5 per cent? Why or why not?

PROBLEMS

1 Use the data for an imaginary economy given in Table 23.3 to compute the following.
 a GDP
 b net investment
 c net exports
 d disposable income
 e saving
 f total leakages from and total injections into the circular flow of income. (Are they equal?)

Table 22.2

Year	Nominal GDP (billions of pounds)	Real GDP (billions of 1986 pounds)	GDP deflator (1986=100)
1986	125	125	100
1993	250	200	
1994	279		122.22

13 Use the data in Table 22.2. What is real GDP in 1994?
 a 225
 b 275

Table 22.3

Item	Amount (billions of pounds)
Consumers' expenditure *(C)*	600
Taxes *(TX)*	400
Transfer payments *(TR)*	250
Exports *(EX)*	240
Imports *(IM)*	220
Government spending on goods and services *(G)*	200
Gross investment *(I)*	150
Depreciation *(Depr)*	60

2 Table 22.4 gives data for an economy in which there are three consumers' goods: bananas, coconuts and grapes.

Table 22.4

| Good | Base period | | | Current period | |
	Quantity in basket (boxes)	Price (pounds per box)	Expenditure (pounds)	Price (pounds per box)	Value of quantities (pounds)
Bananas	120	6		8	
Coconuts	60	8		10	
Grapes	40	10		9	

a Complete the table by computing expenditures for the base period and the appropriate value of quantities in the current year for computing the Retail Prices Index.
b What is the value of the basket of consumption goods in the base period? In the current period?
c What is the Retail Prices Index for the current period?

3 Table 22.5 gives data for an economy in which there are three final goods included in GDP: pizzas, staplers and bombs.

Table 22.5

| Good | Base period | | | Current period | |
	Quantity in basket	Price (pounds)	Expenditure (pounds)	Price (pounds)	Expenditure (pounds)
Pizzas	110		6	8	880
Staplers	50		8	10	500
Bombs	50		10	9	450

a Complete the table by computing expenditure on each good evaluated at base period prices.
b What is the value of nominal GDP in the current period?

c What is the value of real GDP in the current period?
d What is the GDP deflator in the current period?

4 Complete Table 22.6.

Table 22.6

Year	Nominal GDP (pounds)	Real GDP (pounds)	GDP deflator
1988	3,055		94
1989		3,170	100
1990	3,410	3,280	
1991		3,500	108

DATA QUESTIONS

Table 22.7 Prices and GDP in Europe

Country	GDP by volume 1993 (1985 = 100)	Consumer prices (1985 = 100)
Denmark	110.1	128.3
Finland	103.0	139.7
France	118.7	125.6
Germany	122.5	119.9
Netherlands	121.0	113.8
Norway	116.4	146.5
Spain	126.9	160.5
Sweden	106.3	158.2
United Kingdom	116.6	148.7

Source: © OECD 1994, *Main Economic Indicators*. Reproduced by permission of the OECD.

Use the data from Table 22.7.

1 Explain what is meant by 'GDP by volume (1985 = 100)'.

2 Which country had (a) the highest, and (b) the lowest rate of economic growth in the period 1985–1993?

3 Which country had (a) the largest, and (b) the smallest rise in consumer prices?

4 To what extent are GDP statistics a good measure of living standards?

ANSWERS

CONCEPT REVIEW

1 consumption expenditure; investment
2 transfer payments
3 Saving; taxes
4 injections; leakages
5 expenditure; factor incomes; output
6 stock
7 indirect
8 depreciation; net; depreciation
9 value added; intermediate
10 hidden economy
11 Retail Prices Index; GDP deflator

TRUE OR FALSE

1 **T** From circular flow diagram, production is sold (expenditure) and earnings used to pay out income.

2 **F** It is payment for a good.

3 **T** $Y = C + S + T$ so $Y - T$ (that is, disposable income) $= C + S$.

4 **T** T = Net taxes = Taxes – Transfer payments, so $Y - T$ (disposable income) $= Y -$ (Taxes – Transfer payments) $= Y +$ Transfer payments – Taxes.

5 **F** Imports are a withdrawal.

6 **T** Market price = Factor cost + Taxes – Subsidies.

7 **F** See last answer.

8 **T** Definition.

9 **F** Standard of living depends on level of GDP divided by population.

10 **F** GDP deflator = [(Nominal GDP)/(Real GDP)] × 100.

11 **T** Real GDP measures amount of goods and services while nominal GDP measures current money value and includes impact of inflation.

12 **F** Changes in relative prices do not cause inflation.

MULTIPLE-CHOICE

1 **c** This is purchase of a capital asset, not capital stock.

2 **c** Definition; the three ways of measuring the nation's accounts should be equal.

3 **d** Income after tax must be either spent or saved.

4 **a** Definition.

5 **b** Market price = Factor cost + Indirect taxes – Subsidies.

6 **c** Savings take money out of the circular flow; others are injections.

7 **b** Definition.

8 **d** This is depreciation and is part of GDP.

9 **e** RPI = [(Sum of current prices × Base quantities)/ (Sum of base prices × Base quantities)] × 100.

10 **c** Relative price = Change in price (deck chairs) – Inflation rate = 25% – (–5.3%) = 30.3%, where Inflation rate = 94.7 – 100.

11 **a** Definition of a base year.

12 **e** GDP deflator = [(Nominal GDP/Real GDP)] × 100.

13 **a** Real GDP = [(Nominal GDP)/(GDP deflator)] × 100.

SHORT ANSWER

1 When an expenditure is made, firms receive money payments. The amount received by firms in the aggregate is aggregate expenditure. All that firms receive is distributed as income to households who own the factors of production. Remember that profit is income. Since the aggregate amount firms receive is expenditure and firms pay out all they receive as income, in the aggregate economy income equals expenditure.

2 Counting both final goods and the intermediate goods that were combined to produce it will result in 'double counting'. For example, counting the value of the steel that is sold to a car manufacturer to build a car and then counting it again when the car is sold as a final good will overstate the value of final goods and services since the steel is counted twice.

3 **a** Activities that produce goods and services that are not included in GDP are criminal activities, production in the underground economy and non-market activities. The first of these is not reported because the activities themselves are illegal. The second of these refers to goods and services that are legal but are not reported to circumvent taxes or government regulations. The third includes those produc-

tive activities which households perform for themselves. Because they do not hire someone else to mow the lawn or wash the car, it is not included in GDP.

b The seriousness of the problem depends on the actual size of activity and this is difficult to measure precisely.

4 A 5 per cent increase in the RPI does not mean that the cost of living has increased by 5 per cent if relative prices also change (and they generally will). Changes in relative prices will cause consumers to make substitutions from goods whose relative price has risen to goods whose relative price has fallen. This reduces the effect on the cost of living. The fact that some goods disappear from use and new goods appear also means that changes in the RPI do not precisely reflect changes in the cost of living.

PROBLEMS

1 **a** GDP = $C + I + G + (EX - IM)$ = £970 billion
  b Net $I = I - Depr$ = £90 billion
  c $NX = EX - IM$ = £20 billion
  d Disposable income = GDP + $TR - TX$ = £820 billion
  e Saving = Disposable income $- C$ = £220 billion
  f Total leakages = $(TX - TR) + IM + S$ = £590 billion
   Total injections = $I + G + X$ = £590 billion
   So, total leakages = total injections.

2 **a** Table 22.4 is completed here as Table 22.8. Note that the base period quantities are evaluated at current prices to find the value of quantities in the current year.

Table 22.8

| | Base period | | | Current period | |
Good	Quantity in basket (boxes)	Price (pounds per box)	Expenditure (pounds)	Price (pounds per box)	Value of quantities (pounds)
Bananas	120	6	720	8	960
Coconuts	60	8	480	10	600
Grapes	40	10	400	9	360

b The value of the basket of consumers' goods in the base period is the sum of the expenditures in that period: £1,600. The value of the basket of consumers' goods is obtained as the sum of the values of quantities in that period: £1,920.

c The Retail Prices Index is the ratio of the value of quantities in the current period to the base period expenditure, times 100:

$$RPI = (1,920/1,600) \times 100 = 120$$

3 **a** Table 22.5 is shown completed as Table 22.9. Base period expenditure for each item is obtained by evaluating the current period quantity at the base year price.

Table 22.9

| | Base period | | | Current period | |
Good	Quantity in basket	Price (pounds)	Expenditure (pounds)	Price (pounds)	Expenditure (pounds)
Pizzas	110	660	6	8	880
Staplers	50	400	8	10	500
Bombs	50	500	10	9	450

b The value of nominal GDP in the current period is the sum of expenditures in the current period: £1,830.

c The value of real GDP in the current period is the sum of the current period quantities evaluated at base period prices; in other words, what the expenditures would have been at base year prices: £1,560.

d The GDP deflator for the current period is the ratio of nominal GDP to real GDP, times 100:

$$GDP \ deflator = (1,830/1,560) \times 100 = 117.3.$$

4 Table 22.6 is completed here as Table 22.10. The following equation is used:

$$GDP \ deflator = (Nominal \ GDP/Real \ GDP) \times 100.$$

Table 22.10

Year	Nominal GDP (pounds)	Real GDP (pounds)	GDP deflator
1988	3,055	3,250	94
1989	3,170	3,170	100
1990	3,410	3,280	104
1991	3,780	3,500	108

DATA QUESTIONS

1 'GDP' is an abbreviation for 'Gross Domestic Product' which is a measure of the output produced by a country, usually over one year. 'Volume' implies that the figures are in real terms, that is, excluding the effects of inflation.

'1985 = 100' means that 1985 is the base year so that, for example, in the United Kingdom GDP rose by 16.6 per cent in the period 1985 to 1993.

2 a The highest rate of growth of GDP was in Spain.
   b The lowest rate of economic growth was in Finland.

3 a Inflation was highest in Spain.
   b Inflation was lowest in the Netherlands.

4 GDP is probably the best measure of living standards, but it has serious inadequacies. In the first place, a number of economic activities are not included in the figures for GDP. These include non-market activities such as DIY and housework. Then the underground economy is excluded,

and this may amount to 5 per cent of GDP, though there are no precise estimates. Third, the figures contain errors, and it is not possible to estimate these accurately.

Even if all these limitations were overcome, the figures would not be a precise measure of living standards. GDP often rises in times of war because the economy is producing at full capacity, but living standards may be low because the goods produced are weapons of war. Other factors affecting living standards include the amount of leisure time, the quality of the environment and the amount of crime. These are not included in the statistics of GDP. Finally, an average figure for GDP per head says nothing about the distribution of that income. In some countries a small minority may take a large share of the national income.

Chapter 23 Aggregate Demand and Aggregate Supply

Chapter In Perspective, Text Pages 637–663

What determines the amount of goods and services that an economy produces? What causes inflation and how can it be controlled? What are the causes of unemployment, and why does the unemployment rate fluctuate over time? The fundamental purpose of macroeconomic analysis is to address these kinds of issues; issues regarding the behaviour of the national economy as a whole.

In this chapter we begin to build the basic tool of macroeconomic analysis: the aggregate demand–aggregate supply model. This model will prove to be very helpful as we attempt to explain the growth of real GDP and inflation as well as business cycle fluctuations in real GDP and unemployment. In subsequent chapters we take more care in developing the underlying principles of aggregate demand and aggregate supply.

Helpful Hints

1 This chapter discusses the fundamental concepts of aggregate demand, aggregate supply and macroeconomic equilibrium. The model developed is the principal means by which we interpret macroeconomic activity. While later chapters will refine our understanding of these concepts, the basic model is introduced here. As a result, this chapter should be reviewed until it is mastered.

2 Three separate reasons for the negative slope of the aggregate demand curve are discussed: the real money balances effect, the intertemporal substitution effect and the international substitution effect.

The first two of these are consequences of the fact that a change in the price level will change the level of real money. A change in real money has a direct effect on aggregate expenditure (the real money balances effect) as well as an indirect effect: a change in real money will lead to a change in interest rates which then affects aggregate expenditure (the intertemporal substitution effect).

The third effect is a consequence of the fact that a change in the UK price level changes the relative price of UK goods and services in terms of the price of goods and services in the rest of the world. In each of these cases, an increase in the price level will cause a decrease in the aggregate quantity of goods and services demanded, thus explaining a negatively sloped *AD* curve.

3 There is a single important reason for the positive slope of the short-run aggregate supply curve: input prices are held constant. Given constant input prices, a change in the price level, that is the price of output, will affect the amount of goods and services that producers are willing to supply. For example, if the price of output rises but the price of input remains constant, profit-maximizing firms will increase output.

4 As in our study of microeconomics, in macroeconomics we do not define the short run and long run in terms of a length of calendar time but rather in terms of whether or not key variables can change. Here, in the short run, the prices of factors of production do not change, whereas in the long run they do change. The principal implication is that, in the short run, a change in the price level causes the price of output relative to the price of input to change and thus firms will change their rate of output. On the other hand, in the long run, input prices adjust and there is no long-run change in output because the initial price of output relative to input prices is restored.

5 The distinction between the short run and the long run gives rise to the differences between the list of factors that affect the short-run and long-run aggregate supply curves. Since input prices are held constant for the short-run aggregate supply curve but not for the long-run aggregate supply curve, a change in input prices will shift the short-run curve but not the long-run curve.

Key Figures

Figure 23.1   The Aggregate Demand Curve and Aggregate Demand Schedule, text page 639
The aggregate demand curve illustrates the relationship between the quantity of real GDP demanded and the price level, holding other things constant. As a

result of the real money balances effect, the intertemporal substitution effect and the international substitution effect the quantity of real GDP demanded decreases as the price level rises. Thus the aggregate demand curve is negatively sloped.

Figure 23.3   Changes in Aggregate Demand, text page 644
This simply lists those factors that will cause the aggregate demand curve to shift. Changes in the factors listed will cause the aggregate quantity of goods and services demanded either to increase or to decrease *at a given price level*.

Figure 23.4   The Aggregate Supply Curves and Aggregate Supply Schedule, text page 646
The two aggregate supply curves illustrate the relationship between the quantity of real GDP supplied and the price level. The short-run aggregate supply curve (*SAS*) illustrates this relationship holding everything else constant, *including input prices*. The long-run aggregate supply curve (*LAS*) illustrates the relationship holding everything *except input prices* constant.

The *LAS* curve shows that, when input prices adjust to clear factor markets, aggregate supply is independent of the price level. Thus the *LAS* curve is vertical at the full-employment level of GDP. On the other hand, when input prices are held fixed, a rise in the price level will induce firms to increase output. Thus the *SAS* curve is positively sloped. The *SAS* curve becomes vertical at some high level of real GDP, reflecting the fact that once the economy reaches its physical limits, further increases in the price level cannot be met by increases in output.

Figure 23.6   Long-run Growth in Aggregate Supply, text page 649
This lists the factors which increase aggregate supply.

Figure 23.7   Macroeconomic Equilibrium, text page 651
Macroeconomic equilibrium occurs when the level of aggregate GDP demanded is equal to aggregate real GDP supplied. Graphically, this occurs at the intersection of the aggregate demand and short-run aggregate supply curves. This intersection gives the equilibrium value of real GDP and the price level.

SELF-TEST

CONCEPT REVIEW

1 The graphical representation of the relationship between the quantity of real GDP demanded and the price level is called the _____ _____ curve. As the price level increases, the quantity of real GDP demanded _____ .

2 There are three separate effects of the price level on the quantity of real GDP demanded. The first of these is the real money balances effect. As the price level rises, the quantity of real money _____ , which causes the quantity of real GDP demanded to _____ .

3 The second effect involves the substitution of goods now for goods later or vice versa; this is the _____ _____ effect. A lower price level will tend to lead to _____ interest rates, which causes the quantity of real GDP demanded to _____ .

4 The third effect is the _____ substitution effect. If the UK price level rises (holding everything else constant), the quantity of UK-produced goods demanded will _____ and the quantity of foreign-produced goods demanded will _____ .

5 If the quantity of money increases, (holding everything else constant) the aggregate demand curve will shift to the _____ . The aggregate demand curve will shift to the right if the government _____ taxes.

6 A firm's _____ output is the output at which its cost per unit produced is minimized. The level of real GDP that results when all firms are producing at this level of output and when there is full employment is _____ - _____ aggregate supply.

7 With input prices held constant and the economy producing below its physical limit, an increase in the price level will cause the quantity of real GDP supplied to _____ . Thus the _____ - _____ aggregate supply curve is _____ sloped. When the economy reaches its physical limit to produce, this curve becomes _____ .

8 If the quantity of real GDP demanded equals the quantity of real GDP supplied, the economy is in _____ _____ . If this occurs when the economy is on its long-run aggregate supply curve, then the economy is said to be in _____ - _____ equilibrium. If this occurs at a level of real GDP below long-run aggregate supply, a(n) _____ equilibrium has occurred.

9 If the economy is producing below its physical limit, an increase in aggregate demand (other things remaining constant, including input prices) will result in a(n) _____ in the price level and a(n) _____ in the level of real GDP.

10 An increase in the price of raw materials (other things remaining constant) will result in a(n) _____ in the price level and a(n) _____ in the level of real GDP.

TRUE OR FALSE

___ **1** According to the real money balances effect, the lower the quantity of real money, the larger the quantity of real GDP demanded.

___ **2** As interest rates decline, the aggregate quantity of goods and services demanded rises.

___ **3** An increase in the expected rate of inflation will decrease aggregate demand.

___ **4** If the government decides to increase its expenditures on goods and services, the aggregate demand curve will shift to the right.

___ **5** An increase in income taxes will cause the aggregate demand curve to shift to the right.

___ **6** If the economy is on its long-run aggregate supply curve, there is full employment.

___ **7** If the stock of capital increases, both the long-run and short-run aggregate supply curves will shift to the right.

___ **8** It is possible to have a macroeconomic equilibrium at a level of real GDP above full employment.

___ **9** If there is a significant technological advance (other things remaining unchanged), the long-run aggregate supply curve will shift to the right but the short-run aggregate supply curve will not shift.

___ **10** If there is significant technological advance (other things remaining unchanged), the price level will rise.

___ **11** The main force generating the underlying tendency of real GDP to expand over time is increases in long-run aggregate supply.

___ **12** The main force generating a long period of inflation is persistent increases in aggregate demand.

___ **13** A large increase in the price of oil, such as in 1973, will generally result in an inflationary recession.

___ **14** Any factor that shifts the short-run aggregate supply curve to the right will also shift the long-run aggregate supply curve to the right.

___ **15** If an economy is producing at levels above its long-run aggregate supply, we will expect wages to rise.

MULTIPLE-CHOICE

1 The aggregate demand curve (*AD*) illustrates that, as the price level falls, the quantity of
  a real GDP demanded increases.
  b real GDP demanded decreases.
  c nominal GDP demanded increases.
  d nominal GDP demanded decreases.
  e real balances fall.

2 Which of the following is a reason for the downward slope of the aggregate demand curve?
  a the intertemporal substitution effect
  b the international substitution effect

  c the expected inflation effect
  d the nominal balance effect
  e both **a** and **b**.

3 As the price level rises, the quantity of real money balances
  a increases, and thus the aggregate quantity of goods and services demanded increases.
  b increases, and thus the aggregate quantity of goods and services demanded decreases.
  c decreases, and thus the aggregate quantity of goods and services demanded increases.
  d decreases, and thus the aggregate quantity of goods and services demanded decreases.
  e decreases, and this has no effect on the aggregate quantity of goods and services demanded.

4 Which of the following will cause the aggregate demand curve to shift to the right?
  a an increase in interest rates (at a given price level)
  b an increase in expected inflation
  c an increase in taxes
  d a decrease in the price level
  e an increase in the price level

5 Long-run aggregate supply is the level of real GDP at which
  a each firm is producing its capacity output.
  b there is full employment.
  c the economy is producing its physical limit.
  d each firm is producing its capacity output and there is full employment.
  e prices are sure to rise.

6 Short-run aggregate supply is the relationship between the price level and the quantity of real GDP supplied, holding constant the
  a wage rate.
  b quantities of factors of production.
  c level of government spending.
  d price level.
  e prices of factors of production.

7 The short-run aggregate supply curve (*SAS*) is positively sloped but becomes vertical at the level of real GDP at which
  a each firm is producing its capacity output.
  b each firm is producing output at its physical limit.
  c there is full employment.
  d it intersects the aggregate demand curve.
  e hyperinflation starts.

8 A technological improvement will shift
  a both the short-run aggregate supply and the aggregate demand curves to the right.
  b both the short-run aggregate supply and long-run aggregate supply curves to the left.
  c the short-run aggregate supply curve to the right but leave the long-run aggregate supply curve unchanged.
  d the long-run aggregate supply curve to the right but leave the short-run aggregate supply curve unchanged.
  e both the short-run aggregate supply and long-run aggregate supply curves to the right.

9 Macroeconomic equilibrium occurs when the
  a economy is at full employment.
  b economy is producing at its physical limit.
  c aggregate demand curve intersects the short-run aggregate supply curve along its vertical portion.
  d quantity of real GDP demanded equals the quantity of real GDP supplied.
  e aggregate demand curve intersects the long-run aggregate supply curve.

10 Which of the graphs in Fig. 23.1 illustrates an unemployment equilibrium?
  a (a)
  b (b)
  c (c)
  d (d)
  e both (c) and (d)

11 Which of the graphs in Fig. 23.1 illustrates an above full-employment equilibrium?
  a (a)
  b (b)
  c (c)
  d (d)
  e both (c) and (d)

12 If real GDP is greater than long-run aggregate supply, then the economy is
  a not in macroeconomic equilibrium.
  b in a full-employment equilibrium.
  c in an above full-employment equilibrium.
  d in an unemployment equilibrium.
  e in long-run equilibrium.

13 If input prices remain constant and firms are producing at levels less than their physical limits, an increase in aggregate demand will cause
  a an increase in the price level and an increase in real GDP.

  b an increase in the price level and a decrease in real GDP.
  c a decrease in the price level and an increase in real GDP.
  d a decrease in the price level and a decrease in real GDP.
  e an increase in the price level, but no change in real GDP.

14 We observe an increase in the price level and an increase in real GDP. Which of the following is a possible explanation?
  a The money supply has fallen.
  b Aggregate wealth has decreased.
  c The price of raw materials has increased.
  d The stock of capital has increased.
  e The expectation of future profits has increased.

15 The economy cannot remain at a level of real GDP above long-run aggregate supply because input prices will
  a fall, thus shifting the long-run aggregate supply curve to the right.
  b fall, thus shifting the short-run aggregate supply curve to the right.
  c rise, thus shifting the long-run aggregate supply curve to the left.
  d rise, thus shifting the short-run aggregate supply curve to the left.
  e rise, thus shifting the short-run aggregate supply curve to the right.

SHORT ANSWER

1 The intertemporal substitution effect implies that an increase in the price level will lead to a decrease in the aggregate quantity of goods and services demanded. Explain.

2 The international substitution effect implies that an increase in the price level will lead to a decrease in the aggregate quantity of goods and services demanded. Explain.

3 Why is the long-run aggregate supply curve vertical?

4 Why is the short-run aggregate supply curve positively sloped over most of its range?

Figure 23.1

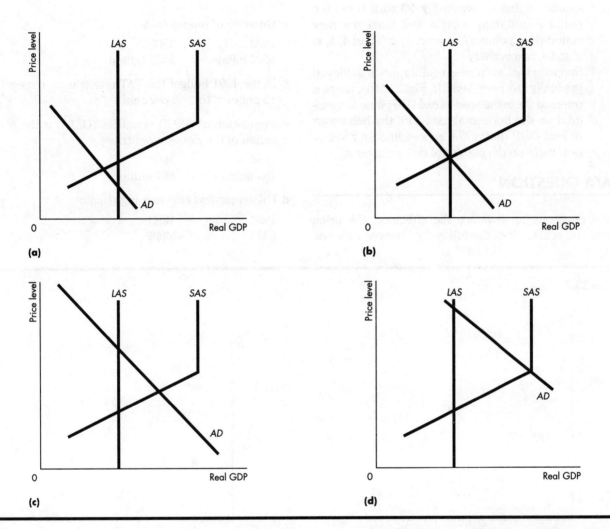

(a) (b) (c) (d)

PROBLEMS

1 Suppose the economy is initially in full-employment equilibrium. Assuming that input prices remain constant, graphically illustrate the effect of an increase in foreign income. What happens to the price level and the level of real GDP?

2 Suppose the economy is initially in full-employment equilibrium. Assuming that input prices remain constant, graphically illustrate the effect of an increase in the stock of human capital. What happens to the price level and the level of real GDP?

3 Suppose the economy is initially in full-employment equilibrium. Graphically illustrate the effect of an increase in wages. What happens to the price level and the level of real GDP?

4 Consider an economy that is initially in full-employment equilibrium. In each of four successive years, an economic event occurs:

Year 1: The government increases its expenditures on goods and services.

Year 2: OPEC increases the price of oil.

Year 3: The government increases the money supply.

Year 4: The government decreases the money supply.

a Graphically illustrate the successive consequences of these four events on a diagram similar to that shown in Fig. 23.2(a). Label the initial equilibrium point *a* and label the new equilibrium points after years 1, 2, 3 and 4, *b*, *c*, *d* and *e*, respectively.

b Suppose that each new equilibrium is achieved gradually over one year. In Fig. 24.2(b), point *a* refers to the initial level of real GDP; time is measured on the horizontal axis. Plot the behaviour of real GDP during the succeeding four years. Comment on the pattern of that behaviour.

DATA QUESTION

Draw diagrams to illustrate the effect on UK price levels and real GDP of the following changes (assume that the economy is originally below full-employment equilibrium).

a Quantity of money (£M4)

1992	1993
£507 billion	£525 billion

b In the 1991 budget the VAT rate was increased from 15 per cent to 17.5 per cent

c Population of OECD countries (OECD is the organization of the richest countries)

1980	1992
780 million	867 million

d UK average weekly earnings (male)

1992	1993
£333	£346

Figure 23.2

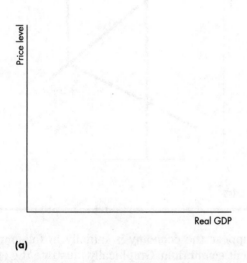

(a)

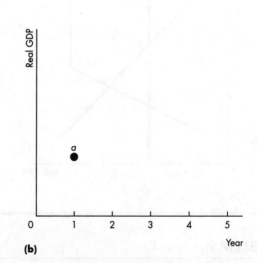

(b)

ANSWERS

CONCEPT REVIEW

1 aggregate demand; decreases

2 falls; decrease

3 intertemporal substitution; lower; increase

4 international; fall; rise

5 right; decreases

6 capacity; long-run

7 increase; short-run; positively; vertical

8 macroeconomic equilibrium; full-employment; unemployment

9 increase; increase

10 increase; decrease

TRUE OR FALSE

1 **F** With lower quantity of real money, individuals cut spending to increase the level of real money.

2 **T** People will have more money to spend.

3 **F** If individuals expect a higher inflation rate they will spend more today to avoid higher prices in the future.

4 **T** Government spending is an injection into the circular flow.

5 **F** Curve will shift to left because people will have less money to spend.

6 **T** Definition.

7 **T** Increase in capital will lead to rise in productivity so that more output is produced at every price.

8 **T** Equilibrium may be at, above or below full-employment level.

9 **F** Anything that shifts *LAS* curve also shifts *SAS* curve.

10 **F** Technological change will increase productivity and lower prices.

11 **T** Increased population, more capital stock and new technology shift *LAS* curve to the right over time.

12 **T** Rises in *AD* not matched by increases in *AS* will pull up prices.

13 **T** It will shift *AS* curve to the left.

14 **F** Changes in factor prices shift only *SAS* curve, not *LAS* curve.

15 **T** Economy will be in above full-employment equilibrium causing extra demand for labour and higher wages.

MULTIPLE-CHOICE

1 **a** *AD* curve is downward sloping owing to three substitution effects. It is real GDP by definition, not nominal and real money balances increase here.

2 **c** **c** shifts *AD* curve, and **d** doesn't exist.

3 **d** Price rises so money buys fewer goods (real money balances fall), so *AD* falls.

4 **b** People will buy now before prices rise.

5 **b** Definition.

6 **e** Definition.

7 **b** At vertical portion of *SAS* curve firms cannot produce more output because they are at their physical limits.

8 **e** Technological improvements mean that labour is more productive leading to increase in supply in both short and long run.

9 **d** Macroeconomic equilibrium always occurs where *AD* = *SAS*; equilibrium *may* occur at answers **a–c**, but it doesn't always occur there.

10 **a** Unemployment equilibrium occurs when *AD* = *SAS* to left of *LAS*.

11 **e** Above full-employment equilibrium occurs when *AD* = *SAS* to right of *LAS*.

12 **c** Equilibrium is where *AD* = *SAS*; if this is greater than *LAS* then there is above full-employment equilibrium.

13 **a** Firms will increase output and prices will also rise (*AD* curve shifts to right).

14 **e** This shifts *AD* curve to the right leading to rise in price and GDP. **a** and **b** shift *AD* curve to the left, while **c** and **d** shift *SAS* and *LAS* curves to the right, respectively, leading to fall in price.

15 **d** If GDP is above *LAS* extra demand for factors will cause their prices to rise leading to increased costs of production and so shift *SAS* curve to the left.

SHORT ANSWER

1 Intertemporal substitution means the substitution of goods now for goods later or vice versa. There are two keys to understanding the intertemporal substitution effect.

The first of these is that changes in interest rates influence households to engage in intertemporal substitution. For example, if interest rates rise, households will tend to borrow and spend less now, thus decreasing the aggregate quantity of goods and services demanded.

The second key is that interest rates are determined by the demand for and the supply of loans and that these are affected by changes in the quantity of real money. In particular, a decrease in real money will make households less willing to lend. This means that the supply of loans will decrease, which will cause the interest rate to rise.

Combining these keys, the intertemporal substitution effect is described as follows: an increase in the price level decreases the quantity of real money, which reduces the supply of loans and thus raises interest rates. The rise in interest rates will lead to a decrease in the aggregate quantity of goods and services demanded.

2 International substitution means substituting domestically produced goods for foreign-produced goods or vice versa. If the price of domestic goods rises and foreign prices remain constant, domestic goods become relatively more expensive, and so households will buy fewer domestic goods and more foreign goods.

This means that there will be a decrease in the quantity of real GDP demanded. Thus, an increase in the price level (the prices of domestic goods), will lead to a decrease in the aggregate quantity of (domestic) goods and services demanded via the international substitution effect.

3 Long-run aggregate supply is the level of real GDP supplied when each firm in the economy is producing at its capacity output and there is full employment. Since this level of real GDP is independent of the price level, the long-run aggregate supply curve is vertical. It should also be noted that this is the level of real GDP attained when input prices are free to adjust so as to clear factor markets.

4 The short-run aggregate supply curve is positively sloped because it holds input prices constant. Thus, when the price level rises, firms see the prices of their output rising, but the prices of their inputs remain unchanged. Each firm is then induced to increase output and so aggregate output increases.

PROBLEMS

1 In Fig. 23.3, the economy is initially at point *a* on the original *AD* curve, AD_0. An increase in foreign income will shift the *AD* curve to the right, from AD_0 to AD_1. At the new equilibrium, point *b*, the price level has risen and the level of real GDP has increased.

Figure 23.3

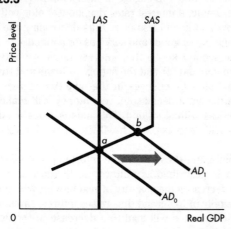

Figure 23.4

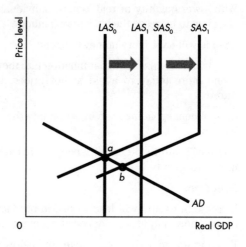

2 The economy in Fig. 23.4 is initially at point *a* on the LAS_0 and SAS_0 curves. An increase in the stock of human capital will shift both the *LAS* and *SAS* curves to the right, to LAS_1 and SAS_1, respectively. At the new equilibrium, point *b*, the price level has fallen and the level of real GDP has increased.

3 In Fig. 23.5, the economy is initially at point *a* on the SAS_0 curve. An increase in wages will shift the *SAS* curve upward, to SAS_1. At the new equilibrium, point *b*, the price level has risen and the level of real GDP has decreased.

Figure 23.5

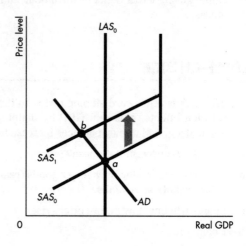

4 a The required diagram is shown in Fig. 23.6(a). The initial equilibrium is at point *a* with AD_0, SAS_0 and *LAS*.

At the beginning of year 1, the increase in government spending shifts the *AD* curve from AD_0 to AD_1 producing a new equilibrium (by the end of the year) at point *b*. We note that real GDP has increased.

At the beginning of year 2, OPEC increases the price of oil, which shifts the *SAS* curve from SAS_0 to SAS_2. Real GDP falls, producing a new equilibrium at point *c*.

At the beginning of year 3, the government increases the money supply (perhaps to combat the fall in output), which causes the *AD* curve to shift from AD_1 to AD_3. The new equilibrium is at point *d* and real GDP has risen.

Finally, in year 4, the government decreases the money supply (perhaps to combat the continuing increase in the price level) and the *AD* curve shifts to the left, from AD_3 to AD_4, say. The consequence is a decline in real GDP and a new equilibrium at point *e*.

b The behaviour of real GDP over time is illustrated in Fig. 23.6(b). At the beginning of year 1, the output level is given by point *a* but the shift in *AD* causes output to rise by the beginning of year 2 (point *b*). Similarly, as indicated in **a**, in years 2, 3 and 4, real GDP falls, rises and falls again (points *c*, *d* and *e*). These real GDP movements are characteristic of the business cycle movements in real GDP.

DATA QUESTION

a Other factors remaining unchanged, an increase in the quantity of money will increase aggregate demand as shown in Fig. 23.7(a).The result will be a move from *a* to *b*, giving a rise in prices and in GDP. Note that if the economy had been at full employment there would have been no rise in GDP.

b An increase in VAT will shift the aggregate supply curve upward as shown in Fig. 23.7(b). The result will be a move from equilibrium *a* to *b*, and a rise in prices and a fall in GDP.

c An increase in population in OECD countries will increase demand for UK goods and services and the result will be identical to that described in **a**.

d A rise in weekly earnings that is not accompanied by any change in productivity will put up firms' costs and shift the short-run *AS* curve upward and the result will be that described in **b**. There may also be an increase in aggregate demand if people expect the inflation rate to increase. This would further push up prices, but would also increase GDP.

Figure 23.6

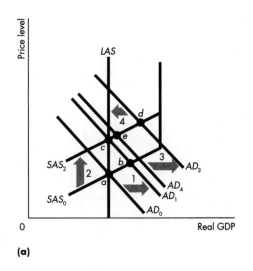

(a)

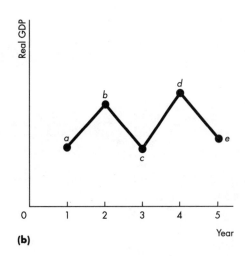

(b)

Figure 23.7

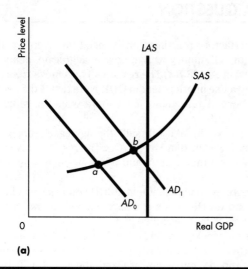

(a)

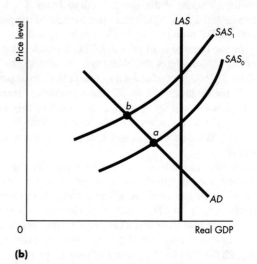

(b)

Chapter 24 — **Expenditure Decisions and GDP**

Chapter In Perspective, Text Pages 664–695

This chapter, as well as the following four chapters, takes a deep look at aggregate demand.

Here we begin by carefully investigating consumption expenditure, investment and net exports, the three private components of aggregate expenditure. We examine the factors that affect the behaviour of each of them. With our enhanced understanding, these components will be brought together in Chapter 25 to help us explain how the levels of aggregate expenditure and GDP are determined.

Helpful Hints

1 Aggregate demand is the relationship between the price level and the quantity of goods and services demanded; in other words, the relationship between the price level and the level of planned aggregate expenditure. The purpose of this chapter is to help us better understand the behaviour of planned aggregate expenditure by separating it into its individual components and examining each of them in isolation. Remember that the ultimate objective is a more complete understanding of aggregate demand, which combines these expenditure components with government expenditure on goods and services.

2 An important concept in this and future chapters is the concept of the marginal propensity to consume *(MPC)*. This is the change in consumption expenditure divided by the change in disposable income. The *MPC* thus shows the impact of some outside change in disposable income on consumption – it measures the incremental change in consumption created by a change in spending power for the consumer.

3 Intuitive explanations for the behaviour of consumption are at the level of the individual household: the *household* consumption function is the relationship between household *consumption expenditure* and household *disposable income*. Our ultimate objective, however, is to examine the behaviour of *aggregate* consumption expenditure as a component of the *aggregate* demand for real GDP. This is why the *aggregate* consumption function is defined as the relationship between aggregate *real* consumption expenditure and real GDP.

Note that the marginal propensity to consume out of real GDP is equal to the marginal propensity to consume (out of disposable income) times $1 - t$ where t is the proportion of an increase in real GDP which goes to net taxes.

4 The aggregate consumption function (which follows from the household consumption function) is a key relationship in our understanding of the behaviour of aggregate demand and thus macroeconomic behaviour. Spending the time necessary to understand thoroughly the behaviour of consumption expenditure in isolation (as discussed in this chapter) will be important in the next chapter where the separate expenditure components are brought together and interaction between them is examined.

5 Investment depends on the real interest rate as well as future profit expectations. For given profit expectations, investment will increase as the real interest rate declines. The real interest rate is defined as the observed interest rate minus the expected inflation rate. The nominal interest rate measures how many pounds one has to pay in interest, while the real interest rate measures how much one has to pay in actual goods and services. Clearly the latter is what one cares about.

Thus, changes in the observed interest rate or the expected inflation rate will affect investment through their effects on the real interest rate. An increase in the observed interest rate (other things held constant) will lead to a decline in investment because the real interest rate has increased. However, an increase in the expected inflation rate (other things held constant) will lead to an increase in investment because the real rate has decreased.

6 Exports are not affected by changes in domestic real GDP, whereas imports increase as domestic real GDP increases. Since net exports are defined as exports minus imports, an increase in domestic real GDP (other things held constant) will cause net exports to decrease.

7 The *AE* curve answers the following question: for a given price level, how is equilibrium aggregate expenditure determined? Aggregate demand relates the resulting levels of real GDP to an array of values of the price level. You should distinguish between movements along the *AD* curve (caused by changes in the price level) and movements of the curve (created by changes in autonomous expenditure not related to the price level).

Key Figures and Table

Figure 24.3 The Paterson Household's Consumption Function and Saving Function, text page 671
The household consumption function is the relationship between household consumption expenditure and household disposable income. Other things held constant, as disposable income increases, consumption expenditure increases.

This relationship is represented graphically in part (a). The 45° line, the line of equality, is a reference line which simply translates values measured on the horizontal axis to the vertical axis. Thus, in this figure, its height is always equal to disposable income. When the consumption function crosses the 45° line, consumption expenditure equals disposable income, which means that saving is zero. When the consumption function lies above the 45° line, saving is negative, and when the consumption function lies below the 45° line, saving is positive.

Part (b) illustrates the implied saving function: saving is negative at low levels of disposable income but increases as disposable income increases and eventually becomes positive.

Figure 24.4 The Consumption Function in the United Kingdom, text page 675
This plots household consumers' expenditure against household disposable income.

There are two interesting facts to note. The first is that, just as the theory of consumption expenditure would suggest, as household disposable income increases, average household expenditure increases. Second, it is interesting that as disposable income increases, the average propensity to consume declines.

Figure 24.6   Investment Demand Curves and Investment Demand Schedules, text page 679
Investment demand is the relationship between investment and the real interest rate, holding other things

constant. This figure illustrates that relationship in two ways: investment demand schedules and the corresponding investment demand curves. Each of these shows that, holding future profit expectations constant, investment increases as the real interest rate declines.

Furthermore, the investment demand schedules and part (b) of the figure also illustrate that, for any given real interest rate, planned investment increases as future profit expectations become more optimistic. This is represented by shifts in the investment demand curve; the curve shifts to the right as optimism increases.

Figure 24.10 Aggregate Expenditure Curve and Aggregate Expenditure Schedule, text page 687

This illustrates the relationship between aggregate planned expenditure and real GDP in two ways: the aggregate expenditure curve and the aggregate expenditure schedule. The *AE* curve is obtained as the vertical sum of each of the separate expenditure component curves:

$$AE = I + G + C + EX - IM$$

where I = investment, G = government purchases of goods and services, C = consumption expenditure, EX = exports and IM = imports.

Table 24.1 Average and Marginal Propensities to Consume and to Save, text page 672

The average propensity to consume *(APC)* is defined as the ratio of consumption expenditure to disposable income. The average propensity to save *(APS)* is defined similarly: the ratio of saving to disposable income.

Part (a) of this table illustrates the computation of the *APC* and *APS* for a hypothetical relationship between disposable income and consumption expenditure. Note that, since disposable income can be used only for consumption expenditure or to add to savings, *APC* + *APS* = 1. Note also that, as disposable income increases, the *APC* decreases and the *APS* increases.

The marginal propensity to consume *(MPC)* is the proportion of an increase in disposable income that is spent on (consumption) goods and services and the marginal propensity to save *(MPS)* is the proportion of an increase in disposable income that is saved.

Part (b) of the table illustrates the computation of the *MPC* and *MPS*. Since an increase in disposable income must be either spent or saved, *MPC* + *MPS* = 1.

SELF-TEST

CONCEPT REVIEW

1 The relationship between consumption expenditure and disposable income is called the _____ _____ . The relationship between saving and disposable income is called the _____ _____ . Negative saving is called _____ .

2 As disposable income increases, consumption expenditure _____ and saving _____ .

3 The ratio of consumption expenditure to disposable income is called the _____ _____ _____ _____ . The ratio of saving to disposable income is called the _____ _____ to save.

4 The fraction of the last pound of disposable income that is spent on consumption goods and services is called the _____ _____ _____ _____ .

5 The relationship between aggregate real consumption expenditure and real GDP is called the _____ _____ _____ .

6 The observed interest rate minus the expected _____ rate gives the real interest rate. As the real interest rate rises, planned investment expenditures _____ . The curve showing the relationship between the real interest rate and the level of planned investment (holding other things constant) is called the _____ _____ curve.

7 As the level of real GDP in the rest of the world increases, UK exports will _____ . As the level of real GDP in the United Kingdom increases, UK imports will _____ . As the foreign exchange value of the pound rises,

UK exports will _____ and UK imports will _____ .

8 The relationship between net exports and UK real GDP (holding constant real GDP in the rest of the world, prices and exchange rates) is called the _____ _____ _____ . As UK real GDP increases, net exports will _____ .

9 The graph of the relationship between the level of aggregate planned expenditure and the level of real GDP is called the _____ _____ curve. As real GDP increases, aggregate planned expenditure _____ .

TRUE OR FALSE

___ **1** The higher a household's expected future income, the greater is its consumption expenditure today.

___ **2** The higher the interest rate, the higher is the level of consumption expenditure.

___ **3** If the average propensity to consume is 0.75, then the average propensity to save must be 0.25.

___ **4** The sum of the marginal propensity to consume and the marginal propensity to save is equal to 1.

___ **5** The average propensity to consume is equal to the slope of the consumption function.

___ **6** A change in expected future income will shift the consumption function.

___ **7** A change in disposable income will shift the consumption function.

___ **8** In the graph of the aggregate consumption function, the gap between the 45° line and the aggregate consumption function is equal to the sum of saving and net taxes.

___ **9** Investment is less volatile than consumption expenditure.

___ **10** The higher the expected rate of inflation, the greater is the amount of investment.

___ **11** An increase in expected profit will shift the investment demand curve to the left.

___ **12** If the level of GDP in the rest of the world declines but GDP remains unchanged in the United Kingdom, we would expect the graph of the net export function to shift.

___ **13** Increases in the degree of specialization in the world economy imply that both imports and exports will increase.

___ **14** The aggregate expenditure schedule lists the level of aggregate planned expenditure that is generated at each level of real GDP.

___ **15** When aggregate planned expenditure exceeds real GDP, stocks will rise more than planned.

MULTIPLE-CHOICE

1 Which is the largest component of aggregate expenditure?
a consumption expenditure
b investment
c government purchases of goods and services
d net exports
e savings

2 The consumption function shows the relationship between consumption expenditure and
a the interest rate.
b the price level.
c real GDP.
d saving.
e nominal income.

3 Consider a household with annual disposable income of £20,000. If the household makes consumption expenditures of £17,000, then its
a marginal propensity to consume is 0.7.
b marginal propensity to consume is 0.85.
c average propensity to consume is 0.7.
d average propensity to consume is 0.85.
e marginal propensity to save is 0.15.

4 The fraction of the last pound of disposable income saved is called the
a marginal propensity to consume.
b marginal propensity to save.
c average propensity to save.
d marginal tax rate.
e average propensity to consume.

5 If the marginal propensity to consume *(MPC)* is less than the average propensity to consume *(APC)* then as disposable income increases the

a *APC* falls.
b *APS* rises.
c *MPC* falls.
d *MPC* rises.
e both **a** and **b** are true.

6 Which of the following would shift the consumption function upward?
a an increase in current disposable income
b an increase in future expected income
c an increase in interest rates
d a change of stage in life from a young household with children at home to an older household with children out of the home and on their own
e a decrease in future expected income

7 Which of the following would lead to an increase in the amount of investment?
a an increase in interest rates
b an increase in the expected inflation rate
c a decrease in expected future profit
d a smaller rate of depreciation
e a decrease in the expected inflation rate

8 If the interest rate is 12 per cent and the expected inflation rate is 8 per cent, then what is the real interest rate?
a 4 per cent
b 8 per cent
c 12 per cent
d 20 per cent
e 4.8 per cent

9 The investment demand curve shows the relationship between the level of planned investment and
a disposable income.
b real GDP.
c expected future profit.
d the real interest rate.
e the expected inflation rate.

10 The acceleration effect implies that if real GDP begins to increase quite rapidly, then the
a investment demand curve will shift to the right.
b investment demand curve will shift to the left.
c consumption function will shift to the right.
d consumption function will shift to the left.
e net export function will shift downward.

11 Which of the following is the most important factor explaining the fluctuations in investment demand? Fluctuations in
a the real interest rate.

b expected future profits.
c depreciation.
d expected inflation.
e the interest rate.

12 Which of the following would increase the demand for UK exports?
a a decrease in the degree of international specialization
b an increase in UK real GDP
c an increase in the level of GDP in the rest of the world
d an increase in the foreign exchange value of the pound
e a decrease in the level of real GDP in the rest of the world

13 Which of the following would increase UK imports from the rest of the world?
a a decrease in the degree of international specialization
b a decrease in UK real GDP
c an increase in the level of GDP in the rest of the world
d an increase in the foreign exchange value of the pound
e a decrease in the foreign exchange value of the pound

14 Which of the following will shift the net export function upward?
a an increase in the foreign exchange value of the pound
b an increase in the level of UK real GDP
c an increase in the level of GDP in the rest of the world
d an increase in interest rates
e a decrease in the level of GDP in the rest of the world

15 The aggregate expenditure curve shows the relationship between aggregate planned expenditure and
a disposable income
b real GDP
c the interest rate
d consumption expenditure
e the price level

SHORT ANSWER

1 What are the four components of aggregate expenditure?

2 What is meant by the marginal propensity to consume and the marginal propensity to save?

3 Explain why the marginal propensity to consume *(MPC)* and the marginal propensity to save *(MPS)* must sum to 1.

4 Explain why a lower interest rate leads to a larger amount of investment.

5 Explain the effect of an increase in German real GDP on UK net exports.

6 Suppose aggregate planned expenditure is greater than real GDP. Explain the process by which equilibrium expenditure is achieved.

7 Explain how the effects of price level changes on the *AE* curve will generate an *AD* curve.

PROBLEMS

1 Figure 24.1 illustrates the consumption function for a household. Compute the following when disposable income is £20,000:
 a *APC* and *APS*.
 b *MPC* and *MPS*.
 c level of saving.

Figure 24.1

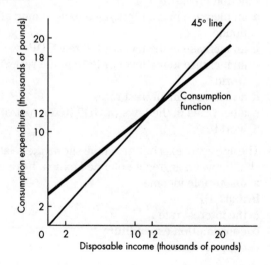

2 From the information given in Fig. 24.1, complete the graph of the saving function for the household in Fig. 24.2.

Figure 24.2

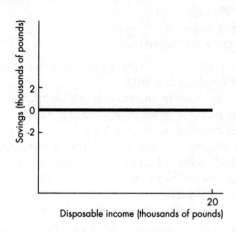

3 Consider an economy of 1 million identical households, each of which has a consumption function as illustrated in Fig. 24.1. Suppose further that net taxes are one-third of real GDP.
 a What is the marginal propensity to consume out of real GDP?
 b Draw the aggregate consumption function for this economy.

4 Table 24.1 gives the rates of return for four individual investment projects under consideration by a firm. Project *A* might be building a new factory and project *B* might be buying a new machine. For the sake of simplicity, suppose that each project costs £1 million. What will be the amount of investment by this firm if the interest rate is
 a 13 per cent?
 b 10 per cent?
 c 7 per cent?
 d 3 per cent?

Table 24.1

Project	Rate of return (per cent)
A	4
B	12
C	8
D	6

DATA QUESTIONS

Consumption and Income

The data in Table 24.2 refers to the UK economy.

1 What is meant by 'real personal disposable income'?

2 What factors might have caused 'real personal disposable income' to change over this period?

3 Explain what is meant by 'real consumers' expenditure 1990 = 100'.

4 What factors other than current disposable income may affect consumption?

Table 24.2

	Real personal disposable income (billions of 1990 pounds)	Real consumers' expenditure (1990 = 100)
1988	356	89
1989	373	95
1990	381	100
1991	378	107
1992	388	112
1993	384	116

Source: *Economic Trends 1994*, Table 1.6. Central Statistical Office. Crown Copyright 1994. Reproduced by the permission of the Controller of the HMSO and the Central Statistical Office.

ANSWERS

CONCEPT REVIEW

1 consumption function; saving function; dissaving

2 increases; increases

3 average propensity to consume; average propensity

4 marginal propensity to consume

5 aggregate consumption function

6 inflation; fall; investment demand

7 increase; increase; decrease; increase

8 net export function; decrease

9 aggregate expenditure; increases

TRUE OR FALSE

1 T Households save less – or borrow – to spend part of future income today.

2 F Higher interest will make it more expensive to borrow to buy goods.

3 T $APS = 1 - APC$.

4 T Because last pound of disposable income is either spent or saved.

5 F MPC = slope of consumption function.

6 T It will change spending plans.

7 F Change in disposable income causes movement along consumption function.

8 T Definition.

9 F Investment is more volatile.

10 T Firms will spend more now on investment goods to avoid higher prices in future.

11 F Higher expected future profits will cause a rise in investment to take advantage of higher future profits.

12 T If there is a fall in real GDP in rest of the world, then exports will fall. If imports are unchanged, then fall in $NX = EX - IM$.

13 T Specialization leads to trade.

14 T Definition

15 F When AE exceeds real GDP this will lead to excess sales and a fall in stocks.

MULTIPLE-CHOICE

1 a Consumer spending is by far the largest item.

2 e Definition.

3 d $APC = C/YD$. There is not enough information to tell marginal propensities.

4 b Definition.

5 e Fall in MPC causes fall in APC and consequently (since income is either spent or saved) a rise in MPS.

6 b Higher expected income in the future causes people to spend more.

7 b This would cut real interest rates and so increase investment. Other answers would lead to fall in investment.

8 a Real interest rate = nominal interest rate – expected inflation rate.

9 d Definition.

10 a Rise in real GDP leads to rise in investment.

11 b See text discussion.

12 c Rise in world GDP causes foreigners to buy more goods from all countries. **b** has no effect on exports, others cause fall in exports.

13 d This makes foreign goods cheaper. **a**, **b** and **d** lower imports, **e** has no impact.

14 c Rise in income causes rest of world to buy more UK goods. **a**, **b** and **e** lead to lower net exports, **d** is irrelevant.

15 b Definition.

SHORT ANSWER

1 The four components of aggregate expenditure are consumption expenditure, investment, government purchases of goods and services, and net exports.

2 The marginal propensity to consume tells us how much consumption changes as disposable income changes, while the marginal propensity to save tells us how much saving changes when disposable income changes. The marginal propensity to consume (save) is the proportion of an increase in disposable income that is added to consumption (saving). It is computed as the change in consumption (saving) divided by the change in disposable income.

3 The *MPC* gives the proportion of an increase in disposable income that is allocated to consumption spending, and the *MPS* gives the proportion that is allocated to saving. There are only two things that a household can do with any increase in disposable income: it can either spend or not spend. The portion that is spent is called consumption expenditure and the portion that is not spent (the rest) is defined as saving. Thus, the proportion of any increase in disposable income that is allocated either to consumption expenditure or to saving (*MPC* + *MPS*) is 1.

4 Investment projects are costly but generate a stream of revenues for the firm. A firm will undertake an investment project if it adds to profit; if it adds more to revenue than it does to cost. Since the interest rate is a part of the cost of any investment project, as the interest rate falls, cost falls, more investment projects become profitable, and thus, investment increases.

5 An increase in German real GDP will lead to an increase in German imports. Since much of German imports come from the United Kingdom, UK exports are likely to rise and thus net exports will increase.

6 If aggregate planned expenditure is greater than real GDP, stocks will fall more than planned and firms will increase output to replenish stocks. As a result, real GDP rises. The process will continue until equilibrium is obtained; when real GDP is equal to aggregate planned expenditure.

7 The aggregate demand curve illustrates the relationship between the price level and aggregate expenditure. The aggregate expenditure diagram shows the level of equilibrium expenditure *holding the price level constant*. If the price level changes the *AE* curve will shift and a new level of equilibrium expenditure will result. Thus for each price level there is a different level of equilibrium expenditure. These combinations of price level and corresponding aggregate expenditure are points on the aggregate demand curve. Since an increase in the price level is associated with a reduction in equilibrium expenditure, the *AD* curve is negatively sloped.

PROBLEMS

1 a From Fig. 24.1, we see that when disposable income is ₤20,000, consumption expenditure is ₤18,000. The *APC* is the ratio of consumption expenditure to disposable income:

$$APC = (18,000/20,000) = 0.9.$$

The *APS* is 1 – *APC*:

$$APS = 1 - 0.9 = 0.1.$$

b The *MPC* is the slope of the consumption function, 0.75. The *MPS* is 1 – *MPC*:

$$MPS = 1 - 0.75 = 0.25.$$

c Saving is equal to disposable income minus consumption expenditure:

$$\text{Saving} = ₤20,000 - ₤18,000 = ₤2,000.$$

2 The saving function is illustrated in Fig. 24.3. This function can be derived from Fig. 24.1 in several ways. We can draw the saving function by noting that saving is zero when disposable income is ₤12,000 and that the slope of the saving function, *MPS*, is 0.25. Alternatively, we can construct the saving function by finding two points on it and drawing a line through them. One possible point has already been mentioned: the point corresponding to disposable income = £12,000 and saving = 0 (point *a* in Fig. 24.3). From **1c** we have a second point: disposable income = £20,000, saving = £2,000 (point *b* in Fig. 24.3).

Figure 24.3

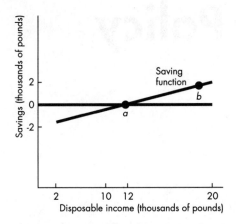

3 a As indicated in the answer to **1b**, the marginal propensity to consume *out of disposable income* is 0.75 or ³/₄. Since net taxes are ¹/₃ of real GDP, disposable income is ²/₃ of real GDP (since disposable income = real GDP – net taxes). This implies that the marginal propensity to consume *out of real GDP* is ²/₃ of ³/₄ or ¹/₂.

b The aggregate consumption function is illustrated in Fig. 24.4. This function can be derived either by finding a point on the line and using the slope of the line or by finding two points on the line.

From **a** we know that the slope of the aggregate consumption function is ¹/₂ (0.5). We can find points on the aggregate consumption function corresponding to points on the individual household consumption functions using the following process.

For example, if each of the 1 million households has a disposable income of £20,000, each will undertake £18,000 in consumption expenditure. Since the households are all identical, this means that when aggregate disposable income is £20 billion, aggregate consumption expenditure is £18 billion. Since aggregate disposable income is ²/₃ of real GDP, when aggregate disposable income is £20 billion, real GDP is £30 billion. Thus, when real GDP is £30 billion, aggregate consumption expenditure is £18 billion. This gives point *a* in Fig. 24.4. Other points can be derived in similar fashion.

4 A project will add to the firm's profit if its rate of return is greater than the interest rate. Thus, the firm will undertake each project for which the rate of return exceeds the interest rate.

a If the interest rate is 13 per cent, investment by the firm will be zero since none of the projects has a rate of return which exceeds 13 per cent.

b If the interest rate is 10 per cent, investment by the firm will be £1 million because project *B* is profitable.

c If the interest rate is 7 per cent, investment by the firm will be £2 million since both projects *B* and *C* are profitable at that lower interest rate.

d If the interest rate is 3 per cent, investment by the firm will be £4 million because the interest rate is now low enough that all four investment projects are profitable.

Figure 24.4

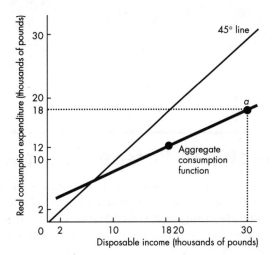

DATA QUESTIONS

1 In 'real personal disposable income', the 'real' refers to data that has been adjusted to remove the effects of inflation. 'Disposable income' is income after income tax has been deducted.

2 Any of the factors which cause shifts in aggregate supply or aggregate demand might cause shifts in real income. One reason for the fall in income was the recession.

3 'Real consumers' expenditure' means that the effects of inflation have been removed; '1990 prices' means that 1990 has been used as a base year. Rather surprisingly consumers continued to spend more even though real income fell in 1991.

4 Apart from current disposable income, the factors which may affect consumption are expected future income, stage in life, degree of patience and the interest rate. They are discussed in detail in the main text pp. 671–674.

Chapter 25 Expenditure Fluctuations and Fiscal Policy

Chapter In Perspective, Text Pages 696–719

The fundamental tool for macroeconomic analysis is the aggregate demand–aggregate supply model. This chapter further deepens our understanding of aggregate demand. In contrast to the previous chapter where we examined the components of aggregate expenditure separately, here we combine these components and examine interactions between them in order to investigate the determination of aggregate expenditure, and thus, of aggregate demand.

Aggregate demand is defined as the relationship between the price level and aggregate expenditure. But, for any given price level, how is aggregate expenditure determined? Furthermore, a shift in the *AD* curve represents a change in aggregate expenditure for each price level. But by how much will aggregate expenditure change? The purpose of this chapter is to answer these questions.

Helpful Hints

1 This chapter distinguishes between *autonomous* expenditure and *induced* expenditure. The difference is that autonomous expenditure is independent of changes in real GDP, while induced expenditure will vary as real GDP varies. In general, a change in autonomous expenditure creates a change in real GDP, which in turn creates a change in induced expenditure. It is important to realize, however, that even though autonomous expenditure may be independent of changes in real GDP, it will not be independent of changes in other variables (for example, the price level).

2 The marginal propensity to buy domestic goods and services is a critical concept in the analysis of this chapter. It is equal to the slope of the aggregate expenditure *(AE)* curve and determines the size of the multiplier. It is thus important to understand the relationship between the marginal propensity to buy and its three main influences: the marginal propensity to consume (out of disposable income), the marginal propensity to import and the marginal tax rate.

To think about the marginal propensity to buy, we consider the increase in spending on domestic goods and services that results from a £1 increase in real GDP. Only consumption and imports have induced components. Furthermore, any increase in imports must be subtracted from the increase in consumption expenditure since we measure expenditure only on *domestic* goods and services. Thus, we see that the marginal propensity to buy is equal to the marginal propensity to consume *out of real GDP* minus the marginal propensity to import.

Sometimes we are not given the marginal propensity to consume out of real GDP but are given the marginal propensity to consume out of disposable income and the (constant) marginal tax rate. In such a case, we can determine the marginal propensity to consume out of real GDP by noting that an increase in real GDP will increase disposable income by $1 - t$ times the change in real GDP, where t is the marginal tax rate. Thus, the marginal propensity to consume out of real GDP is given by the product of the marginal propensity to consume out of disposable income times $1 - t$.

3 Planned expenditure is the desired level of expenditure, given the level of real GDP, and so on. However, this can differ from actual expenditure if firms' sales turn out to be unexpectedly high or low. If planned expenditure is not equal to actual expenditure, the economy will not be in equilibrium, firms will alter their behaviour, and this will alter the level of real GDP. This process is a crucial part of the equilibrium process.

4 The multiplier is a very important concept developed in this chapter. It is a result of the fact that the various components of aggregate expenditure interact with one another.

In particular, an initial increase in autonomous expenditure will increase real GDP directly, but that is not the end of the story. That initial increase in real GDP will generate an increase in *induced* expenditure, which further increases real GDP, and thus induces further increases in expenditure.

5 There are two types of autonomous shocks. One type of shock adds to the instability of the economy – it includes changes in autonomous consumption, investment and exports. Another source of shocks is usually a planned shock that will (hopefully) reduce the instability of the economy – it includes changes in government spending and taxes. However, both shocks work through the same mul-

tiplier process. Therefore the same process that creates the instability is also available to reduce the instability.

Key Figures and Table

Figure 25.1 Aggregate Expenditure, text page 699

This two-part figure illustrates aggregate expenditure. In part (a) consumption expenditure and imports rise as GDP rises. Part (b) makes clear that as GDP rises autonomous expenditure is constant, but induced expenditure rises.

Figure 25.2 An Increase in Autonomous Expenditure, text page 701

From text Fig. 25.1 we note that part of aggregate planned expenditure remains constant as real GDP increases. The sum of all such expenditure components is planned autonomous expenditure. It consists of investment, government purchases of goods and services, exports and the autonomous component of consumption expenditure. This figure shows the effect of an increase in autonomous expenditure and makes it clear that the increase in real GDP is bigger than the increase in autonomous expenditure.

Figure 25.3 The Multiplier and the Slope of the AE curve, text page 702

This graphically illustrates the relationship between the multiplier and the marginal propensity to buy domestic goods and services. Parts (a) and (b) present *AE* curves with two alternative values for the marginal propensity to buy. In each of the two parts of the figure, the initial increase in autonomous aggregate expenditure is the same: £120 billion. This causes the *AE* curve in each case to shift up by £120 billion. As is demonstrated clearly in the figure, when the marginal propensity to spend increases the multiplier increases and there is a bigger rise in GDP.

Figure 25.8 Changes in Autonomous Expenditure and Aggregate Demand, text page 711

This shows that an increase in investment leads to a shift in the *AE* curve; this can also be represented as a shift in the aggregate demand curve.

Table 25.1 Calculating the Multiplier, text page 703

This defines some convenient notations and then demonstrates the derivation of the formula for computing the autonomous expenditure multiplier. Using a straightforward step-by-step procedure, part (b) derives the familiar expression for the ratio of the change in equilibrium GDP to the initial change in autonomous expenditure.

SELF-TEST

CONCEPT REVIEW

1 The components of aggregate expenditure can be classified into two broad groups. The first of these, _____ expenditure, is the sum of those components of aggregate planned expenditure that are not influenced by real GDP. The other, _____ expenditure, is the sum of those components of aggregate planned expenditure that do vary as real GDP varies.

2 The fraction of the last pound of real GDP that is spent on domestically produced goods and services is called the _____ _____ _____ _____domestic goods and services. It is equal to the marginal propensity to consume out of real GDP minus the marginal propensity to _____ .

3 _____ expenditure occurs when aggregate planned expenditure is equal to real GDP. If aggregate planned expenditure exceeds real GDP, _____ investment will exceed _____ investment and _____ will rise.

4 The fraction of the last pound of income paid to the government in taxes is called the _____ _____rate. The higher its value, the _____ is the marginal propensity to spend.

5 The amount by which a change in autonomous expenditure must be multiplied to calculate the ensuing change in equilibrium real GDP is called the autonomous expenditure _____ . The larger is the marginal propensity to spend, the _____ is its value.

6 An increase in the price level will cause the aggregate planned expenditure curve to shift _____ , which _____ equilibrium expenditure and produces a _____ _____ the aggregate demand curve.

TRUE OR FALSE

___ **1** The marginal propensity to buy is equal to the slope of the aggregate expenditure curve.

___ **2** When aggregate planned expenditure exceeds real GDP, stocks will rise more than planned.

___ **3** Equilibrium expenditure occurs when aggregate planned expenditure equals real GDP.

___ **4** Anything that changes autonomous expenditure will shift the aggregate expenditure curve.

___ **5** An increase in autonomous expenditure of £1 million will generate an increase in equilibrium expenditure of more than £1 million.

___ **6** The multiplier is greater than 1 because an increase in autonomous expenditure leads to an induced increase in consumption expenditure.

___ **7** The higher the marginal propensity to buy, the lower is the multiplier.

___ **8** If the marginal propensity to buy is 0.75, the autonomous expenditure multiplier is equal to 3.

___ **9** Taxes and transfer payments that vary as income varies, act as automatic stabilizers in the economy.

___ **10** Multipliers tend to be small when the economy goes into recession and larger in recovery.

___ **11** An increase in the price level will shift the aggregate expenditure curve upward.

___ **12** An increase in government expenditure will shift the aggregate expenditure curve upward and thus the aggregate demand curve to the right.

___ **13** An increase in taxes will shift the aggregate expenditure curve downward and thus the aggregate demand curve to the left.

MULTIPLE-CHOICE

1 Autonomous expenditure is not influenced by
a the interest rate.
b the foreign exchange rate.
c real GDP.
d the price level.
e any other variable.

2 The fact that imports increase as real GDP increases implies that imports are a part of
a marginal expenditure.
b autonomous expenditure.
c consumption expenditure.
d equilibrium expenditure.
e induced expenditure.

3 The slope of the aggregate expenditure curve is equal to
a the marginal propensity to buy domestic goods and services.
b the marginal propensity to consume.
c the marginal propensity to import.
d 1 – marginal propensity to import.
e the autonomous expenditure multiplier.

4 The marginal propensity to buy is equal to
a 1 – marginal propensity to save.
b 1 – marginal propensity to import.
c the marginal propensity to consume out of disposable income minus the marginal propensity to import.
d the marginal propensity to consume out of real GDP minus the marginal propensity to import.
e none of the above.

5 Which of the following will lead to an increase in the marginal propensity to buy?
a an increase in the marginal propensity to import
b an increase in the marginal tax rate
c a decrease in the marginal propensity to consume
d a decrease in the marginal propensity to save
e an increase in the marginal propensity to save

6 A decrease in the marginal tax rate will
a make the AE curve flatter and increase the multiplier.
b make the AE curve flatter and decrease the multiplier.
c make the AE curve steeper and increase the multiplier.
d make the AE curve steeper and decrease the multiplier.
e shift the AE curve upward and leave the multiplier unchanged.

7 If the marginal propensity to buy is 0.75, what is the (autonomous expenditure) multiplier?
a 0.57
b 1.50
c 2.00
d 4.00
e 1.33

8 The government wants to increase aggregate expenditure by £12 billion. If the multiplier is 3, by how much should the government increase its spending on goods and services?
a £3 billion
b £3.6 billion
c £12 billion
d £36 billion
e £4 billion

9 When an economy goes into recession, the multiplier tends to be
a large since income changes are viewed to be temporary.
b large since income changes are viewed to be permanent.
c small since income changes are viewed to be temporary.
d small since income changes are viewed to be permanent.
e constant since income changes are viewed to be temporary.

10 An increase in the price level will
a shift the AE curve up and increase equilibrium expenditure.
b shift the AE curve up and decrease equilibrium expenditure.
c shift the AE curve down and increase equilibrium expenditure.
d shift the AE curve down and decrease equilibrium expenditure.
e have no impact on the AE curve.

11 Suppose that, owing to an increase in expected future profit, investment increases by £10 billion.

If the multiplier is 2, the aggregate demand curve will

a shift to the right by the horizontal distance of £20 billion.

b shift to the right by a horizontal distance greater than £20 billion.

c shift to the right by a horizontal distance less than £20 billion.

d not be affected.

e shift upward by a vertical distance equal to £20 billion.

12 Suppose the multiplier is 2 and the aggregate supply curve is positively sloped. Suppose further that, owing to an increase in expected future profit, investment increases by £10 billion. Equilibrium real GDP will

a increase by £20 billion.

b increase by more than £20 billion.

c decrease by less than £20 billion.

d be unaffected.

e increase by less than £20 billion.

13 Suppose that, owing to an increase in expected future profit, investment increases by £10 billion. Which of the following would reduce the effect of this increase in autonomous expenditure on equilibrium real GDP?

a an increase in the marginal propensity to consume

b a decrease in the marginal propensity to import

c a decrease in the marginal tax rate

d a steeper aggregate supply curve

e a flatter aggregate supply curve

14 Consider an economy where the marginal propensity to consume out of real GDP is 0.70, and the marginal propensity to import out of real GDP is 0.10. In this economy what is the transfer payments multiplier?

a 1.50

b −1.50

c 1.67

d −1.67

e 1.00

15 Consider an economy where the marginal propensity to consume out of real GDP is 0.70, and the marginal propensity to import out of real GDP is 0.10. In this economy what is the balanced budget multiplier?

a 1.50

b −1.50

c 1.67

d −1.67

e 1.00

SHORT ANSWER

1 What is the difference between autonomous expenditure and induced expenditure?

2 Suppose aggregate planned expenditure is greater than real GDP. Explain the process by which equilibrium expenditure is achieved.

3 How do changes in the marginal tax rate affect the marginal propensity to spend?

4 Explain (without algebraic expressions) why the multiplier is larger if the marginal propensity to spend is higher.

5 Explain how the effects of price level changes on the AE curve will generate an aggregate demand curve.

PROBLEMS

1 Consider an economy with the following characteristics:

Autonomous part of consumption expenditure = £10 billion

Investment = £5 billion

Government purchases of goods and services = £40 billion

Exports = £5 billion

Marginal propensity to consume (out of disposable income) = 0.8

Marginal propensity to import (out of real GDP) = 0.14

Marginal tax rate (constant) = 0.2

a What is autonomous expenditure in this economy?

b What is the marginal propensity to spend?

c Draw a graph containing the AE curve for this economy (label it AE_1), as well as a 45° line.

d What is equilibrium expenditure?

2 Return to the economy of Problem 1. Now suppose that the government decides to increase its purchases of goods and services by £20 billion (from £40 billion to £60 billion).

a Using the graph from Problem 1, draw the new AE curve and label it AE_2.

b What is the new equilibrium expenditure?
c What is the multiplier?
d What is the change in consumption, imports and investment after this increase?

3 Now consider a new economy that is identical to the economy of Problem 1 except that the marginal propensity to import is 0.24.
  a What is the marginal propensity to spend in this economy?
  b On a new graph, draw the *AE* curve for this economy, as well as a 45° line.
  c What is equilibrium expenditure?
  d What is the multiplier?

4 Return to the economy of Problem 1. The *AE* curve was constructed under the (implicit) assumption that the price level *(P)* was constant, at *P* = 100, say. If *P* increases to 120, suppose that autonomous expenditure decreases by £20 billion. If *P* decreases from 100 to 80, suppose that autonomous expenditure increases by £20 billion. Using this information, respond to the following:
  a What is equilibrium expenditure when *P* = 100?
  b What is equilibrium expenditure when *P* = 120?
  c What is equilibrium expenditure when *P* = 80?
  d From your answers to **a**, **b** and **c**, draw the three points of the aggregate demand curve on Fig. 25.1 and draw a line through them to represent *AD*.

DATA QUESTIONS

Investment and GDP
The amount of bread we eat next year will be fairly similar to the amount we ate last year. That is because

Figure 25.1

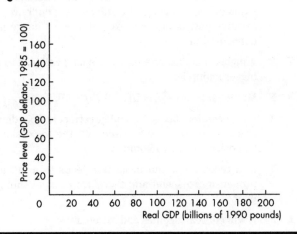

consumption patterns of staple foods such as bread are relatively stable. That is very different from the pattern of investment. When incomes and expenditure are rising, firms buy more machines and order new offices and factories. When national income is constant or falling, firms do not need extra machines and so investment falls. Thus Gross Fixed Capital Formation at constant prices was £8,761 million in 1979 and £6,779 million in 1981. A similar fall took place after 1990. These changes in investment have a multiple effect on national income.

1 How do changes in investment affect GDP?

2 What factors affect the size of the effect on GDP?

ANSWERS

CONCEPT REVIEW

1 autonomous; induced
2 marginal propensity to buy; import
3 Equilibrium; planned; actual; stocks
4 marginal tax; lower
5 multiplier; larger
6 downward; lowers; movement along

TRUE OR FALSE

1 T They both measure the effect of a change in income on *AE*.
2 F They will rise less.
3 T Definition.
4 T Intercept of *AE* curve = Autonomous expenditure; change in autonomous expenditure leads to shift in *AE* curve.

5 T Autonomous expenditure multiplier > 1.

6 T Total change in AE = Change in autonomous expenditure + Change in induced expenditure – Positive part of induced expenditure = Change in consumption.

7 F A higher marginal propensity to spend will lead to a bigger multiplier.

8 F Multiplier = $1/(1-g) = 1/(1-0.75) = 1/0.25 = 4$.

9 T In a recession, taxes fall and government spending rises so reducing the extent of the recession. Opposite is true in a boom.

10 T In a recession, a fall in income leads to a fall in propensity to spend and therefore a lower multiplier.

11 F It will cut real incomes and expenditure.

12 T See text Fig. 25.8.

13 T An increase in taxes has the opposite effect to that shown in text Fig. 25.8.

MULTIPLE-CHOICE

1 c Definition.

2 e Definition of induced.

3 a Both measure change in AE divided by change in Y.

4 d Definition.

5 d An increase in propensity to spend means people have more to spend.

6 c Cut in tax will increase propensity to buy and so the multiplier.

7 d Multiplier = $1/(1-g) = 1/(1-0.75) = 4$.

8 e Change in aggregate expenditure is change in government spending × multiplier, so $12 = 3 \times 4$.

9 c Multiplier becomes smaller due to this effect.

10 d It will cut real incomes.

11 a Multiplier effect raises AE and Y by 2 times original change in autonomous expenditure causing AD to shift to right by same amount.

12 e Multiplier effect of Q 11 is reduced by change in price level owing to positively sloped *SAS* curve.

13 d This leads to more change in P, less change in Y. All others make effect larger.

14 a $g = 0.7 - 0.1 = 0.6$. Transfer payments multiplier = $g/(1-g) = 0.6/(1-0.6) = 1.50$.

15 e Balanced budget multiplier always = 1.

SHORT ANSWER

1 Autonomous expenditure does not change when real GDP changes, whereas induced expenditure does change when real GDP changes.

2 If aggregate planned expenditure is greater than real GDP, stocks will fall more than planned and firms will increase output to replenish those depleted stocks. As a result, real GDP increases. This procedure will continue as long as real GDP is less than aggregate planned expenditure. Thus it will stop only when equilibrium is attained; when real GDP is equal to aggregate planned expenditure.

3 The marginal propensity to consume out of real GDP is equal to $1 - t$ times the marginal propensity to consume out of disposable income, where t is the (constant) marginal tax rate. This implies that the marginal propensity to spend will decrease as the marginal tax rate increases.

4 Any initial stimulus to autonomous expenditure will generate a direct increase in real GDP. The basic idea of the multiplier is that this initial increase in real GDP will generate further increases in real GDP as increases in consumption expenditure are *induced*.

At each round of the multiplier process, the increase in spending, and thus the further increase in real GDP, are determined by the marginal propensity to spend. Since a larger marginal propensity to spend means a larger increase in real GDP at each round, the total increase in real GDP will also be greater. Thus, the multiplier will be larger if the marginal propensity to spend is larger.

5 The aggregate demand curve illustrates the relationship between the price level and aggregate expenditures. The aggregate expenditure diagram shows the level of equilibrium expenditure *holding the price level constant*. If the price level changes, the AE curve will shift and a new level of equilibrium expenditure will result. Thus, for each price level, there is a different level of equilibrium expenditure. These combinations of price level and corresponding aggregate expenditure are points on the aggregate demand curve.

For example, if the price level rises, autonomous expenditure will decline, and the AE curve will shift down. This will lead to a decrease in equilibrium expenditure. Since an increase in the price level is associated with a reduction in equilibrium expenditure, the AD curve is negatively sloped.

PROBLEMS

1 a Autonomous expenditure is the sum of the autonomous part of consumption expenditure, investment, government purchases of goods and services, and exports. This sum is £60 billion.

b The marginal propensity to spend is the additional amount that is spent on domestic goods and services when we increase real GDP by £1, expressed as a fraction of the additional pound.

In this economy, when real GDP increases by £1, only consumption expenditure and spending on imports increase. Since the marginal propensity to import is 0.14, 14 pence of the additional pound of real GDP is spent on imports. In order to determine the amount by which consumption expenditure increases, we must first determine what happens to disposable income. Since the (constant) marginal tax rate is 0.2, 20 pence of the additional pound is collected as tax, leaving an increase in disposable income of 80 pence. The marginal propensity to consume (out of disposable income) is 0.8, thus there will be an induced increase in consumption expenditure of 64 pence (0.8×80 pence). Because we are interested only in the additional amount spent on domestic goods and services, we must subtract the 14 pence spent on imports. This gives an increase in spending on domestic goods and services of 50 pence. Thus, half of the additional pound of real GDP was so spent and the marginal propensity to spend is 0.5.

c See the curve labelled AE_1 in Fig. 25.2. The curve was drawn by noting that the amount of autonomous expenditure (£60 billion) gives the vertical intercept and the marginal propensity to spend (0.5) gives the slope of the AE curve.

Figure 25.2

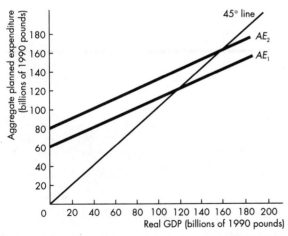

d Equilibrium expenditure occurs at the intersection of the AE_1 curve and the 45° line. Equilibrium expenditure is £120 billion. This can be calculated by multiplying

the level of autonomous expenditure (£60 billion) by the multiplier (2).

2 a See the curve labelled AE_2 in Fig. 25.2. The new curve reflects the fact that autonomous expenditure increases by £20 billion but the marginal propensity to spend remains unchanged.

b The new equilibrium expenditure is £160 billion. This is given by the intersection of the AE_2 curve with the 45° line.

c Since a £20 billion increase in autonomous expenditure generated a £40 billion increase in equilibrium expenditure, the multiplier is 2. This, of course, can be obtained by using the formula for the multiplier:

$$k = \frac{1}{1-g} = \frac{1}{1-0.5} = \frac{1}{0.5} = 2$$

where g is the marginal propensity to spend.

d The total change in real GDP is £40 billion. The marginal propensity to consume out of real GDP is $0.8 \times 0.8 = 0.64$, so the change in consumption is $0.64 \times £40$ billion, or £25.6 billion. The change in imports is the marginal propensity to import out of real GDP (0.14) $\times £40$ billion, or £5.6 billion. Investment is autonomous, and therefore not affected by the change in real GDP. (*Note*: the change in autonomous expenditure (£20 billion) plus the change in induced expenditure (£25.6 billion – £5.6 billion) must add up to the total change in real GDP (£40 billion).)

3 a Using the same analysis as in **1b**, we find that the marginal propensity to spend is 0.4 in this economy.

b See Fig. 25.3. The AE curve, AE_3, was constructed by noting that the amount of autonomous expenditure continued to be £60 billion but that the marginal propensity to spend is 0.4, less than for the economy of Problem 1. Therefore AE_3 is flatter than AE_1, with equilibrium coming at the level where the autonomous expenditure of £60 billion times the multiplier of 5/3 equals £100 billion.

c Equilibrium expenditure is £100 billion, given by the intersection of AE_3 and the 45° line.

d The multiplier is given by the formula:

$$k = \frac{1}{1-g} = \frac{1}{1-0.4} = \frac{1}{0.6} = 1.67$$

4 a Since $P = 100$ was (implicitly) assumed in Problem 1, equilibrium expenditure is £120 billion, as reported in the answer to **1d**.

b When P increases from 100 to 120, autonomous expenditure decreases by £20 billion. Since the multiplier is 2, equilibrium expenditure decreases by £40 billion. Thus, equilibrium expenditure is £80 billion (120 – 40).

c When *P* decreases from 100 to 80, autonomous expenditure increases by £20 billion. Since the multiplier is 2, equilibrium expenditure increases by £40 billion. Thus, equilibrium expenditure is £160 billion (120 + 40).

d See Fig. 25.4. Point *a* reflects the information in the answer to **a**. When *P* = 100, equilibrium aggregate expenditure (the aggregate quantity of goods and services demanded) is £120 billion. This is a point on the aggregate demand curve. Points *b* and *c* are obtained similarly from the answers to **b** and **c** .

DATA QUESTIONS

1 Changes in the level of investment affect GDP via the multiplier process. This process occurs because when investment rises the people who benefit from the investment will in turn increase their spending, and the process will be repeated. The process also occurs when there is a fall in investment; those whose incomes fall as a result of the fall in investment will in turn cut back their spending. The multiplier process is described in the main text on pp. 700–705.

2 The size of the multiplier effect depends on the amount of leakages from the system. If marginal propensities to save, to tax and to import are high, there will be many leakages from the system and the multiplier effect will be small. If these propensities are low, there will be few leakages and a big multiplier.

Figure 25.3

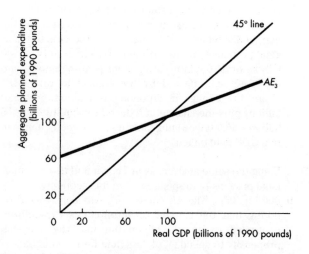

Figure 25.4

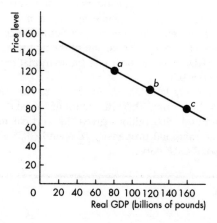

Chapter 26 — Money, Banks and Interest Rates

Chapter In Perspective, Text Pages 720–748

What exactly is money and what are its functions? How does a particular monetary system arise? What role do banks play in the creation of money? These are a few of the important issues addressed in this chapter.

Our major purpose for pursuing a deeper understanding of money and banks, however, is to help us understand the connection between money and macroeconomic activity, especially the behaviour of the price level. The connection is briefly addressed in this chapter and will be pursued further in a later chapter.

Helpful Hints

1 What is money? You should be able to answer this question on several levels. First, at the level of general definition: money is a medium of exchange, and so on. Second, at the level of classification: currency notes are money but cheques are not. Third, at the level of specific definitions such as M4.

2 One of the most important concepts presented in this chapter is the money multiplier process by which banks create money. There are two fundamental facts that allow banks to create money.

First, one of the liabilities of banks is money: chequable deposits. Banks create money by creating new chequable deposits. Second, banks hold fractional reserves. This means that when a bank receives a deposit, it will hold only part of it as reserves and can loan out the rest. Note that the bank is not indulging in a scam – it is still maintaining assets (reserves plus loans) to match its liabilities (the deposits). When that loan is spent, at least part of the proceeds are likely to be deposited in another bank, creating a new deposit (money).

The money multiplier process follows from this last fact: banks make loans when they receive new deposits and these loans are spent and then will return to another bank, creating another new deposit. The process then repeats itself, adding more money (but in progressively smaller amounts) in each round. Practise going through examples until the process becomes second nature.

3 It is crucial to distinguish between real and nominal money. Nominal money is the actual pounds you hold in the form of cash and demand deposits. Real money is the measure of the purchasing power of that nominal money – how many goods and services you can buy with it. Clearly you hold only nominal money for this purpose, so it is the real money balances that you care about.

Therefore, if the average price level rises, and all else stays the same (most especially your desired real spending), you will want the same amount of real money balances as before. In order to achieve this, you will need a rise in nominal money equivalent to the rise in the average price level.

4 Why does the aggregate demand curve shift to the right when there is an increase in the quantity of money?

For the answer, we return to the discussion of aggregate demand in Chapter 23. There we discovered that an increase in the quantity of *real* money caused aggregate demand to increase for two reasons. The first was the real balances effect and the second was the intertemporal substitution effect which is a result of the fact that interest rates will fall when real money increases.

At a given price level, an increase in the quantity of money is an increase in the quantity of real money. Thus, aggregate demand increases through these two effects and, since the price level is given, the aggregate demand curve shifts to the right.

Key Figures and Tables

Figure 26.1 The Official Measure of Money, text page 727
This illustrates the components of M4.

Figure 26.5 Money Market Equilibrium, text page 745
This illustrates an equilibrium in the money market. The supply of real money is £500 billion and does not

vary as the interest rate varies. The real money supply curve is thus a vertical line at £500 billion. On the other hand, the demand for real money is inversely related to the interest rate, and therefore the real money demand curve is negatively sloped. The equilibrium interest rate is determined by the intersection of the demand curve for real money and the supply curve of real money.

In this example, that intersection takes place at an interest rate of 5 per cent. At higher interest rates, the fixed supply of real money is greater than the quantity of real money demanded; households and firms are holding more money than they desire at these higher interest rates. They will therefore try to reduce the excess supply by buying financial assets. As a result of this increase in the demand for financial assets, the price of financial assets will rise and the interest rates earned on these assets will fall. As interest rates fall, the quantity of money demanded increases, reducing the excess supply of money. This process will continue until interest rates have fallen sufficiently so that the quantity of real money demanded is equal to the quantity of real money supplied. Similarly, at interest rates below 5 per cent, the same process will occur, but in the opposite direction, pushing the interest rate back to 5 per cent. Note that the demand for money must do the adjusting, as the supply of money is fixed.

Table 26.2 The Official Definition of Money, text page 726
This simply lists the components of M4 and cash.

Table 26.3 Paying by Cheque, text page 727
This shows why cheques are not money; they merely transfer money.

SELF-TEST

CONCEPT REVIEW

1 Money is defined by its main function: money is a(n) _____ _____ _____ . This means that money is anything that is generally acceptable in exchange for goods and services. The alternative to using money in exchange is the direct exchange of goods for goods, called _____ .

2 Money has four functions, the first of which gives the definition of money. The second function of money is as a(n) _____ _____ _____ since units of money serve as an agreed measure for stating the prices of goods and services. Money also provides an agreed measure that allows contracts to be written for future receipts and payments. Money is thus a standard of _____ _____ .

Finally, money serves as a(n) _____ _____ _____ because it can be held and exchanged later for goods or services.

3 Money takes four different forms. A physical commodity that is valued in its own right and also serves as a medium of exchange is called a(n) _____ money. A paper claim to a commodity that circulates as money is called _____ _____ money. An intrinsically worthless (or almost worthless) commodity that serves the functions of money is called _____ money. Finally, a loan that the borrower promises to pay on demand which is used by the lender in exchange for goods and services is called _____ _____ money.

4 A firm that takes deposits from households and firms and makes loans to other households and firms is called a(n) _____ _____ .

5 Assets that can be quickly converted into a medium of exchange at a reasonably certain price are known as _____ assets. The degree to which an asset has this property is known as _____ .

6 The fraction of a bank's total deposits that are actually held in reserves is called the _____ _____ . The ratio of reserves to deposits that a bank regards as necessary to conduct business is called the _____ _____ _____ . Actual reserves minus desired reserves equal _____ _____ .

TRUE OR FALSE

__ **1** Barter can take place only if there is a double coincidence of wants.

__ **2** Money is anything that is generally acceptable as a medium of exchange.

__ **3** Unpredictable changes in the rate of inflation enhance the function of money as a standard of deferred payment.

__ **4** Only money serves as a store of value.

__ **5** Gresham's law implies that money that has *not* been debased (good money) will tend to drive debased money (bad money) out of circulation.

__ **6** A chequable deposit is an example of private debt money.

__ **7** In our modern economy, credit cards are money.

__ **8** Individual households are generally better at pooling risk than are financial intermediaries.

__ **9** If a depositor withdraws currency from a bank, that bank's reserve ratio declines.

__ **10** An increase in the quantity of money shifts the aggregate demand curve to the right.

__ **11** According to the quantity theory of money, in the long run an increase in the quantity of money will cause the price level to rise but will leave real GDP unchanged.

__ **12** The quantity theory of money implies that a 10 per cent increase in the quantity of money will cause a 10 per cent increase in the price level.

__ **13** On average, the money supply growth rate is exceeded by the inflation rate.

MULTIPLE-CHOICE

1 Which of the following is *not* one of the four functions of money?
 a medium of exchange
 b measure of liquidity
 c standard of deferred payment
 d store of value
 e unit of account

2 When a contract specifies that a certain number of pounds are to be paid in the future for services rendered, money is functioning as a
 a medium of exchange.
 b measure of liquidity.
 c unit of account.
 d store of value.
 e standard of deferred payment.

3 If the prices of goods and services were stated in terms of pounds of salt, then salt is a
 a unit of account.
 b standard of deferred payment.

c store of value.

d quasi-money.

e medium of exchange.

4 UK currency today is an example of

a fiat money.

b commodity money.

c convertible paper money.

d private debt money.

e fractionally backed gold-convertible money.

5 A chequable deposit in a financial institution is an example of

a commodity money.

b fiat money.

c convertible paper money.

d private debt money.

e public debt money.

6 Which of the following is an example of quasi-money or 'almost' money?

a credit cards

b demand deposits

c term deposits

d other chequable deposits

e savings deposits

7 Which of the following is money?

a a chequable deposit

b a blank cheque

c a credit card

d a large time deposit

e a Government Savings Bond

8 Which of the following is a liability of a chartered bank?

a vault cash

b loans

c securities

d demand deposits

e its deposits at the Bank of England

9 Which of the following is most liquid?

a demand deposits

b real estate

c a government bond

d savings deposits

e a cheque

10 A bank can create money by

a selling some of its investment securities.

b increasing its reserves.

c lending its excess reserves.

d printing more cheques.

e converting reserves into securities.

11 According to the quantity theory of money, a decrease in the quantity of money will cause

a both the price level and real GDP to decline in the short run, but in the long run only the price level will fall as real GDP returns to its initial level.

b both the price level and real GDP to increase in the short run, but in the long run only the price level will rise as real GDP returns to its initial level.

c the price level to fall in the short run, but in the long run the price level will return to its initial level.

d the price level to fall and real GDP to rise in both the short run and the long run.

e the price level to fall and real GDP to fall in both the short run and the long run.

12 Which of the following is *not* a principal motive for holding money by households and firms?

a reserve motive

b interest rate motive

c speculative motive

d precautionary motive

e neither **a** nor **b**

SHORT ANSWER

1 What is meant by a double coincidence of wants?

2 What are the four principal functions of money?

3 What are the main disadvantages of a commodity money?

4 Explain why credit cards are not money.

5 How do banks create money?

PROBLEMS

1 Suppose there is a decrease in the quantity of money. Using an aggregate demand–aggregate supply model, show what happens to the price level and the level of real GDP in the short run and in the long run.

2 Consider a perpetuity with an annual coupon payment of £100. What is the interest rate on this financial asset if its price is
a £1,000?
b £900?
c £1,100?

DATA QUESTIONS

Money and Prices

1 Explain what is meant by
a M4
b Index of Retail Prices (1985 = 100)

2 Draw a graph using the figures in Table 26.1 to illustrate the relationship between M4 and the Index of Retail Prices. Comment on your results.

Table 26.1

Year	Quantity of money (M4 £000 million)	Index of Retail Prices (1985 = 100)
1980	111	70.7
1981	129	79.1
1982	155	85.8
1983	175	89.8
1984	199	94.3
1985	226	100
1986	262	103.4
1987	304	107.7
1988	358	113.0
1989	422	121.8
1990	473	133.3
1991	501	141.1
1992	519	146.4

Source: *Economic Trends 1994.* Central Statistical Office. Crown Copyright 1994. Reproduced by the permission of the Controller of the HMSO and the Central Statistical Office.

ANSWERS

CONCEPT REVIEW

1 medium of exchange; barter
2 unit of account; deferred payment; store of value
3 commodity; convertible paper; fiat; private debt
4 financial intermediary
5 liquid; liquidity
6 reserve ratio; desired reserve ratio; excess reserves

TRUE OR FALSE

1 T Buyer must be selling what seller wants to buy and vice versa.
2 T Basic function of money.
3 F Unpredictable inflation makes it difficult to sign long-term contracts eroding value of money as a standard of deferred payment.
4 F Other assets (such as land) can act as store of value.
5 F Agents keep more valuable good money and circulate less valuable bad money.
6 T Definition.

7 F Credit cards are form of identity card used to make short-term loans.
8 F Large size of financial intermediaries allows them to pool risk.
9 T Currency is part of reserve ratio.
10 T Increase in money supply causes *MD* to shift to right for real money balances effect and intertemporal substitution effect.
11 T True in the very long run.
12 T Theory assumes that *V* and *Y* are independent of money supply so that change in money leads to proportionate change in prices.
13 F See Data Questions for evidence.

MULTIPLE-CHOICE

1 b Definition of a function.
2 e Payment is deferred.
3 a Definition.
4 a Definition.
5 d Definition.
6 e Savings deposits are near money because they cannot be used immediately to buy goods.

7 **a** Definition.

8 **d** Demand deposits are a liability because the bank owes them to the depositor.

9 **a** Most readily changed into currency.

10 **c** Lending its reserves is done by crediting borrower's deposits, creating more deposits = more money.

11 **a** In the long run, real GDP is independent of change in money supply.

12 **e** Others cause people to want to hold money.

SHORT ANSWER

1 A double coincidence of wants occurs in barter when an individual who has good A and wants to trade for good B finds an individual who has good B and wants to trade for good A.

2 The four principal functions of money are: medium of exchange, unit of account, standard of deferred payment and store of value.

3 There are two disadvantages of commodity money discussed in the text. First, there is a temptation to cheat on the value of money by clipping or debasing the money. Second, the use of the commodity for money has a high opportunity cost. When the commodity is used as money, it cannot be used in other ways. For example, the opportunity cost of using gold as money is the forgone use of that gold for jewellery or some other function.

4 A credit card is not money, but rather a mechanism for borrowing money, which must later be repaid. The repayment of money takes place when the credit card bill is paid by cheque.

5 Banks create money by making new loans. When the proceeds of these loans are spent, the person receiving the money will deposit much of it in a bank deposit which is new money.

PROBLEMS

1 The consequences of a decrease in the quantity of money are illustrated in Fig. 26.1. The economy is initially in long-run equilibrium at point a, the intersection of AD_0 and SAS_0 (and LAS). The price level is P_0 and GDP is at its full-employment level, Y.

A decrease in the quantity of money will shift the AD curve to the left, from AD_0 to AD_1. The new short-run equilibrium is at point b. The price level falls to P_1 and

real GDP falls to Y_1. In the long run, however, input prices will also fall, which will shift the SAS curve down, from SAS_0 to SAS_1. A new long-run equilibrium is achieved at point c. Thus, in the long-run, the price level falls further to P_2, while real GDP returns to its initial level, Y.

Figure 26.1

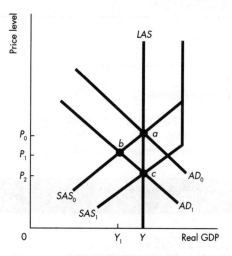

2 The interest rate (r) on a perpetuity is obtained using the formula:

$$r = \frac{c}{p} \times 100$$

where c = coupon and p = price of the bond.

a $r = \dfrac{100}{1000} \times 100 = 10$ per cent

b $r = \dfrac{100}{900} \times 100 = 11.11$ per cent

c $r = \dfrac{100}{1100} \times 100 = 9.09$ per cent

DATA QUESTIONS

1 **a** 'M4' is a measure of the money supply in the United Kingdom which includes cash held outside the Bank of England by the public, and also all sterling deposits at banks and building societies.

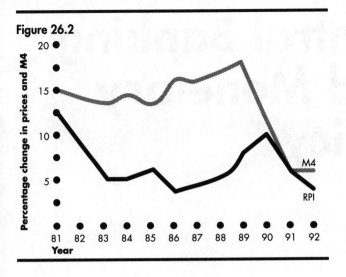

Figure 26.2

b The Index of Retail Prices is a measure of the change in consumer prices bought by a typical household in the United Kingdom. '1985 = 100' means that 1985 has been chosen as the base year.

2 The relationship is shown in Figure 26.2. At first sight, there seems to be little relationship between the quantity of money and the RPI. The two variables since the increases in the quantity of money are always larger than the changes in the Retail Prices Index. However, the pattern of the curves is similar, and a longer run of figures might give a closer match.

The relationship between these two variables is crucial in economic policy – is controlling the money supply a good way to control inflation? This is discussed in more detail in the next chapter.

Chapter 27

Central Banking and Monetary Policy

Chapter In Perspective, Text Pages 749–777

In Chapter 26 we discovered that a new bank deposit will, as it works its way through the banking system, cause a total increase in the quantity of money that is a multiple of the initial new deposit. But how might that new money-creating deposit arise? In this chapter, we find that a central bank, through its use of monetary policy tools, can create such new deposits and thus influence the quantity of money.

The reason we are so interested in the quantity of money of course is that, as we have seen in Chapters 23 and 26, changes in the quantity of money can have important effects on real GDP and the price level. For example, an increase in the quantity of money will increase aggregate demand, thus causing the price level to increase and the level of real GDP to increase, at least in the short run.

How does an increase in the quantity of money affect aggregate demand? We will learn that an increase in the quantity of money will cause an increase in aggregate expenditure primarily through its ability to lower interest rates. Then the question becomes: how does a change in the quantity of money cause interest rates to change? A major purpose of this chapter is to present a model that will allow us to explain the determination of interest rates.

Helpful Hints

1 One restriction on UK monetary policy is created by the international nature of the UK economy – this will come back in later chapters to play a very important role. The fact that UK citizens and foreigners can easily switch between UK and foreign assets is a crucial constraint on policy choices, as we shall see.

2 One of a central bank's most important tasks is to control the money supply. It uses four methods: credit ceilings, changing asset requirements, changing interest rates and open market operations. Since no method is perfect, the actual methods adopted have varied over the years, and you should understand all four.

To remember whether an open market purchase will lead to a decrease or an increase in money, it may be helpful to think of open market operations as an exchange of government securities for cash. For example, think of an open market purchase as the Bank of England acquiring government securities by giving cash to the public. Thus the money supply will increase.

3 Ordinary use of the term *money* does not make some of the important distinctions that are made in economics. In order to avoid confusion regarding the concept of the demand for money, it is important that these distinctions be clear.

For example, we often talk about our income as the amount of *money* we make over a certain period of time. When we use the term in this context, we are speaking of money as a flow – a quantity received over some period of time.

On the other hand, we may talk about how much *money* we have in our bank account or in our wallet at a certain point in time. In this context we are speaking of money as a stock – a quantity at a point in time. The distinction between these two concepts can be very important.

To avoid potential confusion, economists rarely use the term *money* when referring to a flow. Instead, they will use less ambiguous alternative terms like income or wage. In this chapter, *money* always refers to a stock. When we talk about the demand for *money* we are talking about the desire to hold a stock of *money* and not spend it. (However, it *is* being held for future spending purposes.)

Key Figure and Table

Figure 27.4 The Bank of England Changes the Interest Rate, text page 764

This illustrates the ability of the Bank of England to influence the interest rate by conducting monetary policy which changes the supply of real money. For example, in part (a), the Bank of England has purchased government securities in the open market which has led to an increase in the quantity of real money. This is represented by a shift of the real money supply curve to the right, from MS_0 to MS_1. The result is a decline in the equilibrium rate of interest by the process described in the previous discussion of Figure 26.5.

In part (b), the Bank of England has caused the interest rate to rise by reducing the supply of real money through open market sales of government securities.

Table 27.4 Calculating the Money Multiplier, text page 762

A formula for the money multiplier is derived in this table. Part 1 lists the relevant variables and defines symbols. Parts 2 and 3 give definitions of relevant variables and ratios.

Note that the money multiplier depends on two key ratios: the ratio of currency to deposits $(\Delta C/\Delta D)$ and the ratio of reserves to deposits $(\Delta R/\Delta D)$. Increases in either of these will reduce the size of the multiplier.

SELF-TEST

CONCEPT REVIEW

1 The attempt by the Bank of England to control inflation and reduce business cycle fluctuations by changing the quantity of money and adjusting interest rates is called _____ .

2 The Bank of England is an example of a(n) _____ central bank.

3 The Bank of England uses three main policy tools. It can change _____ requirements and also the _____ _____

on lending of last resort. The third tool involves the purchase and sale of government securities by the Bank of England. It is called _____ _____ _____ .

4 There are three main motives for holding money. The first motive, to undertake transactions and minimize the cost of transacting, is called the _____ motive. Money held as a precaution against unforeseen events and required unplanned purchases corresponds to the _____ motive. The final motive, to avoid predicted losses from holding stocks and bonds that are expected to fall in value, is called the _____ motive.

5 The relationship between the quantity of real money demanded and the interest rate, holding other things constant is called the _____ for _____ _____.

6 An increase in real income will shift the demand curve for real money to the _____, and, if the supply of real money is constant, will cause the equilibrium interest rate to _____.

7 The amount by which an initial increase in bank reserves is multiplied to calculate the effect on total bank deposits is called the _____ _____ multiplier. This multiplier will be larger, the _____ is the desired reserve ratio. The real-world multiplier is different in part because there is a tendency for some loans to leave the banking system. This tendency is called the _____ _____.

8 The proposition that an increase in money leads to an equal percentage increase in the price level is the _____ theory of _____. Its original basis follows from certain propositions about the equation of _____. This equation is true by definition since one of its components is defined by it. This component, the _____ of circulation, is the average number of times a pound is used annually to buy the goods and services that make up GDP.

9 If the Bank of England buys government securities in the open market, the interest rate is likely to _____.

TRUE OR FALSE

___ **1** An increase in reserve requirements is intended to increase lending by banks.

___ **2** Bank of England notes are non-convertible.

___ **3** The money multiplier is given as the ratio of the quantity of money to the monetary base.

___ **4** If there is an increase in the fraction of deposits that households and firms hold as currency, the money multiplier will decrease.

___ **5** The higher the banks' desired reserve ratio, the larger is the money multiplier.

___ **6** If the price level increases, there will be an increase in the nominal quantity of money people will want to hold.

___ **7** If the price level increases, there will be an increase in the real quantity of money people will want to hold.

___ **8** The velocity of circulation is given by the ratio of real GDP to real money supply.

___ **9** If interest rates rise, the velocity of circulation is likely to increase.

___ **10** If interest rates rise, the quantity of money demanded is likely to decrease.

___ **11** The development of near-money deposits and growth in the use of credit cards in recent years have caused the demand curve for real money to shift to the right.

___ **12** If the price of a bond rises, the interest rate earned on the bond falls.

___ **13** An increase in the demand for real money will cause the interest rate to fall.

___ **14** If households or firms find that they have more money than they want to hold, they will buy financial assets. This will cause the prices of financial assets to rise and the interest rates earned on those assets to fall.

___ **15** If the Bank of England wants to lower interest rates, it should sell government securities in the open market.

___ **16** The simple money multiplier is equal to 1 divided by the desired reserve ratio.

___ **17** Other things being equal, the currency drain makes the real-world money multiplier larger than the simple money multiplier.

___ **18** If the quantity of money is £50 billion and nominal GDP is £200 billion, the velocity of circulation is $\frac{1}{4}$.

MULTIPLE-CHOICE

1 The international nature of the UK economy
  a means the Bank of England has an expanded range of actions to choose from.

b means the Bank of England must ignore exchange rate determination.

c is due to the many restrictions on capital mobility set by the government.

d means the Bank of England has no independence.

e means the Bank of England cannot ignore interest rate pressures from EU countries.

2 A flexible exchange rate regime is one in which the

a supply of pounds remains flexible.

b demand for pounds remains flexible.

c value of the exchange rate is determined by market forces.

d value of the exchange rate is influenced by the central bank.

e central bank defines and maintains a flexible exchange rate value.

3 A managed exchange rate regime is one in which the

a supply of the pound is managed.

b demand for the pound is managed.

c value of the exchange rate is determined by market forces.

d value of the exchange rate is influenced by the central bank.

e central bank defines and maintains a fixed exchange rate value.

4 Which of the following would *not* affect the size of the monetary base?

a A bank exchanges government securities for a deposit at the Bank of England.

b A bank exchanges vault cash for a deposit at the Bank of England.

c The Bank of England buys government securities from a bank.

d The Bank of England buys government securities from someone other than a bank.

e The Bank of England sells government securities to a bank.

5 An open market purchase of government securities by the Bank of England will

a increase bank reserves and thus increase the monetary base.

b decrease bank reserves and thus decrease the monetary base.

c increase bank reserves and thus decrease the monetary base.

d decrease bank reserves and thus increase the monetary base.

e decrease bank reserves but increase the money supply if banks have excess reserves.

6 If banks want to hold 3 per cent of deposits as reserves and households and firms want to hold 10 per cent of deposits as currency, what is the money multiplier?

a 8.5

b 11.0

c 36.7

d 10.0

e 33.3

7 The money multiplier will increase if either the fraction of deposits that households and firms want to hold as currency

a increases or the desired reserve ratio increases.

b decreases or the desired reserve ratio decreases.

c decreases or the desired reserve ratio increases.

d increases or the desired reserve ratio decreases.

e none of the above.

8 The quantity of real money demanded will increase if either real income increases or the

a price level increases.

b price level decreases.

c interest rate increases.

d interest rate decreases.

e price of bonds falls.

9 Real money is equal to nominal money

a divided by real GDP.

b minus real GDP.

c divided by the price level.

d minus the price level.

e divided by velocity.

10 The higher the interest rate, the

a lower the quantity of money demanded, and the higher is the velocity of circulation.

b lower the quantity of money demanded, and the lower is the velocity of circulation.

c higher the quantity of money demanded, and the higher is the velocity of circulation.

d higher the quantity of money demanded, and the lower is the velocity of circulation.

e higher the quantity of money demanded, but the money supply remains unaffected.

11 Which of the following will cause the demand curve for real money to shift to the left?

a an increase in real GDP

b a decrease in interest rates

c the expanded use of credit cards

d an increase in the quantity of money supplied

e an increase in the price level

12 If households and firms find that their holdings of real money are less than desired, they will

  a sell financial assets, which will cause interest rates to rise.

  b sell financial assets, which will cause interest rates to fall.

  c buy financial assets, which will cause interest rates to rise.

  d buy financial assets, which will cause interest rates to fall.

  e buy goods, which will cause the price level to rise.

13 If the Bank of England buys government securities in the open market, the supply curve of real money will shift to the

  a left, and the interest rate will rise.

  b left, and the interest rate will fall.

  c right, and the interest rate will rise.

  d right, and the interest rate will remain constant as money demand will shift to the right as well.

  e none of the above.

14 If real GDP increases, the demand curve for real money will shift to the

  a left, and the interest rate will rise.

  b left, and the interest rate will fall.

  c right, and the interest rate will rise.

  d right, and the interest rate will fall.

  e right, and the interest rate will remain constant.

15 Money market equilibrium occurs

  a when interest rates are constant.

  b when the level of real GDP is constant.

  c when money supply equals money demand.

  d only under a fixed exchange rate.

  e when both **a** and **b** are true.

16 If all banks hold 100 per cent reserves, what is the simple money multiplier?

  a 0

  b 1

  c 10

  d 100

  e infinite

17 Suppose there is an increase in the tendency for loans to return to banks in the form of reserves; in other words, there is a decrease in the currency drain. Select the best statement.

  a The simple money multiplier will decrease.

  b The simple money multiplier will increase.

  c The real-world money multiplier will decrease.

  d The real-world money multiplier will stay constant.

  e The real-world money multiplier will increase.

18 According to the quantity theory of money, an increase in the quantity of money will lead to an increase in the price level

  a but have no effect on real GDP or the velocity of circulation.

  b as well as increasing both real GDP and the velocity of circulation.

  c as well as increasing real GDP but decreasing the velocity of circulation.

  d as well as decreasing real GDP but increasing the velocity of circulation.

  e but have no effect on real GDP while decreasing velocity.

19 If the price level is 2, real GDP is £100 billion, and the quantity of money is £40 billion, what is the velocity of circulation?

  a 2.5

  b 4

  c 5

  d 10

  e 50

SHORT ANSWER

1 Why do international considerations constrain the Bank of England's actions?

2 How does an open market purchase of government securities lead to an increase in the monetary base?

3 What are the three main motives for holding money?

4 Why do people care about the quantity of real money they hold rather than the quantity of nominal money they hold?

5 Why will the quantity of real money demanded fall when the interest rate rises?

6 The market for money is initially in equilibrium when the Bank of England increases the supply of money. Explain the adjustment to a new equilibrium interest rate.

7 According to the quantity theory of money, what is the effect of an increase in the quantity of money?

PROBLEMS

1 Let D = deposits, C = currency, and R = reserves. Then let $a = \Delta C/\Delta D$, the ratio of change in currency to change in deposits, and $b = \Delta R/\Delta D$, the ratio of change in reserves to change in deposits. Table 27.1 gives a row of alternative values for a and alternative values for b in the first column.

Complete the nine cells of Table 27.1 by computing the money multiplier for each of the nine combinations of a and b. What happens to the money multiplier as the change in currency to change in deposits ratio increases? Note what happens to the money multiplier as the change in reserves to change in deposits ratio increases.

Table 27.1   Money Multipliers

	a		
b	0.1	0.2	0.3
0.05			
0.10			
0.15			

2 Calculate the money multipliers in each of the following cases.
   a The money supply is £50 billion and the monetary base is £20 billion.
   b Deposits = £50 billion, currency = £10 billion and reserves = £5 billion.
   c Reserves = £5 billion, currency = £15 billion and the change in reserves to change in deposits ratio = 0.1.

3 Figure 27.1 illustrates the current equilibrium in the money market where MD is the demand curve for real money and MS is the supply curve for real money. Suppose that the Bank of England wants to stimulate aggregate expenditure by lowering the interest rate to 6 per cent. By how much must the Bank of England increase the nominal money supply if the price level is 2?

4 Having determined the amount by which the Bank of England must increase the nominal supply of money, we now want to determine the open market operation that will be necessary if the change in currency to change in deposits ratio is 0.2 and the desired reserve ratio is 0.1. Will the Bank of England need to buy or sell government securities in the open market and, if so, in what amount?

Figure 27.1

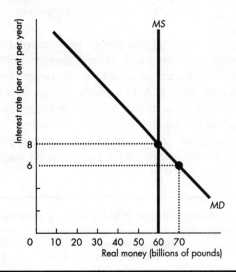

5 Given the values for the change in currency to change in deposits ratio and desired reserve ratio assumed in Problem 4, the round-by-round money multiplier process is examined here.
   a For the open market operation in Problem 4, complete Table 27.2 by following the first six rounds of the process, then specify the effects in all other rounds, and finally give the total effects.
   b What is the total change in money after six rounds?
   c What is the total change in the money supply? Does this number agree with the desired change from Problem 3?

6 We observe an economy in which the price level is 1.5, real GDP is £240 billion and the money supply is £60 billion.
   a What is the velocity of circulation?
   b According to the quantity theory of money, what will be the result of an increase in the quantity of money to £80 billion?

DATA QUESTIONS

The Central Bank of the United Kingdom

What does a central bank do? Essentially it has three functions. The first is to advise on and execute monetary policy – that is policies aimed at safeguarding the value of money in the economy. The second is to ensure the soundness of the nation's financial system, including direct super-vision of banks and other participants in City financial markets. The third is to promote the efficiency and competitiveness of the financial system….

The bank is a very significant participant in both the domestic money markets and foreign exchange markets. This means it is able to influence interest rates domestically and, in certain circumstances, to carry out operations in the foreign exchange markets to smooth fluctuations in the level of sterling. This in turn enables it to use its market operations to put into effect the government's policies for interest rates and

the exchange rate, which are the major elements of monetary policy.

Source: adapted from *Economic Briefing*, May 1991, HM Treasury. Reproduced with the permission of the Controller of Her Majesty's Stationery Office.

1 Explain what is meant by

  a 'monetary policy', and

  b 'City'.

2 What participants other than banks are there in the City?

3 How does the government put into effect its 'policies for interest rates'?

Table 27.2 Money Multiplier Effects (billions of pounds)

Round	Excess reserves at start of round	New loans	Change in deposits	Change in currency	Excess reserves at end of round	Change in quantity of money
1						
2						
3						
4						
5						
6						
All others	–				–	
Totals	–				–	

ANSWERS

CONCEPT REVIEW

1 monetary policy
2 subservient
3 asset; interest rate; open market operations.
4 transactions; precautionary; speculative
5 demand; real money
6 right; rise
7 simple money; smaller; currency drain
8 quantity; money; exchange; velocity
9 fall

TRUE OR FALSE

1 F It will decrease lending.
2 T They are not backed by gold.
3 T Definition.
4 T $mm = (1 + \Delta C/\Delta D)/(\Delta C/\Delta D + \Delta R/\Delta D)$ causes increase in CD and fall in mm.
5 F High reserve ratio means banks can lend less and so create less money.
6 T People will want to hold more money to pay higher prices.

7 F They will want to hold more money in nominal terms.

8 F $V = $ Nominal GDP/M.

9 T People will spend money more quickly.

10 T Because the opportunity cost of holding money will rise.

11 F Demand for money is determined by factors such as level of incomes.

12 T Inverse ratio between bond price and interest rate.

13 F Increases in demand push up prices.

14 T If demand for money exceeds supply, people will use excess to buy assets, so pushing up their price.

15 F Selling government bonds leads to fall in banks' reserves and so to fall in banks' ability to create money.

16 T Definition – see text for explanation.

17 F Currency drain makes money multiplier smaller.

18 F $V = PT/M = 200/50 = 4$.

MULTIPLE-CHOICE

1 e Financial markets are interdependent; hence so are interest rates.

2 c Definition.

3 d Definition.

4 b Others are all examples of open market operations.

5 a Bank of England pays for securities by crediting banks' reserves, which are part of monetary base.

6 a $mm = (1 + 0.1)/(0.1 + 0.03) = 8.5$.

7 b Both decreases mean there are more reserves to create new loans at each stage of the multiplier process.

8 d Opportunity cost of holding money will fall, so people will hold more.

9 c Definition.

10 a Rise in interest rate means rise in opportunity cost of holding money, leading to fall in demand for money and increase in velocity since velocity = Y/MD.

11 c Credit cards will facilitate transactions.

12 a People will sell assets to obtain money; fall in asset prices will lead to higher interest rates.

13 e Buying bonds leads to rise in deposits, reserves and money supply; excess supply of money leads to fall in interest rates.

14 c Rise in GDP means people want more money to finance transactions. Increase in demand for money pushes up its price.

15 c Definition.

16 b Multiplier = 1/(Desired reserve ratio) = 1/1 = 1.

17 e Decrease in currency drain leads to increase in real-world money multiplier.

18 a Owing to assumption that neither is affected by change in money supply.

19 c $V = PY/M = 2(100)/(40) = 5$.

SHORT ANSWER

1 The Bank of England is constrained by international considerations because UK citizens and foreigners can each hold deposits in the other's country. As a result, interest rates are related across borders, a factor that constrains the Bank of England's ability to manipulate domestic interest rates via monetary policy. It is also constrained by membership of the European Union.

2 An open market purchase of government securities by the Bank of England increases the monetary base by increasing one of its components: banks' deposits at the Bank of England. The process by which this takes place depends on whether the securities are purchased from banks or from the non-bank public.

If the purchase is from banks, the process is direct: the Bank of England pays for the securities by crediting the bank's deposit at the Bank of England, which directly increases the monetary base.

If the purchase is from the non-bank public, the Bank of England pays by writing cheques on itself which the sellers of the securities deposit in their banks. The banks in turn present the cheques to the Bank of England, which credits the banks' deposits at the Bank of England. Thus, in either case, the monetary base increases by the amount of the open market purchase.

3 The three main motives for holding money are the transactions motive, the precautionary motive and the speculative motive.

4 Nominal money is simply the number of pounds, while real money is a measure of what money will buy because it will fall as the price level rises and the number of pounds is constant.

What matters to people is the quantity of goods and services that money will buy, not the number of pounds. If the price level rises by 10 per cent, people will want to hold 10 per cent more pounds (given real income and interest rates) in order to retain the same purchasing power.

5 Much of what constitutes money pays no interest; for example, currency and demand deposits. The interest rate is the opportunity cost of holding money, which pays no interest since interest income on alternative financial assets that could have been held is forgone. When interest rates rise, it becomes more costly to hold money, and so people will reduce their money holdings in order to buy other financial assets and take advantage of the higher interest rates.

6 An increase in the supply of real money means that, at the current interest rate, the quantity of money supplied will be greater than the quantity of money demanded. Money holders will want to reduce their money holdings and will attempt to do so by buying bonds. The increase in the demand for bonds will cause the price of bonds to rise and thus interest rates on bonds to fall. As interest rates fall, the quantity of money demanded increases, which reduces the excess supply of money. This process continues until the interest rate has fallen sufficiently that the quantity of money demanded is the same as the quantity of money supplied.

According to the quantity theory of money, an increase in the quantity of money will cause the price level to increase by an equal percentage amount.

PROBLEMS

1 The completed table is shown here as Table 27.3. The entries are values of the money multiplier obtained from the following formula:

$$mm = \frac{1 + a}{a + b}$$

where mm is the money multiplier. For example, for the cell of the table corresponding to $a = 0.2$ and $b = 0.05$, we have:

$$mm = \frac{1 + 0.2}{0.2 + 0.05} = \frac{1.2}{0.25} = 4.8$$

We note that for a given currency to deposits ratio, as the desired reserve ratio increases, the money multiplier decreases. For a given desired reserve ratio, as the currency to deposits ratio increases, the money multiplier also decreases.

Table 27.3 Money Multipliers

		a	
b	0.1	0.2	0.3
0.05	7.33	4.80	3.71
0.10	5.50	4.00	3.25
0.15	4.40	3.43	2.89

2 **a** The money multiplier is the ratio of the money supply (M) to the monetary base (MB):

$$mm = M/MB = 50/20 = 2.5$$

b Here we calculate $a = \Delta C/\Delta D$ and $b = \Delta R/\Delta D$ and use the formula derived in text Table 27.4:

$$a = \Delta C/\Delta D = 10/50 = 0.2$$
$$b = \Delta R/\Delta D = 5/50 = 0.1$$
$$mm = \frac{1 + a}{a + b} = \frac{1 + 0.2}{0.2 + 0.1} = 4$$

c Here we are given that $b = 0.1$ but we must find $a = \Delta C/\Delta D$. We know the value of ΔC but not the value of ΔD. We can find the value of ΔD, however, from our knowledge of b and ΔR: $\Delta D = \Delta R/b$. Therefore,

$$\Delta D = \Delta R/b = £5 \text{ billion}/0.1 = £50 \text{ billion}$$
$$a = \Delta C/\Delta D = 15/50 = 0.3$$
$$mm = \frac{1 + a}{a + b} = \frac{1 + 0.3}{0.3 + 0.1} = 3.25$$

3 The current equilibrium interest rate is 8 per cent and the Bank of England would like to increase the money supply sufficiently to lower the interest rate to 6 per cent. Since the quantity of real money demanded at an interest rate of 6 per cent is £70 billion, the Bank of England will want to increase the supply of real money by £10 billion: from £60 billion to £70 billion.

Real money is nominal money divided by the price level and the Bank of England controls only the supply of nominal money. Since the price level is 2, the supply of nominal money must rise by £20 billion in order to increase the supply of real money by £10 billion. Therefore, the Bank of England will need to increase the nominal money supply by £20 billion.

4 In order to increase the supply of money, the Bank of England will need to buy government securities in the open market because buying government securities will increase bank reserves and the monetary base. The amount of the open market purchase will depend on the money multiplier. Since $a = 0.2$ and $b = 0.1$, we can calculate the money multiplier as follows:

$$mm = \frac{1 + a}{a + b} = \frac{1 + 0.2}{0.2 + 0.1} = 4$$

This means that any initial increase in the monetary base will generate a total increase in money equal to 4 times its size. Thus, if we want a total increase in money of £20 billion, we need a £5 billion increase in the monetary base. This requires an open market purchase of £5 billion in government securities.

5 **a** The completed table is shown here as Table 27.4. The £5 billion open market purchase will create excess reserves of £5 billion which will be loaned out; 20 per cent of the loan or £1 billion will be held as currency, the remainder will be held added to deposits (£4 billion). Of this increase in deposits, 10 per cent or £0.4

billion will be held as desired reserves, and the rest (£3.6 billion) will be excess reserves at the end of round 1. This then becomes the excess reserves at the beginning of round 2 and the process continues.

In subsequent rounds we compute the various entries in the table as follows:

– Excess reserves at start of round = excess reserves at end of previous round
– New loans = excess reserves at start of round
– Change in deposits = 0.8 times new loans
– Change in currency = 0.2 times new loans
– Excess reserves at end of round = 0.9 times change in deposits
– Change in quantity of money = change in deposits + change in currency

The total effects for each relevant column are obtained by using the fact that the money multiplier is 4 (from Problem 4) and the effect of all other rounds is the difference between the final total and the total after six rounds.

b The total change in money after six rounds is £15.25 billion, the sum of the changes in the quantity of money for rounds 1 to 6.

c The total change in the money supply is £20 billion, which can be obtained by using a money multiplier of 4. This is exactly the desired increase in the money supply from Problem 3.

6 a From the equation of exchange, we know that the velocity of circulation is defined by:

$$\text{Velocity of circulation} = \frac{\text{Price level} \times \text{Real GDP}}{\text{Quantity of money}}$$

With the values for the price level, real GDP and the quantity of money given in this problem, we have:

$$\text{Velocity of circulation} = \frac{1.5 \times 240}{60} = \frac{360}{60} = 6$$

b The quantity theory of money predicts that an increase in the quantity of money will cause an equal percentage increase in the price level. An increase in money from £60 billion to £80 billion is a one-third (33 per cent) increase. Thus, the quantity theory of money predicts that the price level will rise by one-third (33 per cent). Since the initial price level is 1.5, the predicted price level will be 2.0.

DATA QUESTIONS

1 a As the article suggests, 'monetary policy' is aimed at safeguarding the value of money in the economy, but it is also used as a means of achieving other economic goals such as a stable exchange rate. It involves controlling the quantity of money, and influencing interest and exchange rates.

b The 'City' sometimes refers to that part of London where banks and insurance companies are concentrated, but usually it refers to the financial institutions themselves.

2 Apart from banks (there are about 530 authorized banks in the United Kingdom), the other participants in the financial market include discount houses, building societies, the stock exchange and insurance firms.

3 The interest rate is determined by the demand for money and its supply. The government influences the interest rate by using methods such as open market operations and by altering the rate on last resort lending. These methods are discussed in detail in the text, pp. 763–766.

Table 27.4 Money Multiplier Effects (billions of pounds)

Round	Excess reserves at start of round	New loans	Change in deposits	Change in currency	Excess reserves at end of round	Change in quantity of money
1	5.00	5.00	4.00	1.00	3.60	5.00
2	3.60	3.60	2.88	0.72	2.59	3.60
3	2.59	2.59	2.07	0.52	1.86	2.59
4	1.86	1.86	1.49	0.37	1.34	1.86
5	1.34	1.34	1.07	0.27	0.96	1.34
6	0.96	0.96	0.77	0.19	0.69	0.96
All others	–	4.65	3.72	0.93	–	4.65
Totals	–	20	16	4	–	20

Chapter 28

Fiscal and Monetary Influences on Aggregate Demand

Chapter In Perspective, Text Pages 782–817

In a somewhat incomplete way, we have seen that monetary policy (Bank of England actions that change the money supply) and fiscal policy (government actions that change taxes or government purchases) can both potentially affect the economy by changing aggregate demand. In this chapter we examine in some detail the channels by which such policy changes work their way through the economy to their final effects on aggregate demand. We also investigate the factors that determine whether a given monetary or fiscal policy will have a large or small effect on aggregate demand and the Keynesian–monetarist controversy about economic policy.

Helpful Hints

1 In Chapter 25 we examined the sector for goods and services in isolation by using the aggregate expenditure model and assuming that the interest rate is given. When the interest rate changes aggregate expenditure changes, and a new (flow) equilibrium level of real GDP results. Similarly, in Chapter 27 we examined the money sector in isolation by using the money supply and money demand model and assuming that the level of real GDP is given. When the level of real GDP changes, the demand for real money changes and a new (stock) equilibrium rate of interest results. So the equilibrium value of real GDP is determined assuming a value for the interest rate and the equilibrium interest rate is determined assuming a value for real GDP. In this chapter we put these two sectors together and determine equilibrium real GDP and the equilibrium interest rate by examining both models at the same time. When the level of real GDP and the interest rate are such that both the market for goods and services and the market for money are in equilibrium at the same time, we have a stock and flow equilibrium. In other words, we have a simultaneous or joint equilibrium in both markets.

2 The major focus of this chapter is on the channels by which an initial change in monetary or fiscal policy is transmitted through the economy to its eventual effect on aggregate demand – the transmission channels of monetary or fiscal policy. The graphical analysis presented in the text is of great value in studying these channels. From this analysis, we can see that the economy initially starts out in equilibrium. Next, either monetary or fiscal policy throws a market out of equilibrium. As this market changes and moves towards a new equilibrium, this triggers off changes in other markets. We eventually arrive at a new, simultaneous equilibrium in all markets.

Some students may find it helpful to augment the graphical analysis with simple 'arrow diagrams' which show the sequence of changes as the economy adjusts to an initial policy change. For example, the interest rate transmission channel of monetary policy is represented by the following arrow diagram.

(1)

$$\uparrow M \to \uparrow MS$$
$$\uparrow MS \to \downarrow r \quad \text{(link 1)}$$
$$\downarrow r \to \uparrow I \quad \text{(link 2)}$$
$$\uparrow I \to \uparrow AE$$
$$\uparrow AE \to \uparrow \text{real GDP}$$
$$\uparrow \text{real GDP} \to \uparrow MD$$
$$\uparrow MD \to \uparrow r$$
$$\uparrow r \to \downarrow I$$
$$\downarrow I \to \downarrow AE$$
$$\downarrow AE \to \downarrow \text{real GDP}$$

This indicates that an expansionary monetary policy (for example, an open market purchase of government securities by the Bank of England) will cause the quantity of money to increase ($\uparrow M$) which leads to ($\to$) an increase in the real supply of money ($\uparrow MS$). This in turn will result in a fall

in the interest rate ($\downarrow r$) which will cause investment, which is a part of aggregate expenditure, to increase ($\uparrow AE$). This will cause real GDP to begin increasing ($\uparrow$ real GDP), which will lead to an increase in the demand for real money ($\uparrow MD$). The increase in the demand for real money will cause the interest rate to rise ($\uparrow r$) and thus investment (aggregate expenditure) will decrease ($\downarrow AE$), which will lead to a fall in real GDP ($\downarrow$ real GDP). This effect offsets the initial changes somewhat, but the economy still eventually converges to a new stock and flow equilibrium. (Ignore the link 1 and link 2 on the arrow diagram for the moment.)

Note that an arrow diagram can be a convenient way of summarizing what we learn from the more detailed graphical analysis. Arrow diagrams can also be useful to help us see what kinds of effects can weaken or strengthen the ability of policy to change aggregate demand. The student may want to draw arrow diagrams for the other transmission channels of monetary policy discussed in the chapter.

3 The principal transmission channel of an increase in government purchases of goods and services (a fiscal policy) is given as follows:

(2)

$$\uparrow G \to \uparrow AE$$
$$\uparrow AE \to \downarrow \text{real GDP}$$
$$\downarrow \text{real GDP} \to \uparrow MD$$
$$\uparrow MD \to \uparrow r \quad \text{(link 1)}$$
$$\uparrow r \to \uparrow I \quad \text{(link 2)}$$
$$\downarrow I \to \downarrow AE$$
$$\downarrow AE \to \downarrow \text{real GDP}$$

The amount of government purchases on goods and services is represented by G. Otherwise the notation is the same as used before. (Once again, ignore the link 1 and link 2 until the next point.)

4 The text indicates that the strength of the effect of a change in the money supply on aggregate demand depends on the responsiveness of the demand for real money to changes in the interest rate and the responsiveness of investment demand to changes in the interest rate. The arrow diagram given by (1) can help us understand how these factors affect the strength of monetary policy by focusing on the 'links' marked 1 and 2. The link between the increase in the supply of real money and the subsequent fall in the interest rate is indicated as link 1. If the demand for real money is very sensitive to interest rate changes (that is, the *MD* curve is very flat), then this link is quite weak: a given increase in the supply of real money will have only a small effect on the interest rate. This in turn means a relatively small effect on investment, and so on. Link 2 captures the effect of a change in the interest rate on investment. If investment is very sensitive to interest rate changes (that is, the investment demand curve is very flat) then this link is quite strong: a given fall in the interest rate will have a very large effect on investment.

We can also examine the factors that determine the strength of the effect of fiscal policy on aggregate demand. Links 1 and 2 of (2) are the relevant links; indeed they are the same as links 1 and 2 for monetary policy. If the demand for real money is very sensitive to interest rate changes (that is, the *MD* curve is very flat), then link 1 is quite weak, the amount of crowding out is small, and fiscal policy is strong. (See Problem 4b.) Similarly, if investment is very sensitive to interest rate changes (that is, the investment demand curve is very flat), then link 2 is quite strong, the amount of crowding out is large, and fiscal policy is weak. Thus links 1 and 2 are the critical links in the transmission process and the focus of the Keynesian–monetarist controversy.

Key Figures

Figure 28.1 Equilibrium Interest Rate and Real GDP, text page 785

This is the basic three-part graph used in this chapter. It illustrates a stock and flow equilibrium: the combination of interest rate and real GDP which corresponds to equilibrium in the money market (stock equilibrium) and equilibrium in the goods market (flow equilibrium). Part (a) illustrates the determination of the equilibrium interest rate in the money market. Once the equilibrium interest rate is determined, the level of investment is determined by the investment demand curve (*ID*) in part (b). Since investment is part of aggregate planned expenditure, the level of investment (along with the other components of aggregate planned expenditure) determines the position of the *AE* curve in part (c). The position of the *AE* curve determines the level of real GDP. (Note that this in turn determines the amount of real money demand and the equilibrium interest rate!)

Figure 28.8 The Effectiveness of Fiscal Policy, text page 796

This may look complicated, but it illustrates the effectiveness of fiscal policy in a logical way. The conclusion reached is that if investment is very sensitive to changes in interest rates, then a change in fiscal policy will have only a small effect on fiscal policy.

At the top right hand of the figure are two curves showing different sensitivities of investment to changes in interest rates. Following the dotted line shows that the effect of an increase in government purchases increases real GDP, but it also increases the demand for money and hence the interest rate. If investment is very sensitive to changes in interest, then the higher interest rate will choke off a lot of investment, so reducing the effect of the rise in government spending.

Figure 28.9 The Effectiveness of Monetary Policy, text pages 797

The larger the effect of a given change in the supply of real money on the interest rate or the larger the effect of a given change in the interest rate on investment, the larger is the effect of monetary policy on aggregate demand. This is illustrated in part (a) of this figure. The effect of a given change in the supply of real money is large because the demand for real money is not very sensitive to changes in the interest rate (that is, the demand curve for real money is relatively steep), creating a large change in the interest rate. Also in part (a), the effect of a given change in the interest rate on investment is large because investment is very sensitive to changes in the interest rate (that is, the investment demand curve is quite flat), creating a large change in the level of investment. Part (b) illustrates the opposite: monetary policy is quite ineffective because the effect of a given change in the supply of real money on the interest rate is small (the *MD* curve is flat) and the effect of a change in the interest rate on investment is small (the investment demand curve is steep).

SELF-TEST

CONCEPT REVIEW

1 The main channel by which an increase in the money supply is transmitted to aggregate demand is through the _____ _____. An increase in the money supply causes the interest rate to _____. This will in turn cause investment to _____, which will _____ aggregate planned expenditure. This change in aggregate planned expenditure will cause real GDP to begin to _____. This change in real GDP will shift the demand curve for real money to the _____, which will cause the interest rate to _____.

2 A change in the money supply will have a larger effect on interest rates the _____ responsive is the demand for real money to changes in the interest rate. A change in the interest rate will have a larger effect on investment the _____ responsive is investment demand to the interest rate.

3 There are three other transmission channels of monetary policy. The _____ _____ _____ effect is the effect of the quantity of real money on the aggregate quantity of real GDP demanded. The _____ effect is the effect of a change in real wealth on aggregate planned expenditure and an increase in money generally increases wealth by its effect on _____ prices. An increase in money can also lead to a depreciation of the pound relative to foreign currencies and thus an increase in exports. This is the _____ _____ effect.

4 The tendency for an increase in government purchases to cause interest rates to rise and thus reduce investment is called _____ _____.

TRUE OR FALSE

___ **1** An increase in the supply of real money will cause the interest rate to rise.

___ **2** An increase in the demand for real money will cause the interest rate to rise.

___ **3** In general, an increase in the supply of real money will be followed by an increase in investment.

___ **4** A decrease in investment will decrease aggregate planned expenditure and equilibrium real GDP.

___ **5** Other things remaining the same, a change in the money supply will have a larger effect on aggregate planned expenditure the more responsive is the demand for real money to the interest rate.

___ **6** Other things remaining the same, a change in the money supply will have a larger effect on aggregate planned expenditure the more responsive is investment demand to the interest rate.

___ **7** A change in the money supply affects interest rates with a time lag but its effect on investment is immediate.

___ **8** An increase in the quantity of money given the price level is an increase in real money balances.

___ **9** An increase in the value of the pound relative to foreign currencies will decrease net exports.

___ **10** An increase in government purchases of goods and services eventually will shift the demand curve for real money to the right, increasing the interest rate.

___ **11** Crowding out will be greater if the investment demand curve is very steep.

___ **12** If aggregate demand is increased by an increase in the money supply, interest rates fall and investment increases.

___ **13** If aggregate demand is increased by an increase in government purchases of goods and services, interest rates fall and investment increases.

___ **14** Keynesians consider the economy to be inherently unstable.

MULTIPLE-CHOICE

1 Which of the following correctly describes the initial steps of the interest rate transmission mechanism? An increase in the money supply will cause investment to
  a increase and thus aggregate planned expenditure to increase.
  b increase and thus aggregate planned expenditure to decrease.
  c decrease and thus aggregate actual expenditure to increase.
  d decrease and thus aggregate planned expenditure to decrease.
  e increase and thus aggregate actual expenditure to increase.

2 Consider Fig. 28.1. Why is the situation depicted there not a stock and flow equilibrium?
  a The level of aggregate planned spending is inconsistent with the interest rate.
  b The money market and the goods market are not individually in equilibrium.
  c The expenditure equilibrium occurs at a different level of real GDP than the level of real GDP assumed when drawing the demand curve for real money.
  d The level of investment in part (c) is inconsistent with the level of investment in part (b).
  e Aggregate expenditure is greater than aggregate supply.

3 Suppose Fig. 28.1 depicts the actual current position of an economy. In stock and flow equilibrium,
  a real GDP will be less than £800 billion and the interest rate will be higher than 4 per cent.
  b real GDP will be less than £800 billion and the interest rate will be lower than 4 per cent.
  c real GDP will be more than £800 billion and the interest rate will be higher than 4 per cent.
  d real GDP will be more than £800 billion and the interest rate will be lower than 4 per cent.
  e none of the above will occur.

4 An increase in the money supply will generally eventually lead to an increase in real GDP, which will shift the demand curve for real money to the
  a left causing the interest rate to fall.
  b left causing the interest rate to rise.
  c right causing the interest rate to fall.
  d right causing the interest rate to rise.
  e right causing the money supply to rise.

5 Monetary policy will have the smallest effect on aggregate demand when the sensitivity of the demand curve for real money to the interest rate is
  a large and the sensitivity of the investment demand curve to the interest rate is large.
  b large and the sensitivity of the investment demand curve to the interest rate is small.
  c small and the sensitivity of the consumption function to the interest rate is large.
  d small and the sensitivity of the investment demand curve to the interest rate is small.

Figure 28.1

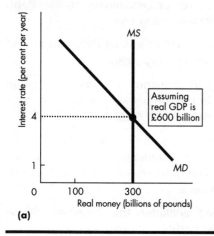
(a)

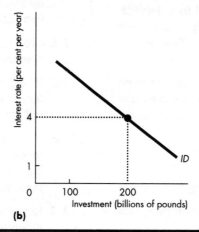
(b)

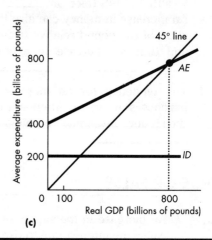
(c)

e small and the sensitivity of the consumption function to the interest rate is small.

6 Which of the following is the main transmission mechanism by which a change in the money supply affects aggregate demand?
a the real money balances effect
b the exchange rate effect
c the wealth effect
d the crowding-out effect
e the interest rate effect

7 Overall, a tax cut will
a increase aggregate planned expenditure by causing disposable income to increase.
b increase aggregate planned expenditure by causing the interest rate to fall.
c decrease aggregate planned expenditure by causing disposable income to fall.
d decrease aggregate planned expenditure by causing the interest rate to rise.
e increase aggregate planned expenditure by causing investment to rise.

8 There will be no crowding out if
a the demand for real money is totally unresponsive to changes in the interest rate.
b the supply of real money is totally unresponsive to changes in the interest rate.
c investment is very responsive to changes in the interest rate.
d investment is totally unresponsive to changes in real GDP.
e the demand for real money is totally unresponsive to changes in real GDP.

9 Aggregate demand can be increased by increasing the money supply (expansionary monetary policy) or by increasing government purchases of goods and services (expansionary fiscal policy). Which of the following is a correct comparison?
a The interest rate will rise under the monetary policy and fall under the fiscal policy, while consumption will increase under both.
b The interest rate will fall under the monetary policy and rise under the fiscal policy, while consumption will increase under both.
c Consumption will rise under the monetary policy and fall under the fiscal policy, while the interest rate will increase under both.
d Consumption will rise under the monetary policy and fall under the fiscal policy, while the interest rate will decrease under both.

e Consumption will fall under the monetary policy and fall under the fiscal policy, while the interest rate will increase under both.

10 A tax cut will cause
a a decrease in the interest rate, which will lead to a decrease in the foreign exchange value of the pound.
b a decrease in the interest rate, which will lead to an increase in the foreign exchange value of the pound.
c an increase in the interest rate, which will lead to a decrease in the foreign exchange value of the pound.
d an increase in the interest rate, which will lead to an increase in the foreign exchange value of the pound.
e no change in the interest rate.

11 Which of the following sets of beliefs is characteristic of a Keynesian?
a The economy is inherently unstable, and fiscal policy is more important than monetary policy.
b The economy is inherently unstable, and monetary policy is more important than fiscal policy.
c The economy is inherently stable, and fiscal policy is more important than monetary policy.
d The economy is inherently stable, and monetary policy is more important than fiscal policy.
e The economy is inherently stable, and crowding out is strong.

12 Which of the following would characterize the extreme monetarist position?
a A horizontal investment demand curve and a horizontal demand curve for real money.
b A horizontal investment demand curve and a vertical demand curve for real money.
c A vertical investment demand curve and a horizontal demand curve for real money.
d A vertical investment demand curve and a vertical demand curve for real money.
e A vertical investment demand curve and a horizontal supply curve of real money.

13 If an economy is in a liquidity trap, then
a a change in the interest rate will have no effect on investment.
b a change in investment will have no effect on aggregate planned expenditure.
c. open market operations will not shift the supply curve of real money.

d an increase in the supply of real money will have no effect on the interest rate.

e fiscal policy is totally crowded out.

14 Counting the first and second round effects, the impact of a contractionary monetary policy is to decrease real GDP,

a reduce the interest rate and reduce investment.

b reduce the interest rate and increase investment.

c increase the interest rate and reduce investment.

d increase the interest rate and increase investment.

e and do none of the above.

SHORT ANSWER

1 Trace the main steps in the interest rate transmission channel following an increase in the supply of real money.

2 Why does an increase in the supply of real money have a smaller effect on aggregate planned expenditure if the demand for real money is very sensitive to changes in the interest rate?

3 How does crowding out take place?

4 Why will more crowding out take place if investment demand is very sensitive to interest rate changes?

PROBLEMS

1 Figure 28.2 depicts an economy. Note that MD_0 corresponds to real GDP = £400 billion, MD_1 corresponds to real GDP = £500 billion and MD_2 corresponds to real GDP = £600 billion.

a What are the equilibrium values for real GDP, the interest rate and investment?

b Is this a stock and flow equilibrium? Why or why not?

2 Consider again the economy depicted by Fig. 28.2. Suppose that the Bank of England increases the supply of real money from £300 billion to £400 billion.

a What is the initial effect on the interest rate?

b What effect will this have on investment?

c As a result of this change in investment, what happens to equilibrium GDP? Why will this level of GDP not be achieved?

d What are the interest rate, investment and real GDP at the new stock and flow equilibrium?

e Show the new stock and flow equilibrium on Fig. 28.2.

3 Figure 28.3 depicts an economy. Note that MD_0 corresponds to real GDP = £400 billion, MD_1 corresponds to real GDP = £500 billion and MD_2 corresponds to real GDP = £600 billion. Suppose

Figure 28.2

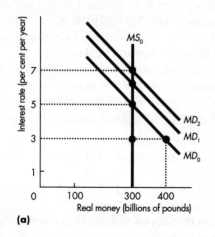

(a)

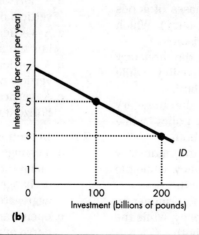

(b)

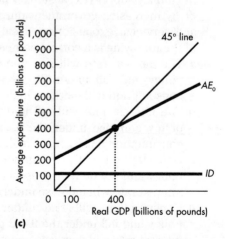

(c)

Figure 28.3

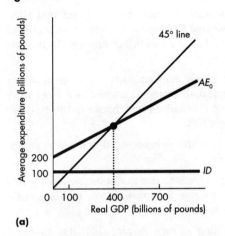

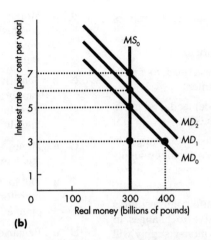

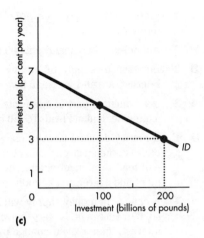

(a)

(b)

(c)

that the government increases its purchases of goods and services by £100 billion.

a What is the initial full multiplier effect on real GDP? Why will the economy not remain at this level of real GDP?

b As a result of this full multiplier effect on real GDP, what happens to the demand curve for real money and to the interest rate?

c What are the interest rate, investment and real GDP at the new stock and flow equilibrium? How much investment is crowded out? (Note the differences in the effects of monetary policy and fiscal policy illustrated by Problems 2 and 3.)

d Show graphically the new stock and flow equilibrium on Fig. 28.3.

DATA QUESTIONS

Government Spending on Public Works

If, for example, a government employs 100,000 additional men on public works, and if the multiplier... is 4, it is not safe to assume that aggregate employment will increase by 400,000. For the new policy may have adverse reactions in other directions.... The method of financing the policy and the increased working cash required by the in-creased employment and the associated rise in prices may have the effect of increasing the rate of interest and so retarding investment in other directions.

Source: J. M. Keynes, *The General Theory of Employment, Interest and Money*, Macmillan, 1936.

1 Define and explain what is meant by 'the multiplier'.

2 Explain with the use of diagram(s) how an increase in government spending may retard investment in other directions.

ANSWERS

CONCEPT REVIEW

1 interest rate; fall; increase; increase; rise; right; rise

2 less; more

3 real money balances; wealth; stock; exchange rate

4 crowding out

TRUE OR FALSE

1 F Increase in supply cuts price (that is, the rate of interest).

2 T An increase in demand puts up price.

3 T Increase in supply of money will lead to fall in interest rate and so rise in investment.

4 T Investment is part of aggregate demand, and fall in aggregate demand leads to fall in GDP.

5 F If money demand is very responsive to changes in interest, then a given small change in money supply will lead to a small change in interest and investment and aggregate expenditure.

6 T A change in money supply will affect interest rates so if investment is very sensitive to changes in interest, then a given change in money supply will have a relatively large effect.

7 F Effect on investment follows from change in interest.

8 T Definition.

9 T Increase in pound will make UK exports cost more and imports will become cheaper.

10 T Increase in government spending leads to rise in GDP, so money demand curve shifts to right leading to increase in supply of bonds. This causes a fall in price of bonds and rise in interest rates.

11 F Steep investment demand curve means investment is not very responsive to changes in interest. Crowding out creates rise in interest rates, but steep investment demand curve means this has little effect.

12 T Increase in supply cuts price (that is, interest rate) and this stimulates investment.

13 F Increase in *AD* will lead to rise in demand for money; rise in demand leads to rise in price (that is, interest rate).

14 T Core of Keynesian approach.

MULTIPLE-CHOICE

1 a Increase in *MS* will cut interest rates and so increase investment, part of aggregate expenditure.

2 c The higher equilibrium real GDP will shift money demand; hence current money demand is inconsistent.

3 a The equilibrium real GDP of £800 billion will raise money demand causing rise in interest rates and

fall in investment so rise in aggregate expenditure and fall in equilibrium real GDP.

4 d Money demand depends positively on real GDP, and higher real GDP leads to increase in supply of bonds and fall in bond prices and rise in interest rates.

5 b Sensitive money demand leads to change in money supply and small change in interest rate; insensitive investment demand means change in interest will have little effect.

6 e Money supply affects interest rate and hence aggregate demand.

7 a Fall in taxes leads to rise in disposable income and therefore to rise in consumption and aggregate planned expenditure.

8 e Because then change in real GDP due to fiscal policy has no impact on real money demand or on interest rates.

9 b Under both, increase in real GDP leads to rise in consumption. Under fiscal policy crowding out leads to rise in interest rate. Under monetary policy rise in money supply leads to fall in interest rate.

10 d Tax cut will lead to rise in real GDP, demand for money, interest rates, demand for financial assets and therefore demand for pounds and a rise in the price of the pound.

11 a Essence of Keynesian approach.

12 b Definition.

13 d Liquidity trap means flat *MD* curve so change in money supply has no impact on interest rate.

14 c Fall in real GDP leads to fall in money demand and interest rate and so a rise in investment, but not enough to overcome original fall in investment.

SHORT ANSWER

1 An increase in the supply of real money

  – will shift the supply curve of real money to the right and lower the interest rate;

  – the lower interest rate will cause investment to increase;

  – the increase in investment means that aggregate planned expenditure increases;

  – the increase in aggregate planned expenditure means that equilibrium GDP is higher and that at the current level of real GDP, inventories are being depleted more rapidly than planned;

  – as inventories fall more rapidly than planned, real GDP begins to rise (toward the new equilibrium);

- rising real GDP causes the demand curve for real money to shift to the right causing the interest rate to rise;
- the higher interest rate will cause investment to decrease;
- the decrease in investment means that aggregate planned expenditure decreases;
- the decrease in aggregate planned expenditure means that equilibrium GDP is lower; and
- as actual real GDP increases and equilibrium GDP decreases, they will converge at a new stock and flow equilibrium.

2 If the demand for real money is very sensitive to changes in the interest rate, the demand curve for real money is very flat. Thus, when the money supply increases and the supply curve for real money shifts to the right, the resulting change in the equilibrium interest rate will be small. A small interest rate change will lead to a small change in investment and a small change in aggregate planned expenditure.

3 Crowding out is the tendency for expansionary fiscal policy to cause the interest rate to rise and thus investment to decline. The expansionary fiscal policy 'crowds out' investment. The increase in the interest rate is a consequence of the fact that the increase in real GDP that occurs as a consequence of an increase in government expenditure on goods and services (say) will cause the demand curve for real money to shift to the right. Thus the equilibrium interest rate will rise.

4 If investment demand is very sensitive to changes in the interest rate, the investment demand curve will be very flat. Thus the increase in the interest rate that initiates the crowding out effect (see Answer 3) will induce a large decrease in investment spending, which means large crowding out.

PROBLEMS

1 a The equilibrium value for real GDP is at the intersection of the AE_0 curve and the 45° line, £400 billion. The equilibrium value for the interest rate is 5 per cent, since the relevant MD curve is MD_1 when real GDP is £400 billion. At an interest rate of 5 per cent, investment is £100 (part b).

b This is a stock and flow equilibrium since equilibrium real GDP is £400 billion when the interest rate is 5 per cent (flow equilibrium) and the equilibrium interest rate is 5 per cent when real GDP is £400 billion (stock equilibrium). That is, it is a stock and flow equilibrium because the values of real GDP and the interest rate that give stock equilibrium and flow equilibrium are the same.

2 a The initial effect of an increase in the supply of real money from £300 billion to £400 billion is to lower the interest rate from 5 per cent to 3 per cent.

b The fall in the interest rate from 5 per cent to 3 per cent will increase investment from £100 billion to £200 billion.

c Equilibrium GDP will increase from £400 billion to £600 billion. This level of GDP will not be achieved because, as real GDP begins to rise above £400 billion, the money demand curve will start shifting to the right causing the interest rate to rise. This will cause investment and thus the AE curve to shift back down somewhat.

d In the new stock and flow equilibrium, we must have a single real GDP and interest rate combination that (given the new money supply) leaves both the money market and the market for goods in equilibrium. This occurs at an interest rate of 4 per cent and real GDP of £500 billion. Investment will be £150 billion.

Figure 28.4

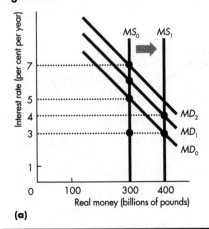

(a)

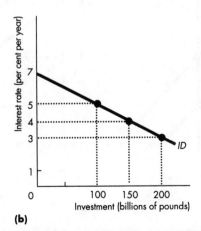

(b)

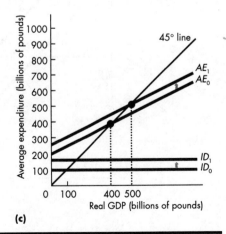

(c)

Figure 28.5

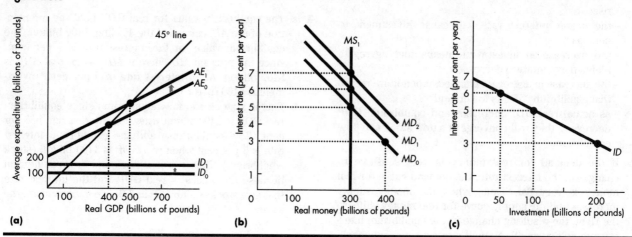

(a)   **(b)**   **(c)**

e See Fig. 28.4. Note that the relevant demand curve for real money is MD_2, which is drawn assuming real GDP = £500 billion. MS_0 has shifted to MS_1, ID_0 has shifted to ID_1, and AE_0 has shifted to AE_1.

3 a The full multiplier effect of an increase in government purchases of £100 billion is to increase equilibrium GDP by £200 billion: from £400 billion to £600 billion. This is not a stock and flow equilibrium.

The economy will not remain here (indeed it would probably never get there) because as real GDP increases, the demand curve for real money will shift to the right, raising the interest rate, which reduces investment, aggregate planned expenditure and equilibrium real GDP.

b If the full multiplier effect on real GDP (from £400 billion to £600 billion) took place the demand curve for real money would shift from MD_0 to MD_2,

Figure 28.6

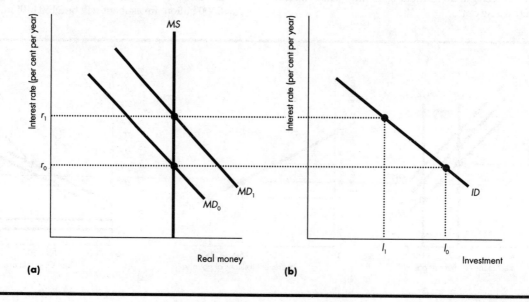

(a)   **(b)**

causing the interest rate to rise from 5 per cent to 7 per cent.

c In the new stock and flow equilibrium the interest rate is 6 per cent and real GDP is £500 billion. Only this combination of interest rate and real GDP gives both a stock (money market) and flow (goods market) equilibrium. Investment has fallen to £50 billion from £100 billion, so £50 billion of investment is crowded out. (Note that both the expansionary monetary policy of Problem 2 and the expansionary fiscal policy of Problem 3 have the same effect on real GDP. The monetary policy, however, reduced the interest rate and increased investment, while the fiscal policy increased the interest rate and reduced investment.)

d See Fig. 28.5. Note that the relevant demand curve for real money is MD_1 which is drawn assuming real GDP = £500 billion. AE_0 has shifted to AE_1, and ID_0 has shifted to ID_1.

DATA QUESTIONS

1 The multiplier is the relationship between an increase in autonomous expenditure and the resultant change in GDP. In essence the multiplier works because the original increase in expenditure leads to additional spending by those who receive the original additional expenditure. The process is described in the main text, pp. 698–700.

2 The overall effect may be diminished because of crowding out. This is illustrated in Fig. 28.6. In part (a) the original increase in public spending increases aggregate planned expenditure and real GDP. However, this increases the demand for money and, if there is no change in the money supply, will increase the rate of interest. The effect of this higher interest rate is shown in part (b) where it leads to a fall in investment. The extent of the fall will depend on the shape of the investment demand curve.

Chapter 29 Productivity, Wages and Unemployment

Chapter In Perspective, Text Pages 818–849

In Chapter 23 it was indicated that the behaviour of the economy (inflation, unemployment, business cycle fluctuations) could be explained using the concepts of aggregate demand and aggregate supply. In Chapters 24 to 28 we have carefully pursued the concept of aggregate demand in order to understand how it is determined and what makes it change. In this chapter, we now turn our attention to the concept of aggregate supply.

The question of aggregate supply is: how does a change in the price level affect the quantity of real GDP supplied? Since the quantity of real GDP supplied depends in large measure on the quantity of labour employed, we find that an understanding of the labour market is critical to a complete understanding of aggregate supply. Thus we examine the labour market in order to understand better the determination of employment and real GDP. We also look at the related issue of the determination of the rate of unemployment.

Helpful Hints

1 Do not lose sight of the fact that the fundamental purpose of this chapter is to deepen our understanding of aggregate supply: the relationship between the price level and the quantity of real GDP supplied.

First we ask a basic question: how is the quantity of real GDP supplied determined in general? In the short run when the capital stock and the state of technology are given, the maximum amount of real GDP that can be produced depends on the quantity of labour employed. This relationship between employment and the quantity of real GDP supplied

is captured by the short-run aggregate production function.

In order to understand the determination of the quantity of real GDP supplied it is therefore necessary to pursue the second issue: how is the level of employment determined? The answer: in the labour market. The demand for labour is determined by firms and the supply of labour is determined by households. If wages are flexible and continuously adjust to clear the labour market, the level of employment will always be the equilibrium level, that is, full employment. If, on the other hand, wages are 'sticky' because the money wage rate is set by a wage contract, the level of employment can deviate from its equilibrium level in the short run.

Since our interest is in aggregate supply, we want to know how the quantity of real GDP varies as the price level varies. This brings us to the third issue: how do changes in the price level affect employment and thereby real GDP? It turns out that if wages are flexible, the level of employment (and thus the quantity of real GDP supplied) is independent of the price level. Whatever the price level, the wage rate will adjust so that the unique equilibrium level of employment is achieved. This implies an aggregate supply curve which is vertical at the full-employment level of real GDP. On the other hand, if wages are sticky, the level of employment (and thus the quantity of real GDP supplied) depends on the actual value of the price level relative to the expected value of the price level. If the price level turns out to be equal to its expected value, the equilibrium level of employment (full employment) results. If the price level is higher than expected, the level of employment turns out to be higher than the equilibrium value and thus real GDP supplied will be larger than full-employment real GDP. If the price level is lower than expected, employment will be less than equilibrium and real GDP supplied will be less than full-employment real GDP. This implies a positively sloped aggregate supply curve when wages are sticky.

2 The following arrow diagram may be helpful in understanding why the short-run aggregate supply curve is positively sloped. It shows the sequence of events that link a change in the price level with the subsequent change in the quantity of real GDP supplied. Let P be the price level, W/P be the real wage rate, L be the quantity of labour employed, and Y be the quantity of real GDP supplied. If wages are sticky we have

$$\uparrow P \rightarrow \uparrow (W/P) \rightarrow \uparrow L \rightarrow \uparrow Y$$

If the money wage rate is fixed by contract, an (unexpected) increase in the price level ($\uparrow P$) will cause the real wage rate to fall ($\downarrow (W/P)$). At the lower real wage rate, firms will want to hire more labour ($\uparrow L$), which implies an increase in the quantity of real GDP supplied ($\uparrow Y$). Thus, the short-run aggregate supply curve is positively sloped.

If wages are flexible, an increase in the price level will have no effect on the quantity of real GDP supplied because the real wage rate will not fall.

Key Figures

Figure 29.1 The Short-run Aggregate Production Function, text page 820

The short-run aggregate production function shows the maximum real GDP attainable at each quantity of labour input, holding constant the state of technology and the quantities of other inputs. Note two things. First, the aggregate production function is positively sloped: an increase in labour input will yield an increase in output. This is the same as saying that the marginal product of labour is positive. Second, the curve becomes flatter as labour input increases. This reflects diminishing marginal product of labour. It is diminishing marginal productivity of labour that gives us downward-sloping labour demand curves.

Figure 29.2 The Growth of Output, text page 822

Both the natural accumulation of capital and the natural advance of technology imply that the short-run aggregate production function will shift upward over time. As illustrated here, this upward shift simply means that now more real GDP can be produced with each quantity of labour than was the case before the increase in capital or the technological advance.

Figure 29.7 Equilibrium with Flexible Wages, text page 829

This illustrates the demand for labour curve (LD), the supply of labour curve (LS) and equilibrium in the labour market. The equilibrium real wage rate is the value that equates the quantity of labour demanded with the quantity of labour supplied. If the real wage rate is below the equilibrium real wage rate, the quantity of labour demanded will exceed the quantity of labour supplied, and if real wages are flexible, the real wage rate will be bid up until equilibrium is achieved. Similarly, if the real wage rate is above equilibrium, the quantity of labour supplied will be greater than the quantity of labour demanded and the real wage rate will fall.

Figure 29.8 Aggregate Supply with Flexible Wages, text page 830

Aggregate supply is the relationship between the price level and the quantity of real GDP supplied (part c). The quantity of real GDP supplied is determined by evaluating the aggregate production at the current level of employment (part b). In the flexible wage model, employment is determined by equilibrium in the labour market (part a). The aggregate supply curve then answers the question: what effect will a change in the price level have on the quantity of real GDP supplied? In order for a change in the price level to affect the quantity of real GDP supplied, it must cause a change in the level of employment. In the case of flexible wages, a change in the price level will have no effect on the level of employment, since the money wage rate will change proportionately so as to leave the real wage rate and employment at their unchanged equilibrium levels. Since a change in the price level has no effect on employment in the flexible wage model, it has no effect on the quantity of real GDP supplied and thus the aggregate supply curve is vertical.

Figure 29.9 A Labour Market with Sticky Money Wages, text page 832

This illustrates the determination of employment in a labour market in which the money wage is fixed (sticky). There is a single real wage rate that is consistent with equilibrium in the labour market. In the example illustrated in this figure, that money wage rate = £15. Thus, for any given price level there is a single money wage rate that results in labour market equilibrium. (Note that a crucial assumption of the theory is that workers will supply whatever labour is desired by firms.)

SELF-TEST

CONCEPT REVIEW

1 A short-run _____ _____ shows how maximum output varies as the quantity of labour employed varies, holding constant the stock of capital and the state of technology. The short-run _____ _____ _____ shows how maximum real GDP varies as total employment of labour varies, holding constant the total stock of capital and the state of technology. It will shift _____ over time as capital accumulates and technology advances.

2 The additional real GDP produced by one additional hour of labour input, holding other inputs and technology constant, gives the _____ _____ of labour. The tendency for this magnitude to decline as the quantity of labour input increases, holding everything else constant, is called the _____ _____ of labour.

3 The _____ _____ _____ is a schedule or curve that shows the quantity of labour demanded at each level of the _____ wage rate. The _____ wage rate is the wage per hour expressed in constant pounds. The _____ wage rate is the wage per hour expressed in current pounds.

4 The _____ _____ _____ is a schedule or curve that shows the quantity of labour supplied at each level of the real wage rate. According to the substitution effect, if the real wage rate rises, households will _____ the quantity of labour they supply. According to the income effect, if the real wage rate rises, households will _____ the quantity of labour they supply.

5 The proportion of the working-age population that is either employed or unemployed (but looking for a job) is called the labour force _____ _____ . The lowest wage at which an individual will supply any labour is called the _____ _____ .

6 There are two leading theories about the labour market. The first of these assumes that the wage rate adjusts continually so as to keep the quantity of labour demanded equal to the quantity of labour supplied. It is called the _____ wage theory. The second, called the _____ wage theory, assumes that the labour market is dominated by wage contracts that set the money wage rate for a specific period of time.

7 If the wage rate adjusts continually to clear the labour market, the aggregate supply curve will be _____ . If the wage rate is set for a period of time by wage contracts, the short-run aggregate supply curve will be _____ sloped.

8 _____ _____ _____ _____ argues that aggregate fluctuations are a consequence of fluctuations in the pace of technological change, and hence are optimal, while the more recent _____ researchers argue that these fluctuations are not necessarily optimal due to factors such as efficiency wages.

9 The _____ wage is a wage that maximizes a firm's profits. It exceeds the competitive market wage and results in _____ .

TRUE OR FALSE

___ 1 The diminishing marginal product of labour implies that the demand for labour curve is negatively sloped.

___ 2 As the real wage rate rises, the quantity of labour demanded decreases, other things remaining constant.

___ 3 Suppose the money wage rate and the real wage rate are initially equal. After an increase in the price level, the money wage rate will be greater than the real wage rate.

___ 4 If the marginal product of each unit of labour increases, the demand for labour curve shifts to the right.

___ 5 An increase in the real wage rate increases the opportunity cost of leisure.

___ 6 If the real wage rate falls, the substitution effect implies that households will increase the time spent working.

___ 7 If the real wage rate falls, the income effect implies that households will increase the time spent working.

___ 8 If the real wage rate is currently high relative to what it is expected to be in the future, workers will tend to supply less labour now and more in the future.

___ 9 According to the flexible wage theory of the labour market, the labour market is always in equilibrium.

___ 10 According to the sticky wage theory of the labour market, if the price level turns out to be higher than expected, the actual real wage will be greater than the equilibrium real wage.

___ 11 According to the sticky wage theory, an increase in the price level will increase employment in the short run.

___ 12 According to the sticky wage theory, fluctuations in real GDP are due only to fluctuations in long-run aggregate supply.

___ 13 If there is an increase in the pace of labour turnover, the unemployment rate will rise.

___ 14 According to the flexible wage model, the unemployment rate is always equal to the natural rate of unemployment.

MULTIPLE-CHOICE

1 The marginal product of labour curve is
 a positively sloped and shifts when there is a change in the capital stock.
 b positively sloped and shifts when there is a change in the quantity of labour employed.
 c negatively sloped and shifts when there is a change in the capital stock.
 d negatively sloped and shifts when there is a change in the quantity of labour employed.
 e negatively sloped and shifts when there is a change in the wage rate.

2 Which of the following would shift the short-run aggregate production function upward?
 a a decrease in the stock of capital
 b a fall in the wage rate
 c an increase in labour employed
 d an increase in the price level
 e a technological advance

3 The demand for labour shows that, holding other things constant, as the
 a price level increases, the quantity of labour demanded decreases.
 b real wage rate increases, the quantity of labour demanded increases.
 c money wage rate increases, the quantity of labour demanded decreases.
 d money wage rate increases, the quantity of labour demanded increases.
 e real wage rate increases, the quantity of labour demanded decreases.

4 Why is the demand for labour curve negatively sloped?

    a At lower wage rates, workers don't work as hard and so firms must hire more of them.

    b Because the marginal product of labour tends to decline as the labour input increases, holding other things constant.

    c As technology advances, less labour is required to produce a given output.

    d As the price of output rises, firms will want to hire less labour.

    e As the marginal product of labour increases, fewer workers are needed.

5 If the money wage rate is £12 per hour and the GDP deflator is 150, the real wage rate is

    a £18 per hour.

    b £12 per hour.

    c £8 per hour.

    d £6 per hour.

    e £15 per hour.

6 A profit-maximizing firm will hire additional units of labour up to the point at which

    a workers are no longer willing to work.

    b the marginal product of labour is zero.

    c the marginal product of labour is a maximum.

    d the marginal product of labour is equal to the real wage.

    e the marginal product of labour is equal to the money wage.

7 According to the flexible wage theory of the labour market, an increase in the price level will cause the

    a real wage rate to fall and therefore increase employment.

    b real wage rate to fall and therefore decrease employment.

    c money wage rate to rise by the same proportion and therefore increase employment.

    d money wage rate to rise by the same proportion and therefore leave employment unchanged.

    e money wage rate to rise by the same proportion and therefore decrease employment.

8 The aggregate supply curve is vertical at full-employment real GDP if

    a the real wage rate adjusts continually so as to leave the labour market always in equilibrium.

    b the money wage rate is fixed but the real wage rate changes because of changes in the price level.

    c employment is determined by the quantity of labour demanded.

    d employment is determined by the quantity of labour supplied.

    e employment is determined by both demand for and supply of labour.

9 According to the flexible wage theory of the labour market, an increase in real GDP implies that

    a long-run aggregate supply has increased.

    b aggregate demand has increased.

    c the economy has moved up its short-run aggregate supply curve.

    d the price level has increased.

    e real wages have fallen.

10 According to the sticky wage theory of the labour market, a wage contract will set the money wage rate at a level

    a equal to the real wage rate.

    b equal to the maximum marginal product of labour.

    c so that the money wage rate is equal to the marginal product of labour.

    d so that, if the actual price level turns out to be what is expected, the labour market will be in equilibrium.

    e so that the real wage is always equal to the marginal product of labour no matter what price level comes about.

11 According to the sticky wage theory, employment is determined by the

    a quantity of labour demanded at the actual real wage rate.

    b quantity of labour supplied at the actual real wage rate.

    c intersection of the demand for labour and supply of labour curves.

    d intersection of the aggregate demand and aggregate supply curves.

    e price level.

12 According to the flexible wage theory, if the price level increases, then in the short run real GDP supplied will

    a remain unchanged but, according to the sticky wage theory, real GDP supplied will increase.

    b increase and, according to the sticky wage theory, real GDP supplied will increase also.

    c increase but, according to the sticky wage theory, real GDP supplied will remain unchanged.

    d decrease but, according to the sticky wage theory, real GDP supplied will increase.

e decrease and, according to the sticky wage theory, real GDP supplied will decrease also.

13 The fact that labour is an economically indivisible factor of production implies that
  a firms will tend to adjust the quantity of labour demanded by changing hours per worker rather than changing the number of workers.
  b firms will tend to adjust the quantity of labour demanded by changing the number of workers rather than changing hours per worker.
  c firms cannot hire fractions of workers.
  d workers will tend to work for a single firm.
  e firms have a difficult time telling the quality of workers.

14 Which of the following would generally increase unemployment?
  a an increase in the number of people entering retirement
  b an increase in the number of people withdrawing from the labour force
  c an increase in the number of people recalled from layoffs
  d an increase in the number of people leaving jobs to go to school
  e an increase in the number of people leaving school to find jobs

15 Figure 29.1 depicts the labour market. The price level, as measured by the GDP deflator, is 150. According to the sticky wage theory, if the price level is expected to remain constant, what money wage rate will be set by a wage contract?
  a £8
  b £12
  c £15
  d £24
  e £18

16 Refer to Fig. 29.1 and again assume that when the money wage was set, the GDP deflator was expected to remain constant at 150. If the GDP deflator actually turns out to be 200, the real wage rate will be
  a £9 and employment will be less than 100 billion hours per year.
  b £9 and employment will be more than 100 billion hours per year.
  c £24 and employment will be less than 100 billion hours per year.
  d £24 and employment will be more than 100 billion hours per year.

  e £6 and employment will be more than 100 billion hours per year.

Figure 29.1

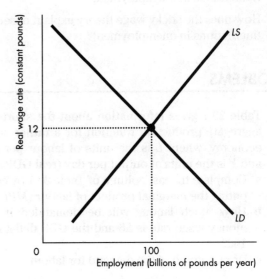

17 If real wages are very flexible, then
  a all unemployment is natural unemployment.
  b aggregate demand has no role to play in determining output.
  c fluctuations in real GDP are associated with shifts in aggregate supply only.
  d monetary and fiscal policy can be used only to affect prices and inflation.
  e all of the above are correct.

SHORT ANSWER

1 Why is the demand for labour curve negatively sloped?

2 a Explain why the labour force participation rate increases as the real wage rate increases.
  b Why does this help explain why the labour supply curve is positively sloped?

3 Suppose the price level increases unexpectedly. According to the flexible wage theory of the labour market, what will happen to the money wage rate, the real wage rate, employment and real GDP?

4 Suppose the price level increases unexpectedly. According to the sticky wage theory of the labour market, what will happen to the money wage rate, the real wage rate, employment and real GDP?

5 How does the flexible wage theory explain observed fluctuations in unemployment?

6 How does the sticky wage theory explain observed fluctuations in unemployment?

PROBLEMS

1 Table 29.1 gives information about the short-run aggregate production function for a rather small economy, where L is the units of labour per day and Y is the units of output per day (real GDP).
  a Complete the last column of Table 29.1 by computing the marginal product of labour (MPL).
  b How much labour will be demanded if the money wage rate is £6 and the GDP deflator is 150?
  c Draw a graph of the demand for labour.

Table 29.1 Short-run Aggregate Production Function

L	Y	MPL
1	8	
2	15	
3	21	
4	26	
5	30	
6	33	

2 Table 29.2 gives the supply of labour schedule for the economy of Problem 1.
  a On the graph from Problem 1c, draw the supply of labour curve.
  b What is the equilibrium real wage rate?
  c What is the equilibrium level of employment?
  d What is the level of output?

3 Suppose the economy presented in Problems 1 and 2 is characterized by flexible wages.
  a If the GDP deflator is 100, what is the equilibrium money wage rate, the level of employment and the level of output?
  b If the GDP deflator is 80, what is the equilibrium money wage rate, the level of employment and level of output?
  c If the GDP deflator is 120, what is the equilib-

rium money wage rate, the level of employment and the level of output?
  d Draw the aggregate supply curve for this flexible wage economy.

Table 29.2 Supply of Labour

Real wage rate	Quantity of labour supplied
8	7
7	6
6	5
5	4
4	3
3	2

4 Now suppose the economy of Problems 1 and 2 is characterized by sticky wages set by wage contract. Use the sticky price model to respond to the following.
  a If the expected value of the GDP deflator over the contract period is 100, what money wage rate will be set?
  b If, during the contract period, the actual value of the GDP deflator is 100, what is the real wage rate, the level of employment and the level of output?
  c If, during the contract period, the actual value of the GDP deflator is 83, what is the real wage rate, the level of employment and the level of output?
  d If, during the contract period, the actual value of the GDP deflator is 125, what is the real wage rate, the level of employment and the level of output?
  e On the graph from Problem 3d, indicate three points on the short-run aggregate supply curve for this sticky wage economy. Draw part of that curve by connecting the points.

5 Now suppose that a technological advance gives a new short-run aggregate production function summarized in Table 29.3.
  a Complete the last column of Table 29.3 by computing the marginal product of labour.
  b On the graph from Problems 1c and 2a, draw the new demand for labour curve.
  c If wages are perfectly flexible, what will be the new equilibrium real wage rate, level of employment and level of output? (The supply of labour curve is unchanged.)

Table 29.3 New Short-run Aggregate Production Function

L	Y	MPL
1	10	
2	19	
3	27	
4	34	
5	40	
6	45	

Table 29.4 The Labour Force in Britain (all figures in millions)

	Estimate 1993	Projection 2006
Men (ages 16–24)	15.4	15.7
Women (ages 16–59)	11.7	12.9

Source: *Employment Gazette*, April 1994. Reproduced with the permission of the Controller of Her Majesty's Stationery Office.

DATA QUESTIONS

Britain's Future Labour Force

1 What is mean by 'labour force'?

2 Describe the main features of the data in Table 29.4.

3 What are the implications for the UK economy of the projected changes in the size of the labour force between 1993 and 2006?

ANSWERS

CONCEPT REVIEW

1 production function; aggregate production function; upward

2 marginal product; diminishing marginal product

3 demand for labour; real; real; money

4 supply of labour; increase; decrease

5 participation rate; reservation wage

6 flexible; sticky

7 vertical; positively

8 Real business cycle theory; Keynesian

9 efficiency; unemployment

TRUE OR FALSE

1 T If firms hire more labour, marginal product will decline so firms will employ more labour only if real wage falls.

2 T Definition of labour demand curve.

3 T Real wage will have fallen.

4 T Increase in marginal product means rise in output per worker so firms will employ more workers at a constant real wage.

5 T More wage is lost for each hour of leisure.

6 F Fall in real wage means fall in opportunity cost of leisure leading to rise in quantity of leisure via the substitution effect.

7 T They will try to maintain their real income.

8 F High current real wage means a higher return to working and more labour supplied.

9 T Money wage adjusts to keep real wage at level where Labour demand = Labour supply.

10 F Lower real wage = Constant money wage rate/ Higher price level.

11 T Because real wages will fall, so firms will take on more labour.

12 F This is a supply-side notion.

13 T There will be higher flows into and out of labour force; hence more search unemployment.

14 T Because there is no sticky wage unemployment.

MULTIPLE-CHOICE

1 c Curve is negatively sloped owing to diminishing marginal product. d and e lead to movements along curve.

2 e Technological advance leads to increased productivity of labour.

3 e Demand for labour depends inversely on real wage rate.

4 b Diminishing marginal product creates downward-sloping labour demand curve.

5 c Real wage = Money wage/Price level × 100.

6 d Profits are maximized at this point.

7 d Money wage rises because flexible, real wage stays the same, so no change in employment.

8 a Definition of flexible wages.

9 a In this theory, real GDP is determined by supply-side factors.

10 d Here, if price turns out as expected there will be no unnatural unemployment.

11 a Firms select labour hired given actual real wage.

12 a For flexible theory money wage will rise so no change in real wage or GDP; for sticky theory money wage will not change so real wage falls, employers take on more workers and so increase GDP.

13 b Because less costly than adjusting hours.

14 e Will increase supply of labour; if demand is unchanged, unemployment will result.

15 e Real wage set where $LD = LS$ at £12, Money wage = Real wage × Price level × 100.

16 b Actual real wage = Money wage/Price level × 100, and lower real wage means more labour is demanded.

17 e There is no sticky wage unemployment, *LAS* curve is vertical and only supply-side factors will affect output and employment.

SHORT ANSWER

1 There are two parts to the explanation of why the demand for labour curve is negatively sloped. The first part is the fact of diminishing marginal product of labour, which implies that the marginal product curve is negatively sloped. The second part is the claim that, for a profit-maximizing firm, the demand curve for labour is the same as the marginal product curve. Thus the demand curve for labour must be negatively sloped.

2 Each individual has a reservation wage below which they will not supply any labour. That is, if the wage rate is below an individual's reservation wage, the individual will not even enter the labour force. In order for an individual to be willing to enter the labour force, the real wage must be at least as great as their reservation wage. As the real wage rate rises, it will exceed the reservation wages of an increasingly larger group of people and thus the labour force increases relative to the size of the working-age population; the labour force participation rate increases. As this rate increases, more individuals are offering to supply labour and thus the quantity of labour supplied increases. Since the original impetus was an increasing real wage rate, the real wage rate and the quantity of labour supplied are positively related.

3 According to the flexible wage theory, an increase in the price level will, at the current money wage rate, reduce the real wage rate. A fall in the real wage rate means that the labour market is now characterized by excess demand for labour; at the lower real wage rate, the quantity of labour demanded exceeds the quantity of labour supplied. Since the wage rate is flexible, the money wage rate will rise until the labour market is again in equilibrium, that is, it will rise until the real wage rate has returned to its previous level. As a result, employment returns to its previous level as does real GDP.

4 According to the sticky wage theory, an unexpected increase in the price level will, at the fixed money wage rate set by contract, reduce the real wage rate. Since the money wage rate cannot adjust during a contract period, this lower real wage rate will remain and, since the level of employment is determined by the demand for labour, the level of employment will increase. This, of course, implies that the quantity of real GDP supplied will increase via the aggregate production function.

5 The natural rate of unemployment is the rate that occurs when the labour market is in equilibrium. According to the flexible wage theory, the labour market is always in equilibrium and thus the rate of unemployment is always equal to the natural rate of unemployment. Thus, any fluctuations in unemployment are the result of fluctuations in the natural rate of unemployment. As discussed in the text, changes in the natural rate of unemployment are the result of changes in the pace of labour market turnover and cannot be avoided.

6 According to the sticky wage theory, the labour market will frequently not be in equilibrium. Thus the observed rate of unemployment will deviate from the natural rate of unemployment. If the real wage rate is above equilibrium, employment will be low and the rate of unemployment will exceed the natural rate of unemployment. If the real wage rate is below equilibrium, employment will be high and the rate of unemployment will be less than the natural rate. Since, according to this view, the natural rate of unemployment is quite stable, the observed rate of unemployment varies principally because of deviations of the observed rate of unemployment about the (almost) constant natural rate.

PROBLEMS

1 a Table 29.1 is completed as Table 29.5. The marginal product of labour is the additional output produced by an additional unit of labour.

b The real wage rate is computed as follows:

$$\text{Real wage rate} = \frac{\text{Money wage rate}}{\text{GDP deflator}} \times 100$$

In our case, the money wage rate is £6 per unit and the GDP deflator is 150. Therefore the real wage is £4. Since a profit-maximizing firm will hire labour until the marginal product of labour is equal to the real wage rate, we can see that the quantity of labour demanded at a real wage rate of £4 is 5 units.

Table 29.5 Short-run Aggregate Production Function

L	Y	MPL
1	8	8
2	15	7
3	21	6
4	26	5
5	30	4
6	33	3

c The graph of the demand curve for labour (labelled LD_0) is given in Fig. 29.2. The demand curve for labour is the same as the marginal product of labour curve (see Table 29.1).

Figure 29.2

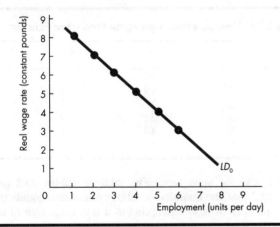

2 a Figure 29.3 illustrates the supply curve of labour (labelled *LS*) on the same graph with the *LD* curve from Problem **1**.

b The equilibrium real wage rate is £5 since the quantity of labour demanded and supplied are both equal to 4 units per day. This can be seen from the graph or the tables.

c The equilibrium level of employment is 4 units.

d From the short-run aggregate production function in Table 29.1, we can see that 4 units of labour will yield 26 units of output per day.

Figure 29.3

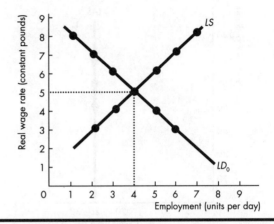

3 Regardless of the value of the GDP deflator, in the flexible wage economy, the equilibrium real wage rate is £5, the level of employment is 4 units per day and the level of output is 26 units per day. If we know the real wage rate and the GDP deflator, the money wage rate can be found by

$$\text{Money wage rate} = \text{Real wage rate} \times \frac{\text{GDP deflator}}{100}$$

a If the GDP deflator is 100, a real wage rate of £5 implies a money wage rate of £5.

b If the GDP deflator is 80, a real wage rate of £5 implies a money wage rate of £4.3.

c If the GDP deflator is 120, a real wage rate of £5 implies a money wage rate of £6.

d The aggregate supply curve (labelled *LAS*) for the flexible wage economy is given in Fig. 29.4. Parts **a**, **b** and **c** of this Problem indicate that at every price level output is 26 units per day.

4 a The contract money wage rate will be set so that if the actual GDP deflator turns out to be equal to the expected value of the GDP deflator (100), the real wage rate will clear the market. The real wage rate that clears the market is £5. So, since the expected GDP deflator is 100, the money wage rate will be set at £5.

b If the actual value of the GDP deflator is 100, since the money wage rate is fixed at £5, the real wage rate is £5. This implies that employment is 4 units and output is 26 units.

c If the actual value of the GDP deflator is 83, since the money wage rate is fixed at £5, the real wage rate is £6 ((5/83) + 100 = 6). Employment is determined by the demand for labour which, at a real wage of £6, is 3 units per day. This implies (from Table 29.1) that output is 21 units per day.

Figure 29.4

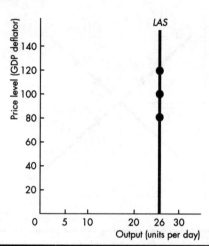

Output (units per day)

d If the actual value of the GDP deflator is 125, since the money wage rate is fixed at £5, the real wage rate is £4. Employment is determined by the demand for labour and is 5 units per day. From Table 29.1, this implies daily output of 30 units.

e Figure 29.5 indicates three points on the short-run aggregate supply curve in the sticky wage economy: point *a* corresponds to output = 26, GDP deflator = 100; point *b* corresponds to output = 21, GDP deflator = 83; point *c* corresponds to output = 31, GDP deflator = 125. The points are connected to give a portion of the short-run aggregate supply curve (labelled *SAS*).

Figure 29.5

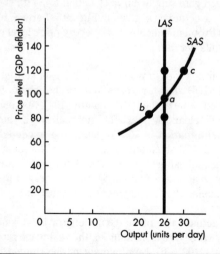

Output (units per day)

5 a Table 29.3 is completed as Table 29.6. Note that the marginal product of each unit of labour has increased as a result of the technological advance.
b Figure 29.6 gives the graph. Notice that the new labour demand curve, LD_1, lies to the right of LD_0.

Figure 29.6

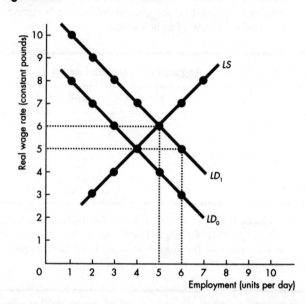

Employment (units per day)

Table 29.6 New Short-run Aggregate Production Function

L	Y	MPL
1	10	10
2	19	9
3	27	8
4	34	7
5	40	6
6	45	6

c It can be seen from Fig. 29.6 or Tables 29.2 and 29.3 that the quantity of labour demanded equals the quantity of labour supplied at a real wage rate of £6. The level of employment is now 5 units of labour per day, which implies output of 40 units per day (from Table 29.3).

DATA QUESTIONS

1 The total labour force includes those in employment, those registered unemployed and those in the armed forces. The civilian labour force excludes those in the armed forces. It does not include such groups as students, retired people or housewives.

2 The main feature is that there is a projected increase in the total labour force from 27.1 million to 28.5 million – over a million.

3 Since there will be a rise in the size of the labour force, it is likely that total output will increase so that GDP will continue to rise. However, this assumes that there will be jobs for these additional workers, and it may be that, unless jobs are created, there will be a rise in unemployment and not an increase in output. Another effect of the increased labour force may be that wages will fall. This will depend partly on the extent to which wages are 'sticky'.

Chapter 30 **Inflation**

Chapter In Perspective, Text Pages 850–876

In previous chapters we have discussed equilibrium real GDP (Chapter 23), equilibrium aggregate expenditure (Chapter 25), the equilibrium interest rate (Chapter 27) and the equilibrium real wage rate (Chapter 29). In Chapter 28 we put the second and third of these together to explain fluctuations in aggregate demand. In Chapter 29 we discussed fluctuations in aggregate supply. In this chapter we bring all of these things together to examine macroeconomic equilibrium.

We find that the nature of macroeconomic equilibrium depends critically on expectations, especially price level (or inflation) expectations. It thus becomes important to consider how expectations are formed and how expectations affect macroeconomic behaviour. The model developed in this chapter is a very powerful tool in explaining the wide variety of macroeconomic events.

Helpful Hints

1 This chapter will be difficult for some students, but it is important because it finalizes the development of the complete modern macroeconomic model. The model developed here is the basic model generally used by macroeconomists as they analyse the economy. It has proven to be a very powerful tool for such analysis.

2 The fourth condition for a macroeconomic equilibrium deserves some additional comment. That condition is that the quantity of labour demanded equals the quantity of labour supplied. It is important to note, however, that this does not mean that employment is determined by the intersection of the demand for labour curve and the supply of labour curve. If that had to be the case, contrary to statements in the text, macroeconomic equilibrium would require full employment. The quantity of labour supplied should be understood to mean the quantity of labour that households want to supply, 'given the wages that prevail, information that they have about available jobs, and the wage and employment contracts that they have accepted.' As we learned in Chapter 29, this last condition indicates that employment can be above or below full employment if wages are sticky and the price level is not correctly anticipated.

3 Recall also from Chapter 29 that if the expected price level turns out to be correct, employment will turn out to be at the full-employment level and thus real GDP supplied will be equal to full-employment (capacity) real GDP. This is why a short-run aggregate supply curve intersects the long-run aggregate supply curve at the expected price level. If the price level is actually equal to the expected price level, the economy must be at full employment, that is, the economy must be on its long-run aggregate supply curve.

4 Note that the rational expectation of the price level will be at the intersection of the expected aggregate demand curve and the expected long-run aggregate supply curve. (This will yield the best possible forecast, the one most likely to be correct on average.) The rational expectations equilibrium, which determines the actual price level, is at the intersection of the actual aggregate demand curve and the actual short-run aggregate supply curve.

5 Be sure you know why each of the following is true.

– If the actual price level is greater than the expected price level, real GDP is above capacity.
– If the actual price level is less than the expected price level, real GDP is below capacity.
– If the actual price level is equal to the expected price level, real GDP is at capacity.

The wise student will understand all nine possible cases that lead to these three outcomes.

6 An important implication of the rational expectations hypothesis is that the consequences of any macroeconomic event (such as a monetary or fiscal policy) depend on expectations. The effect on the price level and real GDP of a given increase in the money supply will be different for different price level expectations. Its effect on the position of the aggregate demand curve does not depend on the expected price level, but the position of the short-run aggregate supply curve does depend on the expected price level and thus so does the macroeconomic equilibrium. The crucial point is whether the actual level of aggregate demand is anticipated or unanticipated.

Key Figures

Figure 30.1 Demand–Pull Inflation, text page 853
In part (a), an increase in aggregate demand (caused by such factors as increased consumer or government spending) shifts the *AD* curve leading to a rise in prices. In turn this forces up wages, causing firms to supply less at each price level and shifting the *SAS* curve to the left. The result is a further increase in prices.

Figure 30.3 Cost–Push Inflation, text page 855
Costs rise – perhaps from an increase in wages, or in the price of raw materials such as oil. The consequence is that the short-run aggregate supply curve shifts to the left and the result is higher prices.

Figure 30.6 Rational Expectation of the Price Level, text page 860
The construction of a rational expectation of the price level is illustrated here. The rational expectation of the price level is the forecast obtained by the intersection of the expected aggregate demand curve and the expected long-run aggregate supply curve. The first step then is to obtain forecasts of the aggregate demand and long-run aggregate supply curves. These are indicated in the figure by *EAD* and *ELAS* respectively. The rational expectation of the price level occurs at the intersection of these two curves. Since the expected price level is at this intersection, the expected short-run aggregate supply curve also intersects these curves at the same point. (This is because its position is determined by the rational expectation of the price level – see Chapter 29.)

Figure 30.7 Anticipated Inflation, text page 861
As illustrated here, if inflation is fully anticipated, real GDP remains at capacity and only the price level rises. The rational expectations equilibrium is given by the intersection of the actual aggregate demand and actual short-run aggregate supply curves. Since expectations are fully correct, these actual curves are the same as their expected counterparts and the equilibrium corresponds to the expected value, and real GDP is capacity real GDP.

SELF-TEST

CONCEPT REVIEW

1 Four conditions must be satisfied when the economy is in macroeconomic equilibrium.

– Real GDP demanded equals _____

_____ _____.

– Aggregate planned expenditure equals

_____ _____.

– Real money demanded equals _____

_____ _____ .

– Quantity of labour demanded equals

_____ _____ _____

_____ .

2 The short-run aggregate supply curve intersects the long-run aggregate supply curve at a price level equal to the _____ _____ _____ . If the price level is higher than expected, then real GDP is _____ than capacity output.

3 If inflation turns out to be higher than expected, borrowers_____and lenders _____ .

4 A forecast that is based on all the available information, is correct on average and minimizes the range of the forecast error is called a(n) _____ expectation. The proposition that the forecasts people make are the same as the forecasts made by an economist using the relevant economic theory as well as all information available is called the _____ _____ hypothesis.

5 The rational expectation of the price level is given by the intersection of the expected aggregate demand curve and the expected _____ - _____ _____ _____ curve.

6 A macroeconomic equilibrium based on expectations that are the best available forecasts is called a(n) _____ _____ equilibrium.

7 The definition of inflation is the percentage rise in the _____ _____ from one year to another. When aggregate demand is expected to increase and it doesn't, actual inflation is _____ its expected level and actual GDP is _____ capacity output.

8 An unanticipated increase in the money supply will cause the price level to _____ and real GDP to _____ .

9 During periods when the rate of inflation is high, nominal interest rates tend to be _____ . If the Bank of England unexpectedly increases the money supply, the immediate effect is to _____ interest rates. If the Bank of England conducts an anticipated and continuous increase in the money supply, interest rates will _____ .

TRUE AND FALSE

____ 1 In a macroeconomic equilibrium the economy will exhibit full employment.

____ 2 The short-run aggregate supply curve intersects the long-run aggregate supply curve at the expected price level.

____ 3 If the expected price level falls, the short-run aggregate supply curve will shift downward by the amount of the fall.

____ 4 Expectations of inflation are partially self-fulfilling.

____ 5 If people expect aggregate demand to increase but it doesn't, the price level will fall and real GDP will increase.

____ 6 A rational expectation is a forecast that is always correct.

____ 7 The rational expectations hypothesis states that people make forecasts in the same way economists do.

____ 8 In a rational expectations equilibrium the economy will exhibit full employment.

____ 9 If the price level at the beginning of 1994 is 120 and the price level at the beginning of 1995 is 130, the rate of inflation is 8.3 per cent.

____ 10 In order for an increase in aggregate demand to raise the price level, the increase in aggregate demand must be anticipated.

____ 11 A large negative supply shock (like the 1973–1974 OPEC oil price increases) will cause the price level to rise and real GDP to decline.

____ 12 If an increase in aggregate demand is correctly anticipated, inflation will not occur.

____ 13 If the inflation rate rises but nominal interest rates remain unchanged, then real interest rates have fallen.

____ 14 If the inflation rate rises but real interest rates remain unchanged, then nominal interest rates have fallen.

__ **15** If an increase in the money supply is unanticipated, its immediate effect will be to raise interest rates.

MULTIPLE-CHOICE

1 Figure 30.1 illustrates an economy initially in equilibrium at point a. What would cause the short-run aggregate supply curve to shift from SAS_0 to SAS_1?
   a an expected increase in the money supply
   b an increase in the price level
   c an increase in the marginal product of labour
   d an increase in the demand for money
   e a decrease in wages

Figure 30.1

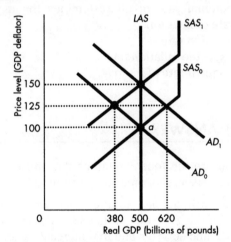

2 Figure 30.1 illustrates an economy initially in equilibrium at point a. If the AD curve is correctly expected to shift from AD_0 to AD_1, the new macroeconomic equilibrium will be real GDP =
   a £380 billion and price level = 125.
   b £500 billion and price level = 150.
   c £500 billion and price level = 100.
   d £620 billion and price level = 125.
   e £500 billion and price level = 125.

3 Figure 30.1 illustrates an economy initially in equilibrium at point a. If the AD curve is expected to shift from AD_0 to AD_1 but it actually remains at AD_0, the new macroeconomic equilibrium will be real GDP =
   a £380 billion and price level = 100.
   b £500 billion and price level = 150.
   c £500 billion and price level = 100.
   d £620 billion and price level = 125.
   e £380 billion and price level = 125.

4 Figure 30.1 illustrates an economy initially in equilibrium at point a. If the AD curve is expected to remain at AD_0 but, in fact, shifts to AD_1, the new macroeconomic equilibrium will be real GDP =
   a £380 billion and price level = 125.
   b £500 billion and price level = 150.
   c £500 billion and price level = 100.
   d £620 billion and price level = 125.
   e £500 billion and price level = 125.

5 If the rate of inflation turns out to be lower than expected, borrowers
   a and lenders both lose.
   b and lenders both gain.
   c gain but lenders lose.
   d lose but lenders gain.
   e lose but lenders are just as well off.

6 If the rate of inflation turns out to be lower than expected, then
   a expectations could not be rational expectations.
   b real GDP will be less than full-employment (capacity) real GDP.
   c the real interest rate will be lower than expected.
   d the real wage rate will be lower than expected.
   e the money wage rate will be higher than expected.

7 A rational expectations equilibrium is the price level and real GDP given by the intersection of the
   a actual aggregate demand curve and the actual long-run aggregate supply curve.
   b actual aggregate demand curve and the expected short-run aggregate supply curve.
   c expected aggregate demand curve and the expected short-run aggregate supply curve.
   d expected aggregate demand curve and the expected long-run aggregate supply curve.
   e aggregate demand curve and the actual short-run aggregate supply curve.

8 According to the rational expectations hypothesis, a correctly anticipated increase in the money supply in an economy with a given long-run aggregate supply will result in

a an increase in the price level and an increase in real GDP.

b an increase in the price level and a decrease in real GDP.

c a proportional increase in the price level and no change in real GDP.

d no change in the price level and an increase in real GDP.

e no change in the price level and no change in real GDP.

9 Suppose OPEC unexpectedly increases the price of oil. This is a negative aggregate supply shock. As a result, the price level will

a rise and real GDP will increase.

b rise and real GDP will decrease.

c fall and real GDP will increase.

d fall and real GDP will decrease.

e rise and real GDP will stay the same.

10 The current year's price level is 180 and the rate of inflation over the past year has been 20 per cent. What was last year's price level?

a 144

b 150

c 160

d 216

e 100

11 Which of the following would cause the aggregate demand curve to keep shifting upward year after year?

a a tax cut

b an increase in government purchases of goods and services

c inflation

d excess wage demands

e a positive rate of growth in the quantity of money

12 Suppose aggregate demand increases by less than anticipated. This will result in an unanticipated

a rise in inflation and real GDP falls below capacity.

b rise in inflation and real GDP rises above capacity.

c fall in inflation and real GDP falls below capacity.

d fall in inflation and real GDP rises above capacity.

e fall in inflation and real GDP stays at capacity.

13 If the actual price level is higher than the expected price level, then real GDP

a must be above capacity.

b must be below capacity.

c must be equal to capacity.

d can be above, below, or equal to capacity depending on the position of the aggregate demand curve.

e can be above or equal to capacity depending on the position of the aggregate demand curve.

14 A correctly anticipated increase in the rate of growth of the money supply will cause nominal interest rates to

a fall and real interest rates to fall.

b fall and leave real interest rates unchanged.

c rise and real interest rates to rise.

d rise and leave real interest rates unchanged.

e rise and real interest rates to fall.

15 The opportunity cost of holding money is the

a real rate of interest.

b nominal rate of interest minus the expected rate of inflation.

c inflation rate.

d expected inflation rate.

e nominal rate of interest.

SHORT ANSWER

1 What are the four conditions that must be satisfied in macroeconomic equilibrium?

2 What will happen to the price level and real GDP if the government increases its purchases of goods and services and that increase is not anticipated (that is, the price level is not expected to change)?

3 What will happen to the price level and real GDP if the government increases its purchases of goods and services and that increase is anticipated?

4 How is a rational expectation of the price level calculated?

5 What is the relationship between the expected rate of inflation and interest rates?

6 It is frequently argued that high wage demands by workers (based on high price expectations) cause inflation. According to the rational expectations model developed in this chapter, is this true or not? Explain briefly.

PROBLEMS

1 Table 30.1 gives the initial aggregate demand and short-run aggregate supply schedules for an economy in which the expected price level is 80.
 a What is capacity real GDP?
 b What is actual real GDP and the actual price level?

Table 30.1 Aggregate Demand and Supply

Price level (GDP deflator)	Real GDP demanded	Real GDP supplied
60	600	400
80	500	500
100	400	600
120	300	700
140	200	700

2 In year 1 the economy is in the macroeconomic equilibrium characterized in Problem 1. It is expected that in year 2, aggregate demand will be as given in Table 30.2.
 a What is the vertical amount of the expected shift in the aggregate demand curve when real GDP is £500 billion?

Table 30.2 Aggregate Demand and Supply

Price level∠ (GDP deflator)	Real GDP demanded	Real GDP supplied
60	800	
80	700	
100	600	
120	500	
140	400	

 b What is the rational expectation of the price level for year 2?
 c The expected shift in aggregate demand will cause the short-run aggregate supply *(SAS)* curve to shift. What will the new *SAS* curve be? For each price level, give the new values of real GDP supplied in the last column of Table 30.2.
 d Suppose that, in fact, aggregate demand does not change but remains as given in Table 30.1. What will real GDP and the price level be in year 2?

 e Compare the actual change in the price level with the expected change.

3 In year 1 the economy is in the macroeconomic equilibrium characterized by Problem 1. It is expected that in year 2, aggregate demand will be as given in Table 30.2. It turns out that expectations are correct: the actual aggregate demand in year 2 is as given in Table 30.2.
 a What is the rational expectation of the price level for year 2?
 b What will real GDP and the price level turn out to be in year 2?
 c Compare the actual change in the price level with the expected change.

4 Graphically illustrate the rational expectations equilibrium in an economy for which aggregate demand is higher than expected. Compare the actual equilibrium with the expected equilibrium.

5 Graphically illustrate the rational expectations equilibrium in an economy for which aggregate demand is higher than expected and long-run aggregate supply is lower than expected. Compare the actual equilibrium with the expected equilibrium.

DATA QUESTIONS

The Phillips Curve

In the traditional explanation of the Phillips curve, expectations were assumed to be static or backward looking. Short-run movements along the curve (for example from *A* to *B* in Fig. 30.2) giving a reduction in unemployment below the natural rate *Un* are possible because workers' expectations of future inflation lag behind reality . However, expectations catch up with reality and unemployment goes back to its natural level at point *C*. The Phillips curve is vertical in the long run. Keeping unemployment below the natural rate therefore requires accelerating inflation so that expectations continually lag behind reality.

With rational expectations workers correctly anticipate inflation (except for random forecasting errors due to uncertainty/random shocks) and there is no short-run reduction of inflation below the natural rate.

Source: adapted from Bob Beachill, 'Teaching Rational Expectations at A Level', *Economics*, Autumn 1987.

Figure 30.2

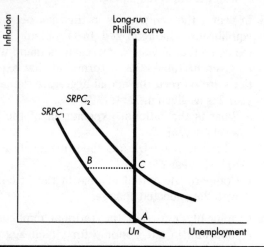

1 Explain what is meant by
  a the 'Phillips curve'.
  b the 'natural rate of unemployment'.

2 Use the rational expectations argument to show why the long-run Phillips curve is vertical.

ANSWERS

CONCEPT REVIEW

1 real GDP supplied; real GDP; real money supplied; quantity of labour supplied

2 expected price level; greater

3 gain; lose

4 rational; rational expectations

5 long-run aggregate supply

6 rational expectations

7 price level; below; below

8 increase; increase

9 high; lower; rise

TRUE OR FALSE

1 **F** Equilibrium can be at, below or above the full-employment level.

2 **T** When expectations are correct, actual real GDP = natural rate.

3 **T** Changes in expected prices cause changes in supply.

4 **T** If people expect higher inflation, firms will put up prices, workers seek higher wages.

5 **F** See Helpful Hint 5.

6 **F** Rational expectations are correct *on average*.

7 **F** Make forecasts in a different way.

8 **F** Equilibrium may not be at full-employment level – depends on expectations.

9 **T** Inflation rate = $[(P_1 - P_0)/P_0] \times 100 = [(130 - 120)/120] \times 100 = 8.3$.

10 **F** See text Fig. 30.1.

11 **T** It will shift *AS* curve to the left.

12 **F** *AD* curve shifts to right, *AS* curve shifts to left because of higher wage demands, hence price level rises.

13 **T** Actual real interest rate = Nominal interest rate – Inflation rate.

14 **F** Nominal rates would have to rise to keep real rate the same.

15 **F** Immediate effect is rise in real money supply leading to fall in nominal interest rates.

MULTIPLE-CHOICE

1 **a** A rise in the price of a crucial input would lead to a shift in *SAS* curve to the left.

2 **b** Expected *P* found from intersection of *EAD* = AD_1, and actual *SAS* is set here leading to new equilibrium where actual *AD* and *SAS* curves cross.

3 **e** Expected P found from intersection of $EAD = AD_1$ and actual SAS is set here leading to equilibrium where actual AD and SAS curves cross.

4 **d** Expected P found from intersection of $EAD = AD_1$ and actual SAS is set here, so new equilibrium where actual AS and SAS curves cross.

5 **d** Borrowers will lose because they will have expected to pay back less.

6 **b** Economy will be in equilibrium at less than full-employment level.

7 **e** Definition.

8 **c** Increase in money supply leads to rise in aggregate demand. Since this is anticipated it causes shift to the left in SAS of equivalent amount so rise in price level and no change in real GDP.

9 **b** SAS curve will shift to left.

10 **b** Invert formula. Inflation rate = $[(P_1 - P_0)/P_0] \times 100$.

11 **e** Others would have only a one-off effect.

12 **c** Because actual price level = expected when SAS curve crosses LAS curve, and equilibrium occurs when $AS = SAS$ – try drawing a graph.

13 **a** Because actual price level = expected when SAS curve crosses LAS curve, and equilibrium occurs when $LAS = AD$.

14 **d** Increased growth rate of money supply leads to rise in inflation rate and increase in nominal rate of same amount (because anticipated); therefore no change in real rate.

15 **e** What is given up is expected losses from inflation.

SHORT ANSWER

1 The four conditions that must be satisfied in macro-economic equilibrium are:

– Real GDP demanded equals real GDP supplied.
– Aggregate planned expenditure equals real GDP.
– Real money demanded equals real money supplied.
– Quantity of labour demanded equals quantity of labour supplied.

2 An increase in government purchases of goods and services will shift the aggregate demand curve to the right. If the price level is not expected to change, the short-run aggregate supply curve remains unchanged and the increase in aggregate demand will cause the price level to rise and real GDP to increase.

3 If the shift in the aggregate demand curve is anticipated, the expected price level will rise by the amount of the ver-

tical shift in the aggregate demand and thus the short-run aggregate supply will shift up by that amount. So, when an increase in aggregate demand is fully anticipated, the aggregate demand curve and the short-run aggregate supply curve will shift upward by the same amount. As a result, the price level will rise and real GDP will remain unchanged.

4 A rational expectation of the price level is obtained by using the aggregate demand and aggregate supply model to predict the price level. The actual price level will be given by the intersection of the aggregate demand curve and the short-run aggregate supply curve. Therefore we want to determine where we expect these curves to be and then see where they intersect. The problem is that the short-run aggregate supply curve depends on the expected price level and that is what we are trying to find. We resolve this problem by recognizing that if the price level turns out to be equal to the expected price level, the short-run aggregate supply curve intersects the aggregate demand curve at the point where the latter curve intersects the long-run aggregate supply curve. Since the long-run aggregate supply curve does not depend on the expected price level, the rational expectation of the price level is obtained at the intersection of the aggregate demand curve and the long-run aggregate supply curve.

5 When the rate of inflation is expected to rise, the interest rate will also rise to compensate for the increased rate at which the purchasing power of money is eroding. The essential point is that lenders and borrowers are interested in the quantity of goods and services that a unit of money will buy. Lenders will insist on the higher interest rate (to compensate for the loss of purchasing power of money) and borrowers will be willing to pay it because they realize that the pounds they pay back will buy fewer goods and services.

6 In the short run, a rise in wages will shift the short-run aggregate supply curve to the left, raising the price level. However, a continuing rise in the price level (that is, an inflation), requires a continuing rise in both the AD and the SAS. This therefore requires a positive growth rate of the money supply to sustain or validate this inflation.

PROBLEMS

1 **a** Capacity real GDP is the quantity of real GDP supplied when the expected price level is equal to the actual price level. The last column of Table 30.1 gives the quantity of real GDP supplied at various price levels assuming that the expected price level is constant at 80. Since when the actual price level is also 80, the quantity of real GDP supplied is $500 billion, that is the value of capacity real GDP.

b Actual real GDP and the actual price level are determined by the intersection of the aggregate demand curve and the short-run aggregate supply curve. Real GDP is $500 billion and the price level is 80, since at a price level of 80 the quantity of real GDP demanded equals the quantity of real GDP supplied ($500 billion).

2 a The price level associated with $500 billion of real GDP demanded for the original aggregate curve (Table 30.1) is 80. The price level associated with $500 billion of real GDP demanded for the new expected aggregate demand curve (Table 30.2) is 120. Therefore the aggregate demand curve is expected to shift upward by 40.

b The rational expectation of the price level is given by the intersection of the expected aggregate demand curve (Table 30.2) and the expected long-run aggregate supply curve. Long-run aggregate supply is equal to $500 billion and is not expected to change. Since the price level associated with $500 billion of real GDP demanded is 120, the rational expectation of the price level is 120.

c The quantities of real GDP supplied for the new *SAS* curve are given in Table 30.3. The original expected price level is 80. From **b** we know that the new expected price level is 120, which implies that the *SAS* curve shifts upward by 40. Thus, at each quantity of real GDP supplied, the price level on the new *SAS* curve is 40 points higher than on the original *SAS* curve (Table 30.1). For example, real GDP supplied of $500 billion now requires a price level of 120 rather than 80. Similarly, real GDP supplied of $400 billion now requires a price level of 100 rather than 60. (Note that the values in parentheses in the table are inferred by extrapolation rather than calculated from Table 30.1.)

Table 30.3 Aggregate Demand and Supply

Price level (GDP deflator)	Real GDP demanded	Real GDP supplied
60	800	(200)
80	700	(300)
100	600	400
120	500	500
140	400	600

d The new macroeconomic equilibrium in year 2 will occur at the intersection of the actual *AD* curve and the relevant *SAS* curve. Since the *AD* curve was expected to shift, the relevant *SAS* curve is the one associated with the expected price level of 120 (the *SAS* curve is completed Table 30.3). But the *AD* curve did not actually shift, so the *AD* curve is given in Table 30.1. The

intersection of these curves is at real GDP of $400 billion and price level of 100 (that is, when the price level is 100, the quantity of real GDP demanded is equal to the quantity of real GDP supplied at $400 billion).

e The price level was expected to rise from 80 to 120 but, in fact, only rises from 80 to 100.

3 a Since aggregate demand is expected to increase, the rational expectation of the price level for year 2 is the same as in Problem 2: 120.

b The rational expectations equilibrium will occur at the intersection of the actual *AD* curve and the relevant *SAS* curve. Since the expected price level is 120, the relevant *SAS* curve is the one given in completed Table 30.3. The actual *AD* curve is also given in Table 30.2. Thus real GDP will be $500 billion and the price level will be 120.

c The price level was expected to rise from 80 to 120, which is exactly what happens.

4 Figure 30.3 illustrates the rational expectations equilibrium. The expected aggregate demand curve is given by *EAD* which intersects the expected long-run aggregate supply curve, *ELAS*, at point *a*. Thus the rational expectation of the price level is P_0, which implies that the relevant short-run aggregate supply curve is *ESAS*. The actual aggregate demand curve, *AD*, is higher than expected and the actual short-run aggregate supply curve is the same as *ESAS*. The rational expectations equilibrium occurs at point *b*, the intersection of the *AD* and *ESAS* curves. The equilibrium price level, P_1, is higher than expected and thus real GDP is above capacity (that is, above Y_0).

Figure 30.3

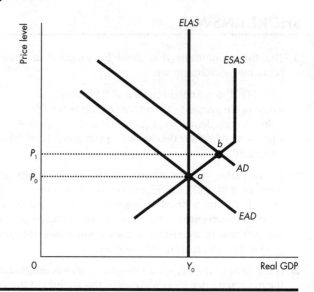

5 Figure 30.4 illustrates the rational expectations equilibrium in this case. The expected aggregate demand curve, *EAD*, intersects the expected long-run aggregate supply curve, *ELAS*, at point *a*. Thus the rational expectation of the price level is P_0, which implies that the expected short-run aggregate supply curve is *ESAS*. The actual aggregate demand curve, *AD*, is higher than expected. Also, the actual long-run aggregate supply curve, *LAS*, is lower than expected, which means that the actual short-run aggregate supply curve corresponding to an expected price level of P_0 is given by *SAS*. The rational expectations

equilibrium occurs at point *b*, the intersection of the *AD* and *SAS* curves. The equilibrium price level is P_1, which is much higher than expected. Real GDP can be above, below, or at the expected capacity real GDP, Y_0, depending on the relative magnitudes of the unanticipated shifts (Fig. 30.4 shows real GDP above expected capacity GDP), but real GDP will be above the new actual capacity real GDP, Y_1.

DATA QUESTIONS

1 a The original Phillips curve was the result of an empirical investigation into the inflational and unemployment rates in the United Kingdom over nearly a century. The results suggested a trade-off between inflation and unemployment; that is, governments could expand output and employment but only at the cost of higher inflation. However, this relationship seemed to break down in the 1960s and 1970s, and some economists suggested that the long-run Phillips curve was vertical.

b The natural rate of unemployment is the unemployment which results when the only unemployment is frictional and structural.

2 In the short run, an expansion of the economy will bring down the unemployment rate and the economy will move along a short-run Phillips curve. However, according to the rational expectations school of economists, this expansion will push up prices, workers will rationally expect this and therefore will not enter the labour market. Consequently, there will be no expansion of output and employment. The only result will be a rise in prices, that is, a move up a vertical Phillips curve.

Figure 30.4

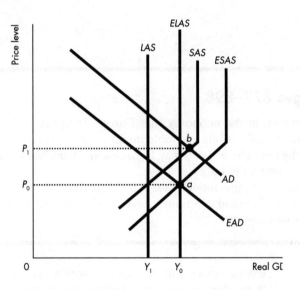

Chapter 31 **Recessions and Depressions**

Chapter In Perspective, Text Pages 877–898

The Great Depression was probably the strongest downturn in the economy that Europe (and the rest of the world) has ever suffered. Real GDP and prices fell substantially, while unemployment rose to record heights. The recessions of 1980–1981 and 1991–1992 were the deepest since the Great Depression. What caused these recessions? Why did the rate of inflation stay positive, although it did fall?

In this chapter we use the aggregate demand–aggregate supply model that has been developed over the last several chapters to interpret the events just mentioned. The model we have developed turns out to be very informative as we use it to analyse real-world macroeconomic events.

Helpful Hints

1 This chapter does not introduce any new analytical structure. Instead, the power of the fully developed aggregate demand–aggregate supply model is demonstrated by analysing some interesting macroeconomic episodes, including the Great Depression.

2 As you are examining various macroeconomic episodes, there are several key factors you should focus on. First, are changes in aggregate demand and/or aggregate supply expected or unexpected? Second, as you follow the various changes, be sure you can follow what is going on in the labour and money markets that underlie the goods and services market. It is these markets that will tell you what is happening to the key variables of employment, unemployment and interest rates.

3 Throughout this chapter we use our two competing theories (flexible wages and sticky wages in the labour market) to explain real-world events. There is no dispute over the facts such as the level of prices or real GDP. The dispute centres around what changes in the economy created the facts (and therefore, also touches on what government policies might affect the economy). It is very important to note that these are theories, and not statements of facts, and that their explanations of the facts could be wrong. Only proper empirical investigation over time will cast light on the validity of the theories.

Key Figures

Figure 31.1 The 1980–1981 Recession in the United Kingdom, text page 879
This illustrates the 1980–1981 recession in the United Kingdom using the aggregate demand and aggregate supply analysis developed in recent chapters.

Figure 31.2 The 1991–1992 Recession in the United Kingdom, text page 880

This explanation focuses on an unexpected fall in investment, largely offset by rises in other components in aggregate demand, but the position was exacerbated by high inflationary expectations which shifted the *SAS* curve to the left.

Figure 31.4 The Labour Market in Recession: Sticky Wage Theory, text page 883

Here the behaviour of the labour market during 1979–1981 is examined assuming that the sticky wage theory is correct. The principal cause was a rise in real wages causing a move along the demand curve for labour. There was also a small shift in the demand curve for labour.

Figure 31.5 The Labour Market in Recession: Flexible Wage Theory, text page 884

This is the counterpart to Figure 31.4 assuming that the flexible wage theory is correct. In this view, the overall fall in employment was caused by a large fall in the demand for labour in goods industries which out-weighed a rise in the demand for labour in services.

SELF-TEXT

CONCEPT REVIEW

1 During a recession, interest rates at first _____ and then _____.

2 The main component of aggregate expenditure that falls during a recession is _____.

3 The 1980–1981 recession led to _____ _____ in the short-run aggregate production function. This shift led to _____ _____ in the marginal product of labour, which implies that the demand for labour curve shifted _____ _____ _____.

4 Modern Keynesians believe that wages are _____. As a result, it is possible for unemployment to _____ the natural rate if there is an unexpectedly low rate of _____.

5 The features of the economy which make severe depression less likely than in the 1930s are the _____ _____ insurance in the United States, the Bank of England's role as _____ _____ _____ _____, taxes and _____ _____, and _____ - _____ families.

TRUE OR FALSE

___ 1 One cause of the 1980–1981 recession in the United Kingdom was the government's policy of monetary restraint.

___ 2 During the early stages of a recession, interest rates tend to fall but later they typically rise.

___ 3 During a recession, the demand for real money grows less rapidly and may even decline.

___ 4 During a recession, the main component of aggregate expenditure that falls is consumption.

___ 5 In order for the flexible wage theory to explain the behaviour of the labour market (real wages and employment), it must be assumed that the natural rate of unemployment rises in a recession.

___ 6 According to the sticky wage model of the labour market, the increase in unemployment during the 1991–1992 recession was due to an increase in natural unemployment because of job market turnover.

___ 7 Modern monetarists and real business cycle theorists tend to believe that wages are flexible and adjust quickly.

___ 8 The stock market crash of 1929 was the cause of the Great Depression.

___ 9 The major initial factor leading to the Great Depression was uncertainty about the future, which led to a reduction in investment and consumer expenditure.

___ 10 A recession today is likely to be much less severe than during the 1920s or 1930s because the government sector is much larger today.

MULTIPLE-CHOICE

1 During the Great Depression, which was caused by an aggregate
  a supply shock, the rate of inflation increased.
  b supply shock, the rate of inflation decreased.
  c demand shock, the rate of inflation increased.
  d demand shock, the rate of inflation decreased.
  e demand shock, the rate of inflation became negative.

2 During a recession
  a what happens to interest rates is irrelevant to the economy.
  b imports usually rise.
  c the decrease in income raises exports.
  d imports usually fall.
  e government transfer payments usually fall.

3 Which of the following describes the typical behaviour of interest rates during a recession?
  a In the early stages of recession interest rates increase but then fall as the recession gets under way.
  b In the early stages of recession interest rates decrease but then rise as the recession gets under way.
  c In the early stages of recession interest rates increase and remain high throughout the recession.
  d In the early stages of recession interest rates decrease and remain low throughout the recession.
  e In the early stages of recession interest rates are unchanged but then fall as the recession gets under way.

4 Modern Keynesians believe that the supply of labour curve is
  a not very sensitive to changes in the real wage rate and that wages themselves are flexible.
  b not very sensitive to changes in the real wage rate and that wages themselves are sticky.
  c very sensitive to changes in the real wage rate and that wages themselves are flexible.
  d very sensitive to changes in the real wage rate and that wages themselves are sticky.
  e none of the above.

5 According to the modern monetarists and real business cycle theorists, the increase in the unemployment rate during the 1991–1992 recession was an increase in the
  a deviation of the rate of unemployment from the natural rate of unemployment resulting from a real wage rate that is too high to clear the labour market.
  b deviation of the rate of unemployment from the natural rate of unemployment resulting from an increase in job market turnover.
  c natural rate of unemployment resulting from a real wage that is too high to clear the labour market.
  d natural rate of unemployment resulting from an increase in job market turnover.
  e rate of new entries into the labour market.

6 According to the real business cycles theorists, why has unemployment increased in recent decades?
  a Too-high real wages kept unemployment from reaching the natural rate of unemployment.
  b Increased job market turnover kept unemployment from reaching the natural rate of unemployment.
  c Too-high real wages increased the natural rate of unemployment.
  d Increased job market turnover increased the natural rate of unemployment.
  e Increased use of contracts prevented wages from being flexible.

7 During the Great Depression, aggregate demand was expected to
  a fall, but it didn't fall as rapidly as expected.
  b fall, but it fell faster than expected.
  c rise, but it actually fell.
  d rise, which it did owing to an increase in the money supply.
  e rise, but it rose less than expected.

8 The major cause of the Great Depression was
  a a dramatic increase in the prices of raw materials during 1929.
  b a fall in the money supply during 1929.
  c a fall in investment and consumer spending because of uncertainty about the future.
  d the stock market crash of 1929.
  e both **b** and **c**.

9 Which of the following is a reason why a recession as deep as the Great Depression is quite unlikely in the United Kingdom today?

a the existence of the European Union
b the value of the pound is linked to other European currencies
c the government is prepared to lend money to companies
d multi-income families
e lower tax rates

10 Multi-income families reduce the probability of another Great Depression by
   a reducing the probability of everyone in the family being simultaneously unemployed.
   b investing more in the economy.
   c paying more taxes.
   d increasing fluctuations in consumption.
   e none of the above.

11 During the Great Depression, real GDP fell and

a consumption fell as well.
b investment fell dramatically.
c exports fell.
d imports fell.
e all of the above.

12 In Fig. 31.1 which graph(s) represent an economy that is recovering from a recession without any government involvement?
   a (a)
   b (b)
   c (b) and (d)
   d (c)
   e (d)

13 In Fig. 31.1, which graph(s) represent an economy where the government is helping it recover from a recession?

Figure 31.1

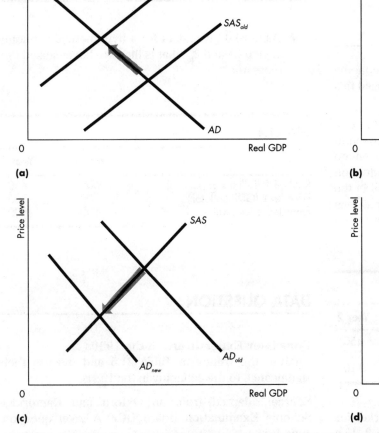

(a)

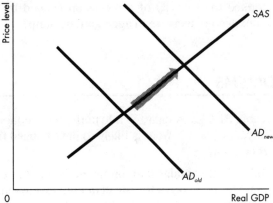

(b)

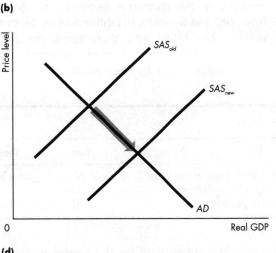

(c)

(d)

a (a)
b (b)
c (b) and (d)
d (c)
e (d)

SHORT ANSWER

1 a What is the basic controversy among economists about the behaviour of the labour market during recession?
b Why is the controversy important for designing an appropriate anti-recessionary economic policy?

2 List the four important features of the UK economy that make severe depression less likely today.

3 How do government transfer payments help to reduce the severity of a recession caused by an unexpected decrease in aggregate demand?

PROBLEMS

1 Table 31.1 gives data for a hypothetical economy in years 1 and 2. What is likely to have caused this recession?

2 Table 31.2 contains data on unemployment, nominal and real wages for the economy discussed in Problem 1. Assuming that there have been no changes in the short-run aggregate production function, and no shifts in labour supply, fill in the rest of the table, and then graph what has happened in the labour market according to the data, assuming a sticky wage model.

Table 31.1

	Year 1	Year 2
Real GDP (billions of pounds)	500	450
Price level (GDP deflator)	100	105
Expected price level	100	110

3 Table 31.3 shows data for the money market for the same economy as in Problems 1 and 2. Use the data from this table and the other tables to interpret what has happened in the money market over the time period in question. Draw a graph as part of your answer.

Table 31.2

	Year 1	Year 2
Nominal wage rate (pounds)	10.00	11.00
Real wage rate (constant pounds)	10.00	
Employment (billions of hours a year)	25	22

Table 31.3

	Year 1	Year 2
Real money supply (billions of pounds)	120	114
Interest rate (per cent per year)	13	19

4 Table 31.4 gives data for a hypothetical economy in years 1 and 2. What is likely to have caused this recession?

Table 31.4

	Year 1	Year 2
Real GDP (billions of pounds)	500	450
Price level (GDP deflator)	100	105
Expected price level	100	100

DATA QUESTION

Consumer Expenditure in the 1930s
Analyse the trends in Table 31.5 and discuss their significance to the economy in the 1930s.

Source: adapted from an Oxford and Cambridge Schools Examination Board GCE A-Level question, June 1986.

Table 31.5

Estimated indices of average annual real earnings (1930 = 100)				Aggregate consumption		Indices of real consumption spending (1929 = 100)		
Year	Average annual money earnings	Cost of living	Average annual real earnings	Year	Consumers' expenditure at 1929 prices (£ million)	Year	Food	Cars and motor cycles
1929	100.2	103.8	96.5	1929	4,062	1929	100	100
1930	100.0	100.0	100.0	1930	4,206	1930	103	96
1931	98.6	93.4	105.6	1931	4,290	1931	107	82
1932	97.0	91.1	106.5	1932	4,267	1932	108	89
1933	96.4	88.6	108.8	1933	4,329	1933	107	103
1934	97.4	89.2	109.2	1934	4,482	1934	110	128
1935	98.8	90.5	109.2	1935	4,554	1935	110	154
1936	100.7	93.0	108.3	1936	4,601	1936	112	171
1937	102.6	97.5	105.1	1937	4,661	1937	113	175
1938	105.7	98.7	107.1	1938	4,680	1938	113	154

Source: H.W. Richardson, *Economic Recovery in Britain 1932–39*, Weidenfeld and Nicolson Ltd.

ANSWERS

CONCEPT REVIEW

1 rise; fall

2 investment

3 no change; no change; not at all

4 sticky; exceed; inflation

5 bank deposit; lender of last resort; government spending; multi-income

TRUE OR FALSE

1 **T** Monetary restraint caused high interest rates.

2 **F** Opposite is true.

3 **T** Fall in real GDP leads to fall in demand for real money.

4 **F** Investment falls most.

5 **T** All unemployment is natural in flexible wage theory.

6 **F** This is flexible wage explanation.

7 **T** They believe flexible wage theory.

8 **F** It was symptom of uncertainty about future that was initial cause.

9 **T** See text discussion.

10 **T** Government sector is now much larger, so automatic stabilizers are also much larger.

MULTIPLE-CHOICE

1 **e** Fall in investor and consumer confidence led to large shift to left in *AD* curve, so fall in price level.

2 **d** Fall in real GDP leads to fall in imports.

3 **a** Observed pattern.

4 **b** Keynesians believe that people do not move in and out of the labour market when wages change by relatively small amounts.

5 **d** Restructuring led to increased labour turnover.

6 **d** In this view, unemployment is caused by increases in the natural rate.

7 **b** Observable fact.

8 **c** See text discussion.

9 d Multi-income families mean that if unemployment rises, some family members will still have unaffected incomes.

10 a See **9**; this leads to smaller fall in consumer confidence when one member becomes unemployed.

11 e See text discussion.

12 e Recession causes unemployment which leads to fall in real wages and *SAS* curve shifts to right.

13 b Expansionary policy causes *AD* curve to shift to right.

SHORT ANSWER

1 a Economists disagree about two aspects of the labour market: (1) the sensitivity of the supply of labour curve to changes in the real wage rate and (2) the speed with which the real wage rate adjusts to clear the labour market. Some economists (modern Keynesians) believe that the labour supply curve is not very sensitive to changes in the real wage rate and that wages themselves are sticky and adjust only slowly. As a consequence, when a recession occurs, the real wage does not fall by enough to clear the labour market in the short run and thus there is an excess supply of labour (unemployment). Other economists (modern monetarists and real business cycle theorists) believe that the labour supply curve is very sensitive to changes in the real wage rate and that wages are flexible. When a recession occurs, the real wage can fall sufficiently to clear the labour market. Any increase in unemployment is thus interpreted to be an increase in natural unemployment. The example in the text, Fig. 31.5, demonstrates a case involving shifts in the composition of labour demand.

b These issues have significant implications for the design of an appropriate policy as a response to recession. If the modern Keynesians are correct, then it may be useful to consider expansionary monetary or fiscal policies to counteract recession. Whereas if the modern monetarist position is correct, since the (short-run) aggregate supply is vertical in that theory, expansionary monetary or fiscal policy will simply increase the rate of inflation and have no effect on real GDP or unemployment.

2 The four important features of the UK economy that make severe depression less likely today are:
– Bank deposits are insured.
– The Bank of England is prepared to be the 'lender of last resort'.
– Taxes and government spending play a stabilizing role.
– Multi-income families are more economically secure.

3 When a recession arises, unemployment increases and disposable income declines. This decline in disposable income will lead to a reduction in consumption expenditure, which will have a multiplied negative effect on real GDP. Transfer payments, however, reduce these secondary effects of a recession by reducing the amount by which disposable income falls. As incomes fall and unemployment increases, government transfer payments increase in the form of higher unemployment benefits or other welfare payments. As a result, the fall in disposable income is reduced and the decline in consumption is less.

PROBLEMS

1 We note that the price level has increased and real GDP has fallen. This would be the result when the upward shift in the short-run aggregate supply curve is greater than the upward shift in the aggregate demand curve. But that would be the case for either a negative aggregate supply shock or an increase in aggregate demand that is less than anticipated. To see which of these has occurred, we look at the price level that was expected in year 2 and compare it to the actual price level. Since the actual price level is lower than the expected price level, it must be the case that the fall in real GDP is due to an increase in aggregate demand that was less than expected. Actual real GDP must be less than capacity.

2 Completed Table 31.2 is shown here as Table 31.6. Clearly, with a sticky wage model, nominal wages are set based on an expected inflation of 10 per cent. However, the actual inflation is only 5 per cent, so that the new level of real wages is higher, from the following formula:

$$\text{Real wage rate} = \frac{\text{Nominal wage rate}}{\text{Price level}} \times 100$$

$$= \frac{11.00}{105} \times 100 = £10.48$$

The rise in real wages, combined with a constant labour demand (owing to an unchanging production function) and no shifts in labour supply, implies a lower level of employment, and a rise in unemployment above the natural rate of (say) 5 billion hours, as shown in Fig. 31.2.

Table 31.6

	Year 1	Year 2
Nominal wage rate (pounds)	10.00	11.00
Real wage rate (constant pounds)	10.00	10.48
Employment (billions of hours a year)	25	22

Figure 31.2

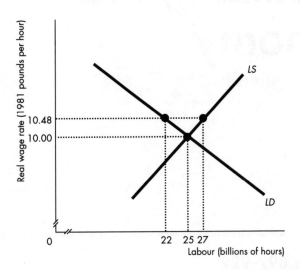

Figure 31.3

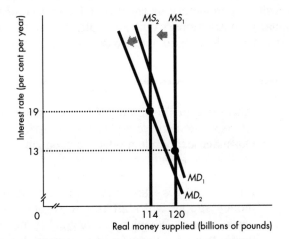

3 Clearly, the real money supply has fallen over this period, because the nominal money supply has risen less than the rise in the price level. In addition, with the fall in real GDP, we would expect a fall in the demand for real money. The results are shown in Fig. 31.3.

4 Once again we note that the price level has increased and real GDP has fallen. In this case, however, the actual price level in year 2 is greater than the price level that was expected. Thus, the fall in real GDP must be due to a negative aggregate supply shock. Actual GDP is greater than capacity but capacity has fallen because of the negative aggregate supply shock.

DATA QUESTION

Table 31.5 shows a fall in money earnings after 1929; it was 1936 before money earnings exceeded their 1929 level. However, prices fell by a greater amount than money wages, so that there was actually a rise in real wages – by over 5 per cent in 1931. One effect of this rise in real wages was that it led to a fall in the demand for labour. After 1931, real wages grew only slowly, and indeed fell towards the end of the period. The rise in real wages led to a rise of 15 per cent in consumers' expenditure in the period 1929–1938. This was a relatively small rise for an entire decade. One reason was that although real earnings were rising, unemployment rose in the years after 1929, and those people that became unemployed cut their spending.

As the table shows, spending on food was comparatively stable, growing by about 13 per cent over the period. Spending on cars and motor cycles was much more volatile, falling by nearly 20 per cent in two years, while it doubled between 1931 and 1937. Increased spending on consumers' durables such as cars contributed to economic recovery during the 1930s, but its fragile nature is shown by the fall in spending on cars in 1938. These swings in consumer spending are still a feature of economies today .

The table does not tell the whole story. An important component of aggregate demand is investment and this fell by 11 per cent between 1929 and 1931. In the same period exports fell by a third. Both of these falls had a multiplied effect on the economy. The result was a substantial fall in aggregate demand as shown in Fig. 31.6 in the main text, p. 891.

Chapter 32 **Stabilizing the Economy**

Chapter In Perspective, Text Pages 899–922

Business cycle fluctuations have been characteristic of the behaviour of the UK economy. Frequently, severe recessions have occurred and at times the United Kingdom has experienced periods of considerable inflation. There is a strong consensus that UK citizens would be better off if these fluctuations could be reduced. In our development of the complete aggregate demand–aggregate supply model, we saw that monetary policy and fiscal policy can be used to shift the aggregate demand curve, and therefore potentially affect these fluctuations.

In this chapter we discuss the use of policy to reduce the magnitude of business cycle fluctuations. It appears, for example, that if the economy enters a recession, expansionary monetary or fiscal policy could be used to increase aggregate demand and eliminate the recession. Similarly, contractionary policies could be used to reduce inflationary pressures. Here we examine the potential and the problems associated with the use of policy to stabilize the economy.

Helpful Hints

1 Like the previous chapter, this chapter introduces some new concepts but no new analytical tools. The model that is used here to analyse the effects of policy is the model whose development was completed in Chapter 30.

2 This chapter is intended to give us a more realistic perspective regarding the use of policy in the real world. In order to simplify our task and thus maximize our learning, in previous chapters we have abstracted from numerous complications that arise in the real-world use of the aggregate demand–aggregate supply model in making policy decisions. In this chapter we learn of the problems that confront a policy maker. Among the most important problems is the inability to predict the magnitude or the timing of factors which affect aggregate demand or aggregate supply.

a Our macroeconomic model is a good guide to the qualitative effects of changes in factors that affect aggregate demand and aggregate supply. For example, we know that an increase in the money supply will shift the aggregate demand curve upward. When conducting policy, however, qualitative knowledge is not enough. We must also have quantitative knowledge. We must know how much a given increase in the money supply will increase aggregate demand. While we may have an understanding of the direction of the effect, knowledge of the magnitude of the effect is much more difficult to obtain and much more limited. This reduces the potential for policy to be used to 'fine tune' the economy.

b In addition to direction and magnitude, we must

also know when. The full effect on aggregate demand of policy changes made today will not be immediate. Much if not most of that effect will occur only with considerable time lag. Thus, it is important that policy makers be able to predict these time lags in order to be confident that the future effect of a policy change made today will be appropriate when the effect actually occurs. Unfortunately, that is extremely difficult. Not only are these lags often long but, to make matters more difficult, they are also variable in length. This makes them unpredictable. As a result, policy makers may initiate a policy today which, when it has its effect sometime in the future, turns out to shift aggregate demand in the 'wrong' direction because circumstances have changed. In such a case, policy will actually turn out to be destabilizing and thus worse than doing nothing at all.

3 It may seem that feedback rules are better than fixed rules, since theoretically they seem to be able to do everything fixed rules can, plus more. However, there are many problems with the actual implementation of feedback rules in the real world:

they require very good knowledge of the economy; they introduce unpredictability into the economy; and they can generate bigger fluctuations in aggregate demand, due to the lags mentioned above. These reasons make it far from obvious that feedback rules are better than fixed rules.

Key Figures

Figure 32.5 Two Stabilization Policies: Aggregate Demand Shocks, text page 907

This compares the effects of different policies when the economy suffers from an aggregate demand shock such as a substantial fall in investment.

Figure 32.6 Two Stabilization Policies: Short-run Aggregate Supply Shocks, text page 911

This is a companion to Fig. 32.5, but this time showing the effect of a supply-side shock. With a fixed-rule policy the economy stays depressed until wages or raw material prices fall. With a feedback rule the government intervenes to raise aggregate demand and the economy returns to full-employment level, but inflation continues.

SELF-TEST

CONCEPT REVIEW

1 Delivering a macroeconomic performance that is as smooth and predictable as possible is the _____ problem.

2 Macroeconomic policy is conducted by choosing policy targets that can be divided into two groups. The first group, _____ targets, includes unemployment at its _____ rate and _____ growth in real GDP. The second group, _____ targets, includes low and predictable _____ .

3 Macroeconomic policies can be classified into two broad categories. A(n) _____ policy rule specifies an action to be pursued regardless of the state of the economy. A(n) _____ policy rule specifies how actions will change when the state of the economy changes.

4 Inflation that has its origins in cost increases is called _____ – _____ inflation.

5 A theory that is based on flexible wages and ascribes aggregate fluctuations to random shocks to the economy's long-run aggregate supply is called a(n) _____ _____ _____ theory.

TRUE OR FALSE

____ **1** One of the goals (targets) of economic policy is to reduce the unemployment rate below its natural rate.

____ **2** The rate of growth of nominal GDP is equal to the rate of growth of real GDP minus the inflation rate.

____ **3** The Bank of England conducts monetary policy.

___ **4** The statement 'Allow the money supply to grow at the constant rate of 3 per cent per year' is an example of a feedback policy rule.

___ **5** The less is known about how the economy operates, the stronger the case for a fixed policy rule.

___ **6** The use of feedback rules can increase the degree of unpredictability in the economy.

___ **7** The use of feedback rules cannot make the business cycle worse.

___ **8** The inflation resulting from expansionary monetary policy is an example of cost–push inflation.

___ **9** The use of a feedback rule rather than a fixed rule increases the likelihood of cost–push inflation.

___ **10** According to real business cycle theory, the short-run and long-run aggregate supply curves are the same.

___ **11** The quantity theory of money implies that a fixed rule is better than a feedback rule.

___ **12** Cost–push inflation cannot persist unless it is accommodated by the central bank.

MULTIPLE-CHOICE

1 Which of the following is an example of a nominal target of macroeconomic policy?
   a unemployment at its natural rate
   b a stable foreign exchange rate
   c steady growth in real GDP
   d low and predictable inflation
   e both **b** and **d**

2 The Bank of England's monetary policy is constrained by
   a the inability of the Bank to change the money supply.
   b the fact that interest rates in England are not influenced by international interest rates.
   c the stubbornness of Parliament.
   d the taxing and spending decisions of Parliament.
   e nothing at all.

3 Which of the following is an example of a fixed 'policy' rule?

   a Wear your boots if it snows.
   b Leave your boots at home if it does not snow.
   c Wear your boots every day.
   d Take your boots off in the house if they are wet.
   e Listen to the weather forecast and then decide whether to wear your boots.

4 Suppose that, starting from equilibrium at capacity real GDP, there is a temporary unexpected decline in aggregate demand. Our feedback rule is: increase the money supply whenever there is a fall in aggregate demand and decrease the money supply whenever there is a rise in aggregate demand. In this case, our rule would result in
   a an increase in real GDP to above capacity and a rise in the price level above its original value.
   b real GDP jumping back to capacity and the price level jumping back to its original value.
   c an increase in real GDP but not back to capacity and no effect on the price level.
   d a slow increase in real GDP back to capacity and a slow rise in the price level.
   e a jump in the price level back to the original level and no change in real GDP.

5 Which of the following is not an argument against a feedback rule?
   a Feedback rules require greater knowledge of the economy than we have.
   b Feedback rules introduce unpredictability.
   c Aggregate supply shocks cause most economic fluctuations.
   d Aggregate demand shocks cause most economic fluctuations.
   e Feedback rules generate bigger fluctuations in aggregate demand.

6 Which of the following is the basic reason for the claim that feedback rules generate bigger fluctuations in aggregate demand? Policy makers
   a use the wrong feedback rules to achieve their goals.
   b must take actions today which will not have their effects until well into the future.
   c do not really want to stabilize the economy.
   d try to make their policies unpredictable.
   e have enough knowledge of the economy.

7 A fixed rule for monetary policy
   a requires considerable knowledge of how changes in the money supply affect the economy.
   b would be impossible for the Bank of England to achieve.

c generates bigger fluctuations in aggregate demand.

d would result in constant real GDP.

e minimizes the threat of cost–push inflation.

8 According to real business cycle theories,

a any decline in real GDP is a decline in capacity.

b wages are flexible but labour market equilibrium does not necessarily imply full employment.

c fluctuations in aggregate demand change capacity real GDP.

d fluctuations in aggregate demand cannot affect the price level.

e flexible rules are best.

9 According to real business cycle theories, if the Bank of England increases the money supply when real GDP declines, real GDP

a will increase but only temporarily.

b will increase permanently.

c and the price level will both be unaffected.

d will be unaffected but the price level will rise.

e will fall due to the inefficiencies introduced into production as a result.

10 Stagflation means that real GDP stops growing or even declines and the

a rate of inflation declines.

b rate of inflation increases.

c rate of inflation remains stable.

d economy experiences deflation.

e rate of inflation becomes negative.

11 What group advocates the viewpoint that there is a very strong connection between money and the price level?

a Keynesians

b neo-Keynesians

c monetarists

d feedback-rule advocates

e none of the above

12 Monetary and fiscal policy are frequently constrained in their ability to affect the economy by other forces. Which of the following statements about these constraints is true?

a Expansionary fiscal policy is constrained by fear of higher interest rates.

b Monetary policy is constrained by interest rate parity.

c Fiscal policy is constrained by the monetary policy that accompanies it.

d All of the above.

e None of the above.

SHORT ANSWER

1 What are the three main macroeconomic policy targets?

2 Distinguish between a fixed rule and a feedback rule.

3 The purpose of policy is to stabilize. How can feedback rules result in even greater variability in aggregate demand?

4 If the Bank of England announced its intention to reduce the rate of inflation by reducing the rate of growth of the money supply, expected inflation would decline accordingly and thus a reduction in the actual rate of inflation could be achieved without a recession. Why does this not seem to be the case?

PROBLEMS

1 Assume that the Bank of England knows exactly how much and when the aggregate demand curve will shift, both in the absence of monetary policy and when the Bank of England changes the money supply. In this environment, compare the effects on real GDP and the price level of a temporary decline in aggregate demand which returns gradually to its previous level over several periods under fixed and feedback policy rules. Assume the economy is initially at capacity real GDP and that capacity real GDP is constant. Illustrate graphically on a separate graph for each of the following rules:

a First, assume that the Bank of England follows the fixed rule: hold the money supply constant.

b Now assume that the Bank of England follows the feedback rule: increase the money supply whenever aggregate demand falls and decrease the money supply whenever aggregate demand rises.

2 Consider an economy which experiences a temporary increase in aggregate demand. The Bank of England follows a feedback rule similar to the one given in Problem 1b but now we assume that the Bank of England does not have perfect knowledge of how much and when aggregate demand will shift. In year 1 the economy is in macro-economic equilibrium at capacity real GDP, but, as the year ends, there is a burst of optimism about the future, which initiates a (temporary) rise in aggregate demand. As a result, in year 2, real GDP increases and the rate of unemployment falls below its natural rate. Given its feedback rule, the Bank of England reduces the money supply 'to keep the economy from overheating'. The effect on aggregate demand, however, takes place only after a time lag of one year. In year 3, this burst of optimism returns to its previous level and thus, so does aggregate demand. In addition, the monetary policy implemented in year 2 finally has its effect on aggregate demand in year 3. Analyse the behaviour of real GDP and the price level using three graphs – one each for years 1, 2 and 3. Assume that all changes in aggregate demand are unanticipated and that capacity real GDP is constant. Did a feedback monetary policy rule stabilize aggregate demand?

3 Assume that real business cycle theories are correct. There is a fall in capacity real GDP. What will be the effect on real GDP and the price level if the Bank of England follows the fixed rule: hold the money supply constant? What will be the effect on real GDP and the price level if the Bank of England follows the feedback rule: increase the money supply whenever real GDP falls and decrease the money supply whenever real GDP rises? Illustrate graphically.

Figure 32.1

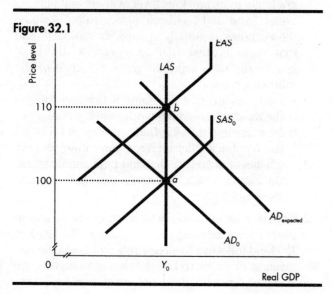

4 Consider a central bank that decides to start an anti-inflationary policy. Figure 32.1 shows the initial state of the economy (point a) and the expected state next period (point b). The bank decides to carry out a gradual policy of inflation reduction. In year 1, it will reduce the growth in aggregate demand to 5 per cent, and in year 2 it will reduce the growth in aggregate demand to 2.5 per cent. If the policy is initially unexpected, show on the graph what will occur over the next few years.

DATA QUESTIONS

Macroeconomic Policy in the United Kingdom

The theoretical case for an active macroeconomic policy was questioned by new classical economics. By the end of the 1980s a reasonable theoretical defence had been constructed. It rested on the observed fact that wages and prices are relatively inflexible, compared for example to exchange rates or the stock market, and on the supposition that they cannot (or should not) be made completely flexible. Thus, for example, when the Chancellor makes his budget judgement he has access to information which was not available to the private sector when the latest annual wage bargain was struck. By using his judgement he can perhaps improve on the outcome for the economy that would result from market behaviour on its own. That seems to be an acceptable defence of stabilization in principle, but there are countervailing arguments in favour of precommitment. Moreover, the conduct of discretionary policy in practice has never been easy.

Source: A.J.C. Britton, *Macroeconomic Policy in Britain 1974–1987*, Cambridge University Press, 1991, p. 305. © Cambridge University Press.

1 Explain what is meant by the 'new classical economics'.

2 Why are wages and prices relatively inflexible?

3 Summarize the arguments in favour of an active interventionist policy.

4 Why is the conduct of discretionary policy not easy?

ANSWER

CONCEPT REVIEW

1 stabilization

2 real; natural; steady; nominal; inflation

3 fixed; feedback

4 cost–push

5 real business cycle

TRUE OR FALSE

1 **F** One goal is to keep unemployment at its natural rate.

2 **F** Nominal rate is real rate plus inflation.

3 **T** For example, by influencing interest rates.

4 **F** The rule is the same regardless of the state of the economy, hence it is fixed rule.

5 **T** Ignorance would lead to interventionist errors.

6 **T** Because wrong decisions might be made.

7 **F** If there are timing lags, feedback policy might be imposed at the wrong time and make matters worse.

8 **F** Cost–push inflation arises from changes in costs such as wages.

9 **T** Feedback rules accommodate wage increases.

10 **T** Because wages are perfectly flexible.

11 **T** Theory suggests that government should increase money supply at regular rate.

12 **T** If not accommodated, unemployment rises leading to fall in factor prices; *SAS* curve shifts to right and price level returns to original level.

MULTIPLE-CHOICE

1 **e** Others are real.

2 **d** Bank is subordinate to Parliament and money variables are affected by fiscal decisions.

3 **c** Same choice regardless of circumstances.

4 **b** Because *AD* will shift back to original value.

5 **d** Others are arguments against a feedback rule.

6 **b** Therefore fluctuations in *AD* are exaggerated.

7 **e** Because it would not accommodate cost–push inflation, reducing likelihood of future cost–push inflation.

8 **a** Because aggregate supply curves are all vertical at long-run real GDP.

9 **d** Because *LAS* curve is vertical.

10 **b** Definition.

11 **c** Name reflects beliefs.

12 **d** All are policy constraints.

SHORT ANSWER

1 The three main macroeconomic policy targets are: unemployment at its natural rate; steady growth in real GDP; and low and predictable inflation.

2 The difference between a fixed rule and a feedback rule is whether or not the specified action depends on the state of the economy. A fixed rule specifies an action that will be pursued regardless of the state of the economy whereas a feedback rule specifies actions that may change depending on the state of the economy.

3 Policy actions, for example an open market operation, will affect aggregate demand only after a time lag. This means that a policy action that is taken today will have its intended effect only sometime in the future. Thus, it is necessary for policy makers to forecast the state of the economy for a year or two into the future in order to be confident that the future effect of the policy action taken today will be appropriate when the effect occurs. This is very difficult to do since the lags are long (one to two years) and unpredictable. As a result, policy makers face a very good chance that the policy action taken today will turn out to have an effect in the future which is the opposite of what would be appropriate at the time, that is, policy could destabilize aggregate demand rather than stabilize aggregate demand.

4 The problem is that expected inflation may not in fact decline as a result of the announcement by the Bank of England. The Bank of England may have a credibility problem since expectations will be much more strongly affected by the record of actions by the Bank of England than by its announcement. If people don't believe the Bank of England, they will not adjust expectations. Then when the Bank of England carries out the policy, a recession will result in spite of the fact that an announcement was made. In addition, if wages are sticky, this could slow down the adjustment of the labour market.

PROBLEMS

1 a The behaviour of real GDP and the price level under the fixed rule is illustrated in Fig. 32.2(a). The economy is initially at point a on the aggregate demand curve AD_0: the price level is P_0, and real GDP is at capacity, denoted Y_0. The temporary decline in aggregate demand shifts the aggregate demand curve downward to AD_1. Since the money supply is held constant under the fixed rule, the new equilibrium is at point b: the price level has fallen to P_1 and real GDP has fallen to Y_1. The economy is in recession. As the aggregate demand curve gradually returns to AD_0, the price level gradually rises to P_0 and real GDP gradually returns to Y_0, capacity.

b The behaviour of real GDP and the price level under the feedback rule is illustrated in Fig. 32.2(b). Once again the economy is initially at point a on the aggregate demand curve AD_0. The temporary decline in aggregate demand temporarily shifts the aggregate demand curve to AD_1. Given the Bank of England's feedback rule, it will increase the money supply sufficiently to shift the AD_1 curve back to AD_0. Thus the Bank of England offsets the decline in aggregate demand and equilibrium remains at point a: the price

level remains at P_0 and real GDP remains at Y_0, capacity. As the temporary causes of the decline in aggregate demand dissipate, the aggregate demand curve will begin gradually shifting upward. The Bank of England will then decrease the money supply just enough to offset these shifts. As a result, the aggregate demand curve will remain at AD_0 and equilibrium will remain at point a.

2 The state of the economy in years 1, 2 and 3 is illustrated in Fig. 32.3, parts (a), (b) and (c), respectively. The initial equilibrium (point a) in year 1 is illustrated in part (a). The economy is producing at capacity real GDP (Y_0) and the price level is P_0. In year 2, the aggregate demand curve shifts to AD_1 in part (b) as a result of the burst of optimism. The Bank of England also reduces the money supply but there is no immediate effect on aggregate demand. Thus the equilibrium in year 2 occurs at the intersection of the AD_1 and SAS curves; at point b in part (b). Real GDP has risen to Y_1, which is above capacity, and the price level has risen to P_1. In year 3 there are two effects on aggregate demand. First, the burst of optimism expires pushing the aggregate demand curve back from AD_1 to AD_0. But, in addition, the Bank of England's reduction in the money supply initiated in year 2 finally has its effect on aggregate demand in year 3. As a result the aggregate demand curve shifts all the way downward to AD_2 and the new equilibrium is at point c in part (c). The price level has fallen to P_2 and real GDP has fallen to Y_2 which is below capacity. The Bank of England's feedback policy in year 2 has caused a recession in year 3 even though it

Figure 32.2

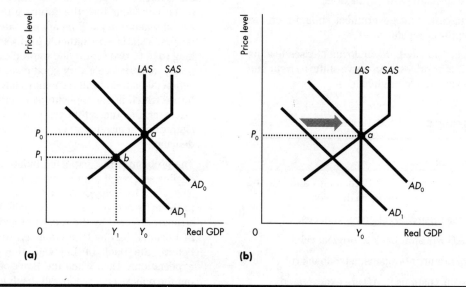

(a)   (b)

Figure 32.3

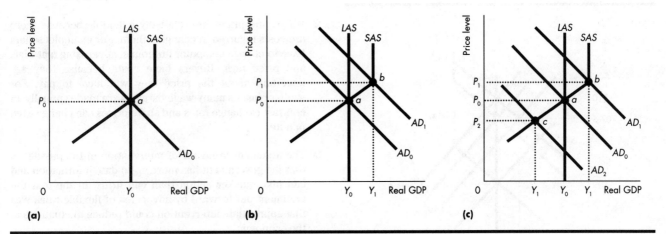

(a) (b) (c)

looked like the right policy when it was implemented. Note that if the Bank of England had been following a fixed rule it would not have changed the money supply in year 2 and as a result, in year 3, the equilibrium would have been at point *a* and real GDP would have been at capacity. Because of imperfect knowledge on the part of the Bank of England and the delayed effect of policy changes, the feedback rule has resulted in destabilizing aggregate demand, that is, policy has increased the variability of aggregate demand.

3 The effects on real GDP and the price level are illustrated in Fig. 32.4. Since we are assuming that real business cycle theories are correct, the only aggregate supply curve is the long-run aggregate supply curve. The economy is initially in equilibrium at the intersection of the AD_0 and LAS_0 curves, point *a*. Real GDP is Y_0 and the price level is P_0. Then capacity real GDP falls and the aggregate supply curve shifts to the left: from LAS_0 to LAS_1. If the Bank of England follows the fixed policy rule, it will hold the money supply constant and the aggregate demand curve will remain at AD_0. Thus the new equilibrium is at point *b*: real GDP will fall to Y_1 (the new capacity) and the price level will have risen to P_1. If, on the other hand, the Bank of England follows the feedback rule, the fall in real GDP will lead the Bank of England to increase the money supply, which will shift the aggregate demand curve to the right: from AD_0 to AD_1. Note that monetary policy will have no effect on capacity real GDP and thus no effect on the (long-run) aggregate supply curve. Thus, under the feedback policy rule, the new equilibrium is at point *c*: real GDP has remained at Y_1 but the price level has risen to P_2. The consequence of a feedback rule is a larger increase in the price level (that is, higher inflation) with no effect on real GDP.

Figure 32.4

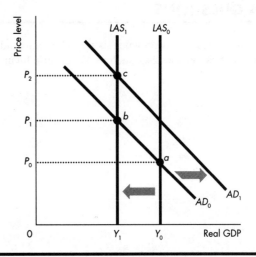

4 The anti-inflationary policy is illustrated in Fig. 32.5. It will reduce the growth of aggregate demand to a (vertical) distance of 5 per cent. However, the actual *SAS* curve will be based on the expected inflation rate of 10 per cent, and therefore SAS_1 is the relevant curve, yielding us an equilibrium in year 1 at point *c*, with a fall in real GDP and a rise in inflation of (say) 7.5 per cent, less than expected. In year 2, the central bank allows aggregate demand to rise a further 2.5 per cent, or a vertical rise to 107.625 (= 105 × 102.5), crossing the long-run aggregate supply curve at the point *d*, where AD_2 and *LAS* cross. The actual impact on the economy depends on how much adjustment of expectations occurs. If the policy is now credible, and if wages can adjust sufficiently, we will get a fall in the short-run aggregate supply curve to SAS_2, and the equilibrium will be at the point *d*, with a very small inflation, and with real GDP back to the natural rate.

Figure 32.5

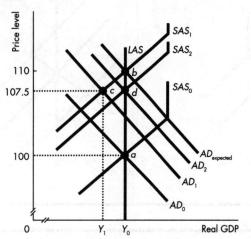

DATA QUESTIONS

1 The 'new classical economics' is the economics advocated by those economists such as Milton Friedman who emphasize the role of markets and control of the money supply. In the context of this chapter they would favour fixed rules, that is, less government intervention.

2 Wages and prices are relatively inflexible because there are costs incurred in changing them. For example, sellers have to change computer programs, advertising materials and price tags. Buyers have costs because they are uncertain about the price they will have to pay. For similar reasons many wage bargains are made annually. In contrast exchange rates and share prices can change each minute.

3 The argument in favour of intervention in the passage is that the government has more up-to-date information and can take quicker action than can firms. In the text the argument put forward by advocates of flexible rules was that appropriate intervention could reduce fluctuations in the economy.

4 Discretionary policy is not easy in practice because of uncertainty and lags. Uncertainty means that we cannot forecast exactly the result of any intervention. Moreover, action taken by the government will take some time to have an effect. Consequently, it is argued by some economists that active intervention can produce greater fluctuations than would result from fixed rules.

Chapter 33

Government Deficits and Borrowing Requirements

Chapter In Perspective, Text Pages 923–949

The government budget deficit is widely discussed and widely misunderstood. How concerned should we be about deficits? What kinds of burdens do large deficits place on current and future generations? Do deficits cause inflation? How can the deficit be eliminated? These are the important issues that are addressed in this chapter.

Helpful Hints

1 To understand why money financing of a deficit is inflationary, it is useful to recall our discussion in Chapter 27 of the conduct of monetary policy by the Bank of England. Money financing is financing a deficit by selling bonds to the Bank of England. The effect on the money supply is just like an open market purchase of government securities. The only difference is that the initial deposit created at the Bank of England when the Bank of England buys these government bonds is owned by the government rather than the public. As these deposits are spent, bank reserves increase and the money multiplier process begins.

2 Note that since tax revenue depends (positively) on real GDP and government transfer payments depend (negatively) on real GDP, the size of the deficit fluctuates with business cycle fluctuations in real GDP. During business cycle recessions the deficit will increase, and during booms the deficit will decrease. We have also noted in discussions of fiscal policy in previous chapters that changes in the deficit are expected to have an effect on real GDP. For example, an expansionary fiscal policy which will increase the deficit will increase real GDP. Thus, in addition to the effect of a change in real GDP on the deficit, a change in the deficit through fiscal policy will affect real GDP. The deficit both affects and is affected by real GDP.

3 The difference between nominal and real deficits is sometimes confusing. The nominal deficit measures the addition to government debt from the current fiscal year, measured in terms of the amount of extra pounds that are owed. The real deficit measures the addition to government debt from the current fiscal year, measured in terms of the amount of extra goods and services owed by the government. Clearly the latter more correctly measures the government's obligations. In times of positive inflation, the nominal deficit overestimates the real obligations of the government.

4 The above discussion of real and nominal deficits implies that arguments about the deficit and its impact on the economy overestimate the problem. The theory of Ricardian equivalence also implies that worries about the deficit are too strong – indeed, the strong version of the theory implies that the size of the deficit is completely irrelevant!

Ricardian equivalence argues that any current government deficit implies that future taxpayers will have to raise taxes in order to pay off the accumulated debt. Rational individuals will take this into account, and realize that they, as taxpayers, have some outstanding debt, and will carefully save up to pay it off when it comes due (or will leave a bequest to their children large enough to pay off the debt). As a result, the strong version of the theory argues that the rise in savings by individuals will match the rise in borrowing from the government, leaving interest rates unchanged, and therefore leaving the economy unaffected by the deficit.

Of course, the crucial (as yet unanswered) question is whether the arguments of the theory are true or not. However, it would seem likely that at the very least, partial Ricardian equivalence is true. As a result, we should discount the problem of the deficit to some degree.

Key Figures

Figure 33.1   Revenue, Expenditure and the Deficit, text page 927

This shows the government sector's revenue, expenditure and deficits over a 25-year period.

Figure 33.4 The Deficit and the Business Cycle, text page 931

A recession leads to a fall in taxes and an increase in government transfer payments (including a rise in unemployment insurance payments). Thus we expect the deficit to rise during recessions. Similarly, a business cycle boom leads to an increase in tax revenue and a fall in government transfer payments. Thus we expect the deficit to decrease during booms. This figure illustrates the historical relationship between the business cycle (measured by the unemployment rate) and the deficit and shows that sometimes other factors alter the expected relationship.

Figure 33.9 The Laffer Curve, text page 943

This illustrates a hypothetical Laffer curve which shows the relationship between tax rates and tax revenue. As the tax rate increases from zero, tax revenue increases since the percentage decrease in income will be less than the percentage increase in the tax rate. Eventually, however, the tax rate is sufficiently high and thus the disincentive to earn additional income sufficiently large that this relationship is reversed and tax revenue falls. Between these ranges is a tax rate at which tax revenue is a maximum.

SELF-TEST

CONCEPT REVIEW

1 The government's budget _____ or _____ is the difference between the taxes it receives and its total expenditure in a given period of time. If a government budget is in neither surplus nor deficit, we say that the government has a(n)_____ _____ .

The total amount the government owes to households, firms and foreigners is called government _____ .

2 The deficit tends to move _____ with the business cycle.

3 The change in the real value of outstanding government debt is the _____ deficit. Because of inflation, this measure of the deficit is _____ than the nominal deficit.

4 Financing the government deficit by selling bonds to the Bank of England is called _____ financing. Financing the government deficit by selling bonds to any holder other than the Bank of England is called _____ financing.

5 The view that debt financing and paying for government spending with taxes are equivalent is called Ricardian _____ .

6 There are two basic ways of eliminating a deficit: _____ _____ and _____ _____ .

7 The percentage of tax levied on a particular activity, like income earning, is called a(n) _____ _____ . The activity on which the tax is levied is called the _____ _____ . The product of these is _____ _____ .

8 The curve that shows the amount of tax revenue that will be collected at each tax rate is called the _____ curve.

TRUE OR FALSE

__ **1** The government deficit is the total amount of borrowing that the government has undertaken.

__ **2** An increase in tax revenues will decrease the budget deficit.

__ **3** The major reason for the increase in the deficit as a percentage of GDP is the fact that tax revenue as a percentage of GDP has remained fairly stable, while government expenditure and interest payments as a percentage of GDP have risen.

__ **4** The budget deficit generally decreases during recessions.

__ **5** If the nominal value of government debt has remained constant between year 1 and year 2, but inflation has been experienced between those years, there will be a real surplus.

__ **6** The real deficit is always below the nominal deficit.

__ **7** To finance a deficit, the government must sell bonds to the public.

__ **8** If the government finances a deficit by selling bonds to households, the money supply must increase.

__ **9** Financing a deficit by selling bonds to the Bank of England is likely to be inflationary.

__ **10** Deficits are inevitably inflationary.

__ **11** For a given level of government expenditure, a deficit causes crowding out of investment only if real interest rates rise.

__ **12** If Ricardian equivalence holds, the real interest rate will not change when the government increases the amount it spends.

__ **13** An increase in the tax rate will always result in an increase in tax revenue.

__ **14** The Laffer curve shows the relationship between the size of the deficit and the real interest rate.

MULTIPLE-CHOICE

1 Suppose the government starts with no debt. Then, in year 1, there is a deficit of £100 billion; in year 2, there is a deficit of £60 billion; in year 3, there is a surplus of £40 billion; and in year 4, there is a deficit of £20 billion. What is government debt at the end of year 4?
  a £20 billion
  b £140 billion
  c £180 billion
  d somewhat greater than £220 billion, depending on the interest rate
  e somewhat greater than £140 billion, depending on the interest rate

2 Which of the following would not increase the budget deficit?
  a an increase in interest on the government debt

b an increase in government purchases of goods and services

c an increase in government transfer payments

d an increase in indirect business taxes

e a decrease in investment income

3 During a recession tax revenue

a declines and government expenditure declines.

b declines and government expenditure increases.

c increases and government expenditure declines.

d increases and government expenditure increases.

e stays constant and government expenditure increases.

4 A large deficit is of greater concern if it occurs during a period of

a recession.

b increasing inflation.

c low inflation and sustained economic growth.

d high unemployment.

e high government debt.

5 The three broad categories of government tax revenue are

a investment income, indirect taxes and income taxes.

b investment income, direct taxes and indirect taxes.

c investment income, income taxes and debt interest.

d transfer payments, income taxes and indirect taxes.

e transfer payments, debt interest and income taxes.

6 Consider the information in Table 33.1. What is the real deficit in year 2?

a £0

b £180 billion

c £198 billion

d £360 billion

e £18 billion

Table 33.1

	Year 1	Year 2
Government debt	£180 billion	£198 billion
Price level	1.0	1.1

7 If, in a given year, government debt increases by 6 per cent and the rate of inflation is 10 per cent,

a the real deficit has increased by 4 per cent.

b the real deficit has increased by 6 per cent.

c the real deficit has increased by 10 per cent.

d there is a real surplus.

e there is a nominal surplus.

8 When the deficit is financed by selling bonds to the Bank of England, it is called

a credit financing.

b debt financing.

c money financing.

d reserves financing.

e bank financing.

9 Money financing of a deficit may be preferred by government because

a the Bank of England is willing to pay a higher price for bonds than households and firms.

b debt financing leaves the government with an ongoing obligation to pay interest.

c it reduces the prospect of inflation.

d it disciplines the government to reduce its level of spending.

e it is easier to sell to the voters.

10 An increase in the deficit will leave future generations with a smaller capital stock if it causes the

a supply of loans to increase more than the demand for loans.

b demand for loans to increase more than the supply of loans.

c demand for loans to increase by the same amount as the supply of loans.

d supply of loans to increase and the demand for loans to decrease.

e supply of loans to decrease and the demand for loans to increase.

11 Ricardian equivalence implies that, for a given level of government spending, as the deficit increases

a the real rate of interest falls.

b the real rate of interest rises.

c saving increases.

d consumption expenditure increases.

e investment decreases.

12 A decrease in tax rates

a can increase tax revenue if the percentage increase in the tax base it causes is greater than the percentage fall in the tax rate.

b can increase tax revenue if the percentage increase in the tax base it causes is less than the percentage fall in the tax rate.

c cannot increase tax revenue since each activity being taxed will be taxed at a lower rate.

d cannot increase tax revenue since the tax base will decline as well.

e both c and d.

13 The curve that relates the tax rate and tax revenue is called the

a tax curve.

b revenue curve.

c Ricardian curve.

d Buchanan curve.

e Laffer curve.

14 Consider Table 33.2. The equilibrium interest rate in the private market is

a 8 per cent.

b 6 per cent.

c 12 per cent.

d 14 per cent.

e 10 per cent.

15 Consider Table 33.2. The government enters the loanable funds market to borrow £200 billion to finance the deficit. If the Ricardian equivalence does not hold, the new equilibrium interest rate will be

a 4 per cent.

b 6 per cent.

c 7 per cent.

d 8 per cent.

e none of the above.

Table 33.2 The Market for Loanable Funds

Private quantity demanded (billions of pounds)	Quantity supplied (billions of pounds)	Real interest rate (per cent)
400	1,600	12
600	1,400	10
800	1,200	8
1,000	1,000	6
1,200	800	4
1,400	600	2

16 Consider Table 33.2. The government enters the loanable funds market to borrow £200 billion to finance the current deficit. If Ricardian equivalence does hold, the new equilibrium interest rate will be

a 4 per cent.

b 6 per cent.

c 7 per cent.

d 8 per cent.

e none of the above.

SHORT ANSWER

1 Why does debt financing of a permanent deficit lead to an ever-increasing deficit?

2 Why will a permanent debt-financed deficit lead to inflation?

3 How might a deficit be a burden on future generations?

4 According to the Ricardian equivalence proposition, why will there be no increase in the real interest rate when government debt finances government spending?

PROBLEMS

1 Table 33.3 gives information about the price level and the government budget in an economy. Based on the information given, complete the table by computing for each year: the surplus or deficit (and noting which by sign; negative for deficit), the government debt, real government debt and the real surplus or deficit (and noting which by sign; negative for deficit).

Table 33.3

Year	Price level	Taxes	Gov't spending	Surplus/ deficit	Gov't debt	Real gov't debt	Real surplus/ deficit
1	1.00	100	120	−20	20	20	−20
2	1.11	110	140				
3	1.20	120	130				
4	1.30	130	135				
5	1.52	140	145				

2 Table 33.4 gives the path of unemployment in an economy over time. In this economy, the natural rate of unemployment is 7 per cent. There is no inflation. When unemployment is at its natural rate, both government spending and taxes are 25 per cent of GDP. Furthermore, if unemployment increases by 1 per cent, government spending increases by 0.75 per cent of real GDP and taxes fall by 1 per cent of real GDP. The effects are symmetric if unemployment decreases. Complete the table by computing the values for taxes, government spending and the actual deficit.

Table 33.4

Year	Unemployment rate (per cent)	Government spending (per cent of real GDP)	Taxes (per cent of real GDP)	Deficit (per cent of real GDP)
1	6			
2	7			
3	7			
4	9			
5	10			
6	8			
7	6			

3 Using a graph of the demand for and supply of loans and a graph of investment demand, show the effect on investment of a decision to finance government spending by way of debt financing if
a the Ricardian equivalence proposition is true.
b the Ricardian equivalence proposition is false and households do not increase saving.

DATA QUESTIONS

The Chancellor's First Budget
In his first budget, the Chancellor of the Exchequer said, 'The overriding need is to place the public finances on a sound footing ... business can plan ahead with confidence only if it knows that government borrowing is under control' .... He said that the measures announced would cut PSBR from just under £50 billion this year to about £38 billion next year. 'It should eliminate borrowing to finance current spending by 1997–8 and eliminate government borrowing entirely by the end of the decade'.

Source: Chancellor's budget speech, 30 November 1993.

1 Explain what is meant by 'PSBR'.
2 Explain how the government finances its borrowing.
3 Is this government borrowing imposing a burden which today's students will have to bear?

ANSWERS

CONCEPT REVIEW

1 surplus; deficit; balanced budget; debt
2 positively
3 real; smaller
4 money; debt
5 equivalence
6 reducing expenditure; increasing revenue
7 tax rate; tax base; tax revenue
8 Laffer

TRUE OR FALSE

1 **F** Deficit = Expenditure – Revenue in current year.
2 **T** Increased revenue will reduce deficit, assuming expenditure is unchanged.
3 **T** See text discussion.
4 **F** It rises because government income falls and spending rises.
5 **T** If nominal is unchanged despite price rise, then real has increased.
6 **F** Only if inflation is positive.
7 **F** It could sell bonds to the Bank of England – money financing.
8 **F** No change in money supply because money flows from households to government which is spent and returns to economy.
9 **T** Money financing is inflationary.
10 **F** Depends on whether they are money or bond financed, and on whether they have any impact on the economy.
11 **T** If interest rates do not rise, then no crowding out.
12 **T** Definition.
13 **F** Extremely high tax rates may discourage work and encourage tax fiddling.
14 **F** Laffer curve shows relationship between tax rates and revenue.

MULTIPLE-CHOICE

1 b Debt = Sum of previous deficits – Previous surpluses.

2 d This is increase in revenue.

3 b Fall in real GDP means fall in tax revenue and rise in unemployment leading to a rise in transfer payments.

4 c Because there will be higher deficits during recessions.

5 a See text discussion.

6 a Real debt in year 2 = (£198 billion/110) × 100 = £180 billion – no change in real debt.

7 d Real debt has fallen because money has lost some of its value.

8 c Definition.

9 b Under money financing, interest is paid to the Bank of England – owned by the government.

10 b Borrowing may cause rise in rate of interest and so cut investment.

11 c Because people save more so they can pay for higher taxes in the future to pay higher interest on debt.

12 a Increase in revenue from higher compliance and wider tax base exceeds loss from higher rate.

13 e Definition.

14 b Here quantity demanded = quantity supplied.

15 c Quantity demanded rises by £200 billion leading to new equilibrium at £1,100 billion.

16 b If Ricardian equivalence holds, then rise in quantity supplied = rise in quantity demanded, therefore same interest rate.

SHORT ANSWER

1 The government pays interest on all of the government debt. Whenever the government has a budget deficit, government debt increases and thus interest payments will increase. This increase in interest payments means that the size of the deficit will be larger next year and thus the debt and interest payments will increase still further. Through this process, the interest payment increases each year and thus adds more to the deficit each succeeding year.

2 A permanent debt-financed deficit will lead to inflation, since the deficit will be ever-increasing as a result of ever-increasing interest payments on government debt (see Question 1). There will be a point beyond which the government cannot or will not continue debt financing the deficit and will turn to money financing. This of course will cause inflation. Since people who buy bonds

know this they will expect higher inflation in the future and the nominal rate of interest will be driven up. This will cause people to reduce their demand for money. The reduction in the demand for money will lead to an increase in the demand for goods and will thus cause inflation now.

3 A deficit will be a burden on future generations to the extent that government debt is owned by foreigners. Future generations will have to pay the higher interest payments on the increased government debt, but to the extent that they also receive those interest payments there is no net burden. However, if part of the debt is owned by foreigners, domestic taxpayers will make all the interest payments but only receive part. The part that is received by foreigners will be a net burden. An additional burden to future generations would occur if the deficit causes real interest rates to rise and thus crowds out investment. In this case, the capital stock inherited by future generations will be less than it would otherwise have been.

4 According to the Ricardian equivalence principle, when the government decides to debt finance its spending, people recognize that taxes must rise in the future in order to cover the additional spending and higher interest payments. In order to be able to pay these higher taxes, they will cut back on consumption and increase saving by enough to meet those future tax liabilities. The increase in saving necessary will be equal to the increase in government spending. An increase in saving is an increase in the supply of loans and an increase in the deficit (government spending) is an increase in the demand for loans. Since the demand for and supply of loans both increase by the same amount, the real interest rate is unchanged.

PROBLEMS

1 Completed Table 33.3 is shown here as Table 33.5. The surplus or deficit is computed as the difference between taxes and government spending. A deficit is a negative value for this difference. Government debt is the sum of all the deficits up to that point in time minus the sum of all the surpluses up to that point in time. Real government debt is actual (nominal) government debt divided by the price level. The real deficit or surplus is the negative of real government debt in the current year minus real government debt in the previous year. Once again, a negative difference indicates a real deficit.

2 Completed Table 33.4 is shown here as Table 33.6. In year 1, unemployment is 1 per cent below the natural rate of 7 per cent, so that government spending falls below 25 per cent by 0.75 per cent to 24.25 per cent, while taxes rise above 25 per cent by 1 per cent to 26 per cent. This creates a surplus of +1.75 per cent of real GDP. Other calculations are similar.

Table 33.5

Year	Price level	Taxes	Gov't spending	Surplus/ deficit	Gov't debt	Real gov't debt	Real surplus/ deficit
1	1.00	100	120	−20	20	20	−20
2	1.11	110	140	−30	50	45	−25
3	1.20	120	130	−10	60	50	−5
4	1.30	130	135	−5	65	50	0
5	1.52	140	145	−5	70	46	+4

Table 33.6

Year	Unemployment rate (per cent)	Government spending (per cent of real GDP)	Taxes (per cent of real GDP)	Deficit (per cent of real GDP)
1	6	24.25	26	+1.75
2	7	25.00	25	0
3	7	25.00	25	0
4	9	26.50	23	−3.50
5	10	27.25	24	−5.25
6	8	25.75	24	−1.75
7	6	24.25	26	+1.75

3 a The effect is shown in Fig. 33.1. Before the decision, the market for loans is in equilibrium at the intersection of the D_0 and S_0 curves. This yields a real interest rate of r_0, which implies that investment is I_0. Once the government decides on debt financing, the demand for loans curve increases from D_0 to D_1. If the Ricardian equivalence proposition is true, the supply of loans curve increases (horizontally) by the same amount: S_0 shifts to S_1. Since the shifts are the same amount, the real interest rate remains at r_0 and thus investment spending remains at I_0. There is no crowding out.

b If, however, households do not increase their saving in response to the increase in the deficit, the demand curve for loans will shift from D_0 to D_1 but the supply of loans curve will remain at S_0. This means that the equilibrium real interest rate will rise to r_1 and that investment will fall from I_0 to I_1. Thus, investment is crowded out.

DATA QUESTIONS

1 'PSBR' is the acronym for 'public sector borrowing requirement' and it results when the public sector spends more than it receives in income.

2 The government finances its borrowing mainly by selling bonds in one of two ways. It can sell bonds to the Bank of England. This is called money financing since it leads to an increase in the money supply. The advan-

Figure 33.1

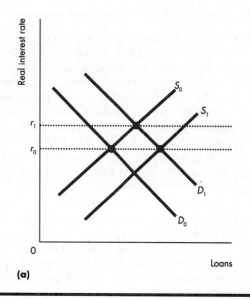

(a)

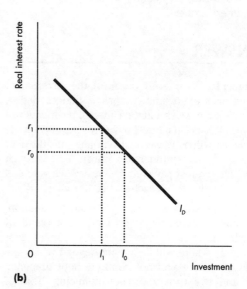

(b)

tage for the government is that the government pays interest to the Bank of England – which it owns. The other way is to sell bonds to the public – called debt financing. This does not increase the money supply but it does lead to an increase in government debt which will have to be repaid.

3 Whether today's students will face a burden depends on several factors. Future standards of living depend on the capacity of the economy to produce goods and services. If the debt means higher interest rates and crowding out, they may be poorer. But if crowding out does not occur and if the money is used for productive investment they may be better off because they will benefit from such things as better communications, and higher standards of health and education.

In narrow financial terms there will be winners and losers. Future generations will face a higher government debt, but the money will also be owed to other citizens, so there will be a redistribution effect.

Chapter 34 · Trading with the World

Trading with the World

Chapter In Perspective, Text Pages 953–978

Why do nations trade? What is the nature of the gains that make trade worth while? What determines which goods a country will import and which it will export? In this chapter we also turn to more difficult issues such as: if there are significant gains to free trade, why do countries frequently restrict imports? What are the effects of a tariff or a quota or some other trade restriction?

Helpful Hints

1 It may be useful to recall the discussion in Chapter 3 of opportunity cost, comparative advantage and gains from trade. The current chapter applies the fundamental concepts of opportunity cost and comparative advantage to the problem of trade between nations. The basic principles are the same whether we are talking about trade between individuals in the same country or between individuals in different countries.

Many students seem confused by the concept of comparative advantage, partially because they implicitly conceive of absolute advantage as the sole reason for trade. A country has an absolute advantage if it can produce all goods using less inputs than another country. However, such a country can still gain from trade if it concentrates its resources where it is *relatively* more efficient.

2 In addition to the gains from trade, this chapter also discusses the economic effects of trade restrictions. One of the important things we learn is that the economic effects of a tariff and a quota are similar.

A voluntary export restraint (VER) is also a quota but imposed by the exporting country rather than the importing country. All these trade restrictions raise the domestic price of the imported good, and reduce the volume and value of imports. They will also reduce the value of exports by the same amount as the reduction in the value of imports. The increase in price that results from each of these trade restrictions produces a gap between the domestic price of the imported good and the foreign supply price of the good. The difference between the alternative trade restrictions lies in which party captures this excess. In the case of a tariff, the government receives the tariff revenue. In the case of a quota imposed by the importing country, domestic importers who have been awarded a licence to import capture this excess through increased profit. When a VER is imposed, the excess is captured by foreign exporters who have been awarded licences to export by their government.

3 The major point of this chapter is that the gains from free trade can be considerable. Why then do countries have such a strong tendency to impose trade restrictions? The key is that while free trade creates overall benefits to the economy as a whole, there are both winners and losers. The winners gain more in total than the losers lose, but the latter tend to be concentrated in a few industries. We are therefore not surprised that free trade will be resisted by some acting on the basis of rational self-interest. Even though only a small minority benefit from any given trade restriction while the overwhelming majority will be hurt, we are not surprised to see trade restrictions implemented. The reason is that the cost of a given trade restriction to each of the many is individually quite small while the benefit to each of the few will be individually large. Thus, the few will have a significant incentive to see that restriction takes place while the many will have little incentive to expend time and energy in resisting trade restriction.

Key Figures

Figure 34.1 UK Exports and Imports, 1992, text page 955

This shows the major types of goods and services that the United Kingdom imports and exports.

Figure 34.6 International Trade in Cars, text page 960

The price at which a good trades internationally and the quantity traded are determined by the international market for the good. This figure illustrates a hypothetical international market for cars using the example of Utopia and Erewhon. Erewhon has a comparative advantage in the production of cars and so supplies cars to the world market. At higher prices, Erewhon is willing to supply more cars although it must receive at least 1 tonne of wheat (its opportunity cost of a car) to be willing to produce. The supply curve in the figure gives Erewhon's export supply of cars. Similarly, the demand curve in the figure gives Utopia's import demand for cars. It shows that as the price of a car falls, the quantity of cars that Utopia wants to import increases although it will not buy any cars at a price above 9 tonnes of wheat (its opportunity cost of a car). The equilibrium price when trade takes place is at the intersection of these two curves. The price of a car (under free trade) is 3 tonnes of wheat, and 4 million cars per year are imported by Utopia from Erewhon.

Figure 34.7 Expanding Consumption Possibilities, text page 962

This clearly illustrates the gains from trade experienced by Utopia and Erewhon. Without trade, each country consumes what it produces. Its consumption is constrained by the production possibility frontier. The gain from trade for each country is that, with trade, while production is constrained by the production possibility frontier, consumption can exceed that frontier. Consumption is constrained only by the consumption possibility curve which (except for a single point) lies beyond the production possibility curve. Part (a) shows the situation for Utopia. Without trade, Utopia produces and consumes at point *a*: 8 million cars and 15 million tonnes of wheat. With trade (at 1 car trading for 3 tonnes of wheat), Utopia produces at point *b*: 5 million cars and 30 million tonnes of wheat. But, because of trade, consumption can be different. Indeed, with trade, Utopia consumes at point *c*: 9 million cars and 18 million tonnes of wheat. This is 1 million more cars and 3 million more tonnes of wheat than were consumed without trade (at point *a*). This additional consumption is the gain from trade for Utopia. A similar analysis in part (b) illustrates that Erewhon also gains from trade.

Figure 34.8 The Effects of a Tariff, text page 966

The effects of a tariff on the price of a good and the quantity traded are shown in this figure by using the Utopia and Erewhon example of trade in cars. Utopia imposes a tariff of £4,000 per car on cars imported from Erewhon. This shifts the export supply curve upward by £4,000 since the price must include the supply price received by Erewhon and the tariff. Thus the price of a car in Utopia increases from £3,000 to £6,000 and the quantity of cars traded falls to 2 million per year. The total revenue from the tariff (which is received by the government of Utopia) is £8,000 million: £4,000 per car times 2 million cars. Although this figure does not show it directly, Utopia's wheat exports will also decrease because Erewhon's income from export of cars has fallen.

Figure 34.9 The Effects of a Quota, text page 971

This illustrates the effects of a quota on domestic price and quantity traded again using the Utopia and Erewhon example. Utopia imposes a quota of 2 million cars per year. This restriction is indicated in the graph by a vertical line at 2 million cars. This becomes the effective supply curve for the purpose of determining the price, which turns out to be £6,000. The quantity traded, of course, is 2 million cars per year, the quota limit. At 2 million cars, Erewhon is willing to supply cars for £2,000 each. This £4,000 per car difference between the selling price and the price received by the exporter is captured by whoever has the import rights.

SELF-TEXT

CONCEPT REVIEW

1 The goods and services purchased from people in foreign countries are called _____. The goods and services sold to people in foreign countries are called _____. The value of exports minus the value of imports is called the _____ of _____ .

2 A country is said to have a(n) _____ _____ in the production of a good if it can produce that good at a lower opportunity cost than any other country. A country is said to have a(n) _____ _____ if for all goods its output per unit of inputs is higher than any other country.

3 The restriction of international trade is called _____ . A tax imposed by the importing country on an imported good is called a(n) _____ . The result of imposing such a tax is to _____ the price that consumers in the importing country pay and _____ the quantity traded. When such a tax is imposed the tax revenue is received by the _____ .

4 A restriction that specifies a limit on the quantity of a particular good that can be imported is called a(n) _____ . The result of such a limit is to _____ the price that consumers in the importing country pay. The extra revenue from such a limit is received by the _____ .

5 An agreement between two governments in which the government of the exporting country agrees to restrict the quantity of its exports to the importing country is called a(n) _____ _____ _____ . Such an agreement will _____ the price that consumers in the importing country pay for the good.

TRUE OR FALSE

1 When a UK citizen stays in a hotel in France, the United Kingdom is exporting a service.

2 If there are two countries, A and B, and two goods, x and y, and country A has a comparative advantage in the production of x, then country B must have a comparative advantage in the production of y.

3 If country A must give up 3 units of y to produce 1 unit of x and B must give up 4 units of y to produce 1 unit of x, then A has a comparative advantage in the production of x.

4 If countries specialize in goods for which they have a comparative advantage, then some countries will gain and others will lose but the gains will be larger than the losses.

5 Trading according to comparative advantage allows all trading countries to consume outside their production possibility frontier.

6 If a country has an absolute advantage, it will not benefit from trade.

7 Countries may exchange similar goods for each other because of economies of scale in the face of diversified tastes.

8 When a government imposes tariffs, it is increasing its country's gain from trade.

9 A tariff on a good will raise its price and reduce the quantity traded.

10 A tariff not only reduces the total value of imports but also reduces the total value of exports.

11 A quota will cause the price of the imported good to fall.

12 The 'excess revenue' created by a voluntary export restraint is captured by the exporter.

13 Elected governments are likely to be slow to reduce trade restrictions even though the gains would be much larger than the losses because there would be many fewer losers than gainers.

MULTIPLE-CHOICE

1 Suppose there are two countries, A and B, producing two goods, x and y. Country A has a comparative advantage in the production of good x if less
   a of good y must be given up to produce one unit of x than in country B.
   b labour is required to produce one unit of x than in country B.
   c capital is required to produce one unit of x than in country B.
   d labour and capital are required to produce one unit of x than in country B.
   e of good x must be given up to produce one unit of y than in country B.

2 Suppose there are two countries, A and B, producing two goods, x and y, and that country A has a comparative advantage in the production of x. If the countries trade, the price of x in terms of y will be
   a greater than the opportunity cost of x in country A and less than the opportunity cost of x in country B.
   b less than the opportunity cost of x in country A and greater than the opportunity cost of x in country B.
   c greater than the opportunity cost of x in both countries.
   d less than the opportunity cost of x in both countries.
   e dependent on the relative size of each economy.

3 International trade according to comparative advantage allows each country to consume
   a more of the goods it exports but less of the goods it imports than without trade.
   b more of the goods it imports but less of the goods it exports than without trade.
   c more of both goods it exports and goods it imports than without trade.
   d less of both goods it exports and goods it imports than without trade.
   e either **a** or **b**; it depends on the price of the goods.

4 In country A, it requires one unit of capital and one unit of labour to produce a unit of x and it requires two units of capital and two units of labour to produce a unit of y. What is the opportunity cost of good x?

   a the price of a unit of capital plus the price of a unit of labour
   b one unit of capital and one unit of labour
   c two units of capital and two units of labour
   d one half unit of y
   e two units of y

5 If country A has an absolute advantage in the production of everything,
   a no trade will take place because country A will have a comparative advantage in everything.
   b no trade will take place because no country will have a comparative advantage in anything.
   c trade will probably take place and all countries will gain.
   d trade will probably take place but country A will not gain.
   e trade will probably take place but country A will be the only one to gain.

6 The imposition of a tariff on imported goods will increase the price consumers pay for imported goods and
   a reduce the volume of imports and the volume of exports.
   b reduce the volume of imports and increase the volume of exports.
   c reduce the volume of imports and leave the volume of exports unchanged.
   d will not affect either the volume of imports or the volume of exports.
   e increase the volume of imports but decrease the volume of exports.

7 Who benefits from a tariff on good x?
   a domestic consumers of good x
   b domestic producers of good x
   c foreign consumers of good x
   d foreign producers of good x
   e no one

8 A tariff on good x which is imported by country A will cause the
   a demand curve for x in country A to shift upward.
   b demand curve for x in country A to shift downward.
   c supply curve of x in country A to shift upward.
   d supply curve of x in country A to shift downward.
   e demand and supply curves of x in country A to shift upward.

9 Country A and country B are currently engaging in free trade. Country A imports good x from country B and exports y to B. If country A imposes a tariff on x, country A's x-producing industry will

 a expand and its y-producing industry will contract.
 b expand and its y-producing industry will expand.
 c contract and its y-producing industry will contract.
 d contract and its y-producing industry will expand.
 e expand and its y-producing industry will be unchanged.

10 Country A and country B are currently engaging in free trade. Country A imports good x from country B and exports y to B. If country A imposes a quota on x, country A's x-producing industry will

 a expand and its y-producing industry will contract.
 b expand and its y-producing industry will expand.
 c contract and its y-producing industry will contract.
 d contract and its y-producing industry will expand.
 e expand and its y-producing industry will be unchanged.

11 When a tariff is imposed, the gap between the domestic price and the export price is captured by

 a consumers in the importing country.
 b the person with the right to import the good.
 c the domestic producers of the good.
 d foreign exporters.
 b the government of the importing country.

12 When a quota is imposed, the gap between the domestic price and the export price is captured by

 a consumers in the importing country.
 b the domestic producers of the good.
 c the government of the importing country.
 d foreign exporters.
 e the person with the right to import the good.

13 When a voluntary export restraint agreement is reached, the gap between the domestic price and the export price is captured by

 a consumers in the importing country.
 b the person with the right to import the good.
 c the government of the importing country.
 d foreign exporters.
 e the domestic producers of the good.

14 Country A imports good x from country B and exports y to B. Which of the following is a reason why country A might prefer arranging a voluntary export restraint rather than a quota on x?

 a So as not to reduce the volume of its own exports of y.
 b To prevent country B from retaliating by restricting country A's exports.
 c To keep the domestic price of x low.
 d To increase government revenue.
 e This will help domestic producers more than the quota.

15 If we import more than we export, then

 a we are going to be unable to buy as many foreign goods as we desire.
 b we will make loans to foreigners to enable them to buy our goods.
 c we will have to finance the difference by borrowing from foreigners.
 d our patterns of trade, including the direction of exports and imports, will be different than if exports equal imports.
 e both **c** and **d**.

SHORT ANSWER

1 What is meant by comparative advantage?

2 How is it that both parties involved in trade can gain?

3 How does a tariff on a particular imported good affect the domestic price of the good, the export price, the quantity imported and the quantity of the good produced domestically?

4 How does a tariff on imports affect the exports of the country?

5 How does a quota on a particular imported good affect the domestic price of the good, the export price, the quantity imported and the quantity of the good produced domestically?

6 Why might a government prefer a quota to a tariff?

PROBLEMS

1 Consider a simple world in which there are two countries, Atlantis and Beltran, each producing two goods, food and cloth. The production possibility frontier for each country is given in Table 34.1.

   a Assuming a constant opportunity cost in each country, fill in the rest of the table.

   b What is the opportunity cost in Atlantis of food? of cloth?

   c What is the opportunity cost in Beltran of food? of cloth?

   d Draw the production possibility frontiers on separate graphs.

Table 34.1

Atlantis		Beltran	
Food (units)	Cloth (units)	Food (units)	Cloth (units)
0	500	0	800
200	400	100	600
400		200	
600		300	
800		400	
1,000			

2 Suppose that Atlantis and Beltran engage in trade.

   a In which good will each country specialize?

   b If 1 unit of food trades for 1 unit of cloth, what will happen to the production of each good in each country?

   c If 1 unit of food trades for 1 unit of cloth, draw the consumption possibility frontiers for each country on the corresponding graph from Problem 1d.

   d Before trade, if Atlantis consumed 600 units of food, the most cloth it could consume was 200 units. After trade, how many units of cloth can be consumed if 600 units of food are consumed?

3 Figure 34.1 gives the import demand curve for shirts for country *A*, labelled *D*, and the export supply curve of shirts for country *B*, labelled *S*.

   a What is the price of a shirt under free trade?

   b How many shirts will be imported by country *A*?

Figure 34.1

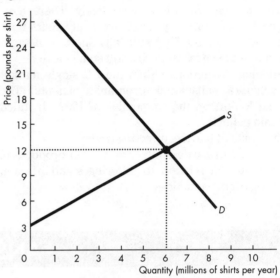

4 Suppose the shirtmakers in country *A* (of Problem 3) are concerned about foreign competition and so the government of country *A* imposes a tariff of £9 per shirt.

   a What will happen to the price of a shirt in country *A*?

   b What is the price the exporter will actually receive?

   c How many shirts will be imported by country *A*?

   d What is the revenue from the tariff? Who captures it?

5 Suppose that instead of a tariff, country *A* imposes a quota of 4 million shirts per year.

   a What will be the price of a shirt in country *A*?

   b What price will the exporter actually receive?

   c How many shirts will be imported by country *A*?

   d What is the difference between the total amount paid by consumers and the total amount received by exporters – the 'excess profit'? Who captures it?

DATA QUESTIONS

A Single European Market

The objective of a 'common' market goes back to the 1957 Treaty of Rome which established the European

Community. The treaty envisaged the creation of a single integrated internal market where people, goods, services and capital could move freely. There have been no intra-Community tariffs for many years now. But the EC (now the EU) still falls short of being a single market because there are still some barriers.

Removing restrictions within the EU single market will generate substantial economic benefits. The Cecchini Report on the economics of 1992 identified four main benefits:
- the removal of barriers affecting trade,
- the removal of barriers affecting overall production, for example in relation to differing standards and other restrictive practices,

- fuller exploitation of economies of scale, and
- gains from intensified competition.

Source: adapted from *Economic Progress Report*, October 1988. Reproduced with the permission of the Controller of Her Majesty's Stationery Office.

1 Explain how the removal of barriers affecting trade will benefit EU citizens.

2 How do differing barriers and other restrictive practices cause barriers to trade?

3 How would the single market allow exploitation of economies of scale?

ANSWERS

CONCEPT REVIEW

1 imports; exports; balance; trade

2 comparative advantage; absolute advantage

3 protectionism; tariff; increase; decrease; government

4 quota; raise; importer

5 voluntary export restraint; raise

TRUE OR FALSE

1 **F** The United Kingdom is importing (using) service.

2 **T** A's comparative advantage means lower units of y lost per units of x than B, higher units of x lost per unit of y produced than B, hence B has comparative advantage of y.

3 **T** A has lower opportunity cost $(3y < 4y)$ = lost y per unit of gained y.

4 **F** All countries gain from specialization and trade, though some groups within countries lose.

5 **T** Countries will specialize and trade to consume outside PPF.

6 **F** If comparative advantage exists, so do gains from trade.

7 **T** Diversified tastes mean that many products are demanded. These can be provided efficiently only if there is specialization and trade.

8 **F** Trade restrictions reduce gains from trade.

9 **T** A tariff leads to shift in export supply curve leading to increase in price and fall in quantity.

10 **T** Since a tariff reduces imports it will reduce incomes in other countries and so foreigners' ability to import will fall.

11 **F** Quota means fall in supply and so rise in price.

12 **T** Exporter owns right to sell good, so captures excess revenue.

13 **T** They would be slow because losers' losses are individually much greater than winners' gains.

MULTIPLE-CHOICE

1 **a** Opportunity cost will be less.

2 **a** Ignoring taxes and so on, prices will be in between differing opportunity costs.

3 **c** Consumption possibilities frontier is outside PPF.

4 **d** Inputs to make one x could make $\frac{1}{2} y$.

5 **c** All countries will gain if they specialize where they have *comparative* advantage.

6 **a** It will reduce volume of imports because their price has increased, it will reduce exports since foreigners' incomes will fall and so they will import less.

7 **b** Domestic producers will benefit from higher price.

8 **c** Tariff leads to rise in domestic price = export price + tariff, leading to upward shift of supply curve.

9 **a** Tariff will reduce imports of x so its x-producing industry will expand; but y industry will contract since foreigners will have less money to buy y.

10 a Quota will reduce imports of x so domestic industry will benefit from higher price, but y industry will suffer because foreigners will have less money to buy y.

11 e Government collects tariff revenue = import price – export price.

12 e Under a quota system, domestic government allocates the licence to import.

13 d Because they have the right to export.

14 b Under a VER, exporting country gains excess revenue so is less likely to retaliate.

15 c Since imports have to be paid for, in long run country has to borrow from foreigners to get foreign exchange to pay for imports.

SHORT ANSWER

1 A country is said to have a comparative advantage in the production of some good if it can produce that good at a lower opportunity cost than any other country.

2 In order for two potential trading partners to be willing to trade, they must have different comparative advantages, that is, different opportunity costs. If they do, then they will trade and both parties will gain. If the parties do not trade, they will each face their own opportunity costs. A price at which trade takes place must be somewhere between the opportunity costs of the two traders. This means that the party with the lower opportunity cost of the good in question will gain because it will receive a price above its opportunity cost. Similarly, the party with the higher opportunity cost will gain because it will pay a price below its opportunity cost.

3 A tariff on an imported good will raise its price to domestic consumers as the export supply curve shifts upward. The export price is determined by the original export supply curve. As the domestic price of the good rises, the quantity of the good demanded falls and thus the relevant point on the original export supply curve is at a lower quantity and a lower export price. This lower quantity means that the quantity imported falls. The rise in the domestic price will also lead to an increase in the quantity of the good supplied domestically.

4 When country A imposes a tariff on its imports of good x, not only does the volume of imports shrink but the volume of exports of y to country B will also shrink by the same amount. Thus a balance of trade is maintained. As indicated in the answer to Question 3, the export price of good x falls when a tariff is imposed. This fall in the price received by the exporter means that the price of imports in the foreign country has risen, that is, if the amount of y that country B gets for an x has fallen, the quantity of x that must be given up to obtain a y has increased. This implies that the quantity of y (A's export) demanded by country B will fall and thus A's exports decline.

5 The effect of a quota on the domestic price of the good, the export price, the quantity imported and the quantity of the good produced domestically is exactly the same as the effects of a tariff discussed in the answer to Question 3. The only difference is that the increase in the domestic price here is not the result of a vertical shift in the export supply curve but the result of the fact that the quota forces a vertical effective export supply curve at the quota amount.

6 The effects of tariffs and quotas on prices and quantities have been discussed in Answers 3 and 5. The difference is that the excess revenue raised by a tariff is captured by the govern-ment whereas the excess revenue raised by a quota is captured by those persons who have been given the right to import by the government. In either case the government is in a position to benefit. It may prefer to use quotas in order to reward political supporters by giving them rights to import and thus allowing them to capture large profits. Second, quotas give the government more precise control over the quantity of imports. Also, it is politically easier to impose a quota than a tariff.

PROBLEMS

1 a Completed Table 34.1 is shown here as Table 34.2. The values in the table are calculated using the opportunity cost of each good in each country (see **b** and **c**).

b In order to increase the output (consumption) of food by 200 units, cloth production (consumption) falls by 100 units in Atlantis. Thus the opportunity cost of a unit of food is $1/2$ unit of cloth. This opportunity cost is constant (as are all others in this problem, for simplicity). Similarly, the opportunity cost of cloth in Atlantis is 2 units of food.

c In Beltran a 100 unit increase in the production (consumption) of food requires a reduction in the output (consumption) of cloth of 200 units. Thus the opportunity cost of food is 2 units of cloth. Similarly the opportunity cost of cloth in Beltran is $1/2$ unit of food.

d Figure 34.2 parts (a) and (b) illustrate the production possibility frontiers for Atlantis and Beltran, respectively (labelled PPF_A and PPF_B). The rest of the diagram is discussed in Problem 2.

2 a Since (from Problem 1b and c) we see that Atlantis has a lower opportunity cost ($1/2$ unit of cloth) in the production of food, Atlantis will specialize in the production of food. Beltran, with the lower opportunity cost for cloth ($1/2$ unit of food) will specialize in cloth production.

Figure 34.2

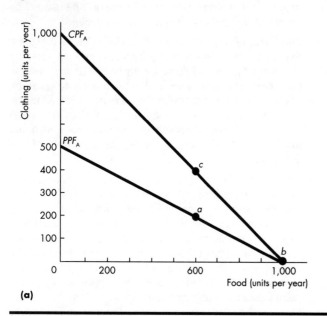

(a)

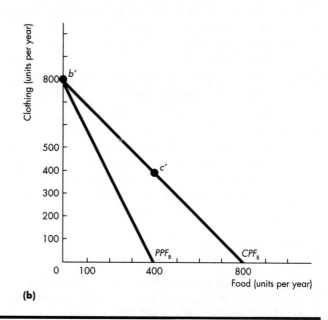

(b)

Table 34.2

Atlantis		Beltran	
Food (units)	Cloth (units)	Food (units)	Cloth (units)
0	500	0	800
200	400	100	600
400	300	200	400
600	200	300	200
800	100	400	0
1,000	0	–	–

b Each country will want to produce every unit of the good in which it specializes as long as the amount it receives in trade exceeds its opportunity cost. For Atlantis, the opportunity cost of a unit of food is $1/2$ unit of cloth but it can obtain 1 unit of cloth in trade. Since the opportunity cost is constant (in this simple example), Atlantis will totally specialize by producing all of the food it can: 1,000 units per year (point *b* in Fig. 34.2a). Similarly, in Beltran, the opportunity cost of a unit of cloth is $1/2$ unit of food but a unit of cloth will trade for 1 unit of food. Since the opportunity cost is constant, Beltran will totally specialize in the production of cloth and will produce 800 units per year (point *b'* in Figure 34.2b).

c The consumption possibility frontiers for Atlantis and Beltran (labelled CPF_A and CPF_B) are illustrated in Fig. 34.2, parts (a) and (b), respectively. These frontiers are straight lines that indicate all the combinations of food and cloth that can be consumed with trade. The position and slope of the consumption possibility frontier for an economy depends on the terms of trade between the goods and the production point of the economy. The consumption possibility frontier for Atlantis (CPF_A), for example, is obtained by starting at point *b* on PPF_A, the production point, and examining possible trades. For example, if Atlantis traded the 400 units of the food it produces for 400 units of cloth, it would be able to consume 600 units of food (1,000 units produced minus 400 units traded) and 400 units of cloth, which is represented by point *c*.

d If Atlantis consumes 600 units of food, trade allows consumption of cloth to be 400 units, 200 units more than possible without trade. The maximum amount of cloth that can be consumed without trade is given by the production possibility frontier. If food consumption is 600 units, this is indicated by point *a* on PPF_A. The maximum amount of cloth consumption for any level of food consumption with trade is given by the consumption possibility frontier. If food consumption is 600 units, this is indicated by point *c* on CPF_A.

3 a The price of a shirt under free trade will occur at the intersection of country *A*'s import demand curve for shirts and country *B*'s export supply curve of shirts. This occurs at a price of £12 per shirt.

b Country *A* will import 6 million shirts per year.

4 a The effect of the £9 per shirt tariff is to shift the export supply curve (*S*) upward by £9. This is shown as a shift from *S* to *S'* in Fig. 34.3. The price is now determined by the intersection of the *D* curve (which is unaffected by the tariff) and the *S'* curve. The new price of a shirt is £18.

b Of this £18, £9 is the tariff, so the exporter receives only the remaining £9.

c Country *A* will now import only 4 million shirts per year.

d The tariff revenue is £9 (the tariff per shirt) times 4 million (the number of shirts imported), which is £36 million. This money is received by the government of country *A*.

Figure 34.3

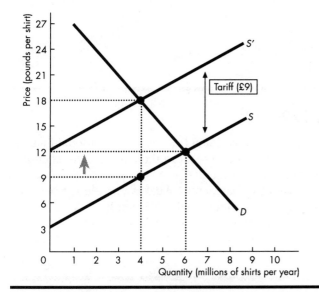

5 a The quota restricts the quantity that can be imported to 4 million shirts per year regardless of the price and is represented by a vertical line in Fig. 34.4 (which corresponds to Fig. 34.1). The market for shirts will thus clear at a price of £18 per shirt.

b This £18 price is received by the people who are given the right to import shirts under the quota. The amount received by the exporter is £9, given by the height of the *S* curve at a quantity of 4 million shirts per year.

c Country *A* will import 4 million shirts per year, the quota limit.

d The 'excess profit' is £9 per shirt (the £18 received by the importer minus the £9 received by the exporter) times 4 million shirts, which is £36 million. This is captured by the importers who have been rewarded by the government of country *A* since they have been given the right to import under the quota. This is essentially a right to make an 'excess profit'.

Figure 34.4

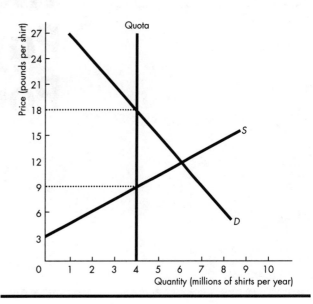

DATA QUESTIONS

1 The removal of barriers will benefit EU citizens in a number of ways. It will allow a better allocation of resources as suggested by the principle of comparative advantage. It will allow firms and individuals to benefit from large-scale production. And it will encourage competition which tends to encourage innovation, to cut costs and to give consumers greater choice.

2 All countries impose restrictions on production. No country allows cars to be sold which have no brakes. Similarly, it is illegal to produce or sell foods which are unfit for consumption. However, some restrictions have the effect of reducing competition. An example is German beer, which for centuries has imposed strict conditions on what ingredients could be used. These conditions benefited consumers who were guaranteed a 'pure' product. However, they also kept out foreign beers, because no other country had similar standards. They therefore constituted barriers to trade. There are thousands of similar barriers.

3 Economies of scale occur as a result of large-scale production. But firms can produce on a large scale only if there is a large market. The single market will create a market of nearly 350 million people – large enough in most cases for economies of scale to be exploited by several firms.

Chapter 35

The Balance of Payments and the Pound

Chapter In Perspective, Text Pages 979–1011

The world is becoming increasingly more interrelated, through both international trade and international finance. In Chapter 34 we explored international trade. In this chapter we continue to explore the international economy by further exploring international finance, and its relation to international trade.

What determines the value of the balance of trade and the balance of payments? What is the relation between the balance of trade and international lending or borrowing? Does a government budget deficit have any effect on the balance of trade? What role does the value of the pound have in determining the balance of trade? Or is the relationship in the opposite direction – does the balance of trade determine the value of the pound? These are some of the basic questions addressed in this chapter.

Helpful Hints

1 The previous chapter demonstrated the gains from trade between countries. Indeed, as noted in Chapter 3, these are the same gains that result from trade within countries as well. However, there is an important difference between trade within a single country and trade between countries. When individuals in the same country engage in trade, they use the same currency and so trade is straightforward. On the other hand, international trade is complicated by the fact that individuals in different countries use different currencies. The person selling the good from Japan will want payment to be in Japanese yen, but the person buying the good in the United Kingdom will probably be holding only UK pounds. This problem complicates trade between individuals in different countries. This chapter addresses this complication by looking at the balance of payments of a country as well as the relation of the balance of payments to the foreign exchange rate.

2 Note that the balance of payments must balance. Individual accounts in the balance of payments can be in deficit or surplus but that will be offset by a surplus or deficit in another account. It may be useful to reconsider the example of Lorraine given in the text.

3 It is important to understand foreign exchange rates as prices determined by supply and demand. They are prices of currency determined in markets for currency. The demand for UK pounds in the foreign exchange market, for example, is the demand for pound sterling (denominated) assets, including UK money. That demand will arise from the desire on the part of foreigners to purchase UK goods and services (which requires pounds) and the desire on the part of foreigners to purchase UK financial or real assets. The supply of sterling assets is determined by the government and depends on the exchange rate regime.

4 The law of one price is not relevant only in the context of international trade. Anytime there is a discrepancy in the price of the same good in two markets, natural economic forces (unless restricted) will eliminate that discrepancy and thus establish a single price.

5 Purchasing power parity is the manifestation of the law of one price in international trade. Purchasing power parity implies that, as long as exchange rates can adjust, they will adjust so that money (of whatever country) will have the same purchasing power in all countries. This means that if one country experiences inflation while others do not, exchange rates will adjust so that the purchasing power of money will be the same in all countries.

6 Note that it is not the edict of a government which fixes the exchange rate of its currency but rather the willingness of its central bank to supply all of the domestic currency denominated assets that are demanded at the fixed exchange rate.

7 With a fixed exchange rate, a country cannot use monetary policy to control inflation. With a flexible exchange rate a country can insulate itself from external shocks by varying the exchange rate. Within the European Union, the exchange rates of the various countries are largely fixed against each other. One reason is that this gives stability and encourages intra-country trade.

Key Figures and Tables

Figure 35.1 The Balance of Payments, 1968–1993, text page 984

The historical record of the three balance of payments accounts is given here.

Figure 35.2 The Three Balances, text page 987

The relationship between the current account balance and the private surplus and government surplus are shown here. The current account fluctuates with fluctuations in the sum of the private surplus and the government deficit.

Figure 35.5 Three Exchange Rate Regimes, text page 995

This illustrates the effects of an increase in the demand for sterling assets under the three exchange rate regimes. Part (a) shows the effects under a fixed exchange rate regime, part (b) shows the effects under a flexible exchange rate regime and part (c) examines the consequences under a managed exchange rate regime. The difference in the effects arises from the difference in the supply curve of sterling assets under each of the three regimes.

Table 35.4 The Demand for Sterling Assets, text page 994

The demand for sterling assets is characterized in this table. The first part indicates that, just like any other case, the demand for sterling assets obeys the law of demand: the quantity of sterling assets demanded is negatively related to the price of a pound in terms of foreign currency. For example, if the yen price of the pound rises, the quantity of sterling assets demanded declines. The second part of the figure lists several factors that will cause the demand curve for sterling assets to shift.

Table 35.5 The Supply of Sterling Assets, text page 994

This is a counterpart to Table 35.4. It characterizes the other half of the foreign exchange market, the supply of sterling assets. As discussed in the text the slope of the supply curve for sterling assets depends on the type of exchange rate regime. Under a fixed exchange rate regime, the supply curve of sterling assets is horizontal at the fixed exchange rate. Under a flexible exchange rate regime, the supply curve of sterling assets is vertical, and under a managed exchange rate regime, it is positively sloped. The bottom section of the table indicates that the supply curve of sterling assets will shift if the Bank of England changes the money supply or there is a government budget surplus/deficit.

SELF-TEST

CONCEPT REVIEW

1 The international trading, borrowing and lending activities of a country are recorded in its _____ of _____ . It consists of two accounts. The expenditures on imported goods and services and the receipts from the sale of exported goods and services are recorded in the _____ account. The second account is transactions in external _____ and _____ .

2 A country that is borrowing more from the rest of the world than it is lending is called a(n) _____ _____ . A country that is lending more to the rest of the world than it is borrowing is called a(n) _____ _____ .

3 A country that during its entire history has borrowed more from the rest of the world than it has loaned is called a(n) _____ nation.

4 The balance of trade deficit is _____ _____ the sum of the government budget deficit and the private sector deficit.

5 Relative prices are determined by_____ and _____ in the _____ market. Money prices are determined by the value of the _____ _____ given the relative prices.

6 The higher the value of the exchange rate, the _____ is the balance of _____ . The equilibrium value of the exchange rate is determined by the demand for and supply of _____ _____ .

7 If the private sector surplus is constant, a higher government sector deficit means a higher _____ _____ _____ _____ .

8 The market in which the currencies of different countries are exchanged for each other is called the _____ _____ market. The price at which one currency exchanges for another is called the _____ _____ _____ .

9 There are three foreign exchange regimes. In the first of these the value of the exchange rate is pegged by a central bank. This is a(n) _____ exchange rate. A(n) _____ exchange rate is a regime in which the exchange rate is determined by market forces without government intervention. A(n) _____ exchange rate is a regime in which the government does not peg the exchange rate but does intervene in the foreign exchange market in order to influence the price of its currency.

10 Buying low and selling high when there is a difference in price in two places is called _____ . This activity implies the law of _____ _____ which states that any given commodity will be available for a single price.

TRUE OR FALSE

___ **1** The sale of Scotch whisky to the United States will be recorded in the current account of the balance of payments accounts.

___ **2** If there is a current account deficit then there must also be a deficit in external assets and liabilities.

___ **3** The balance of payments accounts must always be equal to zero.

___ **4** If a nation is a net borrower from the rest of the world, it must be a debtor nation.

___ **5** If a country is a net borrower for consumption purposes, this is nothing to worry about.

___ **6** If a country has a large government budget deficit and the private sector deficit is small, the balance of trade deficit will be large.

___ **7** If investment is greater than saving, the private sector has a deficit.

___ **8** Net exports is the same as the current account balance.

___ **9** A larger government sector deficit always leads to a higher current account deficit.

___ **10** Money prices are set by the exchange rate, while relative prices are set on the world market.

___ **11** If the Bank of England wishes to prevent the exchange rate from depreciating in value, the best way is to lower the growth rate of the money supply.

___ **12** The balance of trade is a real variable.

___ **13** The exchange rate is a real variable.

___ **14** If the exchange rate between the UK pound and the Japanese yen changes from 130 yen per pound to 140 yen per pound, the UK pound has appreciated.

___ **15** If the foreign exchange value of the pound is expected to rise, the demand for sterling denominated assets increases.

___ **16** Under a fixed exchange rate regime, the supply curve of assets valued in the currency is horizontal at the pegged exchange rate.

MULTIPLE-CHOICE

1 Which of the following is one of the balance of payments accounts?
a current account
b non-traded goods account
c official reserves account
d net interest account
e public account

2 Suppose the United Kingdom initially has all balance of payments accounts in balance (no surplus or deficit). Then UK firms increase the amount they import from Japan, financing that increase in imports by borrowing from Japan. There will now be a current account
a surplus and a capital account surplus.
b surplus and a capital account deficit.
c deficit and a capital account surplus.
d deficit and a capital account deficit.
e deficit and a capital account balance.

3 The country Plato came into existence at the beginning of year 1. Given the information in Table 35.1, in year 4 Plato is a

a net lender and a creditor nation.
b net lender and a debtor nation.
c net borrower and a creditor nation.
d net borrower and a debtor nation.
e net lender and neither a creditor nor a debtor nation.

Table 35.1

Year	Borrowed from rest of world (billions of pounds)	Loaned to rest of world (billions of pounds)
1	60	20
2	60	40
3	60	60
4	60	80

4 Assuming that Plato is on a floating exchange rate, in which year or years in Table 35.1 did Plato have a current account surplus?
a year 1
b year 2
c years 1, 2 and 3
d years 1 and 2
e year 4 only

5 A nation is currently a net lender and a debtor nation. Which of the following statements applies to that nation?
a It has loaned more capital than it borrowed from abroad this year, but borrowed more than it loaned during its history.
b It has borrowed more capital from abroad than it loaned this year and also borrowed more than it loaned during its history.
c It has loaned more capital than it borrowed from abroad this year and has loaned more than it borrowed during its history.
d Its accounting system must be in error if it shows this nation to be a net lender and a debtor nation at the same time.
e Its debts must be currently growing.

6 The distinction between a debtor or creditor nation and a net borrower or net lender nation depends on
a the distinction between the level of saving in the economy and the saving rate.

b the distinction between the level of saving in the economy and the rate of borrowing.

c the distinction between the stock of investments and the flow of interest payments on those investments.

d the distinction between exports and imports.

e really nothing; they are the same.

7 Suppose that in a country, government purchases of goods and services is £400 billion, taxes (net of transfer payments) is £300 billion, saving is £300 billion and investment is £250 billion. Net exports are in a

a surplus of £150 billion.

b surplus of £50 billion.

c deficit of £150 billion.

d deficit of £50 billion.

e deficit of £250 billion.

8 The country of Question 7 has a government budget

a surplus and a private sector surplus.

b surplus and a private sector deficit.

c deficit and a private sector surplus.

d deficit and a private sector deficit.

e surplus and a private sector balance.

9 The link between the public sector deficit and the private sector surplus can be weak because

a the interest rate will tend to do the adjusting to a change in public deficits rather than the private sector.

b real GDP will tend to do the adjusting to a change in public deficits rather than the private sector.

c the economy may not be operating at close to capacity, and changes in public deficits will not affect the private sector.

d international capital mobility may cut any strong link between changes in the public sector deficit and changes in interest rates.

e the government's deficit is partially caused by borrowing abroad.

10 Under a flexible exchange rate regime, if the foreign exchange value of a country's currency starts to rise, that country's central bank will

a increase the supply of assets denominated in its own currency.

b decrease the supply of assets denominated in its own currency.

c decrease the demand for assets denominated in its own currency.

d do nothing.

e do nothing unless there is a government budget deficit, in which case it will increase the supply of assets denominated in its own currency.

11 Which of the following will shift the supply curve of sterling assets to the right under flexible exchange rates?

a An increase in the demand for foreign goods by UK citizens.

b A decrease in the demand for UK goods by foreigners.

c The pound is expected to appreciate.

d The government has a budget deficit.

e None of the above.

12 Under a managed exchange rate regime, a UK government budget deficit will cause the foreign exchange price of the pound to

a fall and the quantity of sterling assets held to fall.

b fall and the quantity of sterling assets held to rise.

c rise and the quantity of sterling assets held to fall.

d rise and the quantity of sterling assets held to rise.

e stay constant, but the quantity of sterling assets held will rise.

13 Which of the following would cause the pound to depreciate against the yen?

a an increase in UK money supply

b an increase in interest rates in the United Kingdom

c a decrease in interest rates in Japan

d an increase in imports from the United Kingdom purchased by Japan

e a government budget surplus

SHORT ANSWER

1 What are the two balance of payments accounts and what do they each record?

2 What is the relationship between a country's trade deficit, its government budget deficit and its private sector deficit?

3 What is purchasing power parity?

PROBLEMS

1 The international transactions of a country for a given year are reported in Table 35.2.

Table 35.2

Transaction	Amount (billions of pounds)
Exports of goods and services	100
Imports of goods and services	130
Transfers to the rest of the world	20
Loans to the rest of the world	60
Loans from the rest of the world	
Increase in official reserves	10

a What is the amount of loans from the rest of the world?

b What is the current account balance?

c What is the capital account balance?

d Does this country have a flexible exchange rate?

2 The information in Table 35.3 is for a country during a given year.

Table 35.3

Variable	Amount (billions of pounds)
GDP	800
Taxes (net of transfer payments)	200
Government budget deficit	50
Consumption	500
Investment	150
Imports	150

a What is the level of government expenditure on goods and services?

b What is the private sector surplus or deficit?

c What is the value of exports?

d What is the balance of trade surplus or deficit?

3 Tables 35.4 and 35.5 give the domestic demand for and supply of imaginary products called widgets and boffs.

Table 35.4

Price of toffs (£ each)	Supply of boffs	Demand for boffs
2	1,000	7,000
4	3,000	5,000
6	5,000	3,000
8	7,000	1,000
10	9,000	0

Table 35.5

Price of widgets (£ each)	Supply of widgets	Demand for widgets
6	2,000	64,000
8	4,000	12,000
12	6,000	10,000
16	8,000	8,000
20	10,000	6,000
24	12,000	4,000

a Draw a graph of the two markets, clearly identifying the domestic equilibrium if there is no international trade.

b Suppose that the world price for boffs is £4 each, while it is £6 each for widgets. Calculate what exchange rate would lead to a balance of trade that is neither a deficit nor a surplus. Show this equilibrium on your graph.

4 Suppose that the exchange rate between the pound and the Deutschmark is 3DM per pound.

a What is the exchange rate in terms of pounds per Deutschmark?

b What is the price in pounds of a camera selling for 250DM?

c What is the price in Deutschmarks of a computer selling for £1,000?

DATA QUESTIONS

Influences on the Balance of Payments

1 Summarize the trends in the three variables.

2 What relationship would you expect to find between the unemployment rate and the exchange rate on one hand and the balance of payments on the other? Do these statistics confirm your expectations?

Table 35.6

Year	Unemployment (thousands)	Sterling exchange rate (1985 = 100)	Current balance (millions of pounds)
1979	1,312	107	−453
1980	1,611	116	2,843
1981	2,482	123	6,748
1982	2,901	113	4,649
1983	3,127	106	3,787
1984	3,158	102	1,832
1985	3,281	100	2,750
1986	3,312	96	−24
1987	2,993	90	−4,182
1988	2,426	97	−15,151
1989	1,784	93	−22,515
1990	1,663	91	−18,268
1991	2,287	92	−7,652
1992	2,267	88	−8,620
1993	2,900	81	−9,500

Source: *Economic Trends 1994*. Central Statistical Office. Crown Copyright 1994. Reproduced by the permission of the Controller of the HMSO and the Central Statistical Office.

ANSWERS

CONCEPT REVIEW

1 balance; payments; current; assets; liabilities

2 net borrower; net lender

3 debtor

4 equal to

5 demand; supply; world; exchange rate

6 higher; trade; sterling assets

7 balance of trade deficit

8 foreign exchange; foreign exchange rate

9 fixed; flexible; managed

10 arbitrage; one price

TRUE OR FALSE

1 T Whisky is a visible export.

2 F There must be a surplus to offset the current deficit.

3 F Settlements vary according to what happens elsewhere in the accounts.

4 F May be true or untrue. Net borrower means that current account net borrowing > 0. Debtor nation means that sum of all net borrowing > 0.

5 F Borrowing will have to be repaid.

6 T Balance of trade (negative) = Government balance (large negative) + Private balance (small negative).

7 T Definition.

8 F See definition.

9 F Perhaps 'uncertain' – it depends on reaction of private sector surplus/deficit.

10 T Exchange rate affects price of goods in international trade.

11 T Lower rate of money supply will increase interest rate and so persuade people to invest in currency to receive higher interest.

12 T Trade is real, not money variable.

13 F Exchange rate is a monetary variable.

14 T Pound is more valuable, so rise in demand for sterling assets.

15 T Rise in foreign exchange value of pound leads to rise in foreign exchange value of sterling assets and so a rise in demand for sterling assets.

16 T Because Bank of England is willing to buy or sell pounds in order to keep exchange rate fixed.

MULTIPLE-CHOICE

1 a Definition.

2 c Imports > exports, therefore current account deficit. Borrowing > lending, so capital account surplus (think about which way money is flowing).

3 b Current lending > borrowing, so net lender. Sum of past borrowing > sum of lending, so debtor nation.

4 e Flexible exchange rate leads to deficit in external assets and liabilities = 0; hence current account surplus = capital account deficit – occurs only when lending > borrowing.

5 a Definitions of net lender and debtor nation. Debts are shrinking.

6 c Net lender – stock of investments rising. Debtor nation – negative flow of interest payments on investments.

7 d Net exports = $(T - G) + (S - I) = 300 - 400 + 300 - 250 = -50$.

8 c Government sector deficit = $G - T = 400 - 300 = 100$. Private sector surplus = $S - I = 300 - 250 = +50$.

9 d Link between government sector deficit and private sector surplus is via higher interest rates – international capital mobility restricts changes in interest rates.

10 d Definition of flexible exchange rate regime.

11 d Others all affect demand for pounds.

12 b Rightward shift positively sloped supply curve. Draw a graph to check.

13 a This increases the supply of pounds. **b**, **c** and **d** increase demand, **e** leads to fall in supply.

SHORT ANSWER

1 The two balance of payments accounts are:
 – The current account, which records the value of exports and the value of imports as well as transfers between countries and interest received from and paid to other countries.
 – Transactions in external assets and liabilities which records all purchases and sales of assets in other countries by UK citizens, and all purchases and sales by foreign citizens of assets in the United Kingdom.

2 The national income accounting identities allow us to show that a country's balance of trade deficit is equal to the sum of its government budget deficit and its private sector deficit.

3 Purchasing power parity follows from arbitrage and the law of one price. It means that the value of money is the same in all countries once the differences in risk are taken into account. For example, if the exchange rate between the pound and the yen is 120 yen per pound, purchasing power parity says that a good that sells for 120 yen in Japan will sell for 1 pound in the United Kingdom. Thus, the exchange rate is such that money (pounds or yen) has the same purchasing power in both countries.

PROBLEMS

1 a The amount of loans from the rest of the world is £100 billion. This is obtained by recognizing that the overall balance of payments must balance; the sum of the positive entries (exports, loans from the rest of the world and increase in official reserves) must equal the sum of the negative entries (imports, transfers to the rest of the world and loans to the rest of the world).

b The current account balance is a £50 billion deficit: exports minus imports minus transfers to the rest of the world.

c The capital account balance is a surplus of £40 billion: loans from the rest of the world minus loans to the rest of the world.

d This country does not have a flexible exchange rate because official reserves increased. Official reserves would have remained unchanged under flexible exchange rates.

2 a Since we know that the government budget deficit is £50 billion and the taxes (net of transfer payments) are £200 billion, we can infer that government expenditure on goods and services is £250 billion.

b The private sector surplus or deficit is given by saving minus investment. Investment is given as £150 billion but we must compute saving. Saving is equal to GDP minus taxes minus consumption: £100 billion. Thus there is a private sector deficit of £50 billion.

c We know that GDP is consumption plus investment plus government expenditure on goods and services plus net exports (exports minus imports). Since we know all these values except exports, we can obtain that value by solving for exports. The value of exports equals GDP plus imports minus consumption minus investment minus government expenditure on goods and services; the value of exports equals £50 billion.

d There is a balance of trade deficit of £100 billion. This can be obtained in two ways. First, we can recognize that the balance of trade surplus or deficit is given by the value of exports (£50 billion) minus the value of imports (£150 billion). The alternative method is to recognize that the balance of trade deficit is equal to the sum of the government budget deficit (£50 billion) and the private sector deficit (£50 billion).

Figure 35.1

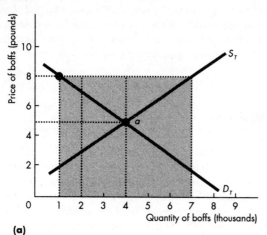

(a)

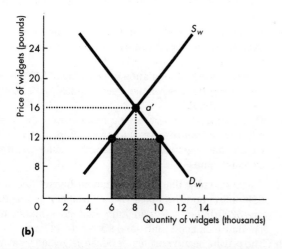

(b)

---

3 a Equilibrium in the market for boffs occurs at a price of £5 each, shown in Fig. 35.1(a), with 4,000 units traded (point *a*), while equilibrium in the market for widgets occurs at a price of £16 each, with 8,000 units traded (point *a'*), shown in Fig. 35.1(b).

b A balance of trade will have the amount earned by exports equal to the amount paid out for imports. To start, pick an exchange rate and see what happens to exports and imports. For example, pick £1 equals $1. In this case, the world price of a boff is equivalent to £4, in which case UK demand is 5,000 units, while UK supply is only 3,000 units, leading to imports of 2,000 units at £4 per unit, for a net payment of £8,000. The world price of a widget is £6, in which case demand is 14,000 units, while supply is only 2,000 units, leading to imports of 10,000 units at £6 per unit, for a total payment of £60,000.

Clearly, at this exchange rate we do not have a balance of trade, since the United Kingdom is trying to

import both goods. To get rid of a deficit, recall that the exchange rate must fall in value. We would therefore try lower and lower values (for example, £1.50 per $1), until by trial and error we arrive at the correct value of £2 per $1. Here, the price of a boff is £8, so that demand is 1,000 units and supply is 7,000 units, leading to exports of 6,000 units, earning £48,000. The price of a widget is £12, leading to a demand of 10,000 units and a supply of 6,000 units, and we import 4,000 units, at a total payment of £48,000, for a balance of trade.

We can see this balance demonstrated on the graphs, with the shaded areas showing the export earnings equal to the import payments.

4 a If £1 can be purchased for 3DM, then the price of a mark is £$\frac{1}{3}$ per Deutschmark.

b At an exchange rate of 3DM per pound, it takes £83.3 to obtain the 250DM needed to buy the camera.

c At an exchange rate of 3DM per pound, it takes 3,000DM to obtain the £1,000 needed to buy the computer.

DATA QUESTIONS

1 Unemployment rose until 1986, then declined and subsequently rose. The exchange rate rose rapidly in the first part of the period, then declined substantially, though with a small rise in 1988. The balance of payments on current account improved until the mid-1980s, then moved into a substantial deficit.

2 As unemployment rises consumer spending falls. We should therefore expect to find that as unemployment rises, imports will fall and the balance of payments move towards a surplus. Figure 35.2(a) shows a clear relationship between unemployment and the balance of payments. In the period 1979–1981 unemployment rose sharply and this was reflected in a rise in the current balance. In the mid part of the graph, the relationship is less clear. After 1986, unemployment fell and the current deficit rose as we would expect.

As the exchange rate of the pound rises, each pound can buy more foreign goods, while UK goods rise in price in foreign markets. We would therefore expect to find that a rise in the exchange rate leads to an increase in imports and a fall in exports, that is, the current account moves towards a deficit. However, there may be time lags while consumers adjust to new prices and producers develop new markets. Thus we can argue that the sharp rise in the exchange rate after 1979 was one reason why the balance of payments moved towards a deficit after 1981. The subsequent fall in the value of the pound could be expected to lead to an improvement in the balance of payments. This does not seem to have happened; the exchange rate effect may have been outweighed by the fall in unemployment, though in the last few years the relationship is as we would expect.

Figure 35.2

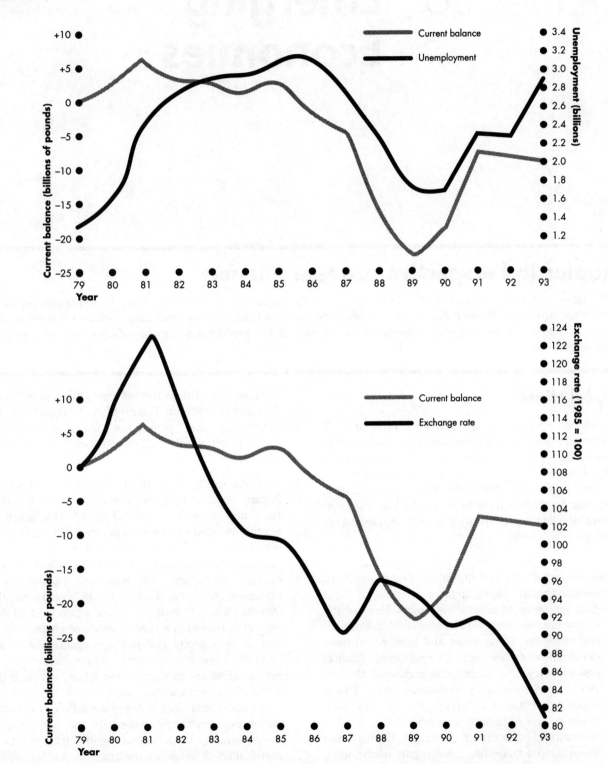

Chapter 36 Emerging Economies

Chapter In Perspective, Text Pages 1012–1042

What makes countries rich or poor? Is it the quantity of natural resources? Why do economic systems differ? What problems do changing economies such as those in China, Russia and Eastern Europe face? In this chapter we address these and related questions as we look at the problems and prospects for economic growth and development.

Helpful Hints

1 Countries become rich by achieving high rates of growth in per capita income and maintaining them over a long period of time. The role of compounding of income can create startling effects here!

The higher the rate of capital accumulation and the faster the pace of technological improvement, the higher the rate of growth in per capita income.

2 It is probably equally important to note the things that are apparently not important determinants of economic growth. These include:

a An abundance of natural resources. Most of the recent success stories of economic development (for example, Hong Kong and Singapore) have occurred with few natural resources. Natural resources can be helpful (for example, the oil-rich countries) but they are not necessary. This is hopeful because a country can do very little about its lack of natural resources.

b Restriction of international trade. Unrestricted international trade has been a part of the most dramatic success stories of economic growth.

From the discussion of the gains from international trade in Chapter 34, it should be no surprise that protection from international competition will decrease the rate of economic growth.

3 It is appropriate that the textbook ends where it began, emphasizing the universal problems that face any economy regardless of the kind of economic system that organizes its economic activity. Foremost among these is the fundamental and universal problem of scarcity, which makes choice necessary. No economic system can eliminate scarcity. Each simply confronts the problem in a different way. Once again we find that opportunity cost is a consequence of choice necessitated by scarcity and not a consequence of the kind of economic system in place. Regardless of how choices are made, the cost of any action is the value of the best forgone alternative.

An additional underlying notion that is relevant under any economic system is the postulate of the rationality of economic agents that has been maintained throughout the text. In particular, we have assumed that individuals will pursue their own best interest as they understand it. It is the case, however, that the specific way in which that pursuit of self-interest will be manifest will be different under different economic systems since alternative systems provide different incentives and constraints.

Key Figures and Tables

Figure 36.1 The World Lorenz Curve, 1985, text page 1015

The Lorenz curve, which was introduced in Chapter 18, graphically illustrates the degree of inequality in the distribution of income. On the horizontal axis is measured the cumulative percentage of the population and on the vertical axis is measured the cumulative percentage of income. The population is ordered from low income to high income. The Lorenz curve for an equal distribution of income would be shown by a 45° line indicating that 20 per cent of the population had 20 per cent of the income, and so on. The world Lorenz curve illustrated here reflects the distribution of average per capita income across countries of the world. It shows substantial inequality.

Figure 36.3 Alternative Economic Systems, text page 1017

Alternative economic systems differ in two dimensions: (1) the degree to which resources are allocated by markets and (2) the degree to which capital is owned by individuals. This figure creates a diagram in these two dimensions to compare the economic systems of different countries easily. On the vertical scale, the range of methods by which resources are allocated is given with pure market allocation at the top and pure planning at the bottom. On the horizontal scale, the range of capital ownership patterns is given with all capital owned by individuals at the left and all capital owned by the state at the right. Using these two scales we can place a country in the diagram according to its actual system. The upper-left corner of the space corresponds to capitalism since all capital is owned by individuals and all resources are allocated by markets. Similarly, the lower-right corner corresponds to socialism, the lower-left corner corresponds to welfare state capitalism, and the upper-right corner corresponds to market socialism. It is useful to note that no country is located exactly at a corner. This reflects the fact that all countries have elements of both capitalism and socialism but differ in degree.

Figure 36.7 Technological Change, text page 1024

This illustrates the consequences of technological change as well as increases in the capital stock on economic growth. The United Kingdom and Ethiopia are assumed to have been using the same technology and thus were on the same per capita production function in 1790. The United Kingdom, however, had more capital per capita and produced further up the production function curve. Output per capita in the United Kingdom exceeded per capita output in Ethiopia in 1790 even though each country used the same technology. From 1790 to 1994 two things happened in the United Kingdom. Technological improvement shifted the per capita production function upward and the per capita stock of capital increased. Both of these increased output per capita and thus were responsible for economic growth. In Ethiopia, however, there was no technological improvement and no accumulation of capital per worker. Thus, output per capita has not increased and Ethiopia has not experienced economic growth.

Table 36.1 A Compact Summary of Key Periods in the Economic History of the People's Republic of China, text page 1026

The People's Republic of China was established in 1949. Since then, the Chinese economic system has undergone several changes. Although at first Mao Zedong followed the Soviet model of socialism, in 1958 he initiated the Great Leap Forward, which was a significant economic reform. It was an economic failure. During the cultural revolution, real GDP actually fell. Since the reforms of 1978 initiated by Deng Xiaoping, however, China has experienced a very rapid rate of growth. These reforms introduced some elements of capitalism into the Chinese economy.

Table 36.2 A Compact Summary of Key Periods in the Economic History of the Soviet Union, text page 1030

In order to understand the nature and consequences of Soviet socialism, it is important to have a knowledge of the economic history of the former Soviet Union since the Bolshevik Revolution. The key aspects of that history are summarized here. As a consequence of the Bolshevik Revolution under Lenin, the Soviet economic system began to change but the fundamental changes took place under Stalin during the 1930s. The system that is described in this chapter was largely put in place by Stalin.

SELF-TEST

CONCEPT REVIEW

1 A country in which there is little industrialization, very little capital equipment, and low per capita incomes is called a(n) _____ country. A country that is poor but is accumulating capital and developing an industrial base is called a(n) _____ country.

2 Countries in which there is a rapidly developing broad industrial base and per capita income is growing quickly are called _____ _____ countries. A country with a large amount of capital equipment and in which people are highly specialized, enabling them to earn high per capita incomes, is called a(n) _____ country.

3 The distribution of income among countries is _____ unequal than the distribution of income among families in the United Kingdom.

4 If poor countries have a slow growth rate of real per capita GDP and rich countries have faster growth rate, the gap between the rich and poor _____ .

5 The relationship between inputs and outputs is called the _____ function. There are three classes of inputs. The first, _____, includes non-produced natural resources. The second, _____, increases as the number of workers increases. The third, _____, includes machines and factories as well as human skills and knowledge.

6 The relationship between per capita output and the per capita stock of capital in a given state of technology is called the _____ _____ function. It will shift _____ if there is a technological advance.

7 Other things being equal, the larger is saving, the _____ will be the rate of capital accumulation. Other things being equal, the larger the government budget deficit, the _____ will be the rate of capital accumulation.

8 The situation in which a country is locked into a low income condition that reinforces itself is called a(n) _____ _____ .

9 The universal fundamental economic problem of _____ cannot be abolished by any economic system.

10 Private ownership of capital and reliance on market allocation of resources are the principal characteristics of the economic system known as _____ . The economic system based on public ownership of capital and centrally planned allocation of resources is called _____ .

11 An in-between economic system that combines public ownership of capital with market allocation of resources is called _____ _____ . Another in-between economic system with private ownership of capital but a high degree of state intervention in the allocation of resources is called _____ _____ _____ .

TRUE OR FALSE

—— **1** The poorest countries in the world are underdeveloped countries.

—— **2** In order for a poor country to close the real per capita income gap between itself and rich countries, it must attain and maintain a high rate of economic growth.

—— **3** Higher levels of average human capital, but with the same level of per capita physical capital, will not raise per capita income.

—— **4** Faster growing countries typically have lower rates of capital accumulation.

—— **5** Countries with higher population growth rates generally have a smaller percentage of the population under age 15.

—— **6** Scarcity is not a problem for capitalist economies.

—— **7** The United Kingdom is an example of a pure capitalist economy.

MULTIPLE-CHOICE

1 Which of the following is not an attribute of a developing country?
a poverty
b a low stock of capital
c a developing industrial base
d a developing commercial base
e a stable and high stock of capital

2 The poorest nations are typically characterized by all of the following except
a high literacy rates.
b high birth rates.
c limited availability of capital.
d low per capita incomes.
e poor capital accumulation.

3 The Lorenz curve depicting the distribution of average per capita income across countries lies
a on the 45° line.
b to the left of the 45° line.
c to the right of the 45° line but not as far out as the Lorenz curve depicting the distribution of income of families within the United Kingdom.
d to the right of the 45° line and further out than the Lorenz curve depicting the distribution of income of families within the United Kingdom.
e to the right of the 45° line, roughly as far out as the Lorenz curve depicting the distribution of income of families within the United Kingdom.

4 Suppose rich country A enjoys a per capita income of £100,000 per year and poorer country B has a per capita income of only £1,000. With constant populations, what happens to the income gap between the two countries (initially £99,000) if per capita income in the poor country grows at a rate of 100 per cent, while growth in the rich country is only 2 per cent?
a The income gap between gap between the two must narrow since the poor country grows faster.
b The income gap stays the same.
c The income gap widens despite the faster growth in the poor country.
d The income gap initially narrows, then widens.
e The income gap initially widens, then narrows.

5 Which of the following is not a characteristic of a per capita production function?

a Per capita output increases as the per capita stock of capital increases.
b The state of technology is held constant for a given per capita production function.
c The law of diminishing returns applies to the per capita production function.
d As the stock of capital increases, the per capita production function shifts upward.
e As technological knowledge advances, the per capita production function shifts upward.

6 As capital is accumulated and capital per unit of labour increases,
a this leads to less output since workers tend to become less hard working when working with big machines.
b this increases the productivity of labour and economic growth.
c the marginal productivity of capital increases.
d this leads to a reduced rate of economic growth as workers lose their jobs to the machines.
e population growth typically increases as a result.

7 As the labour force grows with a constant capital stock,
a there is less output in total since the capital–labour ratio declines.
b the marginal productivity of labour is increased as the marginal productivity of capital is decreased.
c the marginal productivity of labour and capital both increase.
d the marginal productivity of labour and capital both decrease.
e the marginal productivity of labour is reduced.

8 There is a limit to growth induced by capital accumulation in the short run since
a labour growth rates may become negative.
b even as capital per capita increases, the rate of increase in total output will eventually begin to diminish.
c even as capital per capita increases, the rate of increase in total output will eventually begin to increase causing excessive inflation.
d there is a strong limit to the amount of capital that can be accumulated.
e low population growth means too few workers for the amount of new capital.

9 Which of the following is not a principal obstacle to economic growth for poor countries?
a population growth
b high number of dependants as a percentage of population
c low saving rates
d international debt
e multinational corporations

10 Population growth can reduce economic growth if
a per capita productivity increases as well.
b the population increase consists of able-bodied workers.
c the population increase consists of children or other dependants not yet in the work force.
d too many workers push up wages.
e the population increase consists of immigrants.

11 For a given level of saving, investment will be higher the
a higher is the government budget deficit and the higher is the current account deficit.
b higher is the government budget deficit and the lower is the current account deficit.
c lower is the government budget deficit and the higher is the current account deficit.
d lower is the government budget deficit and the lower is the current account deficit.
e higher the income level.

12 The best any economic system can do is to
a produce on its production possibility frontier.
b produce above its production possibility frontier.
c produce below its production possibility frontier.
d eliminate scarcity.
e produce a fair distribution of individual incentives.

13 Which economic system is characterized by private ownership of capital and considerable state intervention in the allocation of resources?
a capitalism
b socialism
c market socialism
d communism
e welfare state capitalism

14 Which economic system is characterized by private ownership of capital and reliance on market allocation of resources?
a capitalism

b socialism
c market socialism
d welfare state capitalism
e communism

15 During the Great Leap Forward in China under Mao Zedong,
a there was a dramatic increase in agricultural production but not industrial production.
b the application of new technologies resulted in a significant general increase in production.
c China experienced very slow economic growth.
d China became a major exporter of grains and cotton.
e China's educational sector boomed.

16 The economic reforms of 1978 under Deng Xiaoping
a moved China off the 'capitalist road' it had been on under Mao Zedong.
b abolished collectivized agriculture.
c have resulted in slower economic growth in China.
d have made China more dependent on food imports.
e led to the closing of universities and schools.

SHORT ANSWER

1 Use the concept of a per capita production function to explain why an increase in the rate of capital accumulation will lead to faster economic growth.

2 Why is international debt generally an obstacle to the economic growth of a poor country?

3 How can an underdevelopment status be self-reinforcing?

4 Distinguish between a capitalist economic system and a welfare state capitalist system.

5 Briefly describe the economic reforms proclaimed by Deng Xiaoping in China in 1978. What has been their effect?

PROBLEMS

1 Consider two countries, High and Low. High currently has a real per capita income of £10,000 while Low currently has real per capita income of only £5,000. The rate of growth of real per capita income in High is 1 per cent per year.

a Suppose the rate of growth of real per capita income in Low is 10 per cent per year. What will the gap in real per capita income between High and Low be after 1 year? After 4 years?

b Suppose the rate of growth of real per capita income in Low is 20 per cent per year. What will the gap in real per capita income between High and Low be after 4 years? How many years will it take for Low to surpass High?

2 This problem illustrates the effect of capital accumulation and technological growth on economic growth. Figure 36.1 shows two per capita production functions for an economy. Suppose we begin on the curve labelled PF_1.

a What is the effect on output per capita of an increase in capital per capita from 1 machine per worker to 3 machines per worker? From 3 machines per worker to 5 machines per worker? From 1 machine per worker to 5 machines per worker directly?

b Now suppose that there is a technological improvement that shifts the per capita production function from PF_1 to PF_2. What is the effect on output per capita of this technological improvement if there is 1 machine per worker? If there are 5 machines per worker?

c Now suppose that the technological improvement that shifts the PF curve occurs at the same time as the capital per capita increases from 1 machine per worker to 5 machines per worker. What is the effect on output per capita?

3 Graveland is a poor country with no natural resources except sand. Initially, income is £500 per year, taxes (and government spending) is £100 per year, all of disposable income is consumed, there are no exports or imports and there is no technological change (all figures are per capita).

a In this economy, what is the level of saving and of investment? Is there economic growth?

b Suddenly, there is a worldwide gravel shortage, and Graveland is able to export gravel at a huge profit. Exports soar from zero to £700, income rises to £1,900, and consumption rises to £1,100 per year. There are still no imports, and initially government spending and taxes are constant. What happens to the current account? What is investment now? Is the growth rate now positive?

Figure 36.1

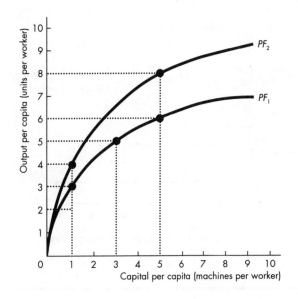

c Suppose that Graveland starts to import capital goods at a rate of £500 per year. What happens to the current account? Savings? Investment? Future growth?

DATA QUESTIONS

Inflation in Poland

Poland introduced a market economy at the beginning of 1990. During the first week of the new year, the Polish people saw the price of bread rise by 40 per cent, ham by 50 per cent, petrol by 100 per cent, electricity by 400 per cent and coal by a staggering 600 per cent. Although all prices increased, some increased by more than others, changing relative prices as shown in Fig. 36.2. The average price increase in January 1990 was 77 per cent. Goods and services with prices that increased by more than this amount experienced an increase in their relative price; goods and services with prices that increased by less than this experienced a decrease in their relative price. Thus the relative price of bread and ham each decreased and the relative price of fuel increased. This led to a substitution effect; many Polish people decided to stop driving their cars altogether.

Figure 36.2

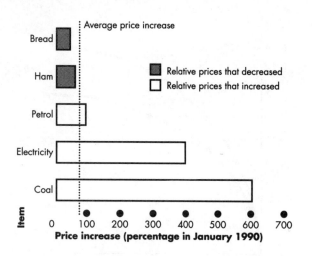

Inflation on the scale experienced in Poland resulted from one main factor – too much money chasing too few goods. When money supply increases quickly, so does aggregate demand. And when aggregate demand grows faster than aggregate supply, the result is inflation.

Source: adapted from M. Parkin, 'Inflation in Eastern Europe', *Economic Times*, Fall 1991.

1 Explain what is meant by
  a Market economy.
  b Substitution effect.

2 Why should aggregate demand increase when money supply increases?

ANSWER

CONCEPT REVIEW

1 underdeveloped; developing

2 newly industrialized; industrial

3 more

4 widens

5 production; land; labour; capital

6 per capita production; upward

7 larger; smaller

8 underdevelopment trap

9 scarcity

10 capitalism; socialism

11 market socialism; welfare state capitalism

TRUE OR FALSE

1 **T** Definition.

2 **T** To close the gap, poor countries must grow at a faster rate than rich countries.

3 **F** Increase in human capital leads to increased productivity and higher per capita incomes.

4 **F** High rates of capital accumulation are associated with rapid growth.

5 **T** High population growth means many children.

6 **F** Scarcity is a problem for all economies.

7 **F** The United Kingdom is a mixed economy.

MULTIPLE-CHOICE

1 **e** Definition.

2 **a** Poor countries usually have low levels of literacy.

3 **d** See text discussion.

4 **e** First year: A's growth = £2,000, while B's = £1,000. By third year A's growth = £2,080.80, while B's = £4,000.

5 **d** This creates a movement along a function.

6 **b** More capital means labour can produce more output per unit.

7 **e** Fall in capital–labour ratio means fall in productivity.

8 **b** Due to fixed technology and labour resources.

9 **e** Multinational corporations can foster growth.

10 **c** Because resources must be spent on child care.

11 c From formula for investment.

12 a Cannot be above the frontier because of resource constraints (scarcity); can do better than just a fair distribution.

13 e Definition.

14 a Pure capitalism relies on market allocation.

15 c See text discussion – slow growth due to resource misallocation.

16 b See text discussion.

SHORT ANSWER

1 The per capita production function illustrates how per capita output increases as the per capita stock of capital increases, given the state of technology. If the rate of capital accumulation increases, then the per capita stock of capital is increasing more rapidly, which means that per capita output is increasing more rapidly, that is, there is faster economic growth. This is illustrated graphically by more rapid movements up the graph of the per capita production function.

2 If a poor country has a large international debt, it needs a current account surplus in order to make interest payments and pay back the debt.

3 The problem with many poor countries is that they have a low per capita stock of capital. In order to increase it, they must increase the saving rate, but the saving rate will not increase because a low per capita stock of capital results in low per capita output which implies low saving. Thus the existence of a low per capita capital stock leads to conditions that generate a low per capita capital stock.

4 Both capitalism and welfare state capitalism are characterized by private ownership of capital. They differ with regard to the role of the state in the allocation of resources. Capitalism relies on market allocation of resources, while welfare state capitalism is characterized by a significant degree of state intervention in the allocation of resources.

5 In 1978 Deng Xiaoping abolished collective agriculture (state-owned and state-operated farms) and raised prices paid to farmers for many crops. Agricultural land was leased to farmers for the payment of a fixed tax and a commitment to sell part of its output to the state. The main thing is that individual farmers were free to decide what to plant and how to produce. Since farmers now were able to profit from their productivity, there were new incentives for efficiency. The effects have been striking. The production of agricultural products increased dramatically with the output of

some products (those for which the set price was increased the most) increasing by many times their previous level. China went from being the world's largest importer of agricultural products to being an exporter of these products. The overall growth rate in the economy increased to 7 per cent per year.

PROBLEMS

1 a Since the rate of growth is 1 per cent per year in High, real per capita income will increase from £10,000 to £10,100 after 1 year. Since the rate of growth is 10 per cent per year in Low, real per capita income will increase from £5,000 to £5,500. Thus the real per capita income gap between High and Low has fallen from £5,000 to £4,600. In High, real per capita income next year will be 1.01 times real per capita income this year. In Low, real per capita income next year will be 1.10 times real per capita income this year. If we carry this out for 4 years, we find that after 4 years, real per capita income will be £10,406 in High and £7,320 in Low. Thus, after 4 years, the real per capita income gap will have fallen to £3,086.

b If the growth rate in Low is 20 per cent, after 4 years real per capita income will be £10,368, while real per capita income in High will be £10,406 (since the growth rate in High is still 1 per cent per year). Thus, after 4 years, the real per capita income gap between High and Low will have fallen from £5,000 to £38. Real per capita income in Low will surpass real per capita income in High early in year 5.

2 a From PF_1 in Fig. 36.1 we see that as the capital per capita increases from 1 machine per worker to 3 machines per worker, output per worker increases from 3 units to 5 units. As the machines per worker increase from 3 to 5, output per worker increases from 5 to 6 units. Thus the law of diminishing returns holds. We note that if we increase the machines per worker from 1 directly to 5, output per worker increases from 3 directly to 6 units.

b If there is 1 machine per worker, the upward shift from PF_1 to PF_2 implies that output per worker increases from 3 units to 4 units. If, however, there are 5 machines per worker, the upward shift from PF_1 to PF_2 implies that output per worker increases from 6 units to 8 units.

c If we increase the machines per worker from 1 to 5 at the same time as the shift from PF_1 to PF_2 occurs, output per worker will increase from 3 units to 8 units.

3 a Given the equation Investment = Saving plus Current account deficit minus Government deficit, since there are initially no deficits, clearly investment equals saving. However, consumption equals disposable income, so saving is zero, as is investment.

b If exports are £700, and imports are still zero, then net exports (the current account in this case) are £700. From our equation, we can see that investment equals saving of £700 plus a current account deficit of –£700 minus government deficit of zero, or investment equals zero. Since investment equals zero, and there is no technological change, growth stays constant at zero after Graveland reaches the new level of income.

c Net exports now equal £700 – £500 or £200. Saving and income are initially unchanged, as is the government deficit, so that investment equals £700 + (–£200) – 0 = £500. Clearly this investment will raise the capital stock, and create future growth.

DATA QUESTIONS

1 a A market economy is one where resources are allocated as a result of the forces of demand and supply. The price system conveys information which allows decentralized decision-making. Market economies usually also involve private ownership of most of the means of production.

b A substitution effect is the effect on the demand for a good or service of a change in the price of a good or service assuming that real income remains unchanged. Thus individuals will move along an indifference curve – in the example above they will consume less of goods such as fuel where the price has increased and more of goods whose relative price has fallen.

2 At least two of the components of aggregate demand will be affected by a rise in the supply of money. Other things remaining equal, the rise in money supply will bring down the rate of interest and so stimulate investment.

The rise in money supply will mean that the demand for money is less than the supply of money; consumers will use the excess supply to buy more consumer goods, hence aggregate demand will rise.